THE U~~NIVERSITY~~
WINCHESTER

Martial Rose Library
Tel: 01962 827306

HARM AND CULPABILITY

Harm and Culpability

edited by
A. P. Simester
and
A. T. H. Smith

CLARENDON PRESS · OXFORD
1996

Oxford University Press, Walton Street, Oxford OX2 6DP
Oxford New York
Athens Auckland Bangkok Bogota Bombay
Buenos Aires Calcutta Cape Town Dar es Salaam
Delhi Florence Hong Kong Istanbul Karachi
Kuala Lumpur Madras Madrid Melbourne
Mexico City Nairobi Paris Singapore
Taipei Tokyo Toronto
and associated companies in
Berlin Ibadan

Oxford is a trade mark of Oxford University Press

Published in the United States
by Oxford University Press Inc., New York

British Library Cataloguing in Publication Data
Data available

Library of Congress Cataloging in Publication Data
Harm and culpability / edited by A.P. Simester and A.T.H. Smith.
p.   cm.—(Oxford monographs in criminal law and justice)
1. Criminal law—Philosophy.   2. Criminal intent.
3. Criminal liability.   I. Simester, A. P.   II. Smith, A. T. H.
III. Series: Oxford monographs on criminal law and criminal justice.
K5018.Z9H37   1996   345'.001—dc20   [342.501]   96–16983
ISBN 0–19–826057–1

1 3 5 7 9 10 8 6 4 2

Typeset by Hope Services (Abingdon) Ltd.
Printed in Great Britain
on acid-free paper by
Biddles Ltd.,
Guildford & King's Lynn

General Editor's Introduction

With this thirteenth volume, the series develops from the traditional mono-graph to the thematic set of essays. The themes germinated and took shape over a two-to-three year period of seminars, a weekend conference and fur-ther exchanges of papers, all under the guiding hands of the two editors. The resulting essays challenge the internal and external boundaries of criminal liability, raising in various ways a number of fundamental issues such as the conditions under which conduct may be justified. The authors share an interest in criminal law theory of the philosophical kind, but the theoretical dimensions of the essays open up several issues with distinctly practical implications—for example, in relation to drug dealing, blackmail, and attempted crimes. Questions of whether or not to criminalize certain con-duct also recur throughout the book, and there is some attention to the most appropriate form in which criminalization (or exemption from liability) might be accomplished. With its considered interweaving of theoretical and practical arguments, *Harm and Culpability* marks a considerable advance in criminal law scholarship.

Andrew Ashworth

Preface

It may be unorthodox for the prefatory remarks to a jointly edited volume to come from the pen (well, word-processor) of only one of the editors, but this way of proceeding enables me to identify the respective roles of the editors, and to acknowledge the enormous input of my co-editor.

The work began its life as a seminar series held in Cambridge throughout the calendar year 1994. It seemed to me that with the arrival in Cambridge of Andrews von Hirsch and Simester, we had the nucleus of a discussion group, at which like-minded colleagues could meet to discuss their joint interests, and possibly to present papers on their current work. Colleagues from other centres were invited to join us, and papers were presented on Friday afternoons. Initially, there was no thought that the papers should be published by us and indeed one of the papers (John Gardner's) was separately published by the *Cambridge Law Journal*.

It soon became apparent, though, that essays were being put together which ought to see the light of day, and that there was a sufficient number of recurring themes and threads that they might constitute a single volume. Thus we approached the publishers with a tentative proposal. Richard Hart proved to be his usual encouraging self, and with his backing (and that of the Oxford University Press Syndicate), we were able to begin phase two of the project, which was to weld what had been somewhat disparate contributions into a more coherent whole. A two-day conference/seminar was held in Caius in December 1994, at which all of the papers were re-presented by their authors (some having been rewritten in the light of comments made at their first airing), and an editorial paper highlighting the editorial themes was given for the first time. The authors then dispersed with the task of rewriting in the light of the editorial introduction, and of discussions with the editors and the other paper presenters.

I have to say that the bulk of the editorial work has fallen upon Andrew Simester. Because of my other commitments, I was unable to devote as much time as I should have wished to taking the project forward, and he played very much the leading part in writing the editorial introduction (mine being the revising hand). He also bore the major burden of making comments on the papers as they were revised and sent to the editors.

Caius College was not merely the place where the papers were presented; it also generously made available both facilities and funding for the conference. The contributors have been quite remarkably conscientious both in their willingness to rewrite and revise, and in sticking to the tight schedules demanded. To all, I am extremely grateful for the support that they have so willingly given to see this project through to a successful conclusion.

A.T.H.S.

July 1995

Contents

Contributors

Peter Alldridge is Senior Lecturer in Law at Cardiff Law School.

Andrew Ashworth is Edmund-Davies Professor of Criminal Law and Criminal Justice at King's College, London.

R. A. Duff is Professor of Philosophy at the University of Stirling.

John Gardner is Fellow and Tutor in Law at Brasenose College, Oxford.

P. R. Glazebrook is Lecturer in Law at the University of Cambridge and Fellow of Jesus College.

Jeremy Horder is Fellow and Tutor in Law at Worcestor College, Oxford.

Grant Lamond is Junior Research Fellow in Law at St Edmund Hall, Oxford.

Paul H. Robinson is Professor of Law at Northwestern University.

A. P. Simester is Fellow of Gonville and Caius College, Cambridge.

A. T. H. Smith is Reader in Law at the University of Cambridge and Fellow of Gonville and Caius College.

G. R. Sullivan is Senior Lecturer in Law at the University of Durham.

Andrew von Hirsch is Senior Research Fellow at the Institute of Criminology and Fellow of Fitzwilliam College, Cambridge; also Professor at the School of Criminal Justice, Rutgers University.

1

Criminalization and the Role of Theory

A. P. Simester and A. T. H. Smith*

Criminal law scholarship tends too often to be conducted exclusively as either traditional blackletter law, as high moral philosophy, or (thirdly) as an exercise in socio-legal or law-in-context theorizing. Yet it is a mistake to think that arguments about the criminal law can be propounded exclusively within any one of these domains, for even the most specific problems can generate especially difficult theoretical questions. Those who seek to formulate and influence the formulation of criminal law will encounter such questions, whether they are attempting to determine the scope of a particular *actus reus*, such as blackmail, or the general criteria of attempts liability. Their responses, like the essays in this volume, must frequently seek the assistance of philosophy.

PHILOSOPHY INFORMING LAW

Perhaps one of the causes of that severance in approaches is the possibility of different types of legal analysis. 'No conviction without blame', say many of our authors. We agree. Yet what sort of claim are we recognizing? The alternative understandings of that proposition correspond to differing theoretical standpoints from which one may approach the analysis of criminal law—whether as descriptive, explanatory, or evaluative inquiries. A legal commentator might choose to give a *description* of the rules which make up the criminal law ('in fact, there is no conviction without blame'), and to a varying extent this is one of the central functions of textbooks; to state what the law is. Such an ambition is not to be belittled. A well-crafted descriptive account that draws together divergent legal strands may make a major contribution to an increased understanding and a more predictable administra-

* We are grateful to the contributors for feedback regarding earlier drafts of this essay, and in particular to Antony Duff, John Gardner, Peter Glazebrook, Bob Sullivan, and Andrew von Hirsch for their detailed comments.

tion of the law. Work of this nature can provide a reference tool of use not only to students but also to practitioners and others who participate in the criminal legal process.

There is much, however, that is incomplete about descriptive analysis. When the law changes, the description becomes obsolete. It no longer has a function, since it merely depicts—and now depicts a legal system that no longer exists. And, one might ask, what of a new case which does not fit the rules precisely? If all we have is a mechanical set of rules, then there is no way of knowing what to do. Nor does description *simpliciter* give us any clues as to how to formulate new laws within the framework of those already in existence.

For instance: what happens when someone fails to give thought to the obvious possibility that his foolish conduct might (say) cause a fire. Is he to be convicted of reckless arson? Sometimes we come to a junction in the law where there is more than one path and we may travel only one. In England, recklessness embraces some cases of inadvertence—but other jurisdictions need not, and many do not, follow that route. Why? When the House of Lords was called upon to decide the issue,[1] it was not enough for the Law Lords just to look at statutory and extant case law.[2] The decision neither is nor should be merely a mechanical application of precedent. A similar statement might be made of cases such as *Lynch*.[3] If the IRA blackmails Albert to participate in murder by (for instance) threatening the lives of his wife and family, should he be convicted of murder? manslaughter? or nothing at all? These are extraordinarily open-ended questions. It is in responding to them that criminal legal 'theory' becomes so important. Indeed, at this point even the semblance of a distinction between criminal law and the theory of criminal law disappears. One cannot answer legal questions in a theoretical vacuum. To decide such cases, one needs an understanding of what underlies the rules—of the doctrines and principles which *explain* them—which can be drawn upon to fill in gaps, or to revise the rules in a principled rather than an *ad hoc* way. In Albert's case, the extent of his criminal liability depends upon whether we conceive of duress as a justificatory defence (in which case he is surely guilty of murder), or as an excuse that acknowledges the frail humanity of defendants (perhaps akin to provocation), or as a denial of the voluntary act requirement (thus begetting an acquittal)—or even as a poorly-understood combination of the three.[4] Whatever the explanation may be, the advantages of providing one should be obvious. The pay-offs are especially to be found in terms of consistency and fairness—in helping us to treat like cases alike. It is only by contemplating their underlying explana-

---

[1] *Caldwell* [1982] AC 341.

[2] For a discussion of the extent to which the House has been unconstrained by precedent, see A.T.H. Smith, 'Criminal Appeals in the House of Lords' (1984) 47 *Modern LR* 133.

[3] [1975] AC 653.   [4] Regard Gardner's view of necessity (at 122, n. 37).

tions that we can even begin to reconcile the rule in *Beckford*,[5] that honest unreasonable mistakes may sometimes afford a defence, with common law liability in manslaughter for negligence. Explanatory theory might not give us answers to all the issues the law raises, but it ought to help us to understand those issues in a clearer light.

So the claim that culpability be a precondition of conviction is, we take it, not descriptive. However, while it might be explanatory ('the principle of no conviction without blame underpins the *mens rea* requirement', say), we do not think it that either. The idea might best be termed *evaluative*, or normative: there *ought* to be no conviction without blame. No analysis of the law is really complete without such argument, for it is not enough, in our view, that an explanation should lead to enhanced consistency; we also want to get the explanation *right*. Fairness is only attained if the underlying explanation isolates the morally-relevant differences between cases and the rules that govern them. As Duff illustrates at the outset of this book, there is often potential for conflicting explanations—varieties of objective and subjective accounts of culpability, for example, are canvassed in his discussion. And some explanations are better than others. One of the truths exemplified by the essays in this volume is that every explanation of a coercive system such as the criminal law stands in need of evaluative support; in need of theory which explains the law we actually have and involves rationales that deserve to be endorsed. Every author in this volume not only asserts and interprets, but also defends.

And, frequently, proposes. If duress is best understood as an excuse, then perhaps it ought to be a palliative to murder also. In this way, where a theory does not explain some aspect of the present law, it may nevertheless be supported. Evaluation, whilst capable of being justificatory, can also be revisionary. Indeed, legitimate reformulation of law characteristically presupposes an imperfect correlation between description and evaluation. This is not, however, to deny the importance of descriptive analysis for theory. Unlike moral theory, legal analysis must attend to the law's practical history—and to the social and institutional constraints that shackle it (and which inform much valuable law-in-context scholarship). One cannot usefully answer theoretical questions in a legal vacuum. To generate legal theory that is not grounded in the system we have is to generate theory about someone else's legal system; one, moreover, of little relevance to us.[6] It is to indulge in erecting fortresses upon ether.

---

[5] [1988] AC 130.
[6] Assuming, as we do, that the social and other costs involved in substantially displacing our present system are prohibitive.

LOCATING CRIMINAL PHILOSOPHY, AND THE CONDITIONS OF
CRIMINALIZATION

The place of any theory depends in part upon its subject matter. What marks
out the criminal law from other branches of law, such as contract or tort?
One obvious factor is its punitive function; as von Hirsch notes in this volume, the dramatic intrusiveness of criminal penalties in the lives of individuals spawns important constraints, including those of fair warning
embodied in the Rule of Law. Yet punishment is not uniquely distinctive of
the criminal law. Punitive damages are available in private law, and a conviction is not always accompanied by further impositions. The proper conditions of punishment are not quite the same as the proper conditions of
criminalization.

HARM

Some of the conditions for criminalization are grounded in its character as
a system directed at guiding or influencing the behaviour of citizens. To
make some action a crime is to declare that it should not be done (and, typically, to deploy contingent sanctions as supplementary reasons not to do it).
That is to say, the criminal law is not meant to be a neutral system—it is
intended to bias and supplant the choices of individuals.[7] We have expressed
our view that such a manipulation of the conduct of others must always
stand in need of philosophical justification;[8] historically, Anglo–American
criminal law has responded to that need in terms of a harm principle. Those
who shape criminal law must therefore consider such questions as, in what
sense is drug dealing wrong—and if so, is it sufficiently harmful to warrant
the State's intervention? Von Hirsch demonstrates here the complexity of
deciding these issues in a principled way; for other questions must also be
asked. There are many legislative interventions which prohibit actions not
because they are intrinsically bad or harmful, but rather (or also) because
they contribute instrumentally to the occurrence of further harms. Suppose,
pace Alldridge, that drug dealing were such a case. Why, von Hirsch would
enquire, should those further harms be made the dealer's responsibility, such
that his dealing was therefore wrong? To answer that question, he suggests
we need a theory of fair imputation.

Certain crimes *mala prohibita* co-ordinate society by settling which one of
alternative possible ways may be adopted in order to satisfy some valuable
but more general goal. Such crimes thereby acquire moral force as a conduit
to the achievement of that indeterminate goal. As Honoré puts it, some

---

[7] This is not, of course, the sole manner in which criminalization may affect the status of
possible actions: compare in particular the essay in this volume by Alldridge.

[8] And see Lamond, more generally, at 218 ff.

moral obligations can be spelled out only by law (this is true, for instance, of the instruction that all must drive on one side of the road rather than the other).[9] But other such crimes might remain open to an objection von Hirsch sees: that wholesale criminalization of actions which are bad only in virtue of the harms to which they conduce—when coupled with the rule that *ignorantia juris neminem excusat*—may lead to systematic violation of precisely that Rule of Law constraint which helps to underpin our prescriptions of *mens rea* standards. Her desire not to injure some remote interest might well not alert the defendant to her imminent transgression of the rule which protects that interest.[10]

One question raised by von Hirsch is whether offences should be understood according to the activity involved or the relevant consequences. In cases of remote harm, the interest being protected may—and, he says, problematically—have little apparent connection with the salient characteristics of the activity which is actually proscribed. It is a point that is placed in starker relief if we acknowledge a proposition implicit in Alldridge's essay: that if criminalization of an *actus* is to be justified by reference to the harm to which that *actus* conduces, then this is the basis upon which offences should be grouped, comprehended, and assessed. Besides being 'property offences',[11] how many characteristics do vandalism and insider dealing share? Sexual violation of animals is not a crime for the same *sorts* of reasons as is rape. Blackmail is misunderstood partly because it is so often regarded as a property offence—whereas, on Lamond's analysis, it is in reality also an offence against the person and analogous to assault as much as to theft. For example, avers Alldridge, it has more in common with drug dealing than does drug possession. We are misled by superficial similarities when we class the latter offences together; only when we clarify our understanding of what is morally significant about the *actus* can we properly decide whether it should be named legally *reus*. Once the nature of the wrong involved is recognized it can readily be seen why, for example, a charge of blackmail may lie even in cases where the civil law does not supply a cause of action (in particular, where the blackmail causes no loss). If Birks is right to explain civil liability by reference to an unjust deprivation of property,[12] then the interest protected by the criminal law is simply different from that safeguarded by the civil action.

Like Alldridge, Horder expresses a dissatisfaction with the received classification of offences. But the aspect with which he is concerned is ulterior intent: with the ways in which accompanying or further intentions change the nature of an action and the wrong it constitutes. If Alex sets fire to her own garden shed, that is probably not a criminal matter. But if she does so hoping to kill the child inside—it most certainly is. Should the fire be put out

---

[9] 'The Dependence of Morality on Law' (1993) 12 *Oxford Journal of Legal Studies* 1.
[10] Cf. the text at n. 23 below.   [11] A. T. H. Smith, *Property Offences* (London, 1994).
[12] See, most generally, *An Introduction to the Law of Restitution* (Oxford, 1989), 174–84.

in time, the harm that results is the same in either instance, yet to describe Alex's action in the latter case as an act of arson entirely fails to capture the essence of the wrong that she does, and of the interest that the criminal law (by prohibiting Alex from doing it) seeks to protect. Duff and Horder concur here about an important claim: we may harm someone just by wronging them, whether or not our action has objectively bad consequences.

As a condition of criminalization, then, the harm requirement is not to be conceived of as speaking only in terms of an *actus reus*. Again Lamond's work is instructive: the difference between a legitimate offer or warning and an instance of blackmail is best understood in terms of the intentions and reasons of the defendant who delivers it. Economic and other consequentialist accounts of the harm principle simply fail to capture that distinction. Similarly, the difference between negligent damage to property and vandalism lies not merely in the degree of culpability but also in the nature of the wrong (though, once again, the physical harm may be the same). They are, that is to say, different actions. Vandalism is not fully specified by its consequence because it expresses a certain sort of contempt for society, and for the victim, which the mere causing of damage does not.

CULPABILITY

Von Hirsch makes the important point in his essay that criminalization of harms cannot be accounted for without reference to fault. Nor should punishment be independent of fault either; as Alldridge observes, the level of sentence is one way in which a court signals the reprehensibleness of the defendant. In addition to punishment and proscription, however, a third aspect of the criminal process, and one central to its distinctiveness from other areas of our legal system, is the conviction itself. In particular, while it enables the imposition of punitive sanctions, a criminal conviction—at least for stigmatic offences—is regarded as a penalty *in its own right*, both by legal officials, such as judges, and by the public; for it has the effect of labelling the defendant as a criminal.[13] In so doing, it makes a public, condemnatory statement about that defendant: that she is blameworthy for doing the *actus reus*—for inflicting the harm or wrong proscribed. If this is so, then we should want the criminal law to cast its conviction-based aspersions truthfully, so as not to defame the people it convicts. And we do not want it to convict people who are not culpable for doing the *actus reus*. The law exists in society, not in the abstract. Correspondingly, the law's labelling of a defendant as 'criminal' should be done with an eye to the social meaning of that term.

Suppose, then, that we were to adjudge some activity a bad thing to do.

---

[13] A point emphasized here by Sullivan (at 152): 'Non-conviction of the blameless should be an informing principle of the substantive criminal law. A conviction for a stigmatic offence is a sanction in its own right and parsimony in the distribution of sanctions should be fostered.'

And suppose, too, that the criminal law (notwithstanding the extra institutional constraints noticed by von Hirsch, including freedom of speech and privacy) were to prohibit it. If Barbara goes ahead and does it anyway, on what footing might we and the law blame her?

Blaming someone is a complicated problem, and the literature is constantly augmented by academic theories that purport to explain how to do so. It is complicated because sometimes actions which are bad or undesirable (say, homicide) do not lead us to blame the defendant—this may happen, for example, when Barbara kills Charles in justified self-defence. Homicide is, in itself, undesirable. And it is the *actus reus* of a crime. But we would not, in Barbara's case, convict or even criticize her for killing Charles. Nor would we blame Deborah, a doctor, who gives a painkiller to the one patient in a million who is unknowably allergic to it and dies as a consequence.

Any explanation of the (dis)connection must recognize that there are different possible types of object of moral assessment. One may form a judgment about some *actus*, activity, or consequence as a good or bad *thing*. Thus, we think that committing homicide (at least, non-consensual killing) is a bad thing to do, and that (unwelcome) death is an undesirable thing when it happens. As such, we have moral reason not to kill. Alternatively, we may form a judgment about a person; especially, about her character. That someone wants to kill people is (*ceteris paribus*) a reason to think less of her. But it is not quite this alternative either that Glover intends when he says, 'to blame a person for an action is more than merely to say that he has brought about something we object to. We disapprove, not merely of the action or its consequences, but of him.'[14] A third sort of moral assessment is of people-with-respect-to-an-action. It is only a moral assessment of this last type that can count as an instance of blame—thus, adverse judgments of this type are the ones that the culpability-conditions of the criminal law must underwrite.

Whatever we think of Deborah as a person (perhaps we know her to be a callous, uncaring doctor who is quite happy for her patients to die), we do not blame her when she kills her patient. Deborah may be faulted as a person, and she causes something that we count undesirable, yet we do not blame her *for doing so*. If this be so, then what are the conditions under which we may attribute fault for a *reus actus*?

The account that one gives may have wide-ranging implications for the criminal law. Consider—by way of example only—two such accounts, which we shall rather arbitrarily christen 'subjective' and 'objective'. Our subjectivist account of culpability concentrates upon the defendant herself.

[14] *Responsibility* (New York, 1970), 64. See also T. Nagel, 'Moral Luck' in *Mortal Questions* (Cambridge, 1979), 24. Note, as do von Hirsch and others in this collection, the implicit requirement here that the *actus* must be initially *reus* before blame for it can attach to the defendant.

There are a variety of such theories, but the one we shall for convenience adopt here (and the one Duff is concerned to attack) asserts that culpability depends upon morally defective *choices*. We blame someone for *choosing* to do something wrong—for instance, for choosing to set fire to the house. Fault is made out whenever someone deliberately puts bad goals or reasons ahead of good ones.

For our subjectivist, there must be advertence because of the way morality operates, which (she claims) is so as to give us ways of evaluating actions.[15] If the action to be evaluated, however, is not foreseen, then the moral reasons for or against it do not affect the defendant's assessment of whether it is right or wrong to act as he does. And it makes sense that someone will not ponder over something she does not know to be relevant. On the subjectivist's view, it is perfectly reasonable to flick a switch if I am unaware the switch is miswired and will cause my friend to be electrocuted. Failing to take account of the risk of electrocution is not something for which I can be blamed. Conversely, it is when a defendant acts for morally-bad reasons (say, takes a risk of killing her friend without having good cause for doing so) that we say not merely that her action in killing somone is bad, but also that *she* is culpable for doing it.

In the law, on this view, defendants must be judged on the facts as they believe them to be. (The emphasis is on the person.) On the other hand, the *objectivist* will argue that culpability depends upon (i) the facts as they actually are, irrespective of the defendant's own beliefs about them; and (ii) the test of what a reasonable person would expect or realize—not to mention, do. Objectivists focus upon the wrongs that defendants actually do. (The emphasis is on the behaviour.) And their argument is that if, say, homicide is an undesirable occurrence, then that is a reason not to do it, whether or not one foresees the risk. Homicide does not become acceptable just because it is done inadvertently. If it is a bad thing, then not only does one have a moral (and, in this case, legal) duty not to do it, but one also has a duty to *take care* so that one does not do it inadvertently either.

How may these alternatives matter to the criminal law? An obvious battlefield has already been noted: the law of recklessness. No minor skirmish, this, for recklessness is the minimum *mens rea* requirement for many stigmatic criminal offences. Suppose that David causes a fire in his house and is charged with reckless arson. In many jurisdictions (lining up behind the earlier English case of *Cunningham*[16]) 'recklessness' requires some degree of actual foresight. So for David to be guilty he must have actually foreseen the risk of setting fire to the house when he did the act that caused it; were he merely negligent (or even grossly so), then he would have to be acquitted. In these jurisdictions, the subjectivist holds sway. On the other hand, following *Caldwell*,[17] the law in England is now objective—one can be convicted

15 Cf. J. L. Mackie, *Ethics* (Harmondsworth, 1977), 208–11.   16 [1957] 2 QB 396.
17 [1982] AC 341.

of reckless arson when one simply fails to think of a risk, provided that the risk created by one's action is obvious and serious. Moreover, the test, whether the risk is obvious, asks whether it would be obvious to a reasonable person, rather than should it have been obvious to the particular defendant.[18]

It makes a big difference. On the *Cunningham* view, neither failure to care nor foolishness is a cause for culpability.[19] By contrast, the *Caldwell* focus is not on beliefs, but upon indifference and risky conduct. A good example is the former offence of reckless driving, which clearly was directed at the behaviour of the driver rather than at his mental state. What is interesting about this offence is that the word 'reckless' was working as an *actus reus* term. Reckless homicide requires that you foresee the risk of death, but reckless driving demanded only that the *manner* of driving be sufficiently dangerous. One might, for example, deliberately drive recklessly. The reason given for making such an apparent extension of the realm of *mens rea* into inadvertence is that indifference to an obvious risk is often just as morally bad as actual foresight of an *actus reus*, and so is amply reprehensible, warranting criminal condemnation. A question may be asked, however, whether this point is systematically true, because—on the view taken in *Caldwell*—we would even convict the defendant in *Elliott* v. *C*,[20] which of course is precisely what an English court did.

One might think that a pertinent question to ask of the defendant in *Elliott* v. *C* would be whether, given her limitations, C's destruction of the shed was even negligent. But is it any longer important to distinguish negligence from recklessness? A subjectivist who opposes liability for *Caldwell* recklessness is going to be hard pressed to justify liability for negligence. And indeed, what we find is that subjectivists often suggest that people should never be convicted for negligence.[21] On the other hand, an objectivist will find negligence liability easier to account for. Negligence is unreasonable *behaviour*, and we do not have to look beyond the unreasonableness of the behaviour to justify criminal culpability.[22] But the objectivist, having

[18] Cf. *Stephen* (1984) 79 Cr. App. R 334.

[19] Compare *Stephenson* [1979] QB 695. Stephenson lit a fire while sheltering in a haystack. He was charged with reckless arson after the haystack caught fire, but successfully claimed that it was not reckless since he did not appreciate the risk.

[20] [1983] 1 WLR 939. C, a subnormal 14-year-old girl, wandered away from home, entering a shed which she subsequently burned down. She had an idea that the white spirit she was playing with was flammable, but had no conception of the scale of the fire it would produce.

[21] J. Hall, 'Negligent Behaviour Should be Excluded from Penal Liability' (1963) 63 *Columbia LR* 632. See also M. S. Moore, 'Choice, Character, and Excuse' in E. F. Paul, F. D. Miller, and J. Paul (eds.), *Crime, Culpability and Remedy* (Oxford, 1990), 29 at 58, who suggests that the place of negligence in the law can only be explained on utilitarian grounds.

[22] It may be possible partially to reconcile the two views, though what we would need in order to do so is that which we do not have: an analysis of the reasonable man test that could show the connection between the reasonable man and the defendant, so that we could be sure the defendant deserves blame for what she does whenever her behaviour fails the reasonable man test. At the moment the standard of care for negligence speaks to the defendant's *behaviour* only; it does not tell us anything about *her*.

conveniently based liability for both recklessness and negligence alike on the defendant's behaviour rather than her beliefs, will now run headlong into a different problem. If the basis of blame is the same, why do we convict in most serious offences for recklessness but not for negligence? A subjectivist can consistently argue that, if inadvertent negligence is blameworthy at all, it is at least *less* blameworthy than is advertent recklessness, and so should not be criminalized as often. An objectivist cannot do that.

There is no obvious answer to this difficulty, except to look in a different direction entirely, and to invoke H. L. A. Hart's Rule of Law principle: that if there is widespread exposure to state interference for inadvertent wrong-doing, then it is going to be much harder for citizens to plan and get on with their lives, without fearing the unforeseen disruption that facing criminal charges entails.[23] But that same principle would count against liability for inadvertent recklessness under *Caldwell*, a case our objectivist champions. Moreover, to the extent that the Rule of Law argument addresses unpredictable interference by the State, liability for negligence is reasonably predictable. Nor should the Rule of Law constraint be overriding; unless negligence liability were no deterrent, the constraint prima facie deprives victims of protection from similarly unlooked-for intrusions by other citizens.

We cannot resolve the problems of recklessness and negligence here. What is striking is how so many other areas of blackletter criminal law are affected by the same subjective/objective debate. Indeed, every paper in this collection which touches on the general part of the criminal law is necessarily informed by some view of what is the essential connection between action and defendant that can ground blame.

Attempts

The implications of Duff's own theory of culpability are well known in the context of recklessness.[24] In this volume he discusses some of its significance for attempts. Any defence of the law of attempts must answer, *inter alia*, two questions: why punish attempts differently from the main crime; and why cannot an attempter be allowed a defence of withdrawal?

As Duff points out, a subjectivist might be expected to argue that since culpability depends upon a defendant's beliefs and intentions, the mere fact that his attempt *fails* when George tries to shoot Harriet dead should make no difference to his culpability. So George should not be treated any differently by the law than if he actually succeeded. If George is successful, he is guilty of murder. In the law, however, if through sheer chance George misses, then George is guilty only of the attempt and is likely to go to jail for a rather shorter term. Yet the only difference is that he missed, and that is

---

[23] See, e.g., H. L. A. Hart, 'Punishment and the Elimination of Responsibility' in *Punishment and Responsibility* (Oxford, 1968), 158 at 181–2.

[24] See, e.g., *Intention, Agency, and Criminal Liability* (Oxford, 1990), ch. 7.

just a matter of luck. So there is, according to the subjectivist, no intrinsic reason why the law should treat George any more leniently than if he were to succeed and Harriet lay dead before him.

As we know, so far as the law is concerned in this area, the views of the objectivist have carried the day. If we look, objectively, at what George has done, the two cases *are* different. In one case George has tried to shoot Harriet. In the other, a much worse thing has happened—he has murdered Harriet. Society would much rather that attempted murderers miss instead of succeed. To put it again: we feel very differently about an attempted bombing, say by the IRA, than we do when the IRA succeeds in killing someone. In one case we say, thank God, they failed. It is not a tragedy, because no-one has died. And it seems natural for the criminal law to reflect the difference.

On the other hand, the objectivist view that the law currently takes of attempts throws up another interesting problem. It makes the line between preparation and attempt all-important. Once a defendant has got past mere preparation and has actually embarked on the attempt, the law in most jurisdictions states that she cannot withdraw from the attempt, because the offence is already committed.[25] But if she withdraws or stops before crossing the preparation line, then there is no offence of attempting to do anything. So the objectivist analysis has resulted in the crucial test being, how far did she go? And what is interesting about this test is that it does not matter *why* the defendant withdraws from the attempt. If she is stopped by a policeman before she crosses the line (as happened recently in the English case of *Campbell*[26]), then she commits no attempt even though the 'withdrawal' was not voluntary. Yet if she does cross it and then for some reason realizes she does not want to go ahead with her planned crime, it does not matter. Because the test depends on her behaviour, it is too late. We acknowledge that objectivism *explains* the law of attempts (at least, rather better than does its rival). Yet in this respect it seems to us to fail to acknowledge a morally-salient difference between these cases.

Justification

Robinson, Simester, and Gardner exhibit some of those same theoretical rivalries over the problem of justification. The problem is illustrated by the well-known case of *Dadson*,[27] in which a policeman shot and wounded a thief who was stealing wood. It was then, as now, an offence intentionally to shoot another, and both the *actus reus* and *mens rea* were made out in Dadson's case. However, the thief was in fact a felon, and a defence existed at that time to the effect that the policeman would be justified in shooting to prevent the escape of a felon. This raised an interesting difficulty, because

---

[25] *Taylor* (1859) 1 F & F 511; *Page* [1933] VLR 351. This rule is not universal: D. Stuart, 'The Actus Reus of Attempts' [1970] *Criminal LR* 505, 519–21; Model Penal Code, § 5.01(4).
[26] [1991] *Criminal LR* 268.   [27] (1850) 4 Cox CC 358.

the policeman had not realized that the person he was shooting was a felon. As far as the policeman knew, he shot without justification. Should he be convicted?

Let us vary the example a little. Suppose that Ian and Julia have been arguing fiercely over some point of law, and Ian becomes so irritated that he pulls out a gun and shoots her. But imagine also that it turns out that Ian did so in the nick of time because, although he did not know it, Julia was also very irritated and was about to shoot Ian. Should Ian be convicted of shooting Julia, or should he be acquitted?

On an objective view, if we look only at the events, then on balance Ian has not done anything wrong at all. The law prohibits unjustified killing, and this is simply not that sort of case. Since there *was* a justication in fact, this is not the sort of harm the law is worried about, and whether or not Ian knew about Julia's intentions just does not matter.

The subjective analysis would convict Ian. It is not a good thing that Julia should be killed, and this is why homicide is the *actus reus* of an offence. Sometimes we allow people to do things which are otherwise undesirable, because they have to—especially, in self-defence. But this is a case where Ian simply decided to commit homicide. Why should we extend the licence we grant people to do otherwise undesirable things to a person who acted for thoroughly bad reasons?

Certain distinctions are thrown into sharp relief by this dispute. As Robinson sees but Gardner denies, reasonableness is not the same thing as justification. A reasonable mistake about the need for self-defence does not make a defendant's conduct *justified*; it merely, and so Robinson contends, excuses. (Here Gardner concurs.) But if this is so how might the objectivist, who is concerned with the reasonableness of behaviour, talk legitimately of justification? Ashworth and Glazebrook point out that disentangling these concepts is vital if one is to address either general or particular defences in a self-consistent manner.

For a reply, Robinson can turn from conditions of culpability to those of harm, with which an objectivist's views might rather neatly dovetail. For if behaviour is reasonable, then surely it is behaviour with which the criminal law ought not to be concerned? Though Gardner finds the institutional objection unconvincing, such a response nevertheless garners persuasive force from its refusal to compartmentalize the law. Von Hirsch argues that the harm principle cannot, and should not, be disjunctive to the ideas of wrongdoing and blame. Ashworth notices that it is so often the good or bad intention that makes a doctor's behaviour right or wrong. Horder sees that same point not merely in the context of the medical profession. So perhaps Robinson is right after all? Yet if he is, this is not because of what objectivism has to say about the ascription of culpability.

DEFEASING CULPABILITY AND PROSCRIBING HARMS

We have identified two types of conditions for criminalization. Correspondingly, some time ago the criminal law was by Kenny and others irreversibly sundered: into a general part, which covers doctrines that apply to all crimes, and a special part, which covers the particular crimes. Rules about *mens rea*, *actus reus*, the voluntary act requirement, omissions, causation, and so forth, are of catholic application and fall within the general part. Rules defining the particular elements of offences such as rape, murder, and burglary are treated within the special part.

Both bifurcations track the further distinction, noticed earlier, between two sorts of moral assessment that we and the criminal law make. One is the judgment that something bad or harmful was done by someone. The second judgment is about the culpability of the person who did it: not only was it a bad thing to do, but that person warrants reproof for doing it. Formulation of the special part of the criminal law is concerned with the former type of judgment—with whether an action is a good or bad thing to do. Before the law proscribes it, of course, it should meet the harm-oriented conditions of criminalization. The principles of culpability, on the other hand, are contained within the general part; and are concerned squarely with the second type of moral judgment—the assessment and blaming of people with respect to their actions. For it is, we have claimed, only judgments of the second type that count as instances of blame.

This is not to say that the *extent* of someone's culpability for an action is independent of the particular substance of that action. One is, we think, deserving of a greater censure for intentionally killing another than for intentionally tripping him up (and this is not merely to say that one has, in the former case, done a worse *thing*). One deserves neither conviction nor blame whatsoever for doing something that is good (and indeed, such an action should not be proscribed). But it *is* to say that the principles which underlie the ascription of culpability for doing an action are independent of the nature of that action. This is, in turn, why they inform the general part of the criminal law. If inadvertent but negligent damage to property is not culpable, for example, then nor is inadvertent but negligent homicide. Similarly, if there should be a voluntary act requirement,[28] it ought to apply across the board of offences.

Let us, though, at once acknowledge one of the dangers of theory. Oversimplification must constantly be guarded against, because (as Horder shows) detail matters. To be sure, the criminal law cannot respond to political and practical ethical niceties as sensitively and flexibly as does an abstract moral system; but to neglect the richness that is to be gleaned from

---

[28] An issue we do not propose to consider here.

the particulars is to slew, in effect, toward the arbitrary. The arguments in favour of a voluntary act requirement, for instance, which are in principle of general application, must heed the egregious need to proscribe some omissions. One might be able to show that there ought to be a general rule against having liability for omissions. However a criminal law that did not admit of specific exceptions (imposing duties, say, on the parents of young children) would be drastically impoverished.

It is a similar mistake to think that theory can result in a clean compartmentalization of the criminal law, with each partition entire unto itself. One of the most important points illustrated by this volume is that the distinction between *actus reus* and *mens rea* cuts across that division between harm and culpability conditions. The point once made in abstract by Glanville Williams[29] and noted here by Simester, that the *mens rea* is often integral to the nature and wrongness of the defendant's action, is placed in practical context by the essays of Ashworth, Horder, and Lamond. Thus questions regarding intention, say, affect both (i) the general issue of under what conditions should criminal culpability for doing an *actus reus* be attributed; and (ii) the discrimination between offers and blackmailing threats. Amongst the considerations that inform Lamond's analysis of (ii) is the point that an intention can change the very nature of what is done: the Thomist doctrine of double effect shares an insight with the House of Lords in this country when it avers that only killings[30] done as ends in themselves or as means to other ends should be termed 'murders'.[31] It may be no better to commit homicide advertently and recklessly, and with that sort of question Simester is concerned, but to do so is not to murder. Killing is bad, yet (as with the relationship between damage to property and vandalism) that does not supply the only reason why murder is wrong. Even if 'harms' can in some narrow sense be specified solely by reference to consequences, wrongs cannot.

We do not doubt that reductionist tendencies should sometimes be resisted. But Glazebrook points out that there are also advantages in being able to generalize. That proof of vandalism, which requires (*inter alia*) proof that the damage to property was intended, at the same time demonstrates a condition of the defendant's culpability for causing the damage does not necessarily mean that the conditions of harm and culpability are irrevocably entangled—rather, it shows that sometimes those conditions can be partially satisfied by the same element. And is there not value in having, for example,

---

[29] 'The act constituting a crime may in some circumstances be objectively innocent, and take its criminal colouring entirely from the intent with which it is done': *Criminal Law: The General Part* (2nd edn., London, 1961), 22. See also A. C. E. Lynch, 'The Mental Element in the Actus Reus' (1982) 98 *Law Quarterly R* 109.

[30] Including (*per Cunningham* [1982] AC 566) inflictions of grevious bodily harm which cause death.

[31] *Moloney* [1985] AC 905; *Hancock and Shankland* [1986] AC 455. See, too, Ashworth's discussion in this volume of the unreported case of *Adams*. This proposition is apparently subject to an exception in respect of side-effects which are foreseen as 'morally certain'. We are not concerned with those here, but they are addressed by Ashworth.

a common understanding of 'intended' when we do so? The criminal law has, *inter alia*, a communicative role:[32] redundant concepts simply confuse.

Conflict between the ambitions to simplify and to particularize is very pertinent to the articulation of defences. One upshot apparent from the earlier discussion of culpability is that neither the subjective nor objective accounts we canvassed present an entirely satisfactory explanation for the criminal law.[33] We suspect that this reflects a certain tension: no unitary account can provide a comprehensive explanation, while no complete explanation can avoid being, in part, piecemeal. Horder may well be right, in that adopting a piecemeal approach may be desirable when it comes to proscribing harms; and Ashworth is no doubt also correct to assert the occasional place for defences specific to the harm from which they exculpate.[34] But Glazebrook perceives the limitations of that approach in the context of exculpation. For if the doctrines that underlie an ascription of blame for wrongdoing are found within the general part of the criminal law, those which deny that ascription should be similarly located.[35]

The recent case of *Kingston* illustrates, however, just how imprecise our ascriptive doctrines can be.[36] In the course of his essay, Ashworth observes that the possibility that all elements of some offence might be present without the defendant's being at fault for wrongdoing was implicitly recognized in *Hyam* and *Gillick*, where it was suggested that an *actus reus* done deliberately in a medical context should be exculpated because it did not involve a 'guilty' intent.[37] This is a view difficult to square with *Kingston*, where Lord Mustill asserted that *mens rea* was merely a technical term; or indeed with the extraordinary reasoning in *Yip Chiu-Cheung*.[38] By contrast with the other cases, perhaps—and even with such excuses as duress and provocation—Kingston's claim to a defence is weakened by the fact that it involves no justificatory element; there is no claim of (albeit unjustified) action arising out of a justified disposition. But it is not clear that the deficiency ought to be decisive: Gardner's remark,[39] that in general supervening

---

[32] A proposition central to Duff's advocacy of an objectivist law of attempts (especially, at 40 ff.). Duff deploys the point in the context of criminal convictions, but it is equally important to the guidance the law gives *ex ante*. Cf. Robinson, at 64 ff.

[33] Compare Duff's contribution to this volume, where he is careful to avoid claiming that the criteria of culpability should be purely objective, while arguing forcefully that they should not be purely subjective.

[34] Especially, perhaps, in the context of medicine: whose practitioners are uniquely placed to assess, in context, cases which for others—including lawyers—lie outside the realms of moral intuition.

[35] See also, in a different vein, the remarks made by Gardner, at 124 ff.

[36] [1995] 2 AC 355. Kingston committed pædophiliac acts while in a state of disinhibition owing to his involuntary intoxication. See the extended discussion of the case by Sullivan in this volume.

[37] See Ashworth's analysis at 178.

[38] (1994) 99 Cr. App. R 406. An undercover police officer was held to be conspiring to export heroin even though he did so only for the sake of exposing the operation. Contrast *Clarke* (1984) 80 Cr. App. R 344; see further Ashworth, at 182, and Sullivan, at 135.

[39] At 122.

defences are recognized by the criminal law only when they operate, at least
in part, as both justification and excuse, would prima facie also preclude
recognition of defences in *Gillick* and *Yip Chiu-Cheung*, the grounds for
neither of which appear to require (though do not forestall) an excusatory
element. Kingston's dispositions, moreover, while not justified, were at least
affected outwith his control. The hesitation we feel over treating his case as
straightforward ought to prompt reflection upon a criminal legal system that
steps simply from those facts to a conviction.

One of the impediments to granting a defence might be that existing legal
excuses seem to reflect choice-oriented constructions of fault. When the law
allows excuses such as duress, it may be influenced by concerns such as
whether the defendant's choice was entirely her own, and whether even if
defective her election to act was at least an understandable option. In an
instructive attempt to find an underpinning account that might 'plug gaps'
in the present law, Sullivan considers the implications of an alternative, subjective approach to the law of excuses. It is in our view a mistake to assume
that inculpation and exculpation theories are complementary: where
Hampton thinks that 'if ignorance excuses then knowledge must convict,'
we find a *non sequitur*.[40] Nonetheless, it seems safe to say that accounts of
inculpation and exculpation ought to be closely related. And Sullivan is right
to notice that culpability does not follow *simpliciter* from the finding that a
defendant's elected action is voluntary rather than compelled. The attraction
of Sullivan's analysis, moreover, is that it is not vulnerable to the objection
typically raised against character-based accounts of fault by choice theorists,
that the law does not criminalize character alone; for his analysis addresses
only those actions which are out of the defendant's character as hitherto
manifested by his behaviour. Of course, it is open for *our* subjectivist to
respond that an 'out-of-character' action may be so described because and
to the extent that it does not genuinely manifest a choice *she* makes—a
choice expressing motives which are very poorly representative of her 'relatively permanent character and personality', as Mackie once put it.[41]
Conversely, however, a character-based approach does circumvent the
'regression' objection. What of actions that manifest a character which the
defendant has not chosen? An adult who kills another out of hate might say,
'I could not help being such a person—my parents instilled that hatred in me
as a child by beating me consistently.' When she says so, she *explains* her
conduct, but does not (we think) excuse it. A character-based analysis such
as Sullivan draws from might tell us that she deserves censure. The theory
refuses to answer the question whether she *deserves* to be a person who
deserves censure; it is enough that she *is*.

---

[40] '*Mens Rea*' in Paul, Miller and Paul (eds.), n. 21 above, 1 at 12.
[41] 'The Grounds of Responsibility' in P. M. S. Hacker and J. Raz (eds.), *Law, Morality and
Society* (Oxford, 1977), 175 at 183.

Theory and Practice

The contributors addressing topics within the law's special part make concrete a view that is shared by all our authors: one should not formulate criminal laws without reference to the underlying principles of criminalization. Not only punishment but also proscription and censure must be justified. From Duff, addressing an issue in the general part, to Lamond, addressing an issue in the specific, the essays contained in this volume are all concerned with the shaping of the criminal law. Whether a contribution discusses the law's conceptions of culpability and harm as doctrines, or in application to more particular areas of legal rules, theory is at work at every stage.

The essays in this collection, then, illustrate some of the ways in which rival accounts of culpability and wrongdoing, over which academics do battle (both in this volume and elsewhere) from their ivory towers, can have real, practical implications for the criminal law. It is in the interests of the criminal law as an institution to have such a theoretical or philosophical underpinning, since public respect for the criminal law depends in part upon its accuracy when labelling defendants as blameworthy. Moreover, public respect depends also upon the law's ability to label defendants consistently. Many questions in the criminal law are intertwined, so that existing attempts to address them separately produce conflict: the solutions offered do not reflect a coherent general theory.[42] Given the legal system's use of precedent, a ruling which leads to an accurate labelling of one defendant may subsequently lead to the defamation of another. If theory can help to avoid that, then there will always be a place for it.

---

[42] Examples of the potential for inconsistency have already been noted here: in the English rule that 'recklessness' should in law embrace unforeseen risks (notwithstanding incapacity to foresee such risks! *per Elliott* v. C [1983] 1 WLR 939), concurrent with the rule that negligence may be sufficient for manslaughter, but also concurrent with the rule that honest unreasonable mistakes are a complete defence (*Beckford* v. R. [1988] AC 130). Another instance of possible conflict is the coexistence of the rule that duress is not a defence to murder with the principle that the absence of a voluntary act is.

2

Subjectivism, Objectivism and Criminal Attempts

R. A. Duff*

'SUBJECTIVISM' AND 'OBJECTIVISM'

It is no doubt sometimes unhelpful to portray controversies about the proper principles of criminal liability as controversies between 'subjectivism' and 'objectivism'.[1] Certainly neither term picks out a single, unitary, position. Furthermore, some disagreements rather concern the scope of the 'subjective' itself: for example, should we analyse recklessness in terms of conscious risk-taking or of 'practical indifference', both of which could be portrayed as 'subjective' aspects of the agent's conduct?[2] Nor can we always draw a clear distinction between the 'subjective' and the 'objective'. If we justify an ascription of recklessness by saying that an agent failed to notice some obvious risk because he did not care about it,[3] we are not simply explaining his failure to notice that risk in morally neutral terms: we are, rather, interpreting his conduct in the light of some normative, non-subjective, standard of appropriate care.[4]

In some contexts, however, there does seem to be a clear distinction between 'subjectivist' and 'objectivist' principles of criminal liability, and controversies which embody that distinction. One such context is the law of attempts. In this paper, I will show that one familiar 'subjectivist' account of the principles of criminal liability has radical implications for the law of attempts—implications far more radical than its proponents seem generally

* I am grateful for helpful comments from the participants in the seminar in Cambridge at which I gave a very early version of this paper, and from Andrew Simester and Andrew von Hirsch.

[1] See Lord Diplock's comments in *Caldwell* [1981] 1 All ER 961 at 965–6; *Lawrence* [1981] 1 All ER 974 at 982.

[2] See my *Intention, Agency and Criminal Liability* (Oxford, 1990), ch. 7.

[3] See, e.g., *Sheppard* [1981] AC 394 at 408; *Pigg* [1982] 1 WLR 762 at 772; and my *op. cit.*, n. 2 above, at 162–3, 170–1.

[4] See A. W. Norrie, 'Subjectivism, Objectivism, and the Limits of Criminal Recklessness' (1992) 12 *Oxford Journal of Legal Studies* 45.

ready to accept. We must then ask why they should be unhappy with the implications of their avowed principles. But we must attend, too, to certain theoretical dichotomies which underpin this type of subjectivism: and I will argue that these dichotomies offer insecure foundations for the subjectivist's principles. Finally, I will sketch an alternative, more 'objectivist', account of the law of attempts.

But I must first say a little more about the distinction between the 'subjective' and the 'objective'.

'Subjectivists' and 'objectivists' disagree about the appropriate criteria for action-ascriptions. An agent is criminally liable only if an action matching the law's definition of an offence can justly be ascribed to her. But how should we decide what actions can justly be ascribed to an agent: what criteria should determine our ascriptions? Subjectivists insist that the criteria should be 'subjective': the actions that are to be ascribed to an agent, for which she is to be held liable, must be described in 'subjective' terms. By contrast objectivists argue that what is 'mine' as an agent cannot be defined or delimited in purely 'subjective' terms, but must be described in partly 'objective' terms.

But what are 'subjective', or 'objective', terms or descriptions? We can say that the 'subjective' is a matter of the agent's psychological states: but that is too vague to be helpful. Any more precise account of the 'subjective', however, would have to be an account of the different conceptions of the 'subjective' expressed in *different* forms of subjectivism. The two most familiar contemporary subjectivist theories, the 'choice' and the 'character' accounts of criminal liability, embody different accounts of the 'subjective'.[5] 'Choice' theorists insist that we can properly ascribe to an agent only those actions that he *chose* to perform; any action for which he is to held liable must be described in terms of his choices. Choice, as constituting the 'subjective', can then be (minimally) defined in terms of intention and belief: I choose to do what I intend to do, or believe myself to be doing. 'Character' theorists, by contrast, hold that we should ground criminal liability in the character traits manifested in the agent's conduct: for them, the 'subjective' consists in those dispositions, attitudes, or motives which constitute legally relevant character traits.

I will focus in this paper on the 'choice' conception of criminal liability, which is the dominant version of subjectivism. Though the objectivist grounding for the law of attempts which I will sketch is opposed to both types of subjectivism, the implications of each type for the law of attempts differ;[6] and the arguments that I will offer against the 'choice' conception

---

[5] See my 'Choice, Character, and Criminal Liability' (1993) 12 *Law and Philosophy* 345.

[6] For instance, a 'character' theorist who focuses on the agent's dangerousness (see Model Penal Code, Commentary to § 5, at 303–33) will see reason to acquit kinds of 'impossible attempt' which do not show the agent to be dangerous (see § 5.05(2)), and to provide a fairly broad specification of the conduct required to constitute an attempt (see § 5.01); whereas 'choice' theorists find it harder to justify acquitting even radically misguided attempts, and

are not the same as those that might be offered against the 'character' conception.

The 'choice' version of subjectivism can be defined by Ashworth's 'intent' and 'belief' principles: agents should be held 'criminally liable for what they intended to do, and not according to what actually did or did not occur', and must be 'judged on the basis of what they believed they were doing, not on the basis of actual facts and circumstances which were not known to them at the time'.[7] This does not mean that agents are to be held liable for their intentions and beliefs *rather than* for their actions. The claim is that the *actions* for which agents are to be held liable should be identified in terms of what they intended to do or believed they were doing: agents are liable for their actions qua chosen.

A subjectivist might argue, or might avow principles which imply, that the action-ascriptions which generate criminal liability should be determined by *purely* subjective criteria: the actions we ascribe to an agent must be described purely in terms of her intentions and beliefs. By contrast, 'objectivists' (as I shall use the notion) do not hold that criminal liability should be based on *purely* objective criteria: that agents' actual intentions or beliefs should be wholly irrelevant to their criminal liability. They deny, rather, that the subjective dimensions of the agent's conduct are all that matter for criminal liability: its 'objective' aspects may also be crucial. But what are these 'objective' aspects?

They are of two kinds. One consists in what actually occurs or is actually the case: for example, in the fact of whether the shot that I intend should hit, or believe will hit, V actually hits or misses; in the fact of whether the woman on whom I press sexual intercourse, believing her to consent to it, actually consents or not. The other consists in what a 'reasonable' person would believe, or realize: in the fact that what I take to be a person is obviously (i.e. would be immediately seen by any reasonable person to be) a tree; or that the means by which I hope to achieve a criminal goal are obviously (i.e. would be seen by any reasonable person to be) utterly inadequate; or that my action creates an obvious risk of harm which would be recognized by any reasonable person.[8]

Now in many contexts subjectivist principles play an *exculpatory* role,

could argue for a narrower specification of the conduct element (see the discussions of 'Impossible Attempts' and of 'The "Conduct Element" in Attempts', text at nn. 22–36 and 50–5 below respectively.

[7] See A. J. Ashworth, 'Criminal Attempts and the Role of Resulting Harm' (1988) 19 *Rutgers LJ* 725 (hereafter, Ashworth, 'Attempts') at 736; and 'Belief, Intent and Criminal Liability' in J. Eekelaar and J. Bell (eds.), *Oxford Essays in Jurisprudence* (3rd Series, Oxford, 1987), 1 (hereafter, Ashworth, 'Belief') at 7.

[8] See *Caldwell* [1981] 1 All ER 961, *Lawrence* [1981] 1 All ER 974; and G. Williams, 'Recklessness Redefined' (1981) 40 *Cambridge LJ* 252 at 254. We need not pursue here the question of how a 'reasonable' person is to be defined (for instance, which, if any, of this particular defendant's characteristics or limitations should be ascribed to the 'reasonable' person); for present purposes we need say only that she or he is a person of ordinary intelligence.

exempting from criminal liability those who might otherwise be held liable. Thus someone who does not realize that her action might damage another's property should not be convicted of criminal damage—even if her act 'in fact creates an obvious risk' (one that would be obvious to the 'ordinary prudent' person) of such damage: for she has not chosen to risk damaging another's property.[9] A man who honestly believed that the woman with whom he had intercourse consented to it should not be convicted of rape—even if his belief was both mistaken and unreasonable: for he did not choose to have, or to take a risk of having, 'intercourse with a woman who [did] not consent to it'.[10] In the law of attempts, however, subjectivist principles more typically play an *inculpatory* role, convicting (or rendering liable to harsher punishments) some who would be acquitted (or be liable to lighter punishments) by objectivist principles. Indeed, we will see that a strict application of subjectivist principles would result in a radical extension of the law of attempts, beyond even its existing (and partly subjectivist) limits.

A Subjectivist Law of Attempts?

A strictly subjectivist law of attempts, which embodied the 'belief' and 'intent' principles, would be very different from our own.

THE PUNISHMENT AND LABELLING OF ATTEMPTS

It is often argued that the mere fact of failure should not alter criminal liability. A failed attempt should be punished as severely as it would have been had it succeeded; a successful attempt should be punished no more severely than it would have been had it failed.

This claim applies to *complete* attempts, whose agent has done all that she can to commit the crime. She has fired the shot, or set the bomb, that is meant to kill; she has appropriated what she believes to be another's property.[11] The difference between success and failure in these cases lies in the objective aspects of the action: does it cause the intended result; are the circumstances as she believes them to be? Whether it succeeds or fails, its subjective aspects are the same: she intends to commit the crime and does what she believes will or might constitute its commission; she has, as far as she can, actualized her choice to commit a crime. Intentions can, of course, be more or less wholehearted; beliefs can be more or less confident or reasonable; attempts can be more or less competent. But a successful attempt can

[9] Contrast, notoriously, *Caldwell* [1981] 1 All ER 961; *Elliott* v. *C (a minor)* [1983] 1 WLR 939.

[10] Sexual Offences (Amendment) Act 1976, s. 1: see *Morgan* [1976] AC 182; *Cogan* [1976] QB 217.

[11] On the distinction between 'complete' and 'incomplete' attempts, see Ashworth, 'Attempts', n. 7 above, at 734.

be half-hearted, unconfident, or incompetent, and failed attempts can be wholehearted, confident, and competent: the mere fact of failure need manifest no relevant difference in the action's subjective character, and so should not affect the agent's sentence.

(Such a conclusion follows directly for subjectivists who believe that sentencing should depend on culpability: the mere fact of failure cannot reduce an agent's culpability as determined by her active choice to commit a crime.[12] If we instead focus on the consequential efficiency of sentences in reducing crime, complex empirical issues arise:[13] we need not discuss these here, since the 'choice' version of subjectivism certainly implies that the mere fact of success or failure should not affect sentence.)

But the position is different with *incomplete* attempts, when the agent desists or is stopped before he has done all that there is for him to do to commit the crime: for he has then done less, in subjective as well as objective terms, than one who completes his attempt. Both chose to embark on the crime. But if criminal liability depends on choice as actualized in *action*, the incomplete attempter has less that he is liable for: he has not actualized his choice to take the final steps towards committing the crime. If he desisted 'voluntarily' from the attempt,[14] we can indeed say that he has chosen not to commit the crime. But even when the non-completion of the attempt is due to external interference, the agent has not done as much as one who completes his attempt. Subjectivists can, therefore, argue that incomplete attempts should be punished less severely than they would have been had they been complete, whatever the reason for their non-completion.[15]

Of course, it may be a matter of luck whether I am able to complete a criminal attempt, just as it may be a matter of luck whether I find myself in a situation in which I am tempted to form, or have the opportunity to actualize, a criminal intention. But this kind of 'situational' luck is not the kind that 'choice' subjectivists think should be irrelevant to criminal liability. I am responsible for the active choices I make in whatever situations I find myself. The kind of luck that should be irrelevant to criminal liability is 'outcome-luck', luck 'in the way one's actions and projects turn out':[16] for only that species of luck is posterior to, and thus supposedly makes no difference to, the moral character of, the agent's active choices.

---

[12] See for instance Ashworth, 'Attempts', n. 7 above, at 741–4; H. L. A. Hart, 'Intention and Punishment', in *Punishment and Responsibility* (Oxford, 1968), 113 at 129–31; J. C. Smith, 'The Element of Chance in Criminal Liability' [1971] *Criminal LR* 63.

[13] For an exhaustive discussion of these, see S. J. Schulhofer, 'Harm and Punishment: A Critique of Emphasis on the Results of Conduct' (1974) 122 *University of Pennsylvania LR* 1497.

[14] On 'voluntary abandonment' see Model Penal Code, § 5.01(4); M. Wasik, 'Abandoning Criminal Intent' [1980] *Criminal LR* 785.

[15] See Ashworth, 'Attempts', n. 7 above, at 739–41.

[16] T. Nagel, 'Moral Luck', in *Mortal Questions* (Cambridge, 1979), 24 at 28; A. J. Ashworth, 'Taking the Consequences' in S. Shute *et al.* (eds.), *Action and Value in Criminal Law* (Oxford, 1993), 107.

But the implications of a strict subjectivism extend further than this. If there is 'no relevant moral difference' between a complete attempt and a successful crime,[17] and especially if, as some argue, what can properly be ascribed to an agent as 'her action' is nothing more than the attempt,[18] why should the law draw any distinction at all between complete attempts and substantive crimes? Why should it not convict of precisely the same crime anyone who completes a criminal attempt, whether that attempt succeeds or not, so ensuring that 'the labels of offences reflected the moral equivalence between substantive offences and "complete" attempts to commit them'?[19]

Ashworth resists this more radical suggestion, since it 'would be alien to ordinary linguistic usage, would sometimes misrepresent the external events which took place, and would in turn blur the distinction between complete and incomplete attempts'.[20] Now the appeal to 'ordinary linguistic usage' sits unhappily with his belief that 'the limitations of language should not be allowed to override moral similarities'.[21] But we could anyway avoid both linguistic deviance and substantive misrepresentation by providing new labels for these new offences: by talking, for instance, not of 'attempted murder' (which implies failure) or of 'murder' (which implies an actual death), but of '(attempted) murder', or 'murderous conduct'. And whilst a simple abolition of the current distinction between attempted and completed offences would fail to mark the morally relevant distinction between complete and incomplete attempts, this suggestion would sharpen that moral distinction: instead of distinguishing substantive crimes from attempts (whether complete or incomplete), we would distinguish complete attempts (whether successful or not) from incomplete attempts.

We see here a strange phenomenon: a subjectivist who is unwilling to accept an apparently direct implication of his avowed principles, but who has no persuasive arguments to support that unwillingness.

'IMPOSSIBLE ATTEMPTS'

For a subjectivist, the fact that it was impossible for a defendant to commit the crime which he 'intended' to commit should not bar conviction for attempting to commit it.[22] One who handles non-stolen goods in the mis-

---

[17] See Ashworth, 'Belief', n. 7 above, at 16–20.
[18] 'See A. J. Ashworth, 'Sharpening the Subjective Element in Criminal Liability', in R. A. Duff and N. E. Simmonds (eds.), *Philosophy and the Criminal Law* (Wiesbaden, 1984), 79 at 79–83; also Ashworth, 'Belief', n. 7 above, at 14–15; D. Lewis, 'The Punishment that Leaves Something to Chance' (1989) 18 *Philosophy and Public Affairs* 53 at 56.
[19] Ashworth, 'Attempts', n. 7 above, at 770.
[20] *Ibid.*; and his 'Defining Criminal Offences without Harm' in P. Smith (ed.), *Criminal Law, Essays in Honour of JC Smith* (London, 1987), 7.
[21] Ashworth, 'Attempts', n. 7 above, at 756.
[22] See Ashworth, 'Attempts', n. 7 above, at 757–64; G. Williams, 'The Lords and Impossible Attempts, or *Quis Custodiet Ipsos Custodes*?' (1986) 45 *Cambridge LJ* 33; H. L. A. Hart, 'The House of Lords on Attempting the Impossible', in *Essays in Jurisprudence and Philosophy*

taken belief that they are stolen is guilty of attempting to handle stolen goods;[23] one who, intending to kill, shoots what is actually a corpse is guilty of attempted murder.[24] Mr Wilson was guilty of attempted forgery in altering the figures on a cheque from '$2.50' to '$12.50', though, since he did not alter the words, he did not alter a material part of the cheque, which was also stamped 'Ten Dollars or less'.[25] For all these agents acted with intentions and beliefs such that, had their intentions been fulfilled and their beliefs true, their actions would have constituted completed crimes. Their actions qua chosen, as described in terms of their intentions and beliefs, constituted crimes (or would have done so had they produced their intended consequences): so they should be convicted, at least, of attempting to commit those crimes. Indeed, given the argument of the previous subsection, a subjectivist should want to see them convicted of the same offence as someone who committed the complete crime, since their 'attempts' were complete.

(Ashworth thinks that 'the fully subjective principle' would also require the conviction of agents who are mistaken about the criminal law: of one who mistakenly believes, for example, that in committing adultery she is committing a crime. To avoid convicting such agents, we must let 'the principle of legality' overrule 'the fully subjective principle' of criminal liability.[26] Now the distinction between 'mistake of fact' and 'mistake of law' is not always easily drawn,[27] but Ashworth is wrong about these cases, for two reasons. First, the principle of legality would not forbid the creation of a new crime, perhaps called 'contempt of law', which would be committed by anyone who did what she (mistakenly) believed to be criminal. But second, a subjectivist could properly oppose the creation of such a crime, on the grounds that the mere willingness to break what she believes to be the law should not make a person criminally liable: that her conduct should manifest a willingness, a choice, to do something which is actually criminal, to injure some interest which the law actually protects—which is not true in these cases.[28])

Here again, however, subjectivists are not always ready to accept the implications of their principles. Williams, for instance, notes that a man who mistakenly thinks his sexual partner is under 16 would be guilty of an

---

(Oxford, 1983), 367; M. Kremnitzer, 'The Punishability of Impossible Attempts' (1984) 19 *Israel LR* 340; Criminal Attempts Act 1981, s. 1, as interpreted (finally) in *Shivpuri* [1987] AC 1; Model Penal Code, § 5.01, Commentary, at 307–20.

[23] *Haughton* v. *Smith* [1975] AC 476; *Anderton* v. *Ryan* [1985] 1 AC 560; *Jaffe*, 78 NE 169 (1906).

[24] *Dlugash*, 363 NE 2d 1155 (1977, New York).

[25] *Wilson*, 38 So. 46 (1905, Mississippi).

[26] Ashworth, 'Attempts', n. 7 above, at 762.

[27] See K. W. Simons, 'Mistake and Impossibility, Law and Fact, and Culpability' (1990) 81 *Journal of Criminal Law and Criminology* 447.

[28] See Nix CJ in *Henley*, 474 A 2d 1115 (1984, Pennsylvania) at 1120; and Law Commission, *Attempt, Impossibility in Relation to Attempt, Conspiracy and Incitement* (No. 102, 1980), para. 2.88; Model Penal Code, Commentary to § 5.01 at 318; Williams, n. 22 above, at 55–6.

attempt, on a subjectivist account. His prosecution would be 'absurd', however, since '(1) The man has not done anything that the law regards as harm
on this occasion. (2) He is very unlikely to make the same mistake again. (3)
The hypothetical facts do not suggest that he is a pædophile.'[29] But the first
consideration holds for many failed attempts, and does not reflect on the
culpability of his choice. The other two considerations look beyond his
choice to the possible dangerousness of the dispositions it manifests, but are
no more persuasive. What matters is not whether he might make the same
mistake again, but whether he is likely to have intercourse with actually
under-age girls; and his conduct on this occasion displays a willingness to do
so. Nor is the law concerned only with pædophiles; it convicts anyone,
pædophile or not, who has sexual intercourse with an under-age girl. This
man chose 'to have intercourse with an under-age girl', thus displaying his
active willingness to injure a legally protected interest: subjectivists must
surely therefore convict him of a criminal attempt.

Williams also thinks that, though recklessness as to the circumstantial
aspects of a complete crime should suffice for an attempt to commit the
crime,[30] punishment is warranted only when those circumstances actually
exist. A man who is reckless as to the consent of a woman with whom he
tries to have intercourse should be convicted of attempted rape if, but only
if, she does not consent. Someone who is reckless as to the possible falsity of
the representations by which he attempts to obtain property should be convicted of attempting to obtain by deception if, but only if, the representations are false. To punish for an attempt, 'where there is both a lack of
intention and a lack of an essential circumstance for the completed offence,
would be stretching the crime of attempt beyond what is tolerable.'[31] But
why would such an extension be intolerable? The culpability of a choice to
take the risk that certain circumstances exist (that this woman does not consent; that these representations are false) is not affected, for a subjectivist, by
the objective fact of whether they actually exist or not. Thus if the reckless
agent is to be convicted of an attempt when those circumstances exist, a subjectivist should also convict him of an attempt when they do not exist.

Another much discussed hypothetical case is that of superstitious
attempts, such as attempts to kill by witchcraft. Many subjectivists want to
acquit in such cases, although some think that this involves qualifying subjectivist principles.[32] Now such a person does choose 'to kill', and acts in a

---

[29] N. 22 above, at 42. See his remarks on *Anderton* v. *Ryan* (see at n. 23 above), in 'Intents
in the Alternative' (1991) 50 *Cambridge LJ* 120 at 129: on which see also Law Commission
No. 102 (n. 28 above) para. 2.97; contrast Ashworth, 'Attempts', n. 7 above, at 760–1.

[30] As any subjectivist should think; see further below at n. 38.

[31] 'The Government's Proposals on Criminal Attempts—III' (1981) 131 *New LJ* 128 at 129.
For his changing views on how such cases should be dealt with see also his 'The Problem of
Reckless Attempts' [1983] *Criminal LR* 365, and n. 29 above.

[32] See, for instance, Law Commission No. 102 (n. 28 above), para. 2.97; Ashworth,
'Attempts', n. 7 above, at 764; Kremnitzer, n. 22 above, at 350–2.

way that, *given* his beliefs, constitutes an attempt to kill. But his beliefs are not merely mistaken, or stupid: they are so radically non-rational that we cannot now treat him as a responsible agent; as someone we can sensibly call to answer for his actions. Since subjectivists hold only responsible agents liable for their criminal choices, they can therefore refuse to convict in such cases without compromising subjectivist principles.[33]

There are, however, radically misguided or stupid attempts which cannot be dealt with in this way, like Mr Wilson's attempt to forge his cheque.[34] Those who focus on the agent's dangerousness might see some reason to treat such agents leniently, since their conduct 'is so inherently unlikely to result . . . in the commission of a crime that neither such conduct nor the actor presents a public danger'.[35] But subjectivists who focus on choice as the determinant of culpability should require that they be convicted, and punished no less severely than they would have been had their attempts been competent or successful: for they have chosen to commit a crime, and actualize that choice in action which they believe is likely to result in its commission. Nonetheless, we might find it hard to regard, and condemn, such agents as 'wicked rather than foolish':[36] That is, our perception of the misguided folly of their enterprises might undermine or qualify our judgment of their culpability.

THE 'FAULT ELEMENT' IN ATTEMPTS

It is typically taken for granted that an attempt must involve an 'intent to commit an offence':[37] discussion normally focuses on such questions as whether 'oblique' intention (constituted by the agent's foresight of the relevant consequence as being practically certain) should suffice, and whether intention should be required as to *every* aspect of the *actus reus* of the complete offence. I will not discuss such questions here. For subjectivists must surely hold that oblique intention, or recklessness as to circumstantial aspects of the complete offence, should suffice for an attempt, if they suffice for the complete offence itself:[38] the mere, objective, fact that an offence is

---

[33] Those of a relativist bent might prefer to say that his beliefs are non-rational only by the norms prevailing in our culture. But it is our legal system that must try him; and someone who is so estranged from our norms of reason cannot properly be called to answer for his actions by our legal system. On this see further my 'Mental Disorder and Criminal Responsibility', in Duff and Simmonds, *Philosophy and the Criminal Law* (n. 18 above), 22.

[34] See n. 25 above.

[35] Model Penal Code, § 5.05(2); see Commentary to § 5.01, at 316.

[36] Ashworth's comment on superstitious attempts; 'Attempts', n. 7 above, at 764.

[37] Criminal Attempts Act 1981, s. 1(1).

[38] On oblique intent, see J. C. Smith and B. Hogan, *Criminal Law* (7th edn., London, 1992), 304–5; Ashworth, 'Attempts', n. 7 above, at 754. On recklessness as to circumstances, see Williams, 'The Problem of Reckless Attempts' (n. 31 above), 'Intents in the Alternative' (n. 29 above); J. C. Smith, 'Two Problems in Criminal Attempts' (1957) 70 *Harvard LR* 422; my 'The Circumstances of an Attempt' (1991) 50 *Cambridge LJ* 100, and 'Recklessness in Attempts (Again)' (1995) 15 *Oxford Journal of Legal Studies* 309.

not completed cannot affect the culpability of the choice made by one who is certain that her action will cause some legally relevant harm, or who is reckless as to the existence of some legally significant circumstance.

Even this modest doctrine, when combined with a subjectivist view of 'impossible attempts', has radical implications: it convicts of a criminal attempt one who is reckless as to the consent or the age of his actually consenting, over-age, sexual partner.[39] But a thorough subjectivism should go further than this: it implies that the 'fault element' in an attempt should be no different from that required for the complete offence.

The obvious difference between a completed crime and its inchoate form is that the *actus reus* is incomplete, although the agent's conduct comes sufficiently close to completing it.[40] So why should the law not define the inchoate crime in just those terms, as being committed by anyone who acts 'with the kind of culpability . . . required for commission of the [complete] crime',[41] and whose conduct is sufficiently proximate to its actual commission? Why should a stricter fault element be required for 'attempts' than for completed crimes?

Someone who acts unjustifiably in a way which she realizes may injure another person or damage another's property, and who actually causes such harm, is guilty of wounding or of criminal damage.[42] The only difference between her and one who acts with like recklessness but causes no injury or damage is in the objective aspects of their actions: in the fortuitous fact that the latter causes no harm. But surely, then, subjectivists should convict the latter of (at least) an inchoate offence, since the subjective character of their actions is the same: each chose to take an unjustifiable risk of causing harm.

Existing laws might convict some such reckless agents: the Model Penal Code includes offences of 'recklessly endangering another person' and 'risking catastrophe';[43] English law has various particular offences of endangerment.[44] But such endangerment offences lack the scope of the law of attempts: the Model Penal Code covers only conduct that threatens death, serious injury, or major property damage; the English offences cover only particular kinds of risk, created by particular activities. The suggestion canvassed here, however, would extend the existing general law of 'attempts' to capture anyone who acts with the fault element appropriate for a complete offence, and whose conduct comes close enough to completing that offence. Such a law would, admittedly, extend well beyond the scope of the ordinary,

---

[39] See nn. 30–1.

[40] See *Cawthorne* [1968] JC 32: the 'vital distinction' between murder and attempted murder is that 'the killing has not been brought off' (Lord Clyde, at 36).

[41] Model Penal Code, § 5.01(1).

[42] Offences Against the Person Act 1861, s. 20; Criminal Damage Act 1971, s. 1(1). See also Model Penal Code, §§ 211.1(1)(a), 220.3.

[43] §§ 211.2, 220.2(2).

[44] See K. J. M. Smith, 'Liability for Endangerment: English Ad Hoc Pragmatism and American Innovation' [1983] *Criminal LR* 127.

extra-legal concept of 'attempt': we would not ordinarily say that a person who takes a reckless risk of causing harm 'attempts' to bring that harm about. But subjectivists should not allow such linguistic niceties to weigh against the substantive arguments that favour such an extensive law of inchoate crimes: we can either give 'attempt' a technical, and much broader, legal meaning or replace that label by a more suitable one, such as 'inchoate crime'.

Few subjectivists have discussed this suggestion, though it seems to follow from subjectivist principles; none favours it. Thus Stuart abandoned his earlier support for it: despite the arguments of principle and logic in its favour, '[o]ur fundamental concerns to give the accused the benefit of reasonable doubt and, in general, to apply the criminal sanction with restraint should tip the scale in favour of restricting the *mens rea* for attempts to actual intent.'[45] Ashworth recognizes that 'the basic principles of culpability and of equality of treatment' favour such a wider law of inchoate offences: but we should hesitate thus to extend the scope of the criminal law, which would 'increase the powers of the police and the individual's liability to both lawful and unlawful police intervention'.[46] Smith also resists such an extension, since it would conflict with 'public sentiment', and so might not be enforced; exempting the lucky reckless agent from liability does not unduly reduce the law's deterrent efficacy; and we should not widen the law merely to 'introduce logic and consistency'.[47]

The fact that reckless agents who fortuitously cause no harm may be just as culpable as those who cause harm thus provides a reason, but not necessarily a decisive reason, for criminalizing their conduct. We should also respect the principle of economy in law-making, creating no more law than is strictly necessary;[48] and we must weigh the costs of any such extension of the law against its probable benefits. Such considerations are then said to favour a law of inchoate crimes not (radically) more extensive than it is now: we should punish reckless agents who cause actual harm, but need not criminalize all those who luckily cause no actual harm.

One problem with this argument is that it depends upon some large empirical claims that are not easily tested. How can we tell whether the costs of thus extending the law would outweigh the benefits? Nor can subjectivists argue that the onus of proof must lie on those who wish to extend the law: 'the basic principles of culpability and of equality of treatment' create a prima facie case for such an extension, which (for subjectivists) puts the onus of proof on those who oppose it.[49]

---

[45] D. Stuart, *Canadian Criminal Law* (Toronto, 1982), 529: contrast his 'Mens Rea, Negligence and Attempts' [1968] *Criminal LR* 647.
[46] 'Attempts', n. 7 above, at 757; and 'Defining Criminal Offences without Harm', n. 20 above, at 18–19.
[47] N. 12 above, at 72–5.
[48] See A. J. Ashworth, *Principles of Criminal Law* (Oxford, 1991), 27–30, 55.
[49] See further below at nn. 56–8.

THE 'CONDUCT ELEMENT' IN ATTEMPTS

Ashworth thinks that the 'fully subjective principle' of criminal liability could imply a 'first act' test for attempts. It requires 'a "trying", which goes beyond a mere intention and requires some effort to put it into effect. Yet this is only a minimal *actus reus*, which might be satisfied by the doing of any overt act with the necessary intention.'[50] He is unhappy with this (supposed) implication of his principle, but thinks that any narrower specification of the conduct element has to appeal to other considerations which outweigh that 'fully subjective principle': in particular, a concern for individual rights and freedom from interference, and a concern to leave intending criminals a *locus poenitentiae*.

Now those who focus on the agent's dangerousness would favour a wider definition of the conduct element than English law provides,[51] though a concern for individual liberty requires something narrower than a 'first act' test.[52] But the 'choice' subjectivist need favour no such broadening of the law. What makes an agent criminally liable is her choice *as actualized in action*.[53] An intending criminal is, of course, culpable as soon as she begins to put her intention into action. But she is less culpable than is one who has progressed further towards the crime, since she has not (yet) chosen to progress beyond that first act; and her criminal culpability is not fully actualized until she has chosen to do the 'last act' which (given her beliefs) there was for her to do to commit the crime.

That is why subjectivists should draw a sharp distinction between complete and incomplete attempts.[54] They can, of course, criminalize incomplete attempts, as involving a partial actualization of a criminal choice: but their 'principles of culpability and of equality of treatment' are not compromised by specifying something much narrower than a 'first act' test for incomplete attempts, since those falling outside the scope of such a test are less culpable than those falling within its scope—and subjectivist principles do not require us to penalize *anyone* who is *to any degree* culpable. To draw the (very rough) boundary between 'mere preparation' and attempt, we must then strike the kind of balance to which Ashworth refers. But this is not (as he implies) a matter of weighing 'subjective principles' against other considerations: it is a matter of deciding how such principles should be applied, in the light of those considerations; and whilst an agent who has taken the first step in some criminal enterprise is already to some degree culpable by subjectivist criteria, a subjectivist respect for choices could also

---

[50] Ashworth, 'Attempts', n. 7 above, at 750.
[51] See *Gullefer* [1990] 1 WLR 1063: the defendant's act is 'more than merely preparatory' (Criminal Attempts Act 1981, s. 1(1)) only if he is 'in the process of committing' the crime itself (at 1065).
[52] See Model Penal Code, § 5.01; Commentary to 5.01, at 326–31.
[53] See text at n. 7 above.   [54] See text at nn. 11–21 above.

point towards as narrow a specification of the conduct element as is feasible, to leave intending criminals every opportunity to choose to abandon their crimes.[55]

The strict application of subjectivist principles would radically revise and extend the law of attempts. We would replace the distinction between substantive crimes and attempts by one between complete attempts (successful or not) and incomplete attempts. This new type of complete crime would be defined 'in the inchoate mode', by removing from the definitions of existing complete crimes any requirement for an actual, objective result: it would not require an 'intent to commit an offence', but only such *mens rea* as is currently required for the substantive offence (in so far as that is consistent with subjectivist principles). The new type of incomplete crime would cover conduct which falls short of the 'last act' (but which has advanced far enough beyond the 'first act' to satisfy whatever test the subjectivist specifies); and, whilst an intention to commit a relevant last act would be required, only such *mens rea* as the complete offence requires would be required as to the objective results of that last act. Finally, what mattered would not be whether the conduct *actually* injured or threatened some legally protected interest, but whether it *would have* threatened such an interest, had the agent's intentions been fulfilled and her factual beliefs true.

Someone who acts, unjustifiably, in a way that she realizes might injure another person or damage his property would thus commit the same crime whether such injury or damage ensues or not. A man who is reckless as to the consent or age of his actually consenting, over-age sexual partner would be guilty of just the same crime as one who is reckless as to the consent of an actually non-consenting woman on whom he forces intercourse, or as to the age of his actually under-age sexual partner.

We have noticed that subjectivists are not always happy with such implications of their avowed principles, but have no very persuasive arguments to offer against them. A further argument should be noted, however. Subjectivist principles, it might be argued, should play an *exculpatory* rather than an *inculpatory* role. They should not be read as requiring us to penalize an agent just so long as he chose to act in a way which would (were his intentions fulfilled, and his factual beliefs true) be criminal; but as requiring us *not* to hold an agent criminally liable *unless* he chose to act in such a way. This argument cannot save the subjectivist, however, for two reasons.[56]

First, it abandons subjectivism. Subjective culpability is only a necessary condition of criminal liability: to construct a sufficient condition we must

---

[55] Thus a concern to leave intending criminals a *locus poenitentiae* is internal to the 'choice' version of subjectivism, not a consideration to be weighed against the 'subjective principle'.

[56] Note, too, that the issue of the punishment and labelling of attempts (considered in the text at nn. 11–21 above) is not whether the agent should be criminally liable at all; it rather concerns the nature of her liability.

add conditions concerning the objective aspects of the agent's conduct—
whether it was actually harmful or dangerous. But this would allow liability
to depend on 'outcome-luck': whereas a central subjectivist principle is that
liability should not thus depend on luck.[57]

Secondly, the subjective aspects of an agent's conduct must play an *inculpatory* role in the law of attempts. What renders my (otherwise innocent)
action of pulling the trigger of an empty gun criminal, as attempted murder,
is my belief that the gun is loaded and my intention to kill the person at
whom I aimed it.[58] Once we recognize this, we must ask why subjectivist
principles should not play the dominant and all-embracing inculpatory role
allotted to them here: my argument has been that the subjectivist has no
answer to this question.

The fact that some subjectivists are thus unhappy with the implications of
their principles suggests that they may be moved by some non-subjectivist
intuitions: intuitions which find no support within a subjectivist perspective.
My task in what follows will be to offer a firmer foundation for such intuitions: but we should first attend to some of the foundations of subjectivism.

SUBJECTIVIST DICHOTOMIES

Subjectivism is often supported by appeal to three related dichotomies: we
can undermine it, and sketch an alternative perspective, by undermining
them. These dichotomies are purportedly analytical or metaphysical—features of the meanings of our concepts, or of the structure of our world. But
they are also supposed to have normative significance, as marking off what
is morally relevant to culpability (and thus to criminal liability) from what
is not. I will argue that they are spurious. More precisely, although they are
related to some (fairly complex) distinctions that we do indeed draw, those
distinctions cannot support or sustain the radical dichotomies to which the
subjectivist wants to appeal.

THE 'INNER' AND THE 'OUTER'

Subjectivism distinguishes the subjective realm of choice, intention, and
belief from the objective realm of actual facts or effects: what the agent
intended and tried to do, or believed to be so, from what actually happened,
or was actually so. Our ordinary understanding of human action embodies
such a distinction: subjectivists often give it, however, a radical metaphysical character which it does not and could not have.

Some take the distinction to mark a profound metaphysical separation
between the 'inner', subjective world of belief, intention, and choice, and the
'outer' world of objective facts. It then becomes a purely contingent matter

---

[57] See n. 16 above, and the discussion of 'Control' and 'Luck' in the text at n. 64 ff. below.
[58] See *Damms*, 100 NW 2d 592 (1960, Wisconsin).

that there is any connection between these worlds: that my beliefs are ever true, my intentions ever fulfilled, or my attempts ever successful. This metaphysical distinction underpins the dualist doctrine that we can never directly know, but can only (and doubtfully) infer, the thoughts and intentions of others.[59] It also underpins the doctrine which some subjectivists assert, that action consists essentially in 'trying': what is strictly 'mine' as an agent is not the actual outcome of my activity, but my 'trying' to bring some outcome about—a 'trying' which consists ultimately in an inner activity of trying to move my body.[60]

I have argued elsewhere that this 'trying' doctrine is untenable: it separates us as agents from our bodies, and from the material and social world in which we live and act.[61] We cannot, as this doctrine implies, understand what it is to act by first understanding what it is to 'try' to act, as a purely 'inner' and subjective activity, and then going on to add the contingent fact of success to some tryings. We cannot understand human agency by first understanding the 'inner' subjective realm of belief, intention, and choice, and then going on to understand how that inner world may contingently connect with the outer, objective world. Rather, we must understand agency and action as an engagement, by essentially embodied beings, with the material and social world that makes human action possible; and we can understand 'trying' only in terms of some such engagement with the world, for instance as an engagement which is difficult or unsuccessful.[62] Wittgenstein's famous remark, 'In the beginning was the deed',[63] is partly a reminder of the way in which human thought and knowledge is embedded in and structured by social activity: the 'deeds' that thus figure 'in the beginning' are not private, inner tryings, but social actions, interactions, by social beings.

I will not rehearse these arguments here, however, or the general critique of the dualist distinction between 'inner' and 'outer': for though subjectivists are often (explicitly or implicitly) motivated by some such distinction, they need not in fact appeal to it.

Even if we cannot draw this metaphysical distinction between the inner and the outer, as two realms which are only contingently connected, we do often distinguish what the agent intends and tries to do from what actually happens; or what a person believes from what is in fact the case. The law of attempts is precisely concerned with cases in which intention and actual result, or belief and actuality, diverge: in which what an agent actually does

---

[59] See my *op. cit.*, n. 2 above, chs. 2.6, 6.   [60] See n. 18 above.

[61] In 'Acting, Trying and Criminal Liability', in S. Shute *et al.* (eds.), *Action and Value in Criminal Law* (Oxford, 1993), 75.

[62] See also P. Winch, 'Trying', in his *Ethics and Action* (London, 1972), 130; P. L. Heath, 'Trying and Attempting' (1971) 45 *Proceedings of the Aristotelian Society (Supp. Vol.)* 193; J. F. M. Hunter, 'Trying' (1987) 37 *Philosophical Quarterly* 392.

[63] L. Wittgenstein, *On Certainty* (trans. D. Paul and G. Anscombe, Oxford, 1979), para. 402, quoting Goethe, *Faust*, I; see also para. 204—'it is our *acting*, which lies at the bottom of the language game'; and see P. Winch, *'Im Anfang war die Tat'* in his *Trying to Make Sense* (Oxford, 1987), 33.

is not what she intended and tried to do, or believed she was doing. All the subjectivist need, therefore, claim is that in such cases criminal liability should depend upon the subjective dimension of intention and belief, rather than on the objective dimension of what was actually done; and that claim can be separated from the spurious metaphysical underpinnings which it is sometimes given. We can understand failed attempts only in terms of the fully-fledged actions which they aspire, but fail, to be: but subjectivists can still consistently hold that the mere fact of failure should not affect our judgment of an agent's culpability.

We still need to know, of course, what justifies this claim. This leads us to the second subjectivist dichotomy.

'CONTROL' AND 'LUCK'

Criminal liability, the argument now goes, should depend on culpability; and culpability requires control. We are responsible, and can properly be held culpable, only for what is within our control—not for what is a matter of luck or chance.

The basic, roughly Kantian, thought here is familiar. Agents cannot claim moral credit for desirable happenings whose occurrence can properly be said to be just a matter of (good) luck; nor can they be properly blamed for undesirable happenings whose occurrence was just a matter of (bad) luck.[64] We will need to examine this thought critically (in the next subsection): but we must first ask whether it is properly applied by subjectivists.

A sharp distinction is drawn between 'control' and 'luck'. We are properly responsible, and so culpable, only for what we control: but in so far as the occurrence of any result depends on factors which are not fully within the agent's control, he lacks complete control over that result, whose occurrence or non-occurrence is therefore to some degree a matter of luck. But this, subjectivists then claim, is true of *all* the actual outcomes of our actions. I do have control over my choices, and over what I try to do: but whether my action (even one as minimal as moving my arm) actually accords with my choice and my attempt is not entirely up to me, since it depends on factors (such as my body's functions) that are not within my control. I am, therefore, culpable only for what I choose and attempt to do: the actual outcomes of my actions cannot affect my culpability, since they are always a matter of luck or chance.[65]

---

[64] Useful discussions of this idea include T. Nagel, 'Moral Luck' (*supra*, n. 16); B. Williams, 'Moral Luck' in *Moral Luck* (Cambridge, 1981), 20; J. Andre, 'Nagel, Williams and Moral Luck' (1983) 43 *Analysis* 202; D. Z. Phillips, 'How Lucky Can You Get?' in D. Z. Phillips and P. Winch (eds.), *Wittgenstein: Attention to Particulars* (London, 1989), 165; A. M. Honoré, 'Responsibility and Luck' (1988) 104 *Law Quarterly R* 530; J. J. Thomson, 'Morality and Bad Luck' (1989) 20 *Metaphilosophy* 203.

[65] See especially Ashworth, 'Belief', n. 7 above; 'Sharpening the Subjective Element in Criminal Liability' (n. 18 above); 'Taking the Consequences' (n. 16 above).

But this claim seems straightforwardly false: we do often control the outcomes of our actions. Unless I am physically impaired, I usually control the movements of my body; a competent marksman controls the direction of his shot; a competent driver controls the movements of her car: indeed, the contrast between competence and incompetence in an activity is often that between the agent who can and does control, and one who cannot control, what happens. If I wilfully smash your valuable vase with my hammer, it would be absurd for me to say that its destruction was a matter of 'luck', since I lacked control over the hammer's movement. Agents are, indeed, criticized precisely for not controlling, or for letting themselves lose control of, what they could, or do, control: a driver might be criticized for failing to control her car, or for driving in a way which predictably caused her to lose control. Correlatively, it seems straightforwardly false to say that actual outcomes are always a matter of luck. It is not a matter of luck that a competent and careful agent achieves what she intends, or that an incompetent or a careless agent does not—what else would we expect? Indeed, the difference between a competent and careful agent and an incompetent or careless agent is that success is not typically a matter of luck for the former, whereas it is for the latter. That is, we would think it (un)lucky that a competent or careful agent *failed*, not that she succeeded; and (un)lucky that the incompetent or careless agent *succeeded*, not that she failed.

Our control over actual outcomes is, of course, vulnerable: since our actions do depend on factors which we do not control, we cannot guarantee that we will never lose control, even over such basics as our bodily movements. But just as the fact that a glass is breakable does not entail that it is broken, the fact that our control is vulnerable does not show that we never have it. The fact that we could lose control *cannot*, indeed, show that we never have it; one cannot lose what one never has.

Here again, however, subjectivists may not need the radical (and untenable) claim which some make, that *all* actual outcomes are matters of luck; a more modest and tenable claim might suffice.

For any particular intended action, it is surely a matter of luck either that it succeeds, or that it fails; for any reckless action, it is surely a matter of luck either that it actually causes harm or that it does not. We would not count it a matter of luck that a competent attempt, made under favourable conditions, succeeds: but such an attempt could still fail; and we would count its failure a matter of luck. We would not count it a matter of luck that an incompetent attempt, or one made under unfavourable conditions, fails: but such an attempt could nonetheless succeed; and we would count its success a matter of luck. Similarly with a reckless action: depending on how great the risk was, we might count it either a matter of (bad) luck that it caused harm, or a matter of (good) luck that it did not.

Thus in any particular case either success or failure, either the occurrence or the non-occurrence of harm, will typically involve an element of luck; and subjectivists can thus argue, without exaggerating the role of luck, that such luck should not affect criminal liability. Someone whose attempt succeeds is not, simply in virtue of that fact, more culpable than he would have been had it failed (whether we count his success, or would have counted his failure, a matter of luck). Someone whose attempt fails is not, merely in virtue of that fact, less culpable than he would have been had he succeeded (whether we count the failure, or would have counted success, a matter of luck). Likewise, someone whose reckless action causes harm is not thereby more culpable than she would have been had it not caused harm; one whose reckless action causes no harm is not thereby less culpable than she would have been had it caused harm. If criminal liability should not depend on 'outcome-luck', the fact or extent of an agent's liability should therefore not depend on whether or not her attempt succeeded, or on whether or not her reckless action actually caused harm.

But this leads us to a third subjectivist dichotomy: between *culpability*, on which criminal liability should supposedly depend, and other aspects or implications of action.

'CULPABILITY' AND OTHER CONCERNS

The actual outcomes of actions matter to us, in various ways; and a subjectivist need not claim (implausibly) that the difference between success and failure in a criminal endeavour, or between harmful and fortuitously harmless reckless actions, should *in no way* affect our responses to the action and its agent. If a criminal attempt to harm someone succeeds, or a reckless action actually causes harm, we will (and will think that the agent should) properly feel sorrow for the harm done, and sympathy for the victim; if compensation for the victim is possible, we may think that it should be paid by the agent who culpably caused the harm. If the attempt fails, however, or the reckless action causes no harm, there is no (or at least less) room for such sorrow or sympathy, and no (or less) harm for which compensation can be required. Our emotional responses, and the wrongdoer's liabilities, are in these ways affected by actual outcomes, although such outcomes may be matters of luck.

But, subjectivists may insist, we must distinguish such emotional responses, and our judgments of an agent's compensatory liabilities, from our *moral* judgment of his *culpability*. His culpability depends, not on the (perhaps fortuitous) actual outcome of his action, but on its subjective aspects—on the moral character of his choice to act in a certain way; and if criminal convictions and punishments are to reflect, as they should, appropriate judgments of culpability, they too should therefore be based on the agent's active choices, not on the actual outcomes of his actions.[66]

[66] See for instance Ashworth, 'Belief', n. 7 above, at 16–19; 'Taking the Consequences', n. 16 above, at 113–17.

We are thus to draw sharp distinctions between our emotional responses, which do indeed depend on actual outcomes, and our judgments of moral culpability; between liability to pay compensation for harm actually caused, and criminal liability to punishment. But can these distinctions be so clearly drawn?[67]

Consider, first, what the wrongdoer owes to her victim. Certainly compensation for whatever material harm was done (if the harm can be compensated, and the wrongdoer has the resources). Also, presumably, apology: an expression of her remorseful recognition of what she has done. But the neat distinction which this implies between compensation for material harm and apology for wrong done cannot be sharply drawn. Compensation can serve (can sometimes only serve), not merely to repair material harm done, but to express the agent's repentance: the wrongdoer aims to 'make up' to the victim not merely (if at all) for whatever material harm he suffered, but for the *wrong* she did to him. Likewise, the wrong for which she has to apologize cannot be so neatly separated from whatever material harm she caused, as if there are two quite distinct items to apologize or express regret for: the culpable wrongdoing, and its actual outcome. If I have attacked you, or recklessly exposed you to risk, I owe you an apology, even if you fortuitously suffer no material harm. If my hostile or reckless action does cause you some material harm, I have more to apologize for: I have done a greater injury to your well-being.[68]

Secondly, consider our emotional responses to wrongdoing (we should distinguish third-person responses to the wrongdoings of others from first-person responses to one's own wrongdoing). Observers may quite properly respond in different ways to different kinds of wrongdoing: the range of emotions that may be appropriate on different occasions include indignation, contempt, and horror, directed at the action and its agent; sorrow, pity, and sympathy for the victim. Such responses are structured in part by our *moral* understanding of what was actually done: consider, for example, the different responses that would be evoked by a successful, as contrasted with a failed, attack; or by a cruel murder, as contrasted with an equally painful natural death. So, too, with a repentant agent's response to his own wrongdoing. The remorse he feels is a remorse for what he has *done*. If his attack succeeded, he does not feel remorse for the intended attack, plus a quite distinct regret (of the kind which an observer might feel) for the harm he

---

[67] They reflect, of course, a (roughly) Kantian conception of morality and moral judgment. Some useful ammunition for the critique of that conception can be found in, amongst others, B. Williams, *Ethics and the Limits of Philosophy* (Cambridge, 1985), especially ch. 10; 'Moral Luck' (n. 64 above); 'Morality and the Emotions', 'Egoism and Altruism' (both in his *Problems of the Self*, Cambridge, 1973, 207, 250); also L. Blum, *Friendship, Altruism and Morality* (London, 1980) and *Moral Perception and Particularity* (Cambridge, 1994).

[68] See my *op.cit.*, n. 2 above, at 111–15. I assume (but cannot argue) here that even if my action causes you no material harm, I have done you an injury: for I have wronged you; and to be wronged is to be harmed.

caused: he feels remorse for the wrongful injury that he did. If his attack failed, he should still feel remorse for the attempt, but that remorse is now tempered by his relief that he failed: his relief both for the victim, that she was not materially harmed, and for himself, that he did not actually bring such harm about.[69]

To all of which subjectivists might reply that punishment should still be distinguished from compensation; that punishment should be determined by blameworthiness; and that blame, as expressing a judgment of culpability, must be distinguished from these other kinds of first- and third-person emotional response. They might add an apparently telling point. The wrongdoer cannot claim moral credit for the fact that her attempt failed, or that her reckless action caused no material harm: how then can that fact reduce her culpability?

Such talk of 'moral credit' is common enough, and may sound harmless. I suspect, however, that it embodies a misguided conception of blame. It suggests that judgments of blame involve making entries on a cosmic balance sheet—crediting moral points to, or debiting them from, agents in virtue of their chosen deeds;[70] and such entries are, of course, ideally made by a detached, impartial observer. But blame, at least in its second-person form, should rather be understood as a *participant* activity of communication with the wrongdoer: a response to him, which expresses and seeks to communicate a moral understanding of what he has done.[71] It is a way of saying 'Look what you have done', and cannot be neatly separated off from those other responses which express our understanding of what was done. Nor, accordingly, can it be focused only on the 'subjective' dimensions of his action. They are crucial to the action's moral character, but do not wholly determine its moral significance as an engagement in our shared social world. For it matters to us whether a criminal attempt succeeds or fails; what the agent has done, what we respond to, attribute to him, and aim to bring him to understand, is what he actually wrought in the world. We want to bring a successful assailant to understand what he has done to his victim: the moral and material injury he has caused her. We want to bring an unsuccessful assailant to understand the wrong he did in attacking his victim—but also to share in our relief that he failed.

The subjectivist's desire to distinguish judgments of blameworthiness, as the proper basis for criminal convictions and punishments, from those other kinds of response to our own and others' wrongdoing which are in part determined by what actually happens, is therefore, I think, misguided: we

---

[69] See my 'Auctions, Lotteries, and the Punishment of Attempts' (1990) 9 *Law and Philosophy* 1, at 33–4.

[70] See J. Feinberg, 'Action and Responsibility' (in his *Doing and Deserving*, Princeton, 1970, 119) at 124–8, on the idea of a 'record'.

[71] See P. F. Strawson, 'Freedom and Resentment', in his *Freedom and Resentment* (London, 1974), 1, on our 'reactive' attitudes; and my *Trials and Punishments* (Cambridge, 1986), ch. 2.

cannot thus separate out a pure form of moral judgment, wholly indepen-dent of the objective dimensions of actions, as an appropriate structure for our moral responses to each other—or as an appropriate basis for the crim-inal law's responses to citizens who break the law.

TOWARDS A MORE OBJECTIVIST LAW OF ATTEMPTS

Objectivists argue that in the context of the criminal law, as in other con-texts, the actions which we are to ascribe to an agent must be described in partly objective terms—in terms, that is, of their actual impact on, their actual relations to, the public social world in which they are done. This is not to say that the objective is *all* that matters: we are not entitled to hold a person liable for an act of killing or wounding, or handling stolen goods, simply because his conduct was causally related to a death or wound, or that he handled what were in fact stolen goods. It is to deny that the subjective is all that matters. We rightly ascribe different actions to a successful and to an unsuccessful assailant: one has killed or wounded, the other has tried but failed to kill or to wound.

In the last section I sketched some of the basis for such a view. That basis consists, partly, in an account of the concept of action: in the argument that we cannot give a purely subjectivist account of what it is to act, since action must be understood as an engagement with and in our shared material and social world. It also involves a rejection of the subjectivist's claim that we can and should distinguish judgments of 'culpability' and blameworthiness, as the proper foundation of ascriptions of criminal liability, from other kinds of response to a person's conduct which depend on its actual impact on the world. Once we understand blame as a feature of our participant social relations, which aims to communicate to the wrongdoer an adequate moral understanding of the nature and significance of what she has done; once we recognize, too, that blame is intimately related to a range of emo-tional responses structured by our moral understanding of the wrongdoer's action and its effects: we can see that the character of the blame that the wrongdoer deserves depends crucially on the actual impact of her action on the world. The subjectivist might now reply that, whilst this is how we *in fact* often respond to wrongdoings (our own and others'), such empirical facts about our actual responses cannot serve to *justify* them.[72] My remarks, however, have been concerned not simply with certain empirical facts about social behaviour, but with the meaning or logic of our moral judgments and responses: whilst I have not aimed to offer any independent justification for these structures of our thought and action (I am not sure what such a justi-fication could be), I have aimed to make plausible moral sense of them, as aspects of our social lives.

[72] See Ashworth, 'Taking the Consequences' (n. 16 above), at 111.

If criminal conviction and punishment are to express appropriate blame or censure, then they too must depend in part on the actual or objective character of the criminal's actions. But what implications does this have for the law of attempts?[73]

It bears most directly on the issue of the punishment and labelling of attempts.[74] A criminal conviction marks a public judgment on, and condemnation of, the offender's wrongdoing: since the difference between a failed attempt and a completed crime matters to us, in the ways sketched above, that difference should be marked in the conviction which the offender receives. If criminal punishment is to serve as a forceful expression of that condemnation, aiming to communicate to offenders an adequate understanding of their crimes,[75] it should also be affected by the fact of success or failure: our response to a failed attempt (a response in which we hope the offender will come to share) is tempered by our relief at its failure; it is therefore appropriate that the offender's punishment should also be tempered.

What of the fault element in attempts?[76] A recognition of the way in which the moral character of an action is determined by the relations between its subjective and its objective aspects can help us to see why this general inchoate crime should be defined in terms of an 'intent to commit an offence': why, that is, it should be defined by the concept of 'attempt'. The paradigm or central case of wrongdoing is that in which there is a unity of subjective and objective: an intended killing, or wounding, or damaging property. Actions that fall short of this paradigm will still count as criminal, so long as they are closely enough related to it: we can still ascribe a killing, or wounding, or damaging, to an agent as his culpably criminal action, for example, even though he did not intend it, if his action displayed a criminal recklessness as to the risk that it would cause death, or injury, or damage.

When the harm which the paradigm crime involves has not actually occurred, however, the difference between intention and recklessness becomes more crucial, as marking the distinction between attacks and (mere) endangerment. One who acts with the intention of causing some

---

[73] I will not discuss the conduct element in attempts here (see the text at nn. 50–8 above), except in so far as it bears on the issue of impossibility in attempts: but see J. Horder, 'Justifying Crimes of Ulterior Intent', this volume, 159–61, for some useful ideas about why it should be defined quite narrowly.

[74] See the text at nn. 11–21 above; and my *op. cit.*, n. 69 above, at 30–7.

[75] For an ambitious version of this communicative conception of punishment, portraying punishment as a kind of secular penance which aims to induce repentance, see my *op. cit.*, n. 71 above. My argument here, however, does not depend on that ambitiously communicative account: all I require here is the more modest thesis that punishment aims at least to communicate, to the offender, an appropriate moral judgment on (and an appropriate moral understanding of) her crime, whether or not it should also aim to persuade her to accept that judgment and repent that wrongdoing. For a more modest version of this communicative account, see A. von Hirsch, *Censure and Sanctions* (Oxford, 1993), especially chs. 2, 8; see also my 'Penal Communications' (1995) 20 *Crime and Justice* 1, ss. III–IV.

[76] See the text at nn. 37–49 above; and my 'Attempted Homicide' (1995) 1 *Legal Theory* 149, s. 5; *op. cit.*, n. 2 above, ch. 8.4.

legally relevant harm is attacking a legally protected interest: her action is intrinsically or essentially harmful even if the harm does not in fact ensue, since it is structured by the prospect of causing that harm; the actual occurrence of harm would simply give objective actualization to the character that the action already has. One who, without intending to cause harm, recklessly creates a risk of causing harm, is endangering but not attacking a protected interest: her action is potentially harmful, in that it might become harmful, but harm is not intrinsic to its structure in the way that it is intrinsic to the structure of an attack. An attack is thus more intimately related to the paradigm of crime than are acts of endangerment: this gives us reason to treat failed attacks more seriously than we treat endangerments which actually cause no material harm, and to define a general law of inchoate crimes that captures attacks but not endangerments (although we might also want to criminalize some relatively serious kinds of endangerment).[77]

What kind of intention should a criminal attempt require? I have argued elsewhere that it should be *an intention such that the agent would necessarily commit an offence in carrying it out.*[78] This specification convicts of an attempt the agent who is reckless as to the existence of some relevant circumstance, if the circumstance exists; and it does so without having to rely on the problematic distinction between 'circumstances' and 'consequences'.[79] A man who attempts to have intercourse with an actually nonconsenting woman is guilty of attempted rape if he is reckless as to whether she consents: for if he succeeded in carrying out his intention to have intercourse with her he would, given her actual lack of consent and his recklessness as to her consent, commit rape. But it does not convict an agent who is reckless as to the possible existence of an actually non-existent circumstance, whose existence is necessary for the commission of the complete crime.[80] Someone who is reckless as to the consent, or age, of his actually consenting and over-age sexual partner is not guilty of a criminal attempt; nor is someone who is reckless as to the possible falsity of the actually true representations by which he tries to obtain property: for these agents would not commit an offence in carrying out their intentions (to have intercourse with this woman; to obtain property by these representations).

---

[77] Several other contributions to this volume offer insights into the significance of intention: see Horder, *op. cit.*, n. 73 above; A. P. Simester, 'Why Distinguish Intention from Foresight', this volume; G. Lamond, 'Coercion, Threats and the Puzzle of Blackmail', this volume.

[78] See 'The Circumstances of an Attempt', n. 38 above; 'Recklessness in Attempts (Again)', n. 38 above; 'Attempted Homicide', n. 76 above; 'Attempts and the Problem of the Missing Circumstance' (1991) 42 *Northern Ireland LQ* 87. This test is clearly related to the slogan, which courts have sometimes applied, that a defendant should not be convicted of an attempt if she did not commit, or would not have committed, the relevant complete offence in doing all that she intended to do: see, e.g., *M'Pherson* [1857] Dears & Bell 197; *Dalton* (1949) 33 Cr. App. R 102; *Haughton* v. *Smith* [1975] AC 476; *Nock* [1978] 3 WLR 57; *Anderton* v. *Ryan* [1985] 1 AC 560; *Wilson*, 38 So 46 (1905, Mississippi); *Jaffe*, 78 NE 169 (1906, New York); *Berrigan*, 482 F 2d 171 (1973). However, it avoids the confusions into which they often fall.

[79] See n. 38 above.   [80] See the text at nn. 30–1 above.

This proposed test is 'objectivist', in that it makes the agent's liability for attempt depend not only on his intentions and beliefs, but also on what is actually the case. It deals neatly with one kind of 'impossible attempt', and avoids some of the implications of subjectivism which even some subjectivists have been uneasy about.[81] Ms Ryan, for example, would be acquitted of attempting to handle stolen goods.[82] She intended to buy this cheap video-recorder, and believed it to be stolen goods. Had it been stolen, she would have committed an offence in carrying her intention out: for she would have handled stolen goods, knowing or believing them to be stolen.[83] But since it was not stolen (as the court had to assume), she did not commit that offence in carrying her intention out, although she believed she was committing it: so she should not be convicted of attempting to commit it.

It is, of course, a matter of luck that Ms Ryan, and the man who is reckless (or mistaken) as to the consent or age of his actually consenting and over-age sexual partner, escape liability by this test: a matter of luck, for which they can claim no moral credit, that the circumstances which would make them guilty (of an attempt, or of the complete offence) do not exist. It is also true that the intentional structure of Ms Ryan's action is no different from that of one who handles what she truly believes to be stolen goods; the intentional structure of the man's action is no different from that of one who has intercourse with an actually under-age or non-consenting woman. Nonetheless, given the actual non-existence of the relevant circumstances, their actions do not constitute attacks on any protected interest: for whether an action constitutes an attack depends not just on its subjective or intentional structure, but also and crucially on how it actually engages with the world. The mere, mistaken belief that what I am doing will or might injure a protected interest is not enough to constitute my action as an attack: if my action does not in fact impinge on, or threaten, a legally protected interest, it is (luckily for me) not an attack on such an interest.

What of radically misguided attempts, like Mr Wilson's attempt to forge his cheque;[84] or the action of one who shoots at what is actually a tree in the mistaken belief that it is a person whom he wants to kill?[85] The proposed test would convict such people: for they act with an intention (to make a cheque for $2.50 appear to be properly worth $12.50; to kill a human being) such that they would commit the relevant complete offence if they succeeded in carrying it out; and their actions thus have the subjective character of an attack (of a would-be attack) on a legally protected interest. But we might, as I noted earlier, feel uneasy about convicting such agents of criminal

---

[81] See the text at nn. 22–31 above; my 'Attempts and the Problem of the Missing Circumstance', n. 78 above.

[82] *Anderton* v. *Ryan* [1985] 1 AC 560; see n. 23, and n. 29 above.

[83] Theft Act 1968, s. 22.   [84] *Wilson*, 38 So 46 (1905); see n. 25 above.

[85] For this kind of hypothetical see *M'Pherson* [1857] Dears & Bell 197 at 201; *Haughton* v. *Smith* [1975] AC 476 at 495; *Berrigan*, 482 F.2d 171 (1973) at 188.

attempts;[86] and both courts and theorists have sometimes argued that they should be acquitted.[87]

The key problem for those who wish to avoid convicting such radically misguided agents is to provide a specification of the kind of would-be criminal acts that should not count as a criminal attempt, which both delimits a plausible category of non-criminal acts (which does not, that is, capture actions which all agree should count as a criminal attempt), and shows *why* they should not be criminal—given that the agent intends to commit a crime, and does what he believes might well bring about its commission. I cannot discuss the efforts such theorists have made to resolve this problem here:[88] but I will suggest a line of thought that might help us.

If we take seriously the idea of a criminal attempt as an attack on a legally protected interest,[89] we must ask whether the intention to injure such an interest, as actualized in conduct which the agent *believes* will injure it, is sufficient to constitute an attack; and I think we can argue that it is not.[90] Whether an action constitutes an attack depends not just on the intention which structures it, but on how it actually engages with the world; and some (would-be) attempts may fail so radically to engage with the actual world that we should not really see them as attacks.

Consider first what kinds of emotion we might feel if we observed Mr Wilson's action, or someone firing at what is obviously a tree in an empty wood in the belief that it is a person (by 'we' here I mean 'reasonable' people of ordinary intelligence and perception,[91] with an ordinary knowledge of how the world works and moderately rational beliefs about the particular situation). Would we feel indignation, horror, anxiety at this criminal attempt? Or would we rather feel an amused contempt or pity for such a radically misguided, inept would-be criminal? In so far as we would respond in the latter way, there is less room for the kind of serious condemnation that criminal conviction and punishment express.[92] Of course he acted culpably: but can we really take his action seriously as an attempted crime?

Secondly, in support of this suggestion, an 'attack' might be seen as an action, done with hostile intent, which could succeed in causing the intended harm: if I hit a normal human being with a feather duster, my action cannot

[86] See nn. 34–6 above.

[87] See, e.g., G. Hughes, 'One Further Footnote on Attempting the Impossible' (1967) 42 *New York University LR* 1005; I. H. Dennis, 'Preliminary Crimes and Impossibility' (1978) 31 *Current Legal Problems* 31; G. P. Fletcher, 'Constructing a Theory of Impossible Attempts', in P. Fitzgerald (ed.), *Crime, Justice and Codification* (Toronto, 1986), 88.

[88] Useful criticisms of some of their efforts can be found in Williams, n. 22 above; Hart, n. 22 above.

[89] But see Hart's criticism (n. 22 above, at 378): so to interpret the concept of 'attempt' is to be misled by 'the clouds of its etymological connection with the word "attack" '.

[90] For a helpful discussion of the notion of an attack, see S. Uniacke, *Permissible Killing* (Cambridge, 1994), 160–2; and especially her distinction (at 162) between failed attacks, and actions which fail to be attacks.

[91] See n. 8 above.

[92] See the section on ' "Culpability" and Other Concerns', in the text at nn. 66–71 above.

be seen as an attack on her life—whatever bizarre beliefs I might hold about the life-threatening potential of such a blow.[93] Perhaps, indeed, an attack is a hostile action whose failure (if it failed) would be a matter of luck: if you hear that I have been attacked, you will be quite ready to hear that I have been killed or injured, and will count me lucky if I am unharmed. But it was not a matter of luck that Mr Wilson's endeavour failed: it would have been a miracle (as we might naturally say) had it succeeded. So, too (unless there were often people in the wood, and the tree could easily have been mistaken for a person), it is not a matter of luck that the tree-shooter does not kill anyone.[94]

Of course, these comments fall well short of specifying any clear category of (would-be) attempts which should not be criminal; nor do I think that one could produce any determinate criteria which would clearly define and delimit such a category. They are intended simply to indicate a direction in which an objectivist concern with the way in which an agent's actions actually engage with the world might be developed to explain why such radically misguided endeavours should not be convicted and punished as criminal attempts: the further development of this suggestion must be a topic for another time.

[93] Compare *Kunkle*, 32 Ind 220 (1869, Indiana), at 231–2.
[94] Contrast *Mitchell*, 71 SW 175 (1902, Missouri). D fired at night into the bed in which V usually slept, but V happened to be sleeping in a different room that night. D was rightly convicted of attempted murder; it was lucky (for V) that he happened to be sleeping elsewhere.

3

Competing Theories of Justification: Deeds v. Reasons

Paul H. Robinson*

Every jurisdiction recognizes that special circumstances can justify conduct that otherwise would be an offence. Unlawful aggression by another can trigger a right to use force in self-defence or in defence of another or of property. Aggressive force is authorized for a police officer making an arrest. Even bus drivers have a right to use some force to maintain order and safety on their vehicles. Beyond the use of force, a person can be justified in taking food from another's forest cabin to avoid dying of starvation or in tying up to another's private dock to avoid the danger of a storm.

In each of these instances, a societal interest[1] is injured or endangered— the elements of an offence are satisfied. Yet, in each instance, whether it is defensive or aggressive force, a trespass, or some other normally criminal conduct, a defence is given under the common theory of all justification defences: although the conduct ordinarily constitutes an offence, when the justifying circumstances exist we are content to have the justified conduct performed. The existence of the justifying circumstances means that, while the harm prohibited by the offence does occur, it is outweighed by the avoidance of a greater harm or by the advancement of a greater good. In other words, there is no *net* societal harm.

This characteristic of justification defences is made explicit in the Model Penal Code's general justification defence, which gives a defence if 'the harm or evil sought to be avoided by such conduct is greater than that sought to be prevented by the law defining the offence charged.'[2] English law has no such general defence, but each justification defence reflects the principle.

* Professor of Law, Northwestern University School of Law. Work on this article was supported by the Stanford Clinton, Sr., Faculty Fund of NULS. The original version of this paper was delivered on 12 December 1994, as part of the Gonville and Caius College Seminar Series on Current Problems in Criminal Theory. The author wishes to acknowledge the research assistance of James R. Lane and the contributions of the participants at the Cambridge Seminar.

[1] By 'societal interest' I mean to include any interest recognized by the society, whether that interest is individual, collective, institutional, tangible, or intangible.

[2] Model Penal Code, § 3.02(1).

Force in self-defence may injure the aggressor, but the injury is outweighed by the societal value of the defensive force—in avoiding the threatened harm to the victim and in condemning and deterring unjustified aggression generally. Force used to effect an arrest may injure the arrestee but the harm is outweighed by the societal interest in effective criminal justice, which requires an effective arrest power.

Justifications are distinguishable from a second type of general exculpatory defence, excuses, of which insanity, duress, and immaturity are examples. In excuse defences, there is no claim that the conduct is right or that it furthers a societal interest. On the contrary, the claim of excuse is an admission that the conduct is undesirable but a plea that, because of special conditions undercutting the actor's ability to avoid performing conduct, the actor ought not be blamed and punished for it. Unlike justified conduct, excused conduct is to be avoided whenever possible, even when the excusing conditions exist. We are content to have the police officer use force in making an arrest but, in contrast, we wish to restrain the psychotic aggressor. We make it an offence to resist an arrest, but we hope the intended victim can successfully resist the psychotic aggressor. We encourage others to assist the officer but disapprove of anyone assisting the psychotic aggressor.

Yet, while one can say all this about justification defences and how they differ in rationale from excuses, the theory of justification remains ambiguous in an important respect. In a typical case, a person knows of the justifying circumstances and, because of them, undertakes the justified conduct. But it is not uncommon that a person believes that his or her conduct is justified—believes that it will produce a net societal benefit—when in fact it is not and will not. The club-wielding attacker, when dragged to the street light, turns out to be a jogger carrying a flashlight whose bulb is out. Whether beating the jogger-mistaken-for-an-attacker is justified depends on whether the justification defence is given (1) because the conduct in fact is justified or (2) because the person acts for a justified reason. Or consider the less common situation in which the actor does not realize that his conduct is justified: he mugs a jogger, only to find out that the victim was a club-wielding attacker. Whether beating the attacker-thought-to-be-a-jogger is justified depends again on whether it is the quality of the *deed* or the actor's *reasons* for it that provide the rationale for justification defences.

The 'reasons' theory of justification (often called the 'subjective' theory[3]) is clearly dominant in the literature and the law. The standard formulation provides that 'an actor is *justified* if he *believes* that the conduct is necessary to' defend against unlawful aggression, to make an arrest, to maintain order on the vehicle, and so on. Under the 'reasons' theory, a person will get a justification defence as long as he or she believes that the justifying circum-

---

[3] I have substituted the 'reasons–deeds' terminology for the 'subjective–objective' because the latter has so many other uses with other meanings in other contexts that its use would seem to invite confusion.

stances exist. Whether they actually exist or not is irrelevant. The force used against the jogger-mistaken-for-an-attacker is justified because it was used for the purpose of self-defence. The actor's reason was right even if the conduct was wrong. It also follows that, if the justifying circumstances do exist but the actor is unaware of them and acts for a different purpose, the 'reasons' theory denies a justification defence. If what matters is the reason for the deed, not the deed itself, the forced used against the attacker-thought-to-be-a-jogger is not justified. While it might have been the right deed, necessary for self-defence, it was for the wrong reason.

As a student twenty years ago I published an article, 'A Theory of Justification: Societal Harm as a Prerequisite to Criminal Liability' ,[4] suggesting that a 'deeds' theory (often termed an 'objective' theory) would be a better way to conceptualize justification defences. I argued that the criterion for justification ought to be whether or not the conduct was something that we were content to have the actor perform under the justifying circumstances and to have others perform under similar circumstances in the future. The test for justification, I argued, ought to be whether on balance the conduct in fact avoided a net societal harm (in the broadest sense of harm). An actor's reasons might be relevant to liability but, if so, they were properly taken into account by other criminal law doctrines: a mistaken reasonable belief that the conduct was justified might exculpate under an excuse defence; a mistaken belief that the conduct was not justified might inculpate as an impossible attempt offence.

The 'deeds' theory suggests different results from the 'reasons' theory at each of these two conflict points: where the actor mistakenly believes the conduct is justified and where the actor mistakenly believes that it is not. Under the 'deeds' theory, whether the deed is in fact objectively justified is what matters; the actor's reasons for acting are irrelevant to the justification defence (although they may be relevant to other doctrines of exculpation or inculpation).

Specifically, under the 'deeds' theory, a person who mistakenly believes that the conduct is justified is not justified (although the person may gain an excuse defence if the mistake is reasonable or perhaps a mitigation even if it is not). Thus, the force used against the jogger-mistaken-for-an-attacker is not justified, although it may be excused if reasonable. In the second kind of case, where a person's conduct in fact avoids a greater societal harm but the person is unaware of this, the conduct is justified despite the actor's ignorance. However, the person's belief that the conduct is not justified may give rise to attempt liability, depending upon whether the jurisdiction punishes legally impossible attempts. Thus, the use of force against the

---

[4] Paul H. Robinson, 'A Theory of Justification: Societal Harm as a Prerequisite to Criminal Liability' (1975) 23 *UCLA LR* 266. George Fletcher wrote a critical response, George P. Fletcher, 'The Right Deed for the Wrong Reason: A Reply to Mr. Robinson' (1975) 23 *UCLA LR* 293.

attacker-thought to-be-a-jogger is justified, although the actor may be liable for an attempt to unjustifiably assault another.

This, then, is the point of dispute in the theory of justification: is the justified nature of the deed central, as the 'deeds' theory would have it, or irrelevant, as the 'reasons' theory suggests?[5]

In the two decades since I wrote, most writers have signed on in support of the 'reasons' theory and in opposition to the 'deeds' theory,[6] some suggesting that the latter is 'absurd',[7] unfair,[8] or unduly burdensome.[9] My views on many things have changed in the past twenty years but my faith in the superiority of the 'deeds' theory of justification has only grown. I have not before directly responded to its critics. I think I understand better now than twenty years ago why others think they prefer the 'reasons' theory. We shall see if my rearticulations and refinements here are any more persuasive.

I argue here that a 'deeds' theory of justification is better in the following senses. First, it generates liability results that are more just and that better match our collective intuitions of what is just. Secondly, even if the competing theories generated identical liability results, a 'deeds' conceptualization lays bare the distinctions that are relevant to determining liability in these cases, while a 'reasons' theory obscures those distinctions. The 'deeds' conceptualization allows a clearer analysis and a better perspective from which meaningfully to debate the competing issues. Finally, a 'deeds' theory of justification improves the criminal law's rule-articulation function.[10] That is, it allows the law to better communicate to the public the conduct rules that it commands they follow.

---

[5] I consider the possibility of some form of hybrid deeds–reasons theory later in the paper. See text accompanying nn. 66–71.

[6] See, e.g., Michael Corrado, 'Notes on the Structure of a Theory of Excuses' (1991) 82 *Journal of Criminal Law and Criminology* 465 at 489 (arguing that state of mind is a necessity and that Robinson's externalist perception is impossible to accept); Kent Greenawalt, 'The Perplexing Borders of Justification and Excuse' (1984) 84 *Columbia LR* 1897 (recognizing that most modern statutes require a subjective belief in justification and that Robinson's fully objective approach is an exception); LaFave and Scott, *Substantive Criminal Law* (St. Paul, Minnesota, 1986), 685 (claiming that in order to have the benefit of justification one must act for that particular purpose); Smith and Hogan, *Criminal Law* (6th edn., London, 1988), 37 (requiring state of mind as well as state of fact for justification is certainly reasonable).

[7] Brian Hogan, 'The Dadson Principle' [1989] *Criminal LR* 679 at 680: 'It seems to me absurd to say that I may *justify* or *excuse* my conduct, however callous it was in the circumstances known to me at the time, by showing that there existed other circumstances which, had I but known of them, would have justified or excused my conduct.' (emphasis in original).

[8] Arnold Loewy, 'Culpability, Dangerousness, and Harm: Balancing the Factors on which Our Criminal Law is Predicated' (1988) 66 *North Carolina LR* 283 at 289 (arguing that, as a matter of fairness, the issue ought to be one solely of culpability rather than result).

[9] Kevin McMunigal, 'Disclosure and Accuracy in the Guilty Plea Process' (1989) 40 *Hastings LJ* 957 at 979: '[A] purely objective view of self-defence . . . is a more difficult factual question for the defendant to resolve than the question of her own subjective belief since calculation of the harm threatened involves a number of variables [which] are beyond the defendants ability to perceive' (emphasis in original).

[10] Paul H. Robinson, 'A Functional Analysis of Criminal Law' (1994) 88 *Northwestern University LR* 857 at 880–2.

Current American law is modelled after the Model Penal Code provision quoted above: an actor is *justified* if he *believes* that the conduct is necessary for defence.[11] Current English law also appears to adopt the 'reasons' theory. Smith and Hogan, for example, conclude that the law 'is stated exclusively in terms of the defendant's belief',[12] citing *Gladstone Williams, Dadson,* and *Thain*.[13] Section 24 of the Police and Criminal Evidence Act 1984 appears to be an exception to the general rule, for it justifies an arrest even if the officer did not at the time know of or believe in the justifying circumstances.[14] Clauses 44 and 185 of the proposed Criminal Code for England and Wales appear to broaden this exception to make it the general rule. That is, they adopt a 'deeds' theory. They provide a defence if the actor 'uses such force as, in the circumstances *which exist,*' is immediately necessary and reasonable for defence.[15] Interestingly, the drafters claim that the provision codifies the common law of self-defence and defence of another.[16] They concede that it modifies the common law of defence of property, arguing that such is necessary to avoid an irrational inconsistency between the rules for the defence of property and person.[17] As will become apparent later in the paper, American law, too, is somewhat ambiguous as to which theory of justification it actually adopts, despite the apparent clarity of first appearances.[18]

INCOMPATIBILITY BETWEEN THE 'REASONS' RATIONALE AND CURRENT LAW'S 'BELIEF' FORMULATIONS

Before diving into a full comparison of the competing theories, consider a few things that ought to raise some initial puzzlement if not suspicion about the 'reasons' theory. As Greenawalt expresses the theory: '[J]ustified action

[11] In text at n. 2 above. See, e.g., Model Penal Code, §§ 3.02(1), 3.03(3)(a), 3.04(1), 3.05(1)(b), 3.06(1), and 3.07(1).

[12] Smith and Hogan, n. 6 above, at 245.

[13] *Gladstone Williams* (1984) 78 Cr. App. R 276; *Dadson* (1850) 4 Cox CC 358; *Thain* (1985) 11 NI 31.

[14] Police and Criminal Evidence Act 1984, ss. 24(4)(a), 24(5)(a), and 24(7)(a) (providing that a person may arrest without a warrant 'anyone who is guilty of the offence' or words to that effect).

[15] *A Criminal Code for England and Wales, Report and Draft Criminal Code Bill* (London, 1989), 61 at 100. The proposed code also provides a defence if the actor 'uses such force as, in the circumstances *which he believes to exist,*' is immediately necessary and reasonable for defence. This does not make the provision one based upon a 'reasons' theory of justification. Nothing in the 'deeds' theory prohibits a defence for mistake as to a justification. On the contrary, it assumes that such a defence will be provided but will be understood to be an excuse. Note that the provision of the proposed code does not identify either defence as a justification or an excuse.

[16] The drafters explain: 'if his defence is that he was defending his person, or that of another, the test at common law is whether what he did *was* reasonable': *ibid.,* 231, § 12.25 (emphasis added).

[17] *Ibid.*

[18] See text accompanying nn. 21–5 below.

is morally proper action . . . [T]o be justified is to have sound, good reasons for what one does. . . .'[19] It is the actor's reasons or motive for the conduct that supports the defence. Yet, the typical justification formulation, requiring that the actor 'believe' in the justifying circumstances, does not fully mirror this rationale. One can have knowledge of justifying circumstances but be motivated entirely by other concerns, perhaps malicious concerns.

Consider this hypothetical. Alphonse wishes to pummel his enemy, Buford, but has not done so for fear of being caught and punished. Alphonse lives in a rough neighbourhood. In the past, while sitting on his porch he has seen many people robbed and beaten but has never intervened on their behalf. One day, to his delight, he sees that Buford is one of several aggressors in a robbery. He immediately intervenes, beating attacker Buford. He is motivated not by a desire to protect the victim but rather by his desire to hurt Buford without risking liability. Does Alphonse deserve a justification defence under the rationale of the 'reasons' theory? Is his conduct 'morally proper'? Are his 'reasons' for pummelling Buford 'sound and good'? No. His reasons for acting are base indeed: his long simmering hatred. Yet, he nonetheless will get a defence under the typical 'believes' formulation of current law.

If current law is based upon a 'reasons' theory, as Greenawalt and other 'reasons' theorists would have us believe, it ought not give a defence on the bare 'belief' that justifying circumstances exist. To require a particular 'reason' for acting, in modern statutory culpability terms, is require a particular 'purpose,'[20] not simply a belief in certain circumstances. If the 'reasons' theory of justification truly lay at the root of present justification defences, those defences would require more than a belief in the justifying circumstances. They would require that the actor's purpose was the justificatory purpose. (Note that giving a justification defence to Alphonse, as current law does, *is* consistent with a 'deeds' theory of justification; his conduct is objectively justified.)

This discrepancy between the standard legal formulation and the 'reasons' theory seems to weaken the claim that current law embraces that theory and that the embrace shows general preference for that theory's liability results. But let us set aside this discrepancy for a moment and compare the liability results for the two theories directly. And, as we do that, let us assume that every person who acts with knowledge of justifying circumstances in fact acts for the justificatory purpose raised by the circumstances.

'Deeds' v. 'Reasons': Liability Results

Where both the deed and the reason are right or where both are wrong, the two theories generate the same liability results: the right deed for the right

---

[19] Greenawalt, n. 6 above, at 1903.   [20] Model Penal Code, § 2.02(2)(a).

reason is free of liability; the wrong deed for the wrong reason is subject to liability. It is only in the case of mistake as to a justification and the case of unknowingly justified actor, in which the theories give different results.

MISTAKE AS TO A JUSTIFICATION

Recall the liability differences in mistaken justification cases. The 'reasons' theory gives a justification defence because the actor believes that the justifying circumstances exist. Whether they actually exist or not is irrelevant. The force used against the jogger-mistaken-for-an-attacker is justified because it was used for the purpose of self-defence. The actor's reason was justified; the actual nature of the deed is irrelevant.

Under the 'deeds' theory, in contrast, the actual nature of the deed is central. The person who mistakenly believes his conduct is justified is not in fact justified, although the person may gain an excuse defence if the mistake is reasonable (or a mitigation even if it is not). Thus, the force used against the jogger-mistaken-for-an-attacker is not justified, although it may be excused.

The availability of an excuse defence under the 'deeds' theory of justification suggests that the liability results under the two theories may not be different. Only the labelling of the results differ. The reasonable mistake as to a justification is 'justified' under the 'reasons' theory but only 'excused' under the 'deeds' theory. Does this mean that there is no real difference in the liability results between the two theories in the adjudication of mistaken justification cases?

Liability for Resisting a Mistaken Justification

Before reaching such a conclusion, look more carefully at the operation of justification defences. Whether conduct is justified can affect liability in two ways. First, whether conduct is justified or not determines whether the actor gains a defence to liability based upon that conduct. But the justified nature of conduct also affects the liability of others for resisting it. As discussed above, it is lawful to use force to resist a robber or even a psychotic aggressor but not a police officer making a justified arrest. Do the two theories give different liability results in this respect?

Recall that a 'reasons' theory of justification holds the actual justified nature of the deed to be irrelevant; only the actor's reason is relevant. Yet application of such a theory gives clearly improper results in defining the situations in which we want persons to be able lawfully to use defensive force. We want people to be able lawfully to defend against people who only mistakenly believe that they are justified, but we do not want people to be able lawfully to defend against people who actually are justified. As the 'deeds' theory insists, the deed's actual objectively justified nature cannot be ignored; by ignoring it, the 'reasons' theory misstates the defensive force rules.

In fact, even codes that at first appear to adopt the subjective 'reasons' formulations concede this point. Having packed both mistaken and actual justification into the same concept, 'justification,' the codes eventually unpack them in order to define the instances in which defensive force lawfully may be used. The obscurity, complexity, and confusion with which this unpacking occurs signals the weakness of the 'reasons' theory in conceptualizing justification.

Consider a hypothetical. Moro is behind in his payments to loanshark Snake. Snake gave Moro a severe beating last week, with a warning that, if Moro missed another payment, he would be killed. The payment is due today but Moro doesn't have the money. He borrows a gun and hangs out at Deffi's Deli, the nieghbourhood grocery store, in the hopes that Snake will leave him alone in public. He is shocked when Snake comes in and walks straight at him. 'I won't let you get me, Snake!' he says as he pulls out his gun and aims. Just as he pulls the trigger, Deffi, the proprietor, who is directly across the counter from him, leans over and punches him. 'That's not Snake. It's his brother, you moron.' Deffi has made a point of learning to tell the difference between the look-alike brothers. Deffi's punch deflects Moro's shot. Snake's brother is wounded but not killed. Moro is cleared of assault charges because of his reasonable belief that he was about to be killed. Moro then files assault charges against Deffi. Is Deffi criminally liable for striking Moro?

The proper result, of course, is no liability for Deffi. If Moro really had been defending himself and Deffi interfered, Deffi might well be liable. But, here, Moro only mistakenly believes that an attack is imminent. Yet, one can see the problem facing the Model Penal Code drafters: the Code includes both mistaken and actual justifications within the term 'justified'. Moro, although mistaken, is 'justified' in the Code's terminology. Having combined mistaken and actual justification, how can the Code authorize lawful intervention in a case of mistaken justification yet prohibit it in a case of actual justification?

Privileged v. Unprivileged Force

Here is the Code's solution. It would analyse the case as follows: under the Model Penal Code, Deffi is not justified in interfering to defend Snake's brother unless Snake's brother would be justified in using the same force in defence of himself.[21] The use of force against Moro by Snake's brother in turn is justified only if Snake's brother satisfies the requirements of self-defence:

Use of Force in Self-Protection. [T]he use of force upon or toward another person is justifiable when the actor believes that such force is immediately necessary for the

---

[21] See Model Penal Code, § 3.05(1).

purpose of protecting himself against the use of *unlawful* force by such other person on the present occasion.[22]

Thus, Deffi and Snake's brother can lawfully resist the mistaken Moro only if Moro's force is 'unlawful'. One might normally assume that 'justified' force is not 'unlawful force'. If that were the case, then, because Moro's shooting of Snake's brother is 'justified', it would not be 'unlawful', and Deffi would have no right to interfere with the shooting. But the Code's definition of 'unlawful force' is somewhat complex and ultimately gives a different result; it includes some kinds of 'justified' force but excludes other kinds. Section 3.11(1) defines 'unlawful force' as:

force, including confinement, which is employed without the consent of the person against whom it is directed and the employment of which constitutes an offence or actionable tort or *would constitute such offence or tort except for a defence (such as the absence of intent, negligence, or mental capacity; duress; youth; or diplomatic status) not amounting to a privilege to use the force.*[23]

In other words, under the Model Penal Code's scheme, two kinds of 'justified' conduct exist: privileged and unprivileged. The former may not lawfully be resisted; the latter may. Unfortunately, the Code gives no definition of what it means by 'privileged'. A review of the commentary suggests that the term is borrowed from tort law and is intended to mean objectively justified;[24] that is, the 'deeds' theory of justification. Having defined their term 'justified' to include mistake as to a justification, the Code drafters no longer have an objective justification concept that they can turn to. Instead, they must try to borrow a concept from tort law, and are left unable to provide defined boundaries for the borrowed concept.

If we assume that the drafters mean 'privileged' to reflect a 'deeds' theory of justification, then Moro's mistaken force is not 'privileged', and, therefore, it is 'unlawful force' and, therefore, Deffi can lawfully defend Snake's brother against it, the proper result.

All codes that define justifications subjectively, as requiring only a 'belief' in the justifying circumstances, must engage in some similar gyrations to allow defensive force against mistaken justifications while prohibiting it against actual, objective justifications. Note, for example, that by including the defences for objective justification and mistaken justification in the same defence provision, the proposed Criminal Code for England and Wales creates the same difficulty for itself. Having packed the two together, section 44(3) must unpack them, using an artificial definition of 'unlawful' that attempts to include within that term conduct for which the actor is acquitted because:

---

[22] Model Penal Code, § 3.04(1) (emphasis added).
[23] Model Penal Code, § 3.11(1) (emphasis added).
[24] Model Penal Code, § 3.11(1), comment 159 (1985).

(a) he was under ten years of age; or
(b) he lacked the fault required for the offence or believed that an exempting circumstance existed; or
(c) he acted in pursuance of a reasonable suspicion; or
(d) he acted under duress, whether by threats or of circumstances; or
(e) he was in a state of automatism or suffering from severe mental illness or severe mental handicap.[25]

As with the Model Penal Code, the proposed Code reaches the right result but only through a definitional scheme that can be confusing. No such scheme is needed if a code's terminology uses 'justified' to refer only to conduct justified under a 'deeds' theory.

This practice of the Model Penal Code of defining 'unlawful force' that lawfully may be resisted as 'privileged force' makes it difficult to describe that Code and the many like it as adopting a 'reasons' theory, as they first appeared to do. In the only instance in which the mistaken-justification liability results differ for the two theories, the law follows the 'deeds' theory's focus on the actual nature of the deed rather than the actor's reasons for the deed. This concedes the primary tenet of the 'deeds' theory of justification: that the *nature of the deed* must be taken as determinative, no matter what the actor's *reasons* for the deed. Perhaps current law's approach to mistake as to a justification ought to be termed one of only a 'reasons' *terminology* rather than a 'reasons' *theory*.

A later section of this paper shows that even adopting 'reasons' terminology is bad policy with serious detrimental effects. But before taking up that issue, let me lay out the liability differences between the two theories, if any, for the cases of the unknowingly justified actor—the case of the attacker-thought-to-be-a-jogger—just as I did above for cases of mistaken justification.

UNKNOWINGLY JUSTIFIED ACTOR

Recall the differing results of the two theories in the case of the unknowingly justified actor. The 'reasons' theory gives no justification defence because the actor does not believe that the justifying circumstances exist. Whether they actually exist or not is irrelevant. The force used against the attacker-thought-to-be-a-jogger is not justified even though it was necessary for self-defence. The actor's reason was wrong; the actual nature of the deed is irrelevant. Under the 'deeds' theory, in contrast, the actual nature of the deed is central. The person whose conduct in fact is justified, although he does not realize it to be so at the time, does receive a justification defence. Thus, the force used against the attacker-thought-to-be-a-jogger is justified, although the actor nonetheless may be liable for an attempt. This, then,

---

[25] N. 15 above, at 61–2.

seems a clear difference in liability results between the two theories, although the difference is only one in grading: the 'reasons' theory would give full liability (no defence), while the 'deeds' theory would give attempt liability (a justification defence to the substantive offence but no defence to the attempt offence).

Disagreement Over the Significance of Resulting Harm

But this disagreement over the proper liability level for the unknowingly justified actor may be simply a manifestation of a larger dispute, going beyond the nature of justification. The grading disagreement may be simply one more battleground for the dispute over the significance of resulting harm. Those who believe that the criminal law ought to focus on culpable state of mind alone, and that the fortuity of resulting harm ought not affect liability, will naturally prefer the result of the 'reasons' theory. Their view is that only the actor's subjective state of mind should matter to liability. That the unknowingly justified actor believes that his conduct is unjustified is enough to impose full liability, they would argue, just as the person who thinks he has bought illegal drugs or believes he has lit a fuse on dynamite sticks ought to be fully liable even if it turns out that the powder is talcum and the dynamite sticks are wooden. The Model Penal Code, for one, seems to take this view when it adopts a rule that generally punishes attempts to the same extent as the substantive offence.[26]

If this is the reason for one's support of a 'reasons' theory of justification, then there is not much more to be said on the liability issue. Even if one were to adopt a 'deeds' theory, which gives only attempt liability, attempts would be graded the same as the substantive offence, erasing any difference in the liability results between the theories. But the next two sections of this essay argue that there are other important reasons for preferring the conceptual scheme and terminology of the 'deeds' theory. Nearly all pure subjectivists (i.e., those believing resulting harm ought to be irrelevant to liability) can skip to the next section.[27]

I do not want to be read as conceding to the pure subjectivists. The fact is, they are a breed that exists (and will probably always exist) only in academia. I know of no jurisdiction that actually takes such a view, whatever the code drafters may say they prefer. Nearly all American jurisdictions, even many of those adopting the Model Penal Code, reject that Code's notion that attempts should be punished the same as the substantive offence.[28]

---

[26] Model Penal Code, § 5.05(1). In reality, however, the Code does not adopt a view that rejects the significance of resulting harm. See Paul H. Robinson, 'The Role of Harm and Evil in Criminal Law: A Study in Legislative Deception?' (1994) 5 *Journal of Contemporary Legal Issues* 299.

[27] Even the pure subjecivist will be interested in the liability analysis for resisting an unknowingly justified actor, below in the text at nn. 42–4.

[28] See authorities cited in Robinson, 'Harm & Evil', n. 26 above, at n. 18.

Even the Code itself is ambivalent in its apparent commitment to a subjectivist view. It creates an exception for attempts to commit a first degree felony, such as murder, so that attempted murder is graded less than murder.[29] More important, if the Code really believed in the subjectivist view that resulting harm is irrelevant, it would simply drop all result elements from its offences. Instead, it retains the standard offence definitions with result elements.[30] Further, it selects the most demanding and traditional definition of causation, the necessary cause ('but for') test.[31] If it were truly an unabashed subjectivist, it would at very least adopt a weaker causation test, perhaps a sufficient cause test (as was proposed during the American Law Institute floor debate on the causation section[32]). If results ought to be irrelevant but for some unpleasant reason we must keep result elements, why not make it as easy as possible to satisfy those elements? It may be that the Code drafters only grudgingly added result elements to offences and adopted a necessary cause test of causation because they thought that people would demand such.[33] But this only concedes that the subjectivist view of criminal law is one that cannot be sold to those who are to be governed by that law.[34]

What theory of justification is preferable if we assume, as the world we know does, that resulting harm ought to increase liability? If people generally think that resulting harm should matter, why do so many nonetheless seem to prefer the 'reasons' theory of justification? Is this simply the product of an untidy world, where the minority subjectivist view is adopted in the formulation of justification because the Model Code took the minority view? Is it that that minority subjectivist view has not been rejected by the state code drafters, who typically hold the majority objectivist view, simply because they do not see the connection between the issues or the inconsistency of rejecting the Model Code's equal grading of attempts but not its subjective formulation of justification? In short, probably yes.

If a jurisdiction admits the significance of resulting harm in assessing liability, if resulting harm may give rise to greater liability than no resulting harm, it seems difficult to see how a jurisdiction can reject the 'deeds' theory of justification, which gives attempt liability to the unknowingly justified actor, in favour of the 'reasons' theory, which ignores the fact that the conduct in reality causes no net harm. The actor may have thought he or she

[29] See authorities cited in Robinson, 'Harm & Evil', n. 26 above, at n. 18.

[30] See, e.g., Model Penal Code, §§ 210.1, Criminal Homicide ('causes the death'); 211.1 Assault ('causes bodily injury to another'); 220.2(1) Causing Catastrophe ('person who causes a catastrophe').

[31] Model Penal Code, § 2.03(1)(a).

[32] A.L.I. Floor Debate on Model Penal Code, § 2.03(1)(a), *A.L.I. Proceedings* (Philadelphia, Pa., 1962), 77–9, 135–9 (proposing that actor's conduct be only 'a substantial factor in producing the result').

[33] See, e.g., Model Penal Code, § 2.03, comment 257 (1985) ('when severe sanctions are involved . . . it cannot be expected that jurors will lightly return verdicts leading to severe sentences in the absence of the resentment aroused by the infliction of serious injuries').

[34] See generally Robinson, 'Harm & Evil', n. 26 above.

was causing a net societal harm but be surprised to find that no such net harm occurs. If the unknowingly justified actor is to be held liable, the liability is analogous to that of the attempter who thinks he is committing an offence, only to be surprised to find out that he is not.

Unknowing Justification as a Legally Impossible Attempt

The propriety of viewing the unknowingly justified actor as an instance of impossible attempt is confirmed by the fact that such an actor clearly comes within the language of the Model Penal Code's attempt provision. Section 5.01(1)(a) provides: 'A person is guilty of an attempt to commit a crime if, acting with the kind of culpability otherwise required for commission of the crime, he purposely engages in conduct which would constitute the crime if the attendant circumstances were as he believes them to be . . .'[35] Under the circumstances as the unknowingly justified actor believes them to be, he is committing an offence.

To deny the analogy between the two situations creates a challenge for the 'reasons' theorists. They must argue that the fortuitous lack of harm that undercuts an offence element—when the victim bends down just as the trigger is squeezed—ought to reduce the grading to that of an attempt, but that the fortuitous lack of a net harm in a justification—maliciously burning the neighbour's field in fact saves the nearby town—ought not reduce the grade to that of an attempt. On what grounds could such a distinction be defended?

Fletcher argues that there is an important difference between violating an offence norm and violating a justification norm; this is the theme of his response to my paper of twenty years ago.[36] I concede that the two certainly are different. Fletcher's arguments in this respect are persuasive, but then most scholars would not disagree with the claim that offences are conceptually distinct from justification defences.[37] What Fletcher must show is why offence rules and justification rules are different in a way that drives us to deviate from our general rule that the presence of resulting harm ought to increase liability over that of an unsuccessful attempt to cause it. I find nothing in his analysis that addresses this central point.

To put the offence-justification dispute in a factual context, consider the following two cases. The actor believes a windstorm is coming but ignores the risk and burns a field's harvest stubble (a common practice by farmers as a low cost way to increase the fertility of the ground) despite the likelihood that the windstorm will cause the fire to burn a nearby town. It turns out that the actor is wrong about the windstorm. There never existed any danger to the nearby town, at least no more than the usual no-wind-storm

---

[35] Model Penal Code, § 5.01(1)(a).
[36] Fletcher, n. 4 above, at 308–18.
[37] There are some important exceptions to this, however, at least among English writers. See, e.g., Glanville Williams, *Textbook of Criminal Law* (2nd edn., London, 1983), 138.

stubble-burning creates. Is the actor guilty of reckless endangerment because she mistakenly believed that she was creating an unlawful danger? I think most would say, no; reckless endangerment requires proof of a real, not just an imagined, unreasonable risk of harm.[38] At most, she could be liable for *attempted* reckless endangerment, if such an offence were recognized.[39]

Now assume the same actor maliciously burns her neighbour's cornfield, but it turns out that the burning serves as a firebreak to an oncoming forest fire about which she did not know. The burning ends up saving the nearby town and is, therefore, justified on the objective facts. I would argue, by analogy, that the actor ought not be held liable for the full offence—i.e., she ought to get a justification defence—because no net harm occurred. She could be held liable for an attempt unjustifiably to burn the field (there is no justifying good that comes from her externalized *intention* unjustifiably to burn the field). If the absence of real danger means the stubble-burner can be punished only for her externalized culpable intention (as an attempt), how, in the absence of any net harm, can the cornfield-burner who saved the town be punished for more than her externalized culpable intention (as an attempt)?

Note that Fletcher's claim that the issue should be resolved differently in the justification context than in the offence definition context runs into some practical difficulty in modern codes. The Model Penal Code defines reck-lessness (and negligence) in a way that incorporates the concept of justifica-tion: It is criminal to disregard a risk (or, in the case of negligence, to be unaware of a risk of which a reasonable person would be aware) that is 'sub-stantial and *unjustified*'.[40] Thus, the application of statutes requiring reck-lessness or negligence requires an assessment of the justification of the risk, making it impossible to isolate justifications for special treatment apart from offence definitions.[41]

---

[38] Model Penal Code, § 211.2, Reckless Endangerment, provides in part: 'A person commits a misdemeanor if he recklessly engages in conduct which places or may place another person in danger of death or serious bodily injury.' Thus if an actor does not fully extinguish a campfire which in turn causes a forest fire to ignite and places a nearby town in imminent danger, the actor will be found guilty of reckless endangerment.

[39] I have argued elsewhere that it should be. See Robinson, 'Functional Analysis', n. 10 above, at 889–96.

[40] Model Penal Code, § 2.02(2)(c)(d) (emphasis added).

[41] They have elsewhere used the term 'justified' to mean 'belief' that the conduct is justified. But under that meaning, one could indeed be liable for an offence of recklessness without ever creating an improper risk. The farmer who mistakenly thinks a windstorm is coming creates no unjustified risk in an objective sense yet, if 'justified' is defined subjectively, he has created an 'unjustified risk' and could be liable for reckless endangerment even in the absence of any real unjustified risk. Such a result might be appropriate for a jurisdiction that looks only to subjec-tive state of mind, but such would be inappropriate in the jurisdiction about which we speak, in which it is recognized that the actual existence or non-existence of results does indeed make a difference to liability.

Liability for Resisting an Unknowingly Justified Actor

Beyond the liability for the actor who performs the justified conduct, the competing theories of justification may have implications for the lawfulness of resisting an unknowingly justified actor. Recall that we undertook an analogous inquiry with regard to liability for resisting mistaken justification.

Under the 'reasons' theory, the actual justified nature of the deed is irrelevant, thus the unknowingly justified actor can be lawfully resisted because he acts for the wrong reason. Yet logic tells us that here again the 'reasons' theory gives improper results. Whether the deed is or is not actually justified is central to whether the law should allow it to be resisted.

Consider a situation similar to that of Moro and Deffi in the earlier hypothetical. This time assume that the person entering the shop really is the loanshark, not his twin brother. He intends to kill the customer—let me call the customer in this variation Duncan—but Duncan does not know of the planned attack. Duncan draws a gun to shoot the loanshark, not because Duncan fears attack, but because he does not want to pay back his gambling debt. In other words, he is unknowingly justified. The shop owner—call him Box—knows of the loanshark's planned attack and is loyal to the loanshark. Can shop-owner Box lawfully interfere with Duncan's shooting? In other words, should one be able lawfully to resist a person that one knows is an unknowingly justified actor?

As before, whether Box can lawfully interfere with Duncan depends upon how we characterize Duncan's conduct. If only reasons count, and Duncan has a bad reason, his conduct is unjustified and presumably we would permit Box to use force to resist it, the 'reasons' theory. If it is the nature of the deed that counts, the 'deeds' theory, Duncan's shooting is justified and cannot lawfully be resisted. Clearly the law must prefer the 'deeds' theory. It is the nature of the deed, not the reasons of the actor, that must determine whether one lawfully can resist it.

What result under the Model Penal Code? Because Duncan does not have the 'belief' required for a justification, his shooting, even though it is necessary for his self-defence, is not justified.[42] Box lawfully can interfere with conduct that is 'unlawful'.[43] Is Duncan's unjustified conduct 'unlawful'? Recall that Model Penal Code, section 3.11(1), defines 'unlawful force' as: 'force . . . which . . . would constitute [an] offence . . . except for a defence . . . not amounting to a privilege to use the force'. Duncan has no defence to his shooting; he will in fact be held fully liable for it. Thus, his shooting is 'unlawful' and Box lawfully can resist it even though he (Box) knows of the justifying facts! In other words, even the contorted definition of 'unlawful force' in section 3.11(1) does not save the Code from improper results. Thus, in the context of the unknowingly justified actor, the Code's 'reasons'

---

[42] Model Penal Code, § 3.02.   [43] Model Penal Code, § 3.06.

approach has a real and a detrimental effect. While its effect is likely inad-vertent—it is hard to believe that the drafters actually intended such a result—it demonstrates the dangers of constructing a code using the 'rea-sons' approach.

Note that the proposed Criminal Code for England and Wales avoids this error by providing an objective form of justification. Whether Box can law-fully interfere with Duncan's shooting under the proposed Code depends upon whether Duncan's shooting is 'unlawful' under section 44(3). Duncan would have a defence to his intended shooting under section 44(1)(c); the circumstances exist that make his shooting necessary to protect himself, even though he does not know of those circumstances. But his defence will not be one of those enumerated in section 44(3), situations in which, despite resulting in an acquittal, the conduct nonetheless is held to be 'unlawful'. Duncan's defence is not that he thought his shooting was necessary, as would be relevant under section 44(c), for example, but rather that his shooting was in fact necessary. Therefore, his conduct is not 'unlawful' under section 44(3) and, therefore, Box cannot lawfully resist it, the proper result.[44]

SUMMARY OF LIABILITY RESULTS

The discussion of the previous section has been rather long. Let me summa-rize the liability results generated by the respective justification theories. In cases of mistake as to a justification, both theories generate the same result—they give defence (or mitigation) for a mistake—but label the defences dif-ferently: The 'reasons' theory calling such defence a 'justification'; the 'deeds' theory calling such defence an 'excuse'. Both theories also allow a person lawfully to resist a mistake as to a justification, although this result takes some complicated manœuvres for the 'reasons' theory because it must allow lawful resistance to what it has labelled as 'justified' conduct.

In cases of unknowing justification, the theories do give different results, for both an unknowingly justified actor and a person resisting such an actor. The 'reasons' theory gives no defence to an unknowingly justified actor, thus full liability. The 'deeds' theory gives a justification defence but the unknow-ingly justified actor nonetheless is liable for an impossible attempt in most modern jurisdictions. Of course, for the pure subjectivist, who believes that resulting harm ought to be ignored and therefore attempts ought to be pun-

---

[44] Duncan may be liable for an impossible attempt under ss. 49 and 50 of the Proposed Code and his conduct might be considered 'unlawful' for the purposes of s. 44 on this ground, which would give the wrong result of allowing Box lawfully to intervene. But this difficulty with the Proposed Code could be fixed with minor changes by making clear that the right to use force depends upon the 'unlawfulness' of the actual conduct, not the conduct mistakenly envisioned in the mind of the person being defended against. This kind of fix is easier to make in the sim-pler formulations of justifications defences described in the text accompanying nn. 52–55 below.

ished the same as the substantive offence, there is again no difference in the liability results for the unknowingly justified actor. But for all others, the 'reasons' theory insists on greater liability for the unknowingly justified actor than that of an impossible attempter even though the former is simply an example of the latter.

The two theories also give different liability results for one who resists an unknowingly justified actor. The 'reasons' theory, having concluded that the unknowingly justified actor's conduct is unjustified, allows a person lawfully to resist the justified conduct. This is the result under the Model Penal Code, but surely it is the wrong result (and may not have been intended by the drafters) for it allows a person lawfully to engage in conduct that the person knows to be against society's interest. The 'deeds' theory, in contrast, properly denies a defence to one who knowingly resists an unknowingly justified actor. (If the resister were unaware of the justifying circumstances, of course, she may be entitled to an excuse for mistaken justification.)

'DEEDS' V. 'REASONS': TERMINOLOGY AND CONCEPTUALIZATION

Even if the liability results of the 'reasons' theory were not objectionable, good reasons exist to prefer a 'deeds' theory: (1) because it clarifies the relevant issues rather than obscures them, as a 'reasons' conceptualization does, and (2) because it better performs the criminal law's function of informing the members of the community of the rules that the criminal law commands they follow.

CLARITY OF CONCEPTUALIZATION: 'JUSTIFICATION AND EXCUSE' V. 'PRIVILEGED JUSTIFICATION, UNPRIVILEGED JUSTIFICATION, AND EXCUSE'

As the previous discussion explains, the 'reasons' theory creates a three-part conceptual structure distinguishing 'privileged justifications', 'unprivileged justifications', and excuses. (I put the phrases 'privileged justification' and 'unprivileged justification' in quotes because they are concepts of special meaning created by the Model Penal Code drafters and, for reasons that will become apparent, have never been adopted by the literature or used in ordinary legal discourse.) What I have called objective or actual justifications are of the 'privileged justification' class. A mistaken belief as to a justification is of the 'unprivileged justification' class. These two kinds of 'justifications' are defined in Article 3 of the Code. The defences of the excuse class, defined in Articles 2 and 4 of the Code, include insanity, duress, involuntary intoxication, immaturity, reliance upon official misstatement, or unavailable law.[45]

---

[45] See generally Paul H. Robinson, 'Criminal Law Defenses: A Systematic Analysis' (1982) 82 *Columbia LR* 199.

What is odd and misleading about this conceptualization is that the second class, 'unprivileged justifications', includes a defence of only one type, a mistaken belief in a justification, which is identical in character to excuses, the third class. Labelling the mistake-as-to-a-justification defence an 'unprivileged *justification*' suggests that it is conceptually similar to the defences of the 'privileged *justification*' group, yet in fact it is conceptually analogous to—indeed, more than that, it is conceptually indistinguishable from—the defences of the excuses group, especially the mistake excuses.

There can be little dispute that a mistaken belief in a justification operates as an excuse. As with all excuses, the claim is: while what I did in fact violated the rules of conduct, I ought not be blamed for the violation. A reasonable person *in my situation* (insane, under duress, involuntarily intoxicated, etc.) similarly would have been unable to avoid the violation. We would have preferred that the excused offender not engage in the conduct. Although we do not hold the excused actor liable, we advise others not to engage in such conduct in the future. We allow others lawfully to resist excused conduct. We prohibit others from assisting excused conduct.

As noted, mistake as to a justification is particularly akin to the other mistake excuses, such as mistake due to reliance upon an official misstatement or due to unavailable law.[46] In each instance the claim is: a reasonable person in my situation would have made the same mistake that I made.[47]

It is possible to conceptualize current criminal law rules in any number of ways. Presumably, the preferred conceptualization is the one that best advances the reason for having a conceptual scheme, and that reason, I would argue, is to help us think most clearly about the issues and to give us the greatest insight into their proper formulation and application. The usefulness of any conceptualization, then, is a function of how much it helps us to see the most meaningful similarities and differences among the rules at issue. The conceptualization inherent in the 'reasons' theory of justification—distinguishing 'privileged justifications', 'unprivileged justifications', and excuses—fails the usefulness test because, for the reasons described, it misleads rather than clarifies the relation among the relevant doctrines.[48]

The best illustration of the 'reasons' theory's potential to confuse is found

[46] See, e.g., Model Penal Code, § 2.04(3).

[47] See generally George P. Fletcher, *Rethinking Criminal Law* (Boston, Mass., 1978), 762–9.

[48] Not all would necessarily agree with my suggestion for a clarity–insight test of a conceptualization. Listen to Kent Greenawalt's explanation of why he prefers the 'reasons' theory of justification: 'Whatever may be true about analogous words in other languages, "justified" is most definitely not a special legal term. In discussions of ethics, justified action is morally proper action. "Justification" is also used in relation to the reasons one puts forward for one's choices; an action is "justified" in this sense when one has defended it with sound arguments. An essentially similar sense is employed when people speak of opinion writing as a process of legal justification. In epistemology, reference is made to "justified" belief—that is, a well founded belief about facts. What joins these various senses is the idea that to be justified is to have sound, good reasons for what one does or believes': Greenawalt, n. 6 above, at 1903. Greenawalt apparently believes that usage of terms in other disciplines is a more sound ground for conceptualising criminal law.

in a well known article by Kent Greenawalt, 'The Perplexing Borders of Justification and Excuse'.[49] After insisting on viewing justifications under a 'reasons' theory, in which mistaken justifications are deemed 'justifications', the author reviews these 'justifications', compares them to excuses, and concludes that the justification–excuse distinction is problematic.[50] His premise, of course, assures his conclusion. The cat owner, who begins with the premise that his beloved Siamese really is his child in every meaningful sense, can then complain that the pet–child distinction is not nearly so clear as people think.

Rather than showing the perplexing borders of justification and excuse, the 'Perplexing Borders' article persuasively demonstrates the potential for confusion in treating mistaken justification as a 'justification'. '[Having] sound, good reasons for what one does',[51] as Greenawalt defines justification, certainly should be grounds for a defence, an excuse defence.

A 'deeds' theory conceptualization, in contrast, is both simpler than the 'reasons' theory conceptualization and clarifies rather than obscures. It is simpler in that it requires only a two-part conceptual scheme—justifications and excuses. It is clarifying because it highlights the conceptual and functional identity of mistake as to a justification with other excuses.

The practical benefit of a better conceptualization is the potential for cleaner and clearer code provisions. Specifically, under a 'deeds' theory formulation, justifications are defined in objective terms that describe the permitted conduct. A mistake as to a justification is defined as a separate excuse defence. In formulating the defensive force defences—self-defence, defence of others, defence of property, etc.—the force an actor lawfully may defend against need not be defined using the unwieldy and obscure definition of 'unlawful', described above, with its undefined terms such as 'privileged'. Instead, the defensive force defences need only provide that an actor may lawfully defend against 'unjustified' force, as defined by the justification defences.

At least one state uses this form,[52] following the lead of the proposed federal criminal code drafted by the Commission for Reform of Federal Criminal Law.[53] Under this approach, the self defence provision need read

---

[49] *Ibid.*   [50] *Ibid.*   [51] *Ibid.*, 1903.

[52] See, e.g., North Dakota Century Code, §§ 12.1–05–03 (self-defence, quoted in text below at n. 54); 12.1–05–04, *Defense of Others* ('A person is justified in using force upon another person in order to defend anyone else if: 1. The person defended would be justified in defending himself; and 2. The person coming to the defense has not, by provocation or otherwise, forfeited the right of self-defense'); 12.1–05–07, *Limitations on the Use of Force—Excessive Force* ('A person in not justified in using more force than is necessary and appropriate under the circumstances'); 12.1–05–08, *Excuse* ('A persons conduct is excused if he believes that the facts are such that his conduct is necessary and appropriate for any of the purposes which would establish a justification . . . under this chapter, even though his belief in mistaken. However, if his belief in negligently or recklessly held, it is not an excuse in a prosecution for an offense for which negligence or recklessness, as the case may be, suffices to establish culpability . . .').

[53] *Final Report of The National Commission On Reform of Federal Criminal Laws* (Washington, D.C., 1971), 43–64 (commonly referred to as the 'Brown Commission', after its chairman, Edmund G. Brown, former Governor of California).

simply, 'A person is *justified* in using force upon another person *to defend himself against* danger of imminent *unjustified* bodily injury . . . by such other person . . .'[54] Conduct is *unjustified* if it is in violation of a substantive offence and is not justified under the (objectively defined) justification defences.[55]

The proposed Criminal Code for England and Wales gets only part way toward this cleaner, clearer approach. It recognizes a defence for the unknowingly justified actor. But it does not segregate force that is necessary from force that the *actor only believes* is necessary. Thus, as with the Model Penal Code, it has no defined concept of objective justification that it can use easily to define the force that lawfully may be resisted. In section 44(3), it must resort to a similar complex and artificial definition of 'unlawful' to make its defensive force provisions work properly.

ARTICULATING THE CRIMINAL LAW'S COMMANDS TO THOSE
BOUND BY THEM

The most objectionable aspect of the 'reasons' conceptualization may be its detrimental effect on the law's ability clearly to communicate its commands to those who are bound by them. The criminal law's rules of conduct include the prohibitions, duties, and permissions contained in the objective elements of offence definitions and justification defences.[56] Conduct that is actually, objectively justified—'privileged justification', in the terminology of the Model Penal Code—is consistent with the rules of conduct. The law wishes to tell others that they can engage in similar conduct in a similar situation in the future. Conduct that is not actually, objectively justified—mistaken justification or 'unprivileged justification'—violates the rules of conduct and should be avoided by others under similar circumstances in the future. The violator at hand is to be excused only because his reasonable mistake renders his improper conduct blameless.

When we give people directions about what they should and should not do, our commands are necessarily descriptions of what conduct we want avoided and under what circumstances. An actor's motive or beliefs may be relevant to an assessment of his blameworthiness but is unnecessary to a description of the rule of conduct. To say 'do not use force against another unless you *think* the other is attacking you' may sound like a rule of conduct but is simply a compression of two distinct points. The rule of conduct says 'do not use force unless another is attacking you'; but we understand that in application *you can only act on what you know or believe*. That second issue, of belief, is not an issue that one must deal with in stating the rule of

[54] North Dakota Century Code, § 12.1–05–03 (emphasis added).
[55] The limitation to 'in violation of a *substantive* offense' avoids the problem discussed at the text accompanying n. 41 above.
[56] Robinson, 'Functional Analysis', n. 10 above, at 876–89.

conduct; it only becomes relevant in adjudicating failures to follow the rule (to satisfy the ideal).[57] By combining objective and mistaken justification within a single 'justification' defence, the Code assures that verdicts of acquittal under a 'justification' defence will always be ambiguous in the message that they announce, frustrating rather than advancing the law's educative effect.

Acquittal in a case where a justification defence is offered might mean either: (1) that the conduct is disapproved, but the actor is excused for it, or (2) that the conduct is approved. Nothing tells the listener which is the case, yet the two possibilities give opposite conclusions about whether the conduct is within the rules of conduct that others are to follow in the future. In each instance, the listener is left to guess: do the rules permit what the actor actually did, or just what he thought he was doing, or both? Each case of mistaken justification can be misinterpreted as a case of true justification, thereby approving conduct that ought to be prohibited. Each actual justification—that is, conduct within the rules of conduct for others in the future—can be misinterpreted as a mistaken justification, thereby improperly discouraging conduct within the rules.

Assume, for example, that the defendant police officer viciously beats a suspect while arresting him because the officer believes such force is necessary to effect the arrest. And assume that the officer is tried and acquitted for the assault. What message does his acquittal carry? Does it mean to tell other officers that they can lawfully use such force in making such an arrest under similar circumstances in the future, or does it mean to tell them that they cannot use such force (that this officer was wrong to use such force but is acquitted only because his mistake was reasonable)?

The point is illustrated by the acquittal of the officers whose severe beating of Rodney King was caught on videotape. There is evidence to suggest that the jurors found the officers' force excessive but that they thought the officers ought not be criminally liable for it because the officers did not realize at the time that their force was excessive. The jury took account of the danger that the officers felt, the confusion and uncertainty of the situation from the officers' perspective, the emotion generated by the preceding high-speed chase, and the possibly inadequate training that the officers may have had for dealing with such situations.

In the words of defense attorney Michael Stone, their goal was to persuade jurors to view the incident 'not through the eye of the camera but through the eyes of the police officers.' . . . On the night in question, [the officers] confronted a 250-pound man who they believed—wrongly—to be intoxicated with the drug PCP, said to endow users with 'superhuman strength'.[58]

---

[57] See Robinson, *ibid.*, and Paul H. Robinson, 'Rules of Conduct and Principles of Adjudication' (1990) 57 *University of Chicago LR* 729.

[58] 'Jury Was Asked to See Events as Police Did; Defense Depicted Officers in Urban Jungle', *Washington Post*, 30 Apr. 1992 at A25. Officer Powell explained to jurors: 'He had very

After hearing the evidence at trial, one juror explained the verdict this way:

At one point, King lunged at and connected with Officer Powell. The cops were simply doing what they'd been instructed to do. They were afraid he was going to run or even attack them. He had not been searched, so they didn't know if he had a weapon. He kept going for his pants, so they thought he might be reaching for a gun . . . I have no regrets about the verdict. I'll sleep well tonight.[59]

Another juror emphasized the difficult circumstances in which the defendants found themselves and which might underlie an excuse-oriented view of the acquittal:

[King] was obviously a dangerous person, massive size and threatening actions . . . They're policemen. They're not angels. They're out there to do a lowdown dirty job. Would you want your husband doing it, or your son or your father?[60]

If one assumes that the jury found that the officers mistakenly believed that their force was not excessive, the traditional 'reasons' terminology would describe the officers as 'justified'. But that description, 'justified', can easily be taken as condoning the officer's conduct. Indeed, many people found the acquittals outrageous specifically because they seemed to condone the use of excessive force:

[The verdict] sends out a message that whatever you saw on that tape was reasonable conduct.[61]

[The verdict] tells me that police can do what they want. Everyone in the world saw that man get whipped and I don't know what the jury was seeing.[62]

What does it take to prove they're guilty? They're saying, 'So what if you videotape me, I still can beat you up.'[63]

[I]t is an outrage that our system can't punish those—particularly police officers—who use the power and majesty of the state to beat some man senseless.[64]

powerful arms. This was a big man . . . I was completely in fear for my life, scared to death that if the guy got up again he was going to take my gun and there would be a shooting, and I did everything I could to keep him down on the ground.'

[59] 'The Jury's View', *Washington Post*, 1 May 1992 at A33.   [60] *Ibid.*
[61] Los Angeles Deputy District Attorney Terry White, reported in 'The Police Verdict', *New York Times*, 30 Apr. 1992 at A1, col. 1.
[62] David Green, 32 year old Northeast Washington construction worker, reported in 'Case Casts Long Shadow', *Washington Post*, 1 May 1992 at A1.
[63] Hilda Whittington, a Chicago nutritionist, who is black, reported in 'Riots in Los Angeles', *New York Times*, 1 May 1992 at A23, col. 1. In the same vein: 'It sends a very scary message to me. I can be driving my car and fitting a description. I try to respect cops as much as I can. I feel they should do the same. I'm very scared that something like this could happen to me. Emilio Henry, a black senior at Texas Southern University, in *ibid.* Similarly: ' The verdict sends two messages. For those who wear the uniform of the law, the message is that anything goes; for those whose only badge is their skin color, the message is to expect no justice from the criminal justice system': Eddie Williams, president of the Joint Center for Political and Economic Studies, a black D.C. think tank, reported in 'A Case of Haunting Images and Perplexing Questions', *Washington Post*, 1 May 1992 at A29.
[64] Jerry Brown, former Governor of California, reported in 'Where's the Out From White America?', *Washington Post*, 1 May 1992 at A27.

If the officers' conduct had been described as 'unjustified' because it was excessive, and the grounds for acquittal laid upon excuse of admittedly mistaken conduct, the verdicts might not have inspired these kinds of reactions. Instead of creating outrage, the finding that the conduct was 'unjustified' could have helped assure citizens that the conduct they saw on tape was indeed disapproved. It might also have made it clearer to police officers that they are not authorized to engage in such conduct under similar circumstances in the future. Instead of clarifying and reinforcing the rules of acceptable conduct, the 'reasons' terminology undercuts and confuses an understanding of the rules.

Indeed, the 'reasons' conceptualization can prevent the system from even properly judging whether conduct is or is not within the rules of conduct. For example, in the case of the beating of Rodney King, even the jurors may not have formed a shared assessment of the excessiveness of the officer's conduct. By packing both mistaken justification and actual justification into the same label, 'justification', different jurors may have come to different conclusions about whether the officers' conduct was proper. Some might have thought it proper, while others thought it improper but excused. It seems hopeless to think that the public adjudication of criminal cases can educate the public about the law's commands when the doctrine's conceptualization and terminology prevents even jurors from having to agree on whether the conduct at issue is within the rules of conduct.

What is needed is a verdict system that distinguishes a justification from an excuse,[65] and an objective, 'deeds' theory of justification that allows judges and juries to make such a distinction.

THE DUAL REQUIREMENT PROPOSAL

I have noted above that current law might be viewed as adopting a 'deeds' theory with regard to mistaken justification (in outcome if not in terminology)[66] and a 'reasons' theory with regard to the unknowingly justified actor.[67] This pattern of liability might lead one to propose a dual requirement for justification: that the actor both perform the right deed and act for the right reason. Such a dual requirement would explain and get support from current law, which justifies defensive force against the attacker who only mistakenly believes he is justified (wrong deed) but denies such justification for force against the attacker who actually, objectively, is justified (right deed) and, at the same time, denies a defence to the unknowingly justified actor (wrong reason).

---

[65] For a discussion of such a proposal, see Robinson, 'Rules of Conduct', n. 57 above, at 766–7. A more detailed proposal is contained in Paul H. Robinson, Peter Greene, and Natasha Goldstein, 'Making Criminal Codes Functional' (1996) 86 *Journal of Criminal Law and Criminology* 304.

[66] See text accompanying nn. 21–5 above.   [67] See text accompanying nn. 35–44 above.

That said, I find such a dual requirement puzzling. I understand the theory behind the 'reasons' approach: a justification defence ought to depend upon whether the actor thought he was justified; many theorists believe that an actor's externalized culpable state of mind ought to be the sole criterion for criminal liability. I also understand, and support, the theory behind the 'deeds' approach: that the defence ought to depend upon the absence of a net resulting harm; no net harm renders the unknowingly justified actor an impossible attempter, who, like any attempter, deserves less liability than one who actually brings about the harm or evil of the substantive offence. I do not, however, understand the theory behind this dual-requirement approach. It seems internally inconsistent in its view on the significance of resulting harm and on the sufficiency of culpability as grounds for full liability. How would one articulate the general theory of liability behind requiring both the right reason and the right deed? Is the absence of a net harm significant or not? Is externalized culpability sufficient for full substantive liability or not? Apparently the answer to these questions is different in different situations—mistakenly justified and unknowingly justified—but it is not apparent why the answers to such questions should depend on the factual situation.

Even if one could articulate a theory for the dual-requirement, it would not necessarily answer my many objections to having the 'belief' requirement, as described in my opposition to the 'reasons' theory. To review, first, current law's expression of the 'reasons' theory—that the actor *believe* that his conduct is justified—fails to implement that theory.[68] Acting for the right reason means having the right motivation. The 'belief' requirement of current law only requires that the actor have certain knowledge when he acts. Why should we irrebutably presume in every instance that the actor is motivated by this knowledge? A true 'reasons' theory would give a defence only if the actor acts for the justificatory purpose.[69]

Secondly, a 'reasons' theory denies the significance of the analogy between the unknowingly justified actor and the impossible attempter.[70] That is, by denying a defence to the unknowingly justified actor, it treats him as indistinguishable from the actor with a similar culpable state of mind who is not objectively justified. This view understandably appeals to those theorists who oppose giving significance to resulting harm, but it seems clear that this view does not reflect our shared intuitions in assessing blameworthiness nor does it reflect current law's treatment of resulting harm. Every known criminal law system gives significance in grading to whether a resulting harm or evil occurs. There is no apparent reason why the significance of resulting

---

[68] See text accompanying nn. 19–20 above.
[69] At least one writer has argued that the *Thain* case might be interpreted to require not only knowledge of the justifying facts, but also a justifactory purpose. See G. R. Sullivan, 'Bad Thoughts and Bad Acts' [1990] *Criminal LR* 559 at 560–1.
[70] See text accompanying nn. 35–41 above.

harm or evil should be denied in the context of the unknowingly justified actor.

Finally, the 'reasons' theory, by denying a justification to the unknowingly justified actor, authorizes others lawfully to resist that objectively justified conduct. Thus, because the unknowingly justified actor is treated as unjustified, even one who knows of the justifying circumstances can lawfully resist him.[71]

SUMMARY AND CONCLUSION

To summarize, current law adopts the terminology of a 'reasons' theory of justification: an actor is justified if the actor believes the conduct is justified; the actual nature of the deed is irrelevant. In reality, however, current law adopts a 'deeds' theory of justification in its treatment of mistaken justification, the most common kind of case on which the two theories give different results. In the case of an unknowingly justified actor, an unusual case, current codes do indeed purport to follow the logic of the 'reasons' theory, but that logic gives bizarre and undesirable results. It allows an actor to interfere with conduct that is objectively justified, even if the interfering actor knows of the justifying circumstances. And it imposes full liability upon the unknowingly justified actor rather than the attempt liability that is appropriate for what is essentially an impossible attempt.

In addition to the 'reasons' theory's problematic performance with regard to liability results, that theory ought to be rejected on independent grounds, because it obscures and confuses the analysis of justification cases. The 'deeds' theory is preferable because it makes the important distinction between mistaken and actual justification and highlights the conceptual and functional identity of mistaken justification as an excuse.

Making the distinction between actual and mistaken justification is particularly important to the law's obligation to communicate its rules of conduct to the public that is bound by those rules. By including both mistaken and actual justification within the single term 'justified', a 'reasons' conceptualization invites the public to misconstrue a finding of 'justified' due to a mistaken belief in justification, to mean that the conduct is truly justified in the sense of being within the rules of proper conduct to be condoned here and in the future. The reverse confusion also can occur. A finding of 'justified' based upon a finding that conduct is proper and condoned, may be misinterpreted as a finding that the conduct actually is disapproved but the actor is excused. A 'deeds' theory, in contrast, uses every case adjudication to tell the community which conduct is approved ('justified') and which conduct is disapproved even though the offender at hand may not be punished for it ('excused').

---

[71] See text accompanying nn. 42–44 above.

The 'deeds' theory of justification, then, is to be preferred because only that theory gives proper liability results, because only its conceptualization accurately describes the important similarities and differences between the doctrines, and because only it educates the public as to the proper rules of conduct.

4

Why Distinguish Intention from Foresight?

A. P. Simester*

Philosophers conventionally distinguish between intentional actions and actions which are merely foreseen. The criminal law endorses that distinction, and applies a condition of unreasonableness before any foreseen action is declared reckless. Why? If we search the law journals for a rationale, our quest is likely to be in vain—a very odd situation indeed, given that the difference is so integral to our legal system. Perhaps there is so little discussion because lawyers simply assume the truth of the view explicated recently by Duff,[1] that *ceteris paribus* intentional wrongdoing is inherently more culpable than advertently-risked wrongdoing (though I have not seen any argument to show, even were that view correct, why unreasonableness might therefore be a condition of culpability specifically for advertent wrongdoings). But in this essay I propose to deny the standard view that intention has moral primacy. Both intended and foreseen wrongful actions are *chosen*, and merit blame because their doing reflects bad deliberative preferences.

Which is not to say that intentional and advertent wrongdoing should be undifferentiated. I shall suggest that the difference between the two cases is not to be measured in degrees of culpability, but is instead worked out in terms of what actions may legitimately be invoked to justify wrongdoing. The central moral distinction between intended actions and those merely foreseen is that the foreseen do not lend any favourable weight to the justification of the intended. In essence, one cannot justify one's intentional doing of a bad action by appeal to the reasonableness of one's behaviour (and, in particular, by appeal to advertent good actions); whereas one may do so to justify advertent bad actions.

* I am grateful for comments from participants in the Cambridge seminars, and to Peter Glazebrook, Jeremy Horder, Grant Lamond, Joseph Raz, and Bob Sullivan for their written remarks.

[1] *Intention, Agency and Criminal Culpability* (Oxford, 1990), 113.

SOME ANALYTICAL AND INSTRUMENTAL CONSIDERATIONS

It is useful to commence briefly by noting the analytical distinction between the two types of advertent agency. I have argued elsewhere that the following are paradigmatically true of an intended *actus reus*:

(a) The agent wants to do that *actus* (for the sake of doing the *actus* itself, or as a means to doing some further *actus*);

(b) She believes that it is possible, by behaving as she does, to do that *actus*;

(c) She behaves as she does because of that want.[2]

We can say, when someone does an action advertently, that it is either done as a means, end, or side-effect. If a means or end, then it is intended. What is interesting, however, is that if the action is an advertent side-effect, then it is only reckless if it is *also* unreasonable:

(i) The agent believes that it is possible, by behaving as she does, to do that *actus*;

(ii) She does not behave as she does because she wants to do that *actus* [it is *not* intended];

(iii) Given her beliefs, it is unreasonable to risk doing that *actus* by behaving as she does.

(In the law, the fact that an evaluative element is 'built into' the notion of recklessness but not into intention is reflected in the forensic phenomenon that, as between accuser and accused, the accused is expected to justify an intended harm; while it is for the accuser to show that a merely foreseen side-effect is unreasonable.) The difference outlined here between a case of intention and a side-effect can be illustrated using two examples proposed by Jonathan Bennett:

Terror Bomber and Strategic Bomber both have as their goal promoting the war effort against Enemy. Both intend to pursue their goal by dropping bombs. Terror Bomber's plan is to bomb the school in Enemy's territory, thereby killing children of Enemy, terrorizing Enemy's population, and forcing Enemy to surrender. Strategic Bomber's plan is to bomb Enemy's munitions plant, thereby undermining Enemy's war effort. However, Strategic Bomber also knows that next to the munitions plant is a school, and that when he bombs the plant he will also kill the children inside the school.[3]

---

[2] See 'Paradigm Intention' (1992) 11 *Law and Philosophy* 235, for a fuller statement. I do not deal in this paper with the rare instances where something not paradigmatically intended on this account is nevertheless 'too close' to what is intended to be termed a side-effect. Such cases do not, I believe, present any particular problems for the discussion here. For their analysis, see my 'Moral Certainty, and the Boundaries of Intention' (1996) 16 *Oxford Journal of Legal Studies* (forthcoming).

[3] J. Bennett, 'Morality and Consequences' in S. M. McMurrin (ed.), *The Tanner Lectures on Human Values* (Cambridge 1980), 45 (hereafter 'Bennett') at 95. The cases are stated here as summarized by M. E. Bratman: 'What is Intention' in P. R. Cohen, J. Morgan, and M. E. Pollack (eds.), *Intentions in Communication* (Cambridge, Mass., 1990), 15 at 23.

Terror Bomber intends the deaths, but Strategic Bomber does not. The essential difference between the two is the non-fulfilment of condition (c), 'she behaves as she does because of that want'. And consider the contemplated causal chains which lead Terror Bomber and Strategic Bomber respectively to conduct themselves as they do:[4]

Terror Bomber: C_{TB} $\longrightarrow$ Kill Children $\longrightarrow$ Win War

Strategic Bomber: C_{SB} $\longrightarrow$ Blow Up Plant $\longrightarrow$ Win War

Kill Children

In the case of Strategic Bomber, the prospect of the children's deaths does not provide him, at least so far as he is concerned, with a reason for his behaviour.[5] Nor does it *explain* his behaviour.[6] Even if he is incidentally happy to kill the children—a case where condition (a) would be satisfied—he does not bomb the plant in order to do so. For Strategic Bomber the deaths are neither a means nor an end, but rather a side-effect: his belief that they may occur does not connect to his motivation.[7]

AN INSTRUMENTAL RATIONALE?

So much for the preliminaries. The question for this paper is, why should that analytical difference between Terror Bomber and Strategic Bomber matter? Before we turn to the question of intrinsic moral distinctions, it is important to consider the possibility that there might also be instrumental reasons for the law to distinguish between intention and advertence. An obvious consideration is deterrence. Kenny proposes that an *actus reus* might be more likely to be done when it is intended by an agent and not merely foreseen:

The argument might go as follows. The purpose of the law is to prevent q, and q is much more likely to occur if A is done in order to bring about q than if A is simply done while q is foreseen as more or less probable. Because, for instance, the latter activity, unlike the former, is compatible with taking precautions against the occurrence of q. . . . In general, incompetent though we humans may be in giving effect to our desires, a state of affairs is more likely to come about, other things being equal, if we set out to bring it about than if we merely passively foresee it as a likely consequence of our other projects. And so, if we are to punish no more than is necessary,

---

[4] I take the idea for such diagrams from Bennett, *ibid*. The 'C' stands for 'Conduct'.

[5] In Bratman's statement of the case (n. 3 above, at 23), 'Strategic Bomber has worried a lot about this bad effect. But he has concluded that this cost is outweighed by the contribution that would be made to the war effort by the destruction of the munitions plant.'

[6] Cf. G. E. M. Anscombe, *Intention* (Oxford, 1957).

[7] Compare R. Audi, 'Intending' (1973) 70 *Journal of Philosophy* 387 at 397; also J. Bentham, *An Introduction to the Principles of Morals and Legislation* (1781; Buffalo, N.Y., 1988), VIII.VI–VII.

there is good reason . . . to attach greater deterrent penalties to an act performed intentionally than to the same act performed recklessly.[8]

This argument faces an objection which Kenny himself recognizes.[9] The requirement for an *actus reus* typically means that the law presently rewards those who take successful precautions against q either with a lesser penalty for the 'attempt' to bring q about or with no penalty at all.[10] Thus the law already contains incentives (i) to take precautions against the foreseen risks of q, (ii) to take precautions against q rather than to seek its occurrence, and (iii) if Kenny's generalization is correct, even passively to risk q without precautions rather than to seek it. Further, the disincentive to risk q, as well as the incentive to take precautions against it, would commensurately be lessened as the penalty for bringing q about advertently were diminished.[11] This is not in itself desirable, since we need to deter the bringing about of q both intentionally and advertently.

Acknowledging the above, I want to outline an objection to the aspect of Kenny's claim which is implicit in (iii): that where she has the option, we should encourage an agent to modify her behaviour so as to risk q (even without precautions) rather than to seek it. Kenny's is not a claim about the relative badness of having done q intentionally versus advertently. And in general, it matters not to the dangerousness of an instance of behaviour whether some *actus* constituted by that behaviour was intended rather than foreseen. So considerations of dangerousness provide no reason *post rem factam* to punish the doing of an *actus* less on account of its merely having been foreseen. His suggestion must be that we may antecedently predict that an agent's behaviour is likely to be less dangerous when the harm proscribed is merely risked and not sought. Now the important type of case to consider here occurs when the harm is sought because it is a means to the agent's motivating end. In some instances of this type there may be alternative ways of seeking the same end; in some of those instances, the alternative may still involve risking that original harm, but as a side-effect rather than as a means. One might think by the last refinement that we are looking at a recondite subset of cases. And the adjective, arcane, certainly vaults to mind regarding Kenny's illustration:

Let us suppose that it is of great importance to Peter that Paul should not be in town on a particular day: perhaps Paul is a witness in a case against Peter, or is coming to claim an inheritance that will otherwise pass to Peter. On the one hand, Peter can kill Paul, giving a 100 per cent certainty that he will be absent on the crucial day. On the

---

[8] 'Intention and Purpose in Law' in R. S. Summers (ed.), *Essays in Legal Philosophy* (Oxford, 1968), 146 at 158.

[9] *Ibid.*, 159; cf. H. Oberdiek, 'Intention and Foresight in Criminal Law' (1972) 62 *Mind* 389 at 398.

[10] Depending in part upon whether conscious risk-taking constitutes a legal attempt.

[11] The alternative option, that of raising the penalty for doing q intentionally, is not always available.

other hand, he can incarcerate Paul in a solitary spot, reducing the certainty of his absence, but also taking a serious risk that he may die before he is rescued. . . . In such a situation, Peter has a greater motive for choosing the less violent course if the law distinguishes between intention and foresight than if it does not.[12]

The example tells us only that cases do exist where there is a choice between intending and risking some *actus reus*, and in which a lesser penalty for advertence might beget safer behaviour on the part of defendants. It does not follow that lesser penalties for advertence tend in general to produce safer behaviour by agents: there is no suggestion in the illustration that the probability of a given harm is systematically reduced whenever that harm is foreseen rather than intended. Without such a suggestion, it seems we are 'to suppose that punishment is a scalpel when in fact it is more like a sledge hammer.'[13]

Even a single such case would at least benefit Kenny's argument if it could also be shown that the probability of harm occurring never goes up when it is merely foreseen. But there seems to be no reason why the alternative route (in which the harm is a side-effect rather than a means) must be less risky. Suppose Terror Bomber^ is just like Terror Bomber, except that Terror Bomber^ has a 75 per cent chance of success. If Strategic Bomber^ is just like Strategic Bomber, but has a 100 per cent chance of hitting the munitions plant because of the plant's size (still with the certain side-effect of killing the children), then—on instrumental considerations of dangerousness—Strategic Bomber^'s behaviour is in greater need of deterrence.[14]

The example reveals that a more general point should be made. Considerations of deterrence always apply to the dangerousness of *behaviour* and not merely to the dangerousness of specific *actus rei*. And there does not seem to be any reason why *behaviour* constituting the doing of—*inter alia*—an *actus* which is intended should be overall any more dangerous, qua behaviour, than behaviour by the same agent constituting—*inter alia*—that same *actus* when merely foreseen.[15] This is where Kenny's generalization that 'a state of affairs is more likely to come about, other things being equal, if we set out to bring it about than if we merely passively foresee it' fails: on the *ceteris paribus* proviso. For in the alternatives here the agent's behaviour is *not* the same, and behaviour is the crucial concern. In particular, the replacement means to the agent's original end may itself be ill also.

I have not shown positively that Kenny's proposal is wrong. But I have shown that it is not clear that an incentive to risk rather than intend harm is

---

[12] N. 8 above, at 159. [13] Oberdiek, n. 9 above, at 398.
[14] Kenny acknowledges a similar difficulty (n. 8 above, at 159) in cases where an unintended effect is foreseen as certain, since the likelihood of that effect occurring is independent of intent. My present point, however, is more general.
[15] One who does an *actus reus* for its own sake might well be a more dangerous *person* than one merely prepared to do it, but this point favours a distinction based upon motive rather than upon intention.

(even typically) an incentive to reduce the risk of harm, or even the risk of a particular harm. And it is not at all clear that cases of the type Kenny envisages occur any more frequently than do those in which it is undesirable for the law to treat foresight differently from intention. Indeed, even if Kenny is right, I suspect that the value to be placed merely upon a difference in the probability of an *actus reus* is rather limited. We may yet say that intending and foreseeing q may both be punished, and punished equally—just as may fatal poisoning and decapitating, though the certainty of death is greater with the latter.

Kenny does advance a second reason for the law to distinguish between intention and foresight. Especially given the use of juries in criminal law, the term 'intention' ought in law to bear the meaning it ports in ordinary usage; thus it should not embrace advertence.[16] Kenny has a point in the context of his paper (addressing, in particular, the case of *DPP* v. *Smith*[17]), but it is not an argument against even-handed punishment of 'intention or foresight'; just against intention subsuming foresight through judicial extensions.

Moreover, it is worth pointing out one consideration in *favour* of assimilating intention and foresight. Since the latter is merely one of the elements of the former, the operation of the criminal law might be simplified considerably (especially regarding rules of evidence and the standard of proof) were it sufficient to prove *mens rea* by showing only advertence to the *actus reus*. The advantage of this move would be substantial, and would weigh heavily against any further instrumental factors which I have not considered and which might count in favour of maintaining the distinction. Its merit, however, is in large part dependent upon there being little intrinsic moral difference between one's doing an *actus reus* intentionally and one's doing it advertently. It is to this issue that I now turn.

Is the Intention–Foresight Distinction a Matter of Degree?

Undoubtedly the most commonly accepted view of the intention–foresight distinction is that, *ceteris paribus*, it is simply morally worse for an agent to do a bad thing intentionally than to do it advertently. Upon reflection, the popularity of that view might surprise, since we should surely be suspicious of a claim that, although the analytical distinction between intention and advertence is one of *kind*, the moral distinction is merely one of *degree*. Let me, however, go further: I think the view is wrong. In the Bomber cases, for example, it is not obvious that we should distinguish morally between the

---

[16] N. 8 above, at 160. Duff points out also the need for the criminal law to be intelligible to ordinary citizens, whom it is expected to guide: 'Intentions Legal and Philosophical' (1989) 9 *Oxford Journal of Legal Studies* 76 at 77.

[17] [1961] AC 290. See however Oberdiek, n. 9 above, at 393–5.

death of the children as a bad means and that same outcome as a bad side-effect. We cannot, for instance, use the fact that death is intended by Terror Bomber as a clue to his having a bad character in a way that merely fore-seeing and 'accepting' death may not be. Indeed, the agents' attitudes towards the harm itself are indistinguishable.[18] There is no reason to sup-pose that either agent would behave in the same fashion were he to have an alternative means to his ultimate end.[19] For the harm itself does not moti-vate either agent—neither agent desires the deaths for their own sakes.[20] Rather, each desires an ultimate (good) end, and is insufficiently different to the means (or side-effect) involved to override that desire.

To my mind, the last proposition is crucial to the blameworthiness of each agent for his action,[21] and moreover suggests the reason why they should not be segregated on the present ground *simpliciter*. We fault the agents because they prefer doing the *actus reus* to not doing it (and thereby failing to achieve their motivating end), and because they deliberately implement that practical preference. Each case involves advertent deficiencies in practi-cal wisdom; advertent failures to give sufficient weight to morally appropri-ate goals.[22] This ground can be expressed in another way. Both agents *chose* to conduct themselves with the consequence that the *actus reus* was done. Thus it may be said of each case that the relevant effect is brought about knowingly and through a volitional exercise of the defendant's agency. Which is enough for Hart; two such cases 'seem equally wicked, equally harmful, and equally in need of discouragement by the law'.[23]

---

[18] As Bennett points out: Bennett, n. 3 above, 99–103. Bennett covers much ground in this paper (at 95–105), and I shall not retrace it all here. See in addition his *The Act Itself* (Oxford, 1995), ch. 11; also T. Baldwin, 'Foresight and Responsibility' (1979) 54 *Philosophy* 347 at 352–3.

[19] The term is Kenny's (n. 8 above, at 160): 'When an agent wants it to be the case that *q* and not in order to make anything else the case, we may say that *q* is his ultimate end.'

[20] Or, if he does, then he does not behave as he does because of that desire. Bennett is pre-pared to cede moral significance to the seeking of something as an end (Bennett, n. 3 above, 99; also Bennett, n. 18 above, at 215).

[21] I pass over the question here whether Strategic Bomber (or indeed Terror Bomber) is to be adjudged blameworthy.

[22] According to J. M. Finnis ('The Rights and Wrongs of Abortion: a Reply to Judith Jarvis Thomson' (1973) 2 *Philosophy and Public Affairs* 117 at 126), 'most moral failings are not . . . straightforward choices against basic values. Rather, they are forms of negligence, of *insuf-ficient* regard for these basic goods. . . .'

[23] 'Intention and Punishment' in *Punishment and Responsibility* (Oxford, 1968), 113 at 127; see also at 121–2. Lord Hailsham spoke similarly in *Hyam* [1974] 2 All ER 41 at 55: 'the two types of intention are morally indistinguishable, although factually and logically distinct. . . .' A sentiment of the same variety appears to move Hector-Neri Castañeda, in 'Intensionality and Identity in Human Action and Philosophical Method' (1979) 13 *Nous* 235 at 255: 'An action that one ponders and places as a side action in a plan leading to a goal action, is an action that one . . . *accepts* in spite of how painful it is, in order to attain that goal. This deliberate tol-eration is of the same family as the acceptance we call intending. It is harsh to cast a tolerated action aside and declare it non-intentional, just because it is not in the path of the goal.'

DOES MORALITY SPEAK PRIMARILY TO INTENTIONS?

There is more to be said, since it is virtually an assumption by many writers that there is something morally primary about intention. Thus we see Foot say of one problem 'explained' by the Double Effect doctrine that 'in one kind of case but not the other we aim at the death of the innocent man'.[24] And my opposition would be misdirected were Mackie right when he claims, without significant argument, that it is morally primary only that we do not desire or seek harm; in his account, the need to limit harm inflicted as a means or side-effect is secondary.[25] But it is not at all clear how this claim follows from his view that moral considerations operate through modifying the agent's appraisal of her prospective actions and of herself were she to do those actions.[26] I have already pointed out that the case of a bad means is not one of desire *stricto sensu* for harm. And surely, rather than just not seeking harm (to the extent that 'seek' embraces more than ends), it ought *also* to be morally primary to not inflict harm (whether as an end, means or side-effect)? Here I concur, at least in part, with Bennett:

The morality I consult as a guide to my conduct does also guide my intentions, but not by telling me what I may or may not intend. It speaks to me of what I may or may not do, and of what are or are not good reasons for various kinds of action; and in that way it guides my intentions without speaking to me about them.[27]

We may doubt that morality speaks to us only regarding what to do.[28] Nevertheless, there seems to me no doubt but that it does (*inter alia*) speak about what to do.

Consider also its manner of speech. When it comes to a bad *actus* or effect, moral norms do not specify for us what to do. They are writ negatively so as to tell us what *not* to do: 'thou shalt not do that *actus*', 'thou shalt not beget that effect'. Thus the two bombers breach the relevant moral norm not because of what they choose or seek to do (they have not failed to 'choose from X', where X is some list containing morally acceptable things which might be done), but because of what they elect not to avoid. In other words, if moral strictures operate to constrain an agent's choices of action, as Mackie himself avers,[29] they should be no less a constraint when the foreseen action will not be done intentionally.

[24] 'The Problem of Abortion and the Doctrine of the Double Effect' (1967) *Oxford Review* 5 at 9.

[25] J. L. Mackie, *Ethics* (Harmondsworth, 1977), 160.

[26] *Ibid.*, 210.   [27] Bennett, n. 3 above, 97.

[28] So, in Raz's example (*Practical Reason and Norms* (2nd edn., Princeton, 1990), 181–2), 'love of one's children is an appropriate motive for performing parental duties towards them. Those who conform with those duties, but for reasons other than love for their children, are at fault: they do not manifest the required moral attitudes which parents ought to possess and to be motivated by.' Bennett himself seems to accept that morality may also speak in particular of ends (n. 20 above). While the considerable literature on virtues will not be addressed here, I have no doubt but that one's character is not merely a function of what one *does*—nor merely of those desires one chooses to satisfy.   [29] N. 25 above, at 108, 110, 210.

So Mackie's proposal for the primacy of intention does not follow from the nature of moral norms. From what then does it follow? We require that which Mackie does not provide: a separate rationale for his claim.

Finnis builds an argument for the moral primacy of intention partly by assimilating means to ends for the purposes of justification. His case is that there are certain basic human goods (including life), and that they are incommensurate. Since they are incommensurate, one must remain open to each basic value, and attentive to some basic value, in each of one's chosen actions.[30] That is, one should not choose to do any action which 'of itself does nothing but' damage a basic good.[31] This is because, *per* Finnis, the only 'reason' that might purport to justify such an action is that the good consequences of the action outweigh the damage done by the action itself. And incommensurability, he avers, means that this cannot occur. So the choice to damage a basic good cannot be justified.

There are known problems with incommensurability. First, let us suppose that basic values are in some way incommensurate. For instance, it would certainly be futile to attempt to compare a unit of liberty with a unit of equality. Does it follow, as Finnis thinks it does, that it is always wrong to attack one value in order to get another? There are two reasons why one might say no. First, one might agree with Williams when he suggests that the claim, conflicts of values can never rationally be resolved,

[I]s certainly a despairing conclusion. *Some* overall comparisons can be made, and if they can, then to some degree, it will be said, these values must be commensurable. . . . [O]bviously there are possible changes by which (say) such a trivial gain in equality was bought by such an enormous sacrifice of liberty that no one who believed in liberty at all could rationally favour it.[32]

That two options are in some way incommensurate does not mean they are morally equal. One option may yet be a greater wrong than the other.[33] If this is so then, for instance, where an agent is forced to choose between doing two such wrongs, his choice to do one of those wrongs can nevertheless be reasonable or unreasonable. He might do wrong without behaving wrongly.[34] I for one would regard the sacrifice of a little knowledge or play[35] as reasonable, were it a means necessary to save my friend's life.

That view is to say that commensurability depends upon reasonable comparisons being possible. But even if we cannot make such comparisons, then it still does not follow that it is wrong to sacrifice one option for the sake of

---

[30] N. 22 above, at 126.   [31] *Natural Law and Natural Rights* (Oxford, 1980), 118.
[32] 'Conflicts of Values' in *Moral Luck* (Cambridge, 1981), 71 at 77.
[33] As Raz notes: *The Morality of Freedom* (Oxford, 1986), 334, 360.
[34] *Ibid.*, 359–60.
[35] Two of the other basic goods identified by Finnis: n. 31 above, chs. III, IV.2.C.

another; since in doing so the agent may be behaving for an undefeated reason.[36] It is not clear why, given incommensurability, the reason motivating
his behaviour must actually defeat, instead of be undefeated by, the reasons
counting against it.

It is not necessary to do more than enunciate the incommensurability objections. Indeed, I am quite content to accept that means and side-effects *are*
incommensurable. What matters here is that thus far Finnis' argument
against doing harm to basic goods as a means may equally be applied to
side-effects. There is nothing in his analysis to suggest that intention should
be morally primary (nor, for that matter, that ends should be either). Finnis
does say elsewhere that the description under which one's behaviour is
intended determines the moral character of that behaviour as a *choice* not to
remain open to one of the basic values.[37] Yet as we have seen, advertent
actions *are* chosen. We choose to do or risk doing them, and so we *choose*
to damage or close ourselves to a basic value. After all, harm may be done
just as much by a side-effect as by a means or an end. And there is no *a priori* reason why side-effects need be any less likely to occur than means in a
given scenario, for the relevant damage may be a side-effect of the behaviour
that begets the intended means, rather than of the means itself.

DO INTENTIONS DETERMINE THE MORAL CHARACTER OF BEHAVIOUR?

Were it implausibly denied that advertent actions are 'chosen', I should in
any case object that the moral character of behaviour is not to be decided
merely by the descriptions under which it is intended. If I burn my house
down to collect the insurance, knowing that a disabled man is asleep inside
with no chance of escape, my behaviour is monstrous.[38] The moral character of my behaviour is not determined by my end, but—glaringly so—by the
foreseen side-effect.[39]

As I have noted, Finnis takes rather a different view about the role of
descriptions. He seeks to confine the point about incommensurability primarily to intended effects through asking how

[36] Raz, n. 33 above, at 339. Cf the 'basic principle of practical rationality' adumbrated by
John Gardner, 'Justifications and Reasons', this volume, 111.

[37] N. 22 above, at 135; also 'Intention and side-effects' in R. G. Frey and C. W. Morris
(eds.), *Liability and Responsibility* (Cambridge, 1991), 32 at 56.

[38] The case is taken from Baldwin, n. 18 above, at 352. R. D. Milo (*Immorality* (Princeton,
1984), 247–8) actually takes the view that indifference is morally worse than deliberate
'wickedness', a possibility that Baldwin (*ibid.*, 353) at least expresses sympathy for. It is not a
possibility that affects the means versus side-effects distinction, however, for one may intrinsically desire, regret, or be indifferent to means and side-effects alike.

[39] Thus I reject Anscombe's reaction ('Modern Moral Philosophy' (1958) 33 *Philosophy* 1
at 12) to Sidgwick's views: 'whereas I should contend that a man is responsible for the bad consequences of his bad actions, but gets no credit for the good ones; and contrariwise is not
responsible for the bad consequences of good actions'.

[T]o determine what is one complete act-that-itself-does-nothing-but-damage-a-basic-good. Human acts are to be individuated primarily in terms of those factors which we gesture towards with the word 'intention'. Fundamentally, a human act is a that-which-is-decided-upon (or -chosen) and its primary proper description is as what-is-chosen. A human action, to be humanly regarded, is to be characterized in the way it was characterized in the conclusion of the relevant train of practical reasoning of the man who chose to do it.[40]

This is a surprising passage. If an act has a 'primary proper description' then it has other descriptions; so Finnis must be referring to instances of raw (that is, undescribed) behaviour with his term, 'act'. And both behaviour and behaviour-under-a-description may be 'what is chosen'. But of course only behaviour-under-a-description 'itself-does-nothing-but-damage-a-basic-good'. There are more important problems here. His precondition for a human action to be humanly regarded may be doubted. The attachment to behaviour of descriptions-which-humans-may-regard depends mainly upon the sorts of criteria discussed by von Wright[41] and Kenny[42]—especially, upon the results and consequences that behaviour conduces to, and the processes it maintains. It is these criteria, rather than my intentions, which inform an observer who names my behaviour as 'breaking the table'. While there are certainly *some* descriptions of behaviour whose application presupposes an intention on the part of the agent,[43] the individuation of most actions constituted by an instance of behaviour has little to do with the agent's practical reasoning.[44] Indeed, some instances of behaviour constitute actions *none* of which are intended (an example might be provided by my idly and inadvertently scratching my nose). The idea that *the* (fundamental) description of an agent's behaviour is that one under which it is intentional—even disregarding the problem posed by the possibility of an agent's having multiple ends when she acts—is unconvincing. Compare the example in the paragraph above; were I to describe my behaviour as being basically an insurance-related arson, then I should be misleading my audience.[45]

Finnis' claim might be modified in two ways. First, he might point out that we paradigmatically ascribe agency through ascribing intention. To this I should respond that the point does not have the moral implications he looks for; moreover, that agency is logically prior to intentional agency. Secondly,

---

[40] N. 31 above, at 122.

[41] See variously *The Varieties of Goodness* (London, 1963), 115–17, 141; *Norm and Action* (London, 1963), 39–42; *An Essay in Deontic Logic* (Amsterdam, 1968); *Practical Reason* (Oxford, 1983), 107–8.

[42] *Action, Emotion and Will* (London, 1963), 171–86; *Will, Freedom and Power* (Oxford, 1975), 54–6.

[43] See for instance the analysis of blackmail by Grant Lamond in 'Coercion, Threats, and the Puzzle of Blackmail', this volume.

[44] As Michael Moore expresses it, it is only a 'minority of action verbs that are intentionally complex': *Act and Crime* (Oxford, 1993), 174.

[45] Cf. E. D'Arcy, *Human Acts* (Oxford, 1963), 18.

Finnis might assert the primacy of intention in that we have to accept that an instance of behaviour is intentional under some description before we can talk about means or side-effects. Again, however, this mere classifactory primacy does not indicate that there is a moral primacy. And the point is a limited one: non-voluntary actions (including my idly scratching my nose) may have side-effects.[46]

Somehow the concept of intentionality has been superimposed upon and is preventing us from addressing the truly morally-relevant concepts involved in practical deliberation. This phenomenon is amply illustrated in Fried's work.[47] Let us grant his assertion that (i) morality is about the right or good way of being in the world as human beings. Then, *per* Fried, because (ii) we relate to the world as human beings through our intentional actions, it follows that (iii) intentional actions are morally primary. How do I object to this? For one thing, the conclusion given (i) and (ii) should be for exclusivity rather than primacy. But my main point is that proposition (ii) is defective. Advertent and even inadvertent actions constitute ways of being in the world as human beings, at least in any sense which might make proposition (i) true. We may, as earlier, evince a monstrous indifference or carelessness in our behaviour. What *is* true is that we conduct ourselves in the world primarily as practical deliberators, and there is nothing in that fact to make intention morally primary. But it is a fact which Fried entirely misses. Consider an alternative formulation of the argument he presents.[48] Let us grant this time his assertion (i) that our moral judgments of right and wrong guide actions. There is nothing in that: advertent actions are no less actions than are intentional ones. But moral judgments (he continues) also (ii) speak about the uniting of outcomes and desires—represented by the concept of intention. This is wrong. Outcomes are united with desires in practical deliberation through an agent adopting her desire for some outcome as part of her motivation: when bringing about that outcome becomes the motivating end for her behaviour. It is certainly a mistake to say that practical deliberation is concerned simply with 'what to intend'.[49] Practical deliberation is concerned with which ends to seek (in the light of what other values are affected) *and* with how to behave in order to fulfil those ends. If there is no way of behaving so as to satisfy an end without incurring harmful side-effects, an agent may be constrained by morality to abandon her pursuit of

[46] Another example (discussed in my review of Moore's *Act and Crime* in [1994] 53 CLJ 173 at 174) occurs when I absently and inadvertently tap my hand against my knee when concentrating upon a discussion, and in doing so spill cigar ash upon the new carpet. See also J. Cornman's reply to Davidson in R. Brinckley, R. Bronaugh, and A. Marras (eds.), *Action, Agent and Reason* (Oxford, 1971), 26 at 32.

[47] 'Right and Wrong—Preliminary Considerations' (1975) 5 *Journal of Legal Studies* 165 at 199.

[48] *Ibid.*, 196.

[49] Cf. G. Harman, 'Practical Reasoning' (1976) 29 *Review of Metaphysics* 431 at 431.

that end. To put it in Finnis' terms, the choice against respecting a basic value is a choice about what to *do*, not simply about what to desire or intend.

An allied point. While it may fairly be said that when we practically deliberate we often think only about means and ends, it does not follow that practical deliberation is paradigmatically a matter of intention. Still less does it follow that intention is morally primary. Failure to consider bad side-effects is a *fault*.[50] Particularly given the role for morality claimed by Mackie, that of counteracting known limitations of men's sympathies, the fault would seem of major moral concern. Indeed, Mackie buttresses the claim that it is morally primary only that we do not desire or seek harm[51] with the contention that '[t]he function of morality is primarily to counteract this limitation of men's sympathies'.[52] Yet when men's sympathies are limited, they tend to bring about harm through side-effects and further consequences in particular.

ARE SIDE-EFFECTS TOO REMOTE TO COUNT?

Finnis does suggest one other ground for differentiating side-effects in the moral assessment of behaviour:

If one is to act intelligently at all one must choose to realize and participate in some basic value or values rather than others, and this inevitable concentration of effort will indirectly impoverish, inhibit, or interfere with the realization of those other values. If I commit myself to truthful scholarship, then I fail to save the lives I could save as a doctor, I inhibit the growth of the production of material goods. . . . These unsought but unavoidable side-effects accompany every human choice, and their consequences are incalculable. But it is always reasonable to leave some of them, and often reasonable to leave all of them, out of account. . . . [W]e can say this: to indirectly damage any basic good . . . is obviously quite different, rationally and thus morally, from directly and immediately damaging a basic good by choosing an act which in and of itself simply (or, we should now add, primarily) damages that good . . . but which indirectly, *via* the mediation of expected consequences, is to promote . . . some other basic good(s).[53]

But we cannot say this at all—at least not qua conclusion. When Finnis claims that it is always reasonable to omit some side-effects from consideration, I ask *which*? Finnis gives no account of when we may ignore particular side-effects. But granted that, as Finnis acknowledges, it is not always reasonable to leave side-effects out of our deliberations, then any such account cannot license us to ignore them in virtue of their being side-effects. Rather than this, perhaps the extraneous features relevant to such an

---

[50] This proposition is subject to certain limitations, especially in the context of emergencies. Confer the brief discussion in my 'Mistakes in Defence' (1992) 12 *Oxford Journal of Legal Studies* 295 at 306.

[51] N. 25 above, at 160.   [52] *Ibid.*, 108.   [53] N. 31 above, at 120.

account are the very features which make Finnis' example look plausible. And it is a *very* peculiar example. We do not have an action so much as the choosing of a life plan. Conceding that the effects of such a choice are incalculable, it might be for this very reason that we may reasonably neglect them—for they are too indeterminate usefully to evaluate. And indeed, it may be debated of the example whether there will be damage to a basic good at all. That I shall not save any lives does not mean that I shall cause the death of some person, or even that anyone will die. The injunction, 'do not harm life', is not breached by the fact that 'I shall not in the future be saving lives'. On the other hand, if I know that a probable side-effect of my doing something will be that Fred dies, then surely it is never[54] morally appropriate for me to go ahead without first taking that risk into account and determining that running it is justifiable.

Regard also Finnis' deployment of 'immediately'. Certainly the remoteness (or lack of 'immediacy') of the effects in his example may contribute to their unsusceptibility of moral assessment. Yet the same is true for ends: if I send an employee to Paris on business in the vague hope that terrorists might blow up the plane *en route*, then her death is not attributable to me when (happy chance!) the plane explodes. Finnis may well be correct when he claims there is a difference between 'direct and immediate' damage and 'indirect' damage. But if immediacy is doing any work in that distinction (and if it is not, why did Finnis introduce the concept?) then the distinction is not one between intention and advertence. For while the death of the children may be an indirect effect of Strategic Bomber's behaviour, it is hardly a less immediate one than the destruction of the munitions plant—and is certainly more calculable and immediate than the winning of Strategic Bomber's war.

RESOLVING CONFLICTS BETWEEN ABSOLUTE PROHIBITIONS

One final matter. There is the hint of a different point in the passage quoted from Finnis: that giving priority to intention (embracing ends and means) resolves the potential for conflict inherent in the prospect that many effects of behaviour might be incommensurably (and unjustifiably) bad.[55] But acknowledging the priority of *ends* would, it seems to me, resolve the potential for conflict with equal efficiency. Notice that I do not preclude primacy

---

[54] Save perhaps in emergencies; see n. 50 above.

[55] Fried makes the point explicitly in n. 47 above, at 190, 193 (and see generally 188–92): 'Attenuation of the absoluteness of absolute prohibitions is required with particular urgency in any moral system that contains more than one such absolute injunction. . . . [B]y paying attention to intention we make possible systems of rules with more than one absolute prohibition or injunction.' As Mackie puts it (n. 25 above, at 162), 'we could not maintain absolute prohibitions if their scope were extended to include obliquely intended actions—side-effects and further consequences'. See also T. Nagel, 'War and Massacre' in *Mortal Questions* (Cambridge, 1979), 53 at 59.

going to ends in morality, just as nothing I have said to date commits me to consequentialism. It is simply that I do not see a reason why morality cannot speak with primary force of *both* desires (or ends) and behaviour.

None of the foregoing is yet to say that I would necessarily disagree with Finnis over specific cases, particularly those where one might be called upon to opine whether a given killing is justifiable. For Finnis will sometimes allow an exception to the general rule, 'thou shalt not kill': 'the "innocence" of the victim whose life is taken makes a difference to the characterizing of an action as open to and respectful of the good of human life, and as an intentional killing'.[56] So the injunction against harming a basic good, 'do not damage human life', mutates here into the formal and absolute proscription, 'do not (intentionally) kill any innocent person'. On my account, the corresponding proscription would be of the form, 'do not (intentionally) kill any person without justification'. And the two proscriptions should normally yield similar results, for I expect that a killing will usually be justifiable only in cases where the victim is not 'innocent'. In particular, I agree with Nagel that there are principles which govern the manner in which we ought to treat other people, and that any justification for harming another must be couched with respect to the behaviour of that other.[57]

As it happens, however, although I have stated that they will normally coincide, the two injunctions may not always do so. I want briefly to consider this point, for three reasons. First, Finnis renders the rationale he has offered more attractive when he claims that it is consistent with the prohibition 'do not intentionally kill innocents', rather than the more draconian stricture 'do not intentionally kill anyone'. I wish to deny him that appeal. Secondly, if my approach is to be preferred in the inconsistent cases, then we have another reason, supplementing my arguments so far, to reject the

[56] N. 22 above, at 141. Thus it is permissible, under certain conditions, intentionally to kill enemy soldiers or to inflict capital punishment: Finnis, *Fundamentals of Ethics* (Washington, D.C., 1983), 130; see also Anscombe, 'War and Murder' in Wasserstrom (ed.), *War and Massacre* (Belmont, 1970), 42.

[57] N. 55 above, at 64 ff. *Per exemplum* (at 65), '[t]here seems to be a perfectly natural conception of the distinction between fighting clean and fighting dirty. To fight dirty is to direct one's hostility or aggression not at its proper object, but at a peripheral target which may be more vulnerable, and through which the proper object can be attacked indirectly.' More generally, the problem cases seem to be where a purported justification for harming X appeals to other factors in the world and not to X personally. See also Fried, n. 47 above, at 187–8. Nagel's proposal neatly deals with Casey's example ('Actions and Consequences' in J. P. Casey (ed.), *Morality and Moral Reasoning* (London, 1971), 155 at 172–3): 'One member of a pair of Siamese twins becomes seriously ill because his liver ceases to function. He will certainly die unless a new liver is transplanted to him. This, however, is impossible because he is of an extremely rare blood group. . . . There is, however, one way in which his life could be saved: his brother is of the same blood group and tissue type. Being of a ruthless nature, he implores a doctor to procure the death of his brother, and save his own life by transferring his brother's liver into him. The doctor refuses the request. On the strong "no moral difference" thesis, the doctor, in refusing to kill the healthy twin, is doing something morally tantamount to killing the unhealthy one. . . . [A] more preposterous conclusion could scarcely be imagined.'

rationale underlying his version of the proscription. Thirdly, I can then be confident that my own analysis of the moral distinctions between ends, means, and side-effects need not cater (as Finnis' must) to the constraints imposed by Finnis' absolute interdiction.

Hart provides us with a case where Finnis and I might diverge:

[O]f which I have been told by an eye-witness, where a man had been trapped in the cabin of a blazing lorry from which it was impossible to free him, and a bystander, in answer to his pleas, shot him and killed him to save him from further agony as he was slowly being burnt to death.[58]

On Finnis' view the lorry driver, who is surely an 'innocent', must not be shot. On my account of the prohibition, killing him may be justifiable; at least, the formal nature of a claim of justification would seem to meet Nagel's constraint. But either way the case is revealing. Because Finnis' account makes it look easy, whereas on my account it is a difficult case. And, in my view, it *is* difficult. Conversely, consider the case of an insane aggressor, who is not responsible for her behaviour when I kill her in the course of defending myself. This is a hard case on Finnis' view, for we hesitate before saying that she is not 'innocent'.[59] But actually this is not a hard case at all, and any account which makes it look difficult must be wrong.

I shall not dwell upon these points here,[60] but notice two other implications of Finnis' view. On that analysis, the killing of a non-innocent person is not harmful to the good of human life (because were it so, then the 'choice' to kill a non-innocent would be a 'choice' to damage a basic good, something that is incommensurably bad (*ergo* unjustifiable) and thus absolutely prohibited). But this is implausible. It certainly harms human life: it is a killing! (albeit a justifiable one). If this is so, then how is an 'innocence' exception compatible with the basis of the original (otherwise absolute) prohibition? It appears *ad hoc*[61]—witness here Finnis' puzzling contention that 'the "innocence" of the victim whose life is taken makes a difference to the characterizing of an action . . . as an intentional killing'.[62] Secondly, on the

---

[58] N. 23 above, at 123.

[59] Thus Suzanne Uniacke contemplates 'a morally innocent unjust aggressor, such as a deranged person or an attacking sleepwalker': *Permissible Killing: The Self-Defence Justification of Homicide* (Cambridge, 1994), 68.

[60] They are also canvassed in my *op. cit.*, n. 50 above, at 302–4.

[61] S. Kagan, *The Limits of Morality* (Oxford, 1989), 134.

[62] N. 22 above, at 141 (the quotation is given in full in the text above at n. 56). Finnis may have in mind here a slightly different point which he later makes in *Fundamentals of Ethics*, n. 56 above, at 129–30. When a public judicial officer deprives a criminal of basic goods in order to restore the order of justice which the criminal violated, he claims, 'the deprivation or suppression will be intended neither for its own sake nor as a means to any further good state of affairs. Rather, it is intended precisely as itself a good, namely the good of restoring the order of justice, a restoration that cannot (logically cannot) consist in anything other than such an act of deprivation or suppression'. Even if Finnis is correct here, however, the deprivation remains intended—albeit as an instance of (rather than means to) the officer's end. Though it may *also* be intended as a restoration of the order of justice, one does not restore justice and incidentally kill the non-innocent; one restores justice *in virtue of* killing him. But if so, then Finnis does not

same analysis one who kills a non-innocent person while believing them innocent has not actually harmed the basic good of human life (and indeed she has not breached the injunction, 'do not intentionally kill any innocent person'). This result, too, seems wrong—at least, unless Finnis were to do rather more to distinguish between the good, human life, and the particulars, individual humans' lives. He shows no inclination to do so when he states that the good of human life is a basic aspect of each person's well-being.[63]

Am I being too literal-minded here? I think not. In allowing an exception based on 'innocence', Finnis has effectively equated 'the basic good of human life' with 'the basic good of innocent human life'. But the lives of non-innocents are just as much human lives as are those of innocents. Human life is a basic good in virtue of its being human life, *simpliciter*; not in virtue of its being innocent.[64] Finnis may well be misled by paradigms: cases involving the intentional killing of an innocent might often be worse than those involving the intentional killing of a non-innocent; the scenarios are not paradigmatically *ceteris paribus*. But the *intrinsic* reasons against killing an innocent—being those reasons grounded in the basic goodness of human life—apply with identical force against killing a non-innocent.

JUSTIFICATION AND THE IMPORTANCE OF MOTIVE

SOME CASES

If intending an *actus reus* is not worse *simpliciter* than foreseeing it, then there is a need to explain why our intuitions so often seem to support the proposition I have rejected. Let me start by setting out four cases. Suppose that Nurse C is in possession of a placebo and of a poison which induces considerable pain. The two drugs are indistinguishable to the eye and have in some way been mixed up in the medicine cabinet so that he cannot tell them apart. Nurse C wishes to find out which one of the commixt drugs is which. Ordinarily it would not be morally acceptable to ascertain the first drug's nature by trial and error.[65] But conjecture also that his patient has a disease of the sort proposed by Kagan:

Imagine a disease which has no painful symptoms for an initial period, but which—if left untreated—eventually erupts, regularly causing the patient excruciating pain, with no chance of remission or treatment. Luckily the disease can be cured, if treated during the initial, dormant stage. Treatment, however, requires inflicting a significant amount of pain upon the unfortunate patient: causing pain to the patient's body

demonstrate why something intended as an instantiation is to be treated like an unintended side-effect rather than a means or end; why we cannot say of that thing that it 'itself-does-nothing-but-damage-a-basic-good'.

[63] N. 31 above, at 85. [64] Cf. *ibid.*, 86. [65] Kenny, n. 8 above, at 160.

stimulates it to release certain hormones and antibodies (which cannot be otherwise produced) that destroy the disease-causing virus.[66]

As with Bennett's Bombers, we may illustrate the difference with diagrams which represent the chain of actual or possible actions contemplated by Nurse C:

Case 1: C_1 ───────────→ Neutral End [Determine Drug Identity][67]
(Experiment Case) |
                        Bad Side-effect [Pain] ───────→ Good Side-effect [Cure]

By hypothesis, were the drug known to be a poison then it might justifiably be injected in order to bring about the patient's cure.[68] This would be a straightforward case of doing something bad as a means to a good end:

Case 2: C_2 ──→ Bad Means [Pain] ──→ Good End [Cure]
(Justified Case)

In the Experiment Case$_1$, the promise of a cure makes the nurse's behaviour, in taking the risk of causing pain to his patient, reasonable though not praise-worthy. He knows that even if the drug he tests proves to be pain-inducing, there would be a good reason to use it on the patient. While we might disap-prove of Nurse C as a person,[69] and while his explanation of his behaviour might be unreasonable, the behaviour itself needs no further explanation. At the same time, however, we would not accept Nurse C's action were he sadis-tically to inject the patient in order to bring pain about, knowing of but not wanting (perhaps even regretting) the beneficial consequences:

Case 3: C_3 ───────────→ Bad End [Pain]
(Sadistic Case) |
                     Good Side-effect [Cure]

---

[66] N. 61 above, at 168. The example is credited by him to Parfit.

[67] The term, 'neutral', is here used rather loosely, to indicate that Nurse C's end is unim-portant by comparison with the other actions her behaviour constitutes; and that, even disre-garding those other actions, the reason for action her end supplies counts only toward its being by itself permissible, rather than creditable or in need of justification.

[68] Kagan continues, '[s]ince the pain necessary for treatment, although significant, is far less than that caused by the disease itself, we may have good reason to deliberately induce pain in one who has recently contracted the disease.' Bob Sullivan has asked me whether this case really does involve a bad means—suggesting that the pain caused, however unpleasant, is not a harm but rather treatment, since it is just what the patient needs. He proposes substituting an exam-ple where a protected interest of the victim is more obviously invaded. An alternative would no doubt be less controversial. But I am sceptical that it is needed. In my instance, Nurse C *does* inflict pain, and deliberately. It is hard to see how doing so stands other than in need of justifi-cation; or, were this not so, how Sullivan would be able to condemn Nurse C in Cases 3 and 4 (to follow). He is beguiled, I suspect, by the same sort of phenomenon that misleads Finnis (n. 62 above), for the harm is intended not as a means to but rather as an instance of treatment. Yet it is still intended. This special case is dealt with further in my 'Moral Certainty, and the Boundaries of Intention', n. 2 above.

[69] The *extent* to which we do so will be affected in part by his attitude to the side-effects. He may yet—albeit incidentally—welcome, regret or be indifferent to them.

Of course, the Sadistic Nurse does not cause pain as a means. In order to draw a closer analogy with the Justified Case₂, suppose this time that Nurse C causes pain because of a bribe:

Case 4:   C₄ ⟶ Bad Means [Pain] ⟶ Neutral End [Money Receipt]
(Bribery Case) |
                    Good Side-effect [Cure]

Here is a central asymmetry. Though Case 2 [Justified] is in this instance morally acceptable, and although Nurse C's actual behaviour is the same for both cases, this last Bribery Case₄ is not.

A PRELIMINARY DISCUSSION

The examples suggest that there are some important moral differences between means, ends, and side-effects. In the present section I will propose an account of those distinctions; in the next I shall offer certain arguments in support of that account. It is not possible, or even desirable, for me to attempt a complete analysis of the foregoing cases, but I want at least to assay some indicative remarks.

Justifying Ends? Cases 2 and 3

Let us begin with the Justified₂ and Sadistic₃ Cases. I take it that Case 2 would be one of those where an intrinsically[70] bad means is justified by the good end to which it conduces.[71] Such cases exist because we can say—subject to certain constraints,[72] and recollecting my opposition to Finnis over this—that where an agent's behaviour constitutes both a bad action and a good action, and if those actions stand respectively in a means–end relationship so far as the agent's motivation for doing them is concerned, then the agent's doing of the bad action (intentionally and as a means to the good action) may sometimes thereby be justified. In effect, a defence of justification may be claimed for an intentional action if the doing of the action-that-is-to-be-defended was *motivated* by the further action which (it is claimed) justifies it.

However if, as in the Sadistic Case₃, the two actions stand in an end–side-effect relationship, then in my view the agent cannot be justified in doing the bad action by the fact that his behaviour also involved a good action. For

[70] My usage is conventional. Roughly speaking, I take it that doing an action is intrinsically good (neutral, bad) when its doing is good (neutral, bad) after discounting the value (whether good or bad) that the action has in virtue of its consequences. The value of the action in virtue of its consequences is termed its instrumental value.

[71] Subject (cf. in Kagan's example, 'requires'), to the possibility of a preferable means being available to cure the patient. See further the note next following.

[72] In particular: (i) a constraint of the sort envisaged by Nagel, and discussed earlier (n. 57 above); (ii) a proportionality constraint, that the end be sufficiently grave to warrant the means; (iii) that no (sufficiently) preferable alternative means is available; and (iv) that the means may in any case be unacceptable because of its side-effects.

many people, this generalization will be plausible enough. It is never morally acceptable to desire a bad *actus*; correspondingly, it ought never to be morally acceptable to do a bad action for its own sake, since to do so is to act motivated by such a desire. As Bennett puts it, there 'is moral significance in what an agent intends as an end'; in what he is motivated to seek by an intrinsic desire therefor. 'It would be a bad man who wanted civilian deaths for their own sakes'.[73] And it would be a bad thing for him to kill them for that reason.

Incidentally, given the difference between the Justified$_2$ and Sadistic$_3$ Cases, I should concur with philosophers who contend that the question, 'was it the right action?', is not to be answered by replying to the utilitarian enquiry, 'did it have the best consequences?' The limited potential for intended bad actions to be justified in these cases neatly disposes of that equation through an asymmetry, for while an end might sometimes justify a means or side-effect, no means or side-effect can justify an end.

It is also worth interposing that the distinctiveness of ends carries over into questions of eligibility for moral credit or praise; for which neither means nor side-effects qualify. I do not warrant approval if my carelessness saves a life. Nor do I deserve to be praised[74] for saving another's life if I did so only because my inheritance depended upon it, a contingency but for which I should have let her die.[75]

Justifying Means? Cases 2 and 4

So there is moral asymmetry between ends and means or side-effects, at least in respect of praise for good actions. Compare now the Justified$_2$ and Bribery$_4$ Cases. In each instance the same good and bad actions are done. And if the agent's raw *behaviour* is morally acceptable in Case 2 then, qua behaviour, it must be morally acceptable in the Bribery Case$_4$. Yet, *ceteris paribus*, we think less of Nurse C as a person in the Bribery Case$_4$ than we do in the Justified Case$_2$. And it seems to me that, correspondingly, the agent's action of inflicting pain for a bribe is not acceptable. Those who concur with me are likely to accept a restriction upon the generalization drawn above from the Justification Case$_2$. If it is ever acceptable to do a bad action intentionally, then this ought to be the case only when (though not whenever) that action is done by the agent *because* it is a means to a further, good

[73] Bennett, n. 3 above, at 99.
[74] At least, to be praised morally. A surgeon might merit praise for the skill he displays during an operation, but not in the sense with which I am concerned here.
[75] D'Arcy concurs (n. 45 above, at 126; see also at 161–2, and at 166 for an example involving a morally neutral end): 'Suppose that A, who in his undergraduate days had belonged to some Fascist or Communist organization, which he has long since quit, is about to be appointed to high office; B happens to know of A's past association, but refrains from making it known, with the result that A is appointed. This may be to B's credit; but not if his reason was the prospect of blackmailing A once he was in office.'

action; and it should not assist such an agent that his behaviour happens also to constitute some other good but unsought action. We shall return to this restriction below.

Justifying Side-Effects? Case 1

The Experiment Case₁ raises the problems of foresight and recklessness more squarely, since in that case the bad action is advertent rather than intentional—the agent inflicts pain only as a bad side-effect of doing what she intends. Moreover, and owing to the curative side-effect that accompanies it, the bad side-effect, though foreseen, is not reckless. We say that the agent's behaviour is reasonable, despite the risk of the pain.

Although I have suggested earlier that recklessness of this sort involves an advertence-based deficiency on the part of the defendant,[76] recklessness is nevertheless analogous to negligence in respect of the nature of that deficiency. The key test for blame in either case is whether it is reasonable to run the risk of (unintentionally) doing that *actus reus*. Such a test is in effect a test of whether the agent's behaviour is reasonable, notwithstanding its potential to involve doing the *actus reus*.

It might look somewhat odd to appose justification with reasonableness, for they are certainly different things. Indeed, implicit in my view of Cases 3 [Sadistic] and 4 [Bribery] is that one is not always justified in doing an *actus reus* by the reasonableness of the behaviour that constitutes it. But if the connection is adopted in the context of negligence, it ought to be embraced here: *ceteris paribus*, one is justified in bringing about an intrinsically bad side-effect if—and only if—it is reasonable in the circumstances to risk doing so by behaving as one does. Once this is accepted, it follows that, when considering whether the advertent but unintentional doing of an *actus reus* is justified, then as well as ends the divers means and side-effects may all be admitted to the assessment—because the question whether or not it is reasonable to behave in a given fashion, and thereby risk the bad side-effect at issue, may be affected by any of the ramifications of that behaviour; by any of the *actus* it has the potential to constitute, whether good or bad; and whether or not in fact intended by the defendant. We shall return also to this discussion below.

Summary: Moral Differences Between Ends, Means and Side-effects

An upshot of these proposals, and one which explains the case *exempla*, is a structural asymmetry that I claim exists between intention and foresight. The central moral distinction between intended actions and those merely foreseen is not (as Mackie *et al.* have claimed) simply a matter of degree, but rather that the foreseen do not lend any favourable weight to the

---

[76] See the text above at n. 22. Note that my suggestion is not meant to prejudge the possibility of indifference-based recklessness; it is made only in the context of advertent wrongdoing.

justification of the intended.[77] They can lend moral weight in favour of the agent only when considering the reasonableness of other merely foreseen actions (as, for instance, in the Experiment Case₁). By contrast, Case 2 [Justified] illustrates that good ends, which motivate the choice to risk the side-effect or to essay the means, may sometimes be offset against the bad-ness of another *actus*. Indeed this prospect is explicitly countenanced in a relatively recondite proviso of the doctrine of double effect, that the unin-tended (bad) action ought to be proportionate to the intended (good) action.[78]

So far as means and side-effects are concerned, the cases suggest that the difference between the two is that (as with ends) one cannot justify one's doing of something bad qua means by appeal to the reasonableness of one's behaviour (and, in particular, by appeal to good side-effects); whereas one may do so to justify one's choice to do something bad as a side-effect.

DEFENDING THE EXPLANATION: TWO TYPES OF JUSTIFICATION

Not everyone will accept what has been suggested here. A consequentialist, for instance, will demur: of course actions done as ends have no further jus-tification qua ends, but why may they not be justified qua actions? That is, if some bad *actus* done by the defendant as an end is in fact justifiable as a means to another albeit unintended consequence, then why should we or the criminal law reprove that defendant for doing it? Here is a crux case for morality and law: where the defendant's motive for inflicting harm is not good enough, but where her behaviour is itself reasonable. On the analysis presented here, the defendant is morally culpable and to be convicted for inflicting the harm, and may not justify her doing so by reference to those

---

[77] Except to offset the adverse weight of other foreseen actions. I emphasize here that the difference is over what counts to *credit*, not discredit. We might say, for instance, that an agent was not justified in doing some intrinsically good action because her doing so had another, dis-proportionately bad side-effect.

Note that while I take this to be the central moral difference, it need not be the only one. In particular, it seems to me plausible that an agent who cannot distribute the blame for acts she does as an end or means can sometimes do so in the case of side-effects. For Strategic Bomber, it may be relevant that the enemy chose to locate the munitions plant next to the school; for Terror Bomber, on the other hand, this cannot matter. (I owe this thought to Bob Sullivan.) Such situations, where the side-effect is in part attributable to the agency of a third party, lie outside the scope of this essay.

[78] J. T. Mangan ('An Historical Analysis of the Principle of Double Effect' (1949) 10 *Theological Studies* 41 at 43) formulates the principle of double effect in the following way:

A person may licitly perform an action that he knows will produce a good effect and a bad effect provided that four conditions are verified . . .
(1) That the action itself from its very object be good or at least indifferent;
(2) that the good effect and not the evil effect be intended;
(3) that the good effect be not produced *by means* of the evil effect;
(4) that there be a proportionally grave reason for permitting the evil effect.
See also Finnis, n. 22 above, at 134–5; J. G. Hanink, 'Some Light on Double Effect' (1975) 35 *Analysis* 147 at 150; Fried, n. 47 above, at 167, n. 6, including additional references cited there.

other, unintended consequences which happen to make her behaviour reasonable. Crudely summarized, the importance of intention is that it knocks out of consideration, rather than outweighs, those good side-effects.

Rather earlier in this essay,[79] I suggested that it might be an error to assume that either intention or behaviour must be morally primary. My own view is that it would indeed be an error to make that assumption. I think that, in effect, moral fault for what one does may be grounded in *either* behaviour *or* motivating reasons. Each ground yields a sufficient but not necessary set of conditions for blame: each approach yields a necessary but not sufficient account of justification.

We can see this even in the *language* of justification. Imagine that a defendant does some intrinsically bad action. If she then purports to justify herself, she makes a claim along the following lines: notwithstanding that she did something bad, nevertheless in the circumstances she did the right thing—or at least, she did not do the wrong thing. But what is it to do the right thing here? That depends upon whether she acts intentionally or unintentionally. She claims her intentional action was the right (or an acceptable) thing to do because it was the best[80] (at least, a permissible) means to do some further action. By contrast, she claims she acted acceptably when she unintentionally did something bad because other actions liable to be constituted by her behaviour made it a reasonable risk to run. Notice the different locution. We complain that she (deliberately) does something bad when it is intentional; but that she *unreasonably* does something bad when it is a side-effect.

That is to say: a defendant's justification for doing an *actus reus* takes a different form regarding side-effects than it does for means. He justifies risking a bad side-effect when he shows that the reasons for and against his behaviour make it reasonable to do so, but he justifies doing that *actus* as a means when he shows that his end gives him good reason to.

The 'Justification' of Side-effects: Behaviour

Correspondingly, in my view there are two alternative bases for blaming an agent. Consider first the case of doing harm as a side-effect. As proponents of the doctrine of double effect impliedly accept,[81] to proscribe unintended harming outright would be intolerable; because we cannot always avoid taking risks and because the side-effects of our actions are so often incalculable. This is why we base culpability upon a very general assessment, one dependent upon the agent's behaviour as a whole; and do not blame someone for doing harm in such a case unless she does so recklessly or negligently—in

---

[79] See the text above at n. 26.
[80] Subject to the constraints noted above n. 72. Even the best means may be so bad that the end does not justify doing it.
[81] Mark the assertions by Fried and Mackie, n. 55 above.

particular, unless her doing so is unreasonable. For whenever we say that an agent's risking harm as she did was unreasonable, then we can also say, on the same grounds, that her behaviour was unreasonable. If blame for foreseen actions attaches to the agent, it is because such actions—in common with intended actions—provide reasons for and more importantly against an agent's behaviour. Those reasons are not contingent upon the agent's own intentions.[82]

This may be put in another way. Side-effects are relevant to blame since, *irrespective* of their role in the agent's own practical reasoning, they provide reasons why her behaviour is reasonable or unreasonable; and because we do not blame a defendant for choosing to run the risk of a bad side-effect[83] unless that choice is on the whole unreasonable—unless that choice does not conform to the reasons by which a reasonable man might be guided. Thus in the Experiment Case₁, Nurse C's behaviour is—qua behaviour—acceptable, although he did not intend the cure that makes it such. He has not inflicted pain recklessly, even though his own reason for doing so is by itself an insufficient warrant. It is always morally acceptable to choose to incur a risk which is reasonable to run.

The Justification of Means: Motive

The other basis is where a defendant does harm intentionally. And the problem occurs when the question, did he do the right thing, is asked of a case where the harm was an acceptable way for him to do something further, but where he did not do the harm for that reason: in a sense, where the harm was justifiable but not actually justified. So while an agent's behaviour may be acceptable, his motives might not be. I think that we may validly blame the agent for the wrong he does by inflicting harm in such a case, and that—

---

[82] They are, in the terminology adopted by John Gardner, guiding rather than explanatory reasons: 'Justifications and Reasons', this volume. Gardner's view (at 105) that 'No action or belief is justified unless it is true *both* that there was an applicable (guiding) reason for so acting or so believing *and* that this corresponded with the (explanatory) reason why that action was performed or the belief held' raises the possibility of an alternative, if rather severe, view of justification, one he does not discuss; requiring that even bad side-effects be risked only for sufficiently good, motivating, (that is, both guiding and explanatory) reasons. On this analysis even the Experiment Case₁ would be unacceptable. But to hold this view would be wrongly to fuse behavioural with motive-based culpability. Blame for behaviour is grounded upon a finding that, independent of the defendant's intentions, the reasons in fact applicable to her behaviour are on balance against. They are, as Gardner might say, defeated *in gross*. Conversely however, if the guiding reasons in favour of one's behaviour are *un*defeated, they are undefeated in gross. The behaviour is, qua behaviour, permissible; so far as side-effects are concerned, the risks are reasonable and there is nothing further to justify. This does not, of course, entitle one to act for bad explanatory reasons, but that is quite a different matter. Since explanatory reasons simply do not apply to side-effects, there seems no basis on which to restrict the eligibility of reasons applicable to justify the choice to risk them to only those guiding reasons which are also explanatory. Gardner's claim (at 113) that 'it is quite pointless to cite, by way of justification, an undefeated reason for which one did not act' presents a consistent but potentially misleading picture of which reasons are doing the work in these cases.

[83] *A fortiori* for bringing it about.

provided his action be an offence—the law ought to convict him for doing so; as indeed English law currently does.[84] Observe that in both law and morality the primary thing proscribed (the *actus reus*) is not the *behaviour* generally, but rather the wrong: the particular *actus* (such as bringing about death), when done with *mens rea*. It is only when that proscription is restricted by a qualifier, unreasonable, that we look to the agent's behaviour—to the other actions that were or might have been done. Otherwise, there seems no reason to do so; nor to relax my stricture that the justification of intentional action operate just as a species of exculpatory explanation.

The denial of blame in the Sadistic[3] and Bribery[4] Cases rests, if anywhere, upon the fact that intending to inflict pain is justifi*able* as a means to cure Nurse C's patient: hence the claim that inflicting pain is not in this case a bad thing to do. We should make no mistake, however: it remains, in itself, a bad thing to do. This is why, *ceteris paribus*, it is morally and may be legally proscribed. I have accepted that it is not proscribed absolutely (compare the Experiment[1] and Justified[2] Cases), but since it is a bad thing to do then both the law and morality have grounds to restrict the basis upon which its doing is permitted. It seems to me that the restriction ought to be: unless Nurse C is not blameworthy for doing it. And it is patently the case that he deserves reproof—as a person, to be sure, but *in respect of* his choice to inflict pain—in cases such as 3 and 4.

I have suggested elsewhere that the proper interpretation of situations where there is a justificatory defence to (what I there term) a prima facie offence is that the circumstances underlying the justification partially liberate the defendant from her prima facie legal (and moral) duty not to commit that offence.[85] But they only do so *in virtue of* the prima facie offence being a means to the justificatory end. An extension to cover side-effects as well as ends (embracing, for instance, Case 3 [Sadistic] as well as Case 2 [Justified]) would be gratuitous. Since the *actus reus* is intrinsically bad, the licence ought not to be extended beyond that which is necessary; beyond circumstances where the agent is not blameworthy for her doing it. And the sort of case at issue here does not involve any denial of her

---

[84] *Thain* [1985] NI 457; also *Dadson* (1850) 2 Den. 35, though in that case the justificatory factor was not recognized by the defendant. In *Thain*, the defendant shot and killed someone escaping from an army foot-patrol, in circumstances where he may have been permitted to do so in effecting an arrest. Although he was apparently aware of those circumstances, the defendant admitted that he was not seeking to arrest the victim, and was consequently convicted of murder. In *Dadson*, a policeman shot and wounded a thief. The thief was, unbeknown to the defendant, a felon, and the policeman would have been justified in shooting to prevent the escape of a felon. See the discussion by G. R. Sullivan, 'Bad Thoughts and Bad Acts' [1990] *Criminal LR* 558. In the United States, only *Dadson* would be good law under the Model Penal Code (*per* §§ 3.02–3.07), which favours allowing a defence provided merely that the defendant believes the justifying circumstances exist.

[85] N. 50 above, at 304.

blameworthiness for doing it. Even if there is no 'net' harm the agent still does a wrong.[86]

The argument can also be expressed in terms of the nature of practical reasons. An agent's positive reasons for making a choice (to behave in some particular fashion) have to do with ends and means. We have seen that one can give no justification for doing something bad for its own sake (that is, qua end), but that one might be able to give reasons to justify doing something bad as a means. Suppose that Fred steals a diamond in response to a credible threat that three strangers will be murdered if he refuses to do so.[87] Then there is, and Fred has, an (instrumental) reason to steal a diamond—because doing so will save lives. He also has a (non-instrumental) reason to save lives, and a concomitant, second-order reason to *steal the diamond in order to save lives*.[88]

The existence of an instrumental reason to do something (in this case, to steal a diamond) is always contingent upon—and in virtue of—there being a second-order reason to do so for the sake of some further thing (in this case, to save lives) which the agent has a non-instrumental reason to

[86] In 'Competing Theories of Justification: Deeds v. Reasons', this volume, 68, Paul Robinson asks, 'Is the absence of a *net* harm significant or not?' (my emphasis). My response should now be apparent: it is not. What is significant is the absence of resulting harm *per se*. Hence I am untroubled by Robinson's proposition (at 68–9) that 'There is no apparent reason why the significance of resulting [net] harm or evil should be denied in the context of the unknowingly justified actor.'

The reply also helps to explain why I would reject Robinson's contention that a defendant who kills another when 'unknowingly justified' should, instead of murder, be convicted only of the attempt to kill; for the homicide occurred. She did not attempt to kill—she succeeded. Robinson's conclusion that his analysis leads to a better performance of the criminal law's communicative function is undermined here. The are other difficulties with the communication argument. At one point (65) Robinson criticizes an ambiguity in the 'reasons' theory he opposes: 'Acquittal in a case where a justification defence is offered might mean either: (1) that the conduct is disapproved, but the actor is excused for it, or (2) that the conduct is approved.' But, although Robinson has argued elsewhere for a verdict system which differentiates justifications from excuses, there is no likelihood of such a system being implemented; especially given that the distinction is an impractical one to apply (cf. K. Greenawalt, 'The Perplexing Borders of Justification and Excuse' (1984) 84 *Columbia LR* 1897 at 1906) and is not tracked by recognized legal defences (cf. Gardner, 'Justifications and Reasons', this volume, 122). Hence, even if 'mistaken justification' is properly recognized as a mere excuse, a consequent acquittal would remain susceptible of either interpretation. The relevant public announcement of what actions are approved is not made by the trial verdict (which is identical on either theory), but rather by the criminal legal rules which determine that verdict. Moreover, as I have argued elsewhere (n. 50 above, at 302–4), it is not obvious that conduct of the sort that occurred in *Dadson* is to be condoned. Given his ignorance of the justificatory circumstances, an actor ought to be commanded by those rules *not* to behave as he does.

[87] The example is taken from Greenawalt, n. 86 above, at 1912, where it is used in a different context. Oddly enough a similar case occurs in Milo, n. 38 above, at 223, n. 7. Neither author credits it to the other.

[88] And, I think, a second-order reason to save lives for the sake of doing so. Here I am helping myself to Raz's point that a (first-order) reason for conduct is different in type from a (second-order) reason for conducting oneself for a reason: n. 28 above, at 39. See also, on second-order reasons, John Gardner, 'Justifications and Reasons', this volume, 114 ff.

do.[89] Correspondingly, Fred behaves for an instrumental reason only in virtue of his complying with (that is, acting for the sake of) rather than merely conforming to (that is, not acting inconsistently with) the reason whence that instrumental reason is derived.[90] This seems to me important. Justification of a bad means requires *compliance* with the reasons for doing that means. Such reasons are reasons to comply, to make the justifying *actus* an end, and not merely reasons to conform. By contrast, first-order reasons to conform are merely reasons to *do* an *actus*, whether as means, end, side-effect or further consequence.

Raz posts an objection to the idea that reasons for behaviour are (save in special cases) anything more than reasons to conform:[91]

[T]here is nothing wrong in not being aware of, and not being motivated to act for, reasons which are overriden or otherwise defeated. . . . The view that reasons must guide might suggest that on such occasions I should consider the defeated reason and become aware of its existence.

That the first statement is true does not mean that such reasons cannot also be reasons to comply. In my analysis their importance as reasons for compliance is limited, and does not extend to cases of the type Raz envisages; my failure to comply with them means only that they cannot explain (let alone justify) any bad means I seek. The suggestion mentioned in Raz's second statement is not borne out. As is true for undefeated reasons, I should advert to defeated reasons only in so far as it is unreasonable not to do so. So far as my behaviour is concerned, the existence of unperceived defeated reasons for behaviour does not prevent it from conforming with the undefeated reasons for behaviour by which a reasonable man would be guided.

For all this, it might be objected that the instrumental reason (to steal a diamond) exists even if Fred's end is not to save the strangers' lives. And that is true, but also, I have contended, immaterial. If an unintended action cannot explain why one intentionally does harm, then it does not justify one's doing so.[92] We should not permit a defendant (hypocritically) to avail

---

[89] Thus Raz remarks (*ibid.*, 182) that an instrumental reason disappears if its end is achieved in some other way.

[90] Raz illustrates the distinction between conformity and compliance as follows: 'If the need to give Jane moral support while she struggles with her homework is a reason for Derek to stay at home, then he conforms with that reason if he does stay at home. Generally people conform with a reason for a certain act if they perform that act in the circumstance in which that reason is a reason for its peformance. If Derek not only stays at home but does so because he realises Jane's need and that it is a reason for him to so act, then we would say that he complies with the reason': *ibid.*, 178.

[91] *Ibid.*, 180–1.

[92] Cf. the demand, 'explain thyself!' It is no straightforward matter to reconcile my claim here with Gardner's position, especially when he asserts (this volume, 112–13) that since the reasons in favour of one's action are undefeated in gross, the defendant need only act upon *any* one undefeated reason. Suppose that I may justifiably smash another's table in order to interrupt a potentially lethal fight that is going on. I do not, however, care about the fatalities—yet I could use some kindling, and so I smash the table. I have acted upon an undefeated reason, but it is the wrong one. One possible riposte (as to which see Gardner, at 115–17) is that

herself of a convenient defence by which she was not motivated. And the overall reasonableness of her behaviour should excuse neither a repugnant intention nor the action it spawns.

Different Rather than Worse?

A realistic objection remains. Leaving aside *actus rei* which are done for their own sake, it has been proposed that there are alternative bases upon which to fault a defendant for some aspect of her behaviour, and that there is no reason to suppose that one of those bases has a greater primacy than the other. Nevertheless, it is true that we intuitively think it worse to do something intentionally rather than advertently. Sometimes this is because one's intention constitutively changes the nature of the wrong done, a point made in this volume by Horder, and to which I shall refer below. But leaving that extraneous factor aside, the only other explanation I can offer for such an intuition is that we are influenced by paradigms. First, perhaps the cases where a means is not justified by the end it conduces to are typically also cases where the behaviour evinced is unreasonable—for the obverse surely does not hold. Secondly, in many cases the intended *actus reus* is sought as an end; there may be a popular association between instances where the *actus reus* is sought as a means and the former, more serious cases of intention.[93] Finally, I have claimed that, unlike advertent ones, an intended *actus reus* may not be mitigated by good foreseen *actus*. It follows that where there are also good unintended *actus*, then *ceteris paribus* the latter will actually be a worse case.

A Rationale?

Finnis, whose analysis has been opposed here, sought to rationalize as well as describe the moral distinctions between ends, means, and side-effects. But his explanation has been rejected: what, beyond description, does this essay offer?

Certainly not a complete rationale. Indeed, it may be that none such exists. The essay does, hopefully, provide support for excluding unintended actions from the defence of those which are intended. More difficult perhaps is the proposition that some intentional bad actions can be justified, which is inconsistent both with the doctrine of double effect[94]and with Finnis'

there is a second-order protective reason excluding certain reasons for damaging the table. Three points, however, should be made. First, on this view protected reasons are much more pervasive than we commonly recognize. Secondly, the rationale for having a protective reason in my example is not as such the one Gardner discusses (being the advantage of having pre-emptive rules); it lies in the property rights and corresponding duties which arise in virtue of another's having ownership of the table. Thirdly, the response does not exclude the possibility of there being two unexcluded reasons, only one of which is by itself sufficient to defeat the first-order part of the protected reason.

[93] Cf. Bennett's concession, n. 20 above.

[94] As traditionally formulated: see Mangan's statement of the doctrine, n. 78 above.

assimilation of means with ends. In this matter one can point to three aspects of the opposition to Finnis' own analysis: first, to the recognition that blame for a means involves, in common with side-effects, condemnation for an agent's being insufficiently different during her practical deliberation, rather than (as in the case of ends) for her being intrinsically desirous of it; secondly, to the rejection of Finnis' point about incommensurability, with its implications for the possibility of justification; and thirdly, to the relative plausibility of the version presented here of the formal proscription against intentional killing.[95]

There is a further source of support. The preliminary statement of structural moral differences between ends, means, and side-effects has been considerably elaborated here, and I hope that out of its elaboration has emerged a sense of the justness of the distinctions which have been drawn: that they are no longer simply brute facts. In particular, the distinctions have been revealed to be consistent with the places of ends, means and side-effects in the structure of an agent's practical deliberation.

LEGAL IMPLICATIONS

For the criminal law, two main implications arise from the bifurcated view of justification that I have presented. The first is that defences which seek to justify (rather than excuse or deny responsibility for) intentional doings of an *actus reus* should require that there be a nexus between the facts giving rise to the defence and the agent's doing of the *actus reus*, such that the justification actually lies in the end toward which the agent sought the proscribed *actus* as means. Both *Thain* and *Dadson* were correctly decided.[96] The second is that the law ought to distinguish intention from advertence, in order that a general defence of reasonableness may apply to the latter.

It seems to me desirable to convict persons who deliberately do an *actus reus* without doing so for good cause. Indeed, these are the sorts of persons with whom the criminal law ought most to be concerned. It certainly does not appear unjust, or defamatory, to convict such persons. Moreover their conviction should derive support from character-based theories of criminal culpability, since the choice to do harm stems from deficiencies of practical reasoning for which they may properly be faulted.

All this having been said, the law *may* have evidential grounds for acquitting where the justificatory side-effect is foreseen, based upon the desirability of simplifying the elements required to prove an offence, and given that the agent recognizes his action would, for instrumental reasons, be on balance acceptable. But these considerations appear to me to provide

---

[95] Though this third point would not refute the argument of one who does not accept that one could ever intentionally kill even non-innocents, including for example enemy soldiers.
[96] N. 84 above.

insufficient reason to ignore his blameworthiness and to permit an agent freely to act whenever such circumstances arise. Moreover the burden of proving his defence was unintended (despite being foreseen) would normally fall upon the prosecution—who may be expected in any case to introduce evidence of intention and motive. The location of the onus ought to forestall concerns about unjust convictions when the defendant does in fact act in order to bring about the justificatory end.

As it happens, the analysis in this essay offers support for an additional feature of Anglo–American law: that recklessness, as much as intention, is characteristically a sufficient *mens rea* element for stigmatized criminal offences. If there is no moral priority of means over side-effects, then in general (subject to a defence of reasonableness) advertence ought, as it currently does, to suffice for criminal culpability. On the other hand, I do not mean by this claim to suggest that the mental element in the definition of murder should be akin to that favoured by certain of the Law Lords in *Hyam*:[97] an intention to bring about, or foresight of the possibility of, death or grievous bodily injury. For terms such as 'murder' are not transparent. When the law states, 'do not murder', people should be entitled to assume that by this it means, do not murder. Ordinary language here respects a distinction unrelated to the one we have considered in this essay. Murder and manslaughter are both actions that are wrong, but they are different actions and different wrongs—and the difference owes itself to the killer's intentions. Murder is a distinctive, and particularly serious, kind of killing, marked by the fact that the killer does so by means of an intentional infliction of serious violence. Hence, for example, the causing of death through deliberately dangerous driving is not regarded as murder. *This* is why reckless killing is not murder; not because recklessness is systematically less culpable than intention.

A similar argument might even exempt advertence as a ground of liability entirely, with respect to some cases where the defendant's intention is constitutive of the criminal wrong. If Lamond is right to argue that 'threats involve the intention to bring about unwelcome consequences *because* they are unwelcome to the recipient; they thus represent an intentional attack upon what the recipient values',[98] then the law would appear to have reason to differentiate blackmail from other cases involving forced choices in part by requiring that the defendant intend that her victim's choice be forced. Blackmail is an instance where the *reus* quality of her *actus* is not independent of the defendant's *mens*.

One last observation. While the moral requirement for a nexus between means and justification forecloses having a general defence of reasonable-

---

[97] [1975] AC 55.
[98] Grant Lamond, 'Coercion, Threats and the Puzzle of Blackmail', this volume, 230 (my emphasis).

ness for intentional doings of an *actus reus*, it does not preclude a general defence of 'good motive'. Why should the law permit only specific defences for intention? The question takes us outside the realm of this essay, but it deserves comment. The most important reason is that not all good ends justify a given bad means. If the sort of limitation proposed by Nagel (and endorsed earlier in this essay) is correct, for instance, then it would not be acceptable for Dudley and Stephens to save themselves and their companion from starvation by killing and eating Parker.[99] Nor, in Nagel's example, to distract and thereby capture an enemy who is casting hand grenades at one by machine-gunning his nearby family.[100] Since there are limitations upon when an end might justify a means, it would seem desirable to specify these limitations in advance, through permitting only specific defences to intentional commissions of *actus rei*. The announcement of such defences provides guidelines by which an individual's choice to commit some *actus reus* is likely to be constrained. Absent such guidelines, there would be a risk of undermining the authority of the law, were its prima facie 'absolute' prohibitions to be defeasible at the individual's own initiative.

This is not to say that the law ought to ignore matters of motive. There are at least three areas where it does and should attend: in the requirement of a nexus, stated here; in the establishing of intention; and in the identification of certain criminal wrongs, for example through the requirement for 'dishonesty' in theft. Perhaps there are others.

---

[99] *Dudley and Stephens* (1884) 14 QBD 273.　　[100] N. 55 above, at 69.

5

Justifications and Reasons

John Gardner*

ISOLATING THE ISSUE

Nobody seriously denies that there is a close relationship between justifications and reasons. To claim that one has justification for doing or believing as one does is to claim, at the very least, that one has reasons for so doing or so believing. The question which arouses disagreement is merely how the reference to 'reasons' here is to be interpreted. For reasons may be either *guiding* or *explanatory*.[1] Guiding reasons are reasons which apply to one. They bear on what one ought to do or believe. One may, however, overlook or ignore these reasons. Then, even though one acts or believes exactly as the guiding reasons would have one act or believe, they are not the reasons *for* which one so acts or believes. They are not, in other words, the explanatory reasons. Explanatory reasons are logically related to guiding reasons, for it is necessarily true of every explanatory reason that the person who acts on it, or holds beliefs on the basis of it, also believes it to be a guiding reason for the action or belief in question.[2] But it may or may not be the guiding reason that she believes it to be. Just as guiding reasons need not be explanatory reasons, in other words, so explanatory reasons need not be guiding reasons. Thus there arises an issue, current in epistemology as well as moral and legal philosophy, about whether justification depends on guiding reasons or on explanatory reasons. Are one's actions and beliefs

* This paper was written during my tenure of a British Academy research leave award, and I am grateful to the Academy for the opportunity to develop this and the larger project of which it forms part. Versions of the paper were presented at seminars in Glasgow, Edinburgh, and Tel Aviv. I benefited greatly from the ensuing discussions, and would like to thank all those who contributed. For incisive written comments, thanks also to Tony Honoré, Stephen Shute, Andrew Simester, and Andrew von Hirsch.

[1] See Joseph Raz, *Practical Reason and Norms* (2nd edn., Princeton, 1990), 16–20.

[2] Some apparent counter-examples to this are mentioned by E. J. Bond in *Reason and Value* (Cambridge, 1983), 29. They cannot be dealt with here. But I should stress that 'believes' here, and throughout this paper, carries its widest connotations. It covers everything from the firmest conviction to the merest inkling, everything from knowing to imagining, and everything from explicit awareness to latent or subconscious recognition. Cf. the remarks on 'vindication' in n. 39 below.

justified by the reasons which actually applied to one, or by the reasons which, perhaps mistakenly, one thought applied to one and accordingly treated, in one's acting or believing, as if they were reasons which actually applied to one? Faced with this question, some have come to the view that there are two different perspectives or points of view from which one's actions or beliefs may be justified. On the one hand there is so-called 'subjective' justification, which depends on explanatory reasons, and hence bows to one's mistakes about the applicable guiding reasons when these mistakes affect what one believes or how one acts. Then there is 'objective' justification, which depends on guiding reasons, and hence extends justification even to some who had no inkling of those reasons, let alone acted or believed anything on the basis of them.[3] In the eyes of some writers, these two modes of justification simply represent irreconcilably different ways of looking at our actions and beliefs. For some purposes or in some contexts we may favour one perspective, while for other purposes and in other contexts we resort to the other.

The terminology of 'subjective' and 'objective' which is used to draw this contrast is notoriously treacherous. It is particularly likely to be misleading for criminal lawyers, who also customarily use these labels to mark a number of quite different distinctions. One of these distinctions needs to be mentioned at this stage in order to move it out of the way. It is a distinction between those who attach justificatory importance to how our actions turn out, and those who decline to do so. In the lingo of some criminal law scholarship and commentary, an 'objectivist' might say that murder is harder to justify than attempted murder, because a death actually comes about; a 'subjectivist' would have to demur.[4] It is a profound and interesting disagreement. But it is not the same as the disagreement about whether justification depends on explanatory reasons or guiding reasons. Rather, it is an internecine dispute, among those who accept that justification turns in part on guiding reasons, about what kinds of guiding reasons there can be. Some hold that (a) there can in principle be no guiding reasons for or against doing what cannot be done (thus the proposition 'ought implies can') and (b) the most we can ever do is try, with no guarantee of success. It means that they insist on regarding all guiding reasons as merely reasons for or against trying, not as reasons for or against succeeding.[5] But in fact there may be rea-

---

[3] See, e.g., Alvin Goldman, *Epistemology and Cognition* (Cambridge, Mass., 1986), 73; Jonathan Kvanig, 'Subjective Justification' (1984) 93 *Mind* 71; William P. Alston, 'Concepts of Epistemic Justification' (1985) 68 *The Monist* 71. This is also, I believe, the distinction with which Paul Robinson is mainly concerned in his 'Competing Theories of Justification: Deeds v. Reasons', this volume.

[4] See, e.g., Andrew Ashworth, 'Taking the Consequences' in Stephen Shute, John Gardner, and Jeremy Horder (eds.), *Action and Value in Criminal Law* (Oxford, 1993), 107 at 109–10, or Antony Duff, 'Subjectivism, Objectivism and Criminal Attempts', this volume.

[5] This appears to be the argument of W. D. Ross in *Foundations of Ethics* (Oxford, 1939), 160, relied upon by Andrew Ashworth in 'Sharpening the Subjective Element in Criminal Liability', Antony Duff and Nigel Simmonds (eds.), *Philosophy and the Criminal Law* (Wiesbaden, 1984), 79.

sons to succeed as well as reasons to try. Moreover the two do not automatically go hand in hand. Sometimes I have reasons to try without having reasons to succeed. Suppose that people will mistakenly take against me if I do not try to help with an unjust war effort. Then I have a perfectly obvious reason to try, but (other things being equal) no reason to succeed. Conversely, I may have reason to succeed but no reason to try. Suppose that, since I cannot swim a stroke, it would be pointless for me to try to rescue someone from a stormy sea. Then (other things being equal) I have no reason to try to rescue them, but it scarcely means that I have no reason to rescue them.[6] If I had no reason to rescue them, after all, I would not be so horrified at the realization that it is pointless for me to try. I could walk past without compunction. That shows why we should give short shrift to 'ought implies can': my horror as I look on helplessly reflects the fact that I ought to save this life even though I cannot. But it also shows why, if the justification of an action depends in part on the guiding reasons for performing that action, the justification of an action may sometimes be partly hostage to the action's results and sometimes not. It simply depends on what particular action the reasons in question are reasons to perform, i.e., whether they are reasons to get or avert certain results or merely reasons to try to get or avert those results. That, however, does not suggest for a moment that sometimes, in relation to some actions, one should look to explanatory reasons rather than guiding reasons to do the justificatory work. On this issue, so far as I can see, the justificatory role of explanatory reasons is neither here nor there.

In what follows, my central concern will not be with the question of what guiding reasons there are in favour of particular actions or particular kinds of actions, but with the more fundamental conceptual question of whether justification depends upon guiding reasons or explanatory reasons. The answer, irritating but unavoidable, is that it depends upon both. No action or belief is justified unless it is true *both* that there was an applicable (guiding) reason for so acting or so believing *and* that this corresponded with the (explanatory) reason why the action was performed or the belief held. It follows that the common view that there are two different perspectives on justification, a 'subjective' (explanatory reason) perspective and an 'objective' (guiding reason) perspective, must be rejected. To cite explanatory reasons

---

[6] Some who accept that I have reason to save in this case may doubt whether I have no reason to try. They picture me momentarily wavering on the cliff's edge, incapacitated by indecision, now leaning forward to jump, now pulling back. Does this not suggest the impetus of a reason to try to save? It may do: it may suggest that I believe myself, contrary to fact, to be capable of effecting a rescue, and so think there is a reason to try, and feel its pull. But my wavering may also be interepreted as the action of a man who is, in momentary defiance of logic, trying to succeed without trying, because he has reason to succeed but no reason to try. This interpretation presupposes that sound practical reasoning follows what Anthony Kenny calls 'the logic of satisfactoriness' (by which one automatically has reason to do whatever is sufficient to achieve what one has reason to achieve) and not 'the logic of satisfaction' (by which one automatically has reason to do whatever is necessary to achieve what one has reason to achieve). For argument, see Kenny 'Practical Inference' (1966) 23 *Analysis* 65.

as well as guiding reasons is not to provide justifications from two different points of view, nor even to provide two partial justifications, but merely to provide the two essential parts of one and the same (partial or complete) justification. Of course this is not to deny that some actions and beliefs may be justified from one point of view and not from another. A certain belief may be justified from my point of view and not from yours, or justified from the Benthamite point of view but not from the Kantian. A certain action may be justified from the point of view of a Christian but not from the point of view of a Muslim, or justified from the point of view of the army's rules of engagement but not from the point of view of the criminal law. My only proviso is that, from whatever point of view one claims justification for one's actions or beliefs, one claims justification only if one claims *both* that there were, from that point of view, reasons for one to act or believe as one did *and* that one's reasons for performing the act or holding the belief were among these reasons. Notice that this is perfectly compatible with a recognition that, within certain systematic points of view or perspectives, the word 'justification' may sometimes be appropriated to do other jobs, e.g. to refer to something falling short of, or going beyond, justification. The legal point of view, in particular, is widely noted for putting its own specialized glosses on everyday words. But English criminal law, at any rate, has not yet paid that particular compliment to the word 'justification'. So far as I can see, our judges persist in using the word 'justification' to refer mainly to legal justifications proper, i.e., to legally recognized reasons for acting which were also the relevant agent's reasons for acting in the case under consideration. This is the essence of the famous *Dadson* doctrine.[7] But even if English criminal law were found to use the word 'justification' in some different, technical sense, that would be a matter of little concern for present purposes. Our interest is not in the legal meaning of the word 'justification'. Our interest is in the ordinary phenomenon, that of justification, which still plays a major role in the thinking of most criminal courts, and indeed in evaluative thinking at large, whatever the local lawyers and legal commentators may choose to call it.

---

[7] *Dadson* (1850) 4 Cox CC 358. *Per* Erle J: 'The prosecutor not having committed a felony known to the prisoner at the time when he fired, the latter was not justified in firing at the prosecutor.' There are two conditions of justification implicit in this: (1) that the prosecutor must have been a felon and (2) that the prisoner firing upon him must have known (or, more broadly, believed) this at the time when he fired. Condition (1) specifies the necessary guiding reason, while (2) is needed to ensure that it is also the explanatory reason. It is true that believing that the prosecutor is a felon is not the same as acting because he is a felon. But the former is a necessary condition of the latter, and since the court in *Dadson* expresses the doctrine negatively, the absence of this necessary condition is all that is needed to dispose of the case. It does not mean that the knowledge condition is being elevated to the status of a sufficient condition—*pace* Paul Robinson, 'Competing Theories of Justification: Deeds v. Reasons', this volume. See further *Thain* [1985] NI 457, in which the distinction between beliefs and explanatory reasons becomes pivotal.

Pros and Cons: the Basic Asymmetry

What calls for justification? I already mentioned actions and beliefs, and we may add to the list a wide range of phenomena which are logically related to actions and beliefs, such as emotions, attitudes, desires, decisions, practices, and rules. But in a way, that is not an answer to the question. We still need to know whether such things always call for justification, or only *sometimes* do. The answer has to be an equivocation. In a loose sense, justification is always called for. That is just to say that actions, beliefs, etc. are always answerable to reason. One may always ask 'why?' But in the stricter and more important sense which concerns us here, justification is called for only when one also has some reason *not* to act, believe, etc. as one does. The unobjectionable, in other words, is in no need of justification. In this stricter sense, justification may be either partial or complete. What one claims if one claims *partial* justification is that the prima facie reasons against one's action or belief are countered by some reasons in favour. What one claims if one claims *complete* justification is that the reasons in favour are, moreover, strong enough to prevail over the reasons against. Thus by claiming full justification one denies that the prima facie judgment against performing the action or accepting the belief should be elevated to the status of an 'all-things-considered' judgment against its performance or acceptance. All things considered, the action or belief was alright in spite of the prima facie objections to it.

Criminal lawyers should already be at ease with this distinction between prima facie and all-things-considered judgments, and should quickly be able to see its relevance to the idea of a justification. For this distinction is highly visible, as Kenneth Campbell has observed, in the familiar demarcation between criminal offences and (justificatory) criminal defences.[8] In classifying some action as criminal, the law asserts that there are prima facie reasons against its performance—indeed reasons sufficient to make its performance prima facie wrongful. In providing a justificatory defence the law nevertheless concedes that one may sometimes have sufficient reason to perform the wrongful act, all things considered. Yet the very familiarity of this point has led many criminal lawyers to underestimate its significance. They have looked upon it rather shamefaced as a kind of artificial legalistic divide. Some have thought that it can only be a matter of expository convenience whether one treats a certain issue as going to the presence of an offence or the absence of a defence.[9] Others have conceded at most an evidential significance to the demarcation, relating it only to the question of

---

[8] See K. Campbell, 'Offences and Defences' in Ian Dennis (ed.), *Criminal Law and Justice* (London, 1987), 73. Campbell does not seem to limit the point, as I do, to *justificatory* defences.
[9] Glanville Williams, 'Offences and Defences' (1982) 2 *Legal Studies* 233 at 233–4.

who should normally bear the burden of adducing initial evidence.[10] Things are not helped here by the fact that criminal lawyers are also accustomed to use the label 'prima facie' itself to mark an evidential classification. To say that an action was prima facie wrongful normally signals, to the legal mind, that there is some reason to believe that a wrong was committed, but that it may yet, once more evidence is presented, turn out not to be so. But in the sense which matters for an understanding of the demarcation between offences and justificatory defences, to identify a prima facie wrong is to identify an *actual* wrong, not just an apparent or putative wrong.[11] It is to claim that there were indeed legally recognized reasons against an action, not merely that there are now legally admissible reasons to believe that there were such reasons. To be sure, the reasons against the action, which are also the reasons for its criminalization, may all have been defeated in the final analysis. It may have been alright for the defendant to act against them, all things considered. But it does not mean that they dropped out of the picture. That a reason is defeated does not mean that it is undermined or cancelled. It still continues to exert its rational appeal. It may indeed be a matter of bitter regret or disappointment that, thanks to the reasons which justified one's action, one nevertheless acted against the prima facie reasons for avoiding that action. It may even be a matter of regret or disappointment to the criminal law. The law certainly need not welcome it. But by granting a defence the law concedes that any regret or disappointment must be tolerated, and that no liability can attach to the person who by her prima facie wrongful actions occasioned it. By granting a *justificatory* defence the law concedes that this is true by virtue of the fact that the defendant had, at the time of her prima facie wrongful action, sufficient reason to perform it.[12]

Whether one accepts this account of the role of justification in the law and beyond is not a matter of merely academic importance. It has far-reaching practical implications. One implication is of immediate significance to us. It stems from the fact that, as I have explained them, claims of justification cannot but exhibit one of the most striking asymmetries in all human thought and experience. This is the asymmetry between the pursuit of positive value and the avoidance of negative value, between reasons in favour

[10] See Michael S. Moore, *Act and Crime: The Philosophy of Action and its Implications for Criminal Law* (Oxford, 1993), 179

[11] For further discussion of this point, see John Searle, 'Prima Facie Obligations' in Joseph Raz (ed.), *Practical Reasoning* (Oxford, 1978), 81.

[12] Compare Paul Robinson, 'A Theory of Justification: Societal Harm as a Prerequisite for Criminal Liability' (1975) 23 *UCLA LR* 266 at 274: 'Justified behaviour is correct behaviour and therefore is not only tolerated but encouraged.' Robinson assumes that a justification operates to cancel or undermine the countervailing considerations rather than to defeat them. So the law has nothing to regret. It is surprising that Robinson apparently remains attached to this position to this day in spite of his own highly effective attack on it in 'Criminal Law Defences: A Systematic Analysis' (1982) 82 *Columbia LR* 199 at 220: 'Where conduct is covered by an offence modification, it is not in fact a legally recognised harm. . . . Justified conduct, on the other hand, causes a legally recognized harm or evil. . . . It is tolerated only when, by the infliction of the intermediate harm or evil, a greater societal harm is avoided or benefit gained.'

and reasons against, or, as we might say in ordinary conversation, between *pros* and *cons*. The asymmetry is brought to the surface by claims of justification only because such claims implicate both reasons in favour of and reasons against the justified action or belief. If the role of justification were that of cancelling or undermining the reasons against an action or belief—if it were, in lawyers terms, a matter of 'negating an element of the offence'— then no question of the relationship between reasons for and reasons against would arise in cases of justification, since in such cases all reasons against would be 'negated', i.e., cancelled or undermined, and would not exert any countervailing force. But since a justification merely defeats the reasons against an action or belief without cancelling or undermining them, the conflict between pros and cons, and hence its asymmetrical structure, is very much at the centre of attention when claims of justification are made.

To understand the asymmetry of rational conflict properly one must begin by thinking a little about the logic of guiding reasons. The first question is: what are guiding reasons there to guide? It may seem like a silly question. Surely it goes without saying that guiding reasons for and against action are there to guide action, guiding reasons for and against belief are there to guide belief, guiding reasons for and against emotion are there to guide emotion, and so on. But there is an alternative view. Perhaps guiding reasons of all kinds are merely there to guide reasons. Thus reasons for or against action are there to guide the reasons for which we act, reasons for or against belief are there to guide the reasons for which we believe, etc. It is not a circular or regressive proposal so long as one remembers the distinction between guiding reasons and explanatory reasons. The suggestion that guiding reasons guide reasons is the suggestion that the real point of there being a guiding reason is that one should act, believe etc. *on the basis of that reason*, i.e., that it should also be the explanatory reason for one's so acting or believing. Thus if one merely acts or believes as the guiding reason would have one act or believe, but one's explanatory reasons are quite different, then strictly speaking one did not follow the guidance. Some have thought that guiding reasons do indeed work in this way by default, or at least that they work in this way by default if they belong to certain families, e.g., moral reasons, reasons of duty, altruistic reasons, etc.[13] If this were true then it would immediately introduce a very radical asymmetry between reasons for and reasons against action and belief. That is because, as I have pointed out elsewhere, explanatory reasons are necessarily reasons *for* action or belief rather than reasons *against*.[14] Explanatory reasons explain. They are the

---

[13] See, famously and starkly, Kant's *Groundwork of the Metaphysic of Morals* (ed. H. J. Paton, New York, 1964), 65–8. For interpretation and discussion of Kant's point, see e.g., Bernard Williams, 'Persons, Character and Morality' in his *Moral Luck: Philosophical Papers 1973–1980* (Cambridge, 1981), 1 at 16–19; Barbara Herman, 'Integrity and Impartiality' (1983) 66 *The Monist* 233; Samuel Scheffler, *Human Morality* (Oxford, 1992), 19 ff.

[14] 'Action' and 'belief', at this point and throughout this paper, must be interpreted widely enough to include inaction and disbelief.

reasons that the agent or believer had for acting or believing as she did. To say that she also acted or believed *in spite of* certain countervailing reasons is necessarily to return to the discourse of guiding reasons, and to leave the discourse of explanatory reasons behind. For the whole point of what one says is that these reasons, since the agent or believer did not act or believe on the basis of them, do not explain her action or belief.[15] The effect of this, if we share the view that guiding reasons exist to guide explanatory reasons, is that guiding reasons against action and belief are to a large extent a debased currency. They can only exert their purchase in a derivative way. After all, to the question 'for what reason should I act?', the answer 'here's a reason not to' is, to say the least, evasive. One cannot, as a matter of logic, act for reasons against so acting (unless, of course, one mistakes them for reasons in favour). The most one can do is modify one's reasons for so acting in the light of reasons against. This endows reasons against with at most an indirect motivational role, subsidiary to that of reasons in favour. The claim is not, I should stress, that reasons against an action cannot be appreciated, considered, taken into account, given their due weight, etc. alongside reasons in favour. The point is only that they cannot, qua reasons against one's action, be the reasons for which one acted. It means that, on any view according to which the point of guiding reasons is to guide explanatory reasons, reasons against action and belief are bound to be poor relations which lack the independent rational force of their positive cousins.

If it were accurate, this broadly Kantian account would make it easy to explain how justifications come to take the form I claimed for them. Since on this account one follows reasons in favour of an action only if one actually acts for those reasons, there is no justificatory ground to be gained by citing a guiding reason in favour of what one did if one did not act for that reason. On the other hand, one can readily lose justificatory ground by citing a guiding reason against one's action without claiming to have acted on it, since reasons against action are merely reasons to modify the reasons for which one acted, and cannot themselves be acted on.[16] Unfortunately, however, the Kantian account quickly descends into confusion. It is not surprising that those who have espoused it, including Kant himself, have had great difficulty understanding the nature of moral, legal, and other rational conflict. For this view of theirs, by debasing the independent rational force of negative guiding reasons, ultimately forces them to reinterpret such reasons as mere cancelling conditions on positive guiding reasons.[17] Thus it turns

---

[15] See John Gardner and Heike Jung, 'Making Sense of Mens Rea: Antony Duff's Account' (1991) 11 *Oxford Journal of Legal Studies* 589 at 569–73.

[16] Qua reasons against. They may of course be reasons for some other action as well as reasons against this one.

[17] Needless to say, some regard this as a positive merit of the Kantian line of thought: see Barbara Herman, 'Obligation and Performance: A Kantian Account of Moral Conflict', in Owen Flanagan and Amélie Rorty (eds.), *Identity, Character, and Morality* (Cambridge, Mass., 1990), 311.

out that the correct view, for once, is the obvious one. Fundamentally, guiding reasons for and against action are there to guide *actions*, not to guide explanatory reasons for actions. This is the grain of truth in Paul Robinson's view that a 'deeds' account of justification should be preferred to a 'reasons' account.[18] It means that negative guiding reasons retain in full their independent rational force. Although one cannot in principle act for these reasons, one can act as they would have one act, and, other things being equal, that is all that guiding reasons, be they positive or negative, envisage that one should do. But does it follow that explanatory reasons do not matter at all so far as guiding reasons are concerned? Do guiding reasons wash their hands of the quality of our reasoning, so long as we do the right thing in the end? Not a bit of it. In a moment we will come to the special 'second-order' cases of reasons to act for reasons, and reasons not to do so. But even before we come to these, there are two ways in which ordinary guiding reasons for action and belief necessarily have something to say on the subject of explanatory reasons. The first point is permissive. Other things being equal, the fact that such-and-such is a reason for a given action or belief makes it *alright* for this to be the reason why one performs the action or holds the belief. The second point of contact is rather more prescriptive. For it is a basic principle of practical rationality, which is at the root of the whole pros/cons asymmetry, that one should always act for *some* undefeated reason, i.e., that at least one of the (guiding) reasons in favour of doing as one did should have been one's (explanatory) reason for doing it.

You may well be suspicious of any appeal to the 'basic principles of practical rationality'. Is this not just a device to win an argument by fiat, to make its conclusion sound incontrovertible when in fact it should be vigorously interrogated? I sincerely hope not. In one way, it is true, principles of practical rationality are more fundamental than other practical principles. For they apply across the boundaries between different fields of practical reasoning. They apply equally in legal reasoning, moral reasoning, strategic reasoning, etc., and do so just by virtue of the fact that these are fields of practical reasoning. This may mean that they have a slight air of the *a priori* about them. But in fact this air is deceptive. Principles of rationality have a rather more mundane, *a posteriori* basis than many ordinary moral and legal principles. For principles of rationality exist purely to guide us towards conformity with moral reasons, legal reasons, and so on, whatever those reasons may happen to be. They are sound or valid principles of rationality if it is true that, when we conform our reasoning to them, we also better conform our actions and beliefs to whatever reasons for action and belief apply to us. Thus principles of rationality stand or fall, in large measure, on their straightforwardly instrumental merits.[19] The basic principle of practical

---

[18] See his 'Competing Theories of Justification: Deeds v. Reasons', this volume.

[19] That explains why, in the work of some philosophers, the label 'principles of rationality' has been appropriated to designate the principles we should adopt if we are better to secure

rationality that tells us always to act for some undefeated reason is no exception. For while it is true that, by default, guiding reasons are there to guide actions and beliefs rather than to guide explanatory reasons for actions and beliefs, it is also important to remember that the only way in which actions and beliefs can be guided is through the guidance of explanatory reasons. Reasons can only move us, if you like, by motivating us. And the principle that we should always act for some undefeated reason is a principle which identifies what we should be looking for, in the way of motivation, if we are to maximize our prospects of acting as reason demands. We should look for an undefeated reason to act as we do. There is no point in going further and looking for *all* the undefeated reasons to act in that way.[20] That would be ridiculous overkill. The very fact that the reason for which one acts is undefeated is enough by itself to guarantee that, all things considered, it is on the winning side in the whole overarching conflict of reasons.[21] Thus the basic principle of rationality which I cited, although modest, is as strong a principle as we need to ensure that our explanatory reasons for action reliably push us towards an action that ought, all things considered, to be performed.

These claims cut against a familiar model of rational conflict. On this model, the reasons for and the reasons against some action or belief are always up to a point mutually defeating. Some of the reasons in favour of an action or belief devote their entire motivating energy to defeating the reasons against that action or belief, and in the process become spent forces, so that the only undefeated reasons in the end are those which were not needed for the battle, the reasons which make up, so to speak, the *net advantage* which the pros had over the cons in terms of their rational force. These are therefore the only reasons left for us to act upon, if it is true that one should always act for an undefeated reason. But my claims in defence of the principle that one should always act for some undefeated reason suggest an alter-

---

whatever ends we each happen to have, without touching on the intrinsic merit of those ends. See, e.g., Derek Parfit, *Reasons and Persons* (Oxford, 1984), 4. This also underlies the popular use of 'rational' when associated with the calculating pursuit of personal advancement.

[20] But is it not necessary to survey all the reasons, if only in order to *work out* that the reason for which one acts is indeed undefeated? Not necessarily. On the view defended here, the fact that one acted for an undefeated reason by instinct or habit need not in any way detract from one's justification. Sometimes we identify undefeated reasons better without stopping to think. There is no basis for the view that fully deliberated action is more reliably sound than spontaneous action: often, the more we think about it the worse our predicament gets. That is one reason (among many) why such things as emotions, passions, and raw desires are so crucial to any well-rounded life. It incidentally helps to dispel another criminal lawyer's myth: that justifications are more at home in situations where there is proper scope for clear thinking, while in situations of emergency, calling for immediate reactions, we must make do with excuses.

[21] Or perhaps we should say, to accommodate cases of incomparability, 'not on the losing side'. In some cases one acts on undefeated reasons whichever way one acts, and one is justified either way, since incomparability prevents the reasons in favour from defeating the reasons against or vice versa. Where the undefeated reasons on both sides are *protected* reasons (on which see below) these are normally known as 'dilemma' cases. For a good account of these, see Ruth Marcus, 'Moral Dilemmas and Consistency' (1980) 77 *Journal of Philosophy* 121.

native picture, according to which, if the reasons in favour of some action defeat the reasons against, then in the ordinary case it is only the reasons against which end up defeated. The reasons in favour are *all of them* undefeated, i.e., they are undefeated *in gross*. The principle of rationality which demands that one always acts for some undefeated reason is therefore compatible, in the ordinary situation of an action with more pros than cons, with our acting on any one of the various reasons in favour of the action. This makes it a much more modest principle than at first sight seems to be needed to defend my promised strong conclusion that reasons in favour of an action are only justificatory if they are also the reasons for which one performed that action. And yet the modesty of this principle of rationality is also, in another way, its strength. For what this principle means is that it is quite pointless to cite, by way of justification, an undefeated reason for which one did not act, even though it would have been alright for one to act upon it if one had been minded to do so. Once one has attempted to make justificatory capital out of such a guiding but non-explanatory reason, one must still go on to identify some *other* undefeated reason which one *did* act upon in order to clinch the justification. For one must always act for some undefeated reason. But once one achieves this, the original non-explanatory reason one cited simply drops out of the picture. It adds nothing to one's case. The citation of the second reason was both necessary (it was acted upon) and sufficient (it was undefeated) to identify one's action as justified. Essentially, that is why justifications must have two matching parts: in the first place, an undefeated guiding reason, which is also, secondly, the explanatory reason for the justified action.

Notice that the reasons against one's action, which a full justification is needed to defeat, are not similarly two-pronged. It is enough that they were guiding reasons against one's action. For as I already said, there is no such thing as an explanatory reason against an action, so there can be no demand, concerning the reasons against an action, that in order to be counted against that action's performance, they must also play some explanatory role in that performance. What this means, in the everyday terms most familiar to lawyers, is that undesirable side-effects as well as undesirable intended results can count against an action, while only desirable intended results can ever count in its favour.[22] This is the basic all-pervading asymmetry between

---

[22] Compare Andrew Simester, 'Intention, Recklessness, and Morality', this volume. My position in this essay directly confronts Simester's view that there are two alternative bases of blame, one connected with 'motive' and the other with 'reasonableness'. Reasonableness in action depends straightforwardly on the reasons for which one acts. Simester's examples do not contra-indicate. In what he calls the 'Experiment Case', a great deal turns on the fact that (as Simester confesses in his n. 67) the 'neutral end' is not in fact neutral, but is a reason in favour of administering the drug. On my account, *if* this reason in favour is undefeated, which on the information given by Simester it might indeed be, *then* the administration of the drug can indeed be justified. It matters not that the motive is not good, so that the action is not creditable. As I explain in the next section, the question whether a reason for acting is good, worthy, etc. is not the same as the question whether it is undefeated.

pros and cons, between reasons in favour and reasons against, between the pursuit of positive value and the avoidance of negative, that comprehensively carves up our lives as rational beings.

FORTIFYING THE ASYMMETRY

This basic asymmetry makes its presence felt in many ways. Most obviously and famously, it structures the distinction between people's virtues and their failings, and the related distinction between credit and blame. Ironically, this may be one of the factors which leads some to suppose that the asymmetry can have no impact on the logic of justification.[23] Their thinking goes something like this. It is one thing to say that an action is fully justified, so that blame can be eliminated. But it is a long way from there to the conclusion that the action is positively creditable. It is only when we take this further evaluative step that the claimed asymmetry between pros and cons can have a real impact. For there can be little doubt that whether an action is creditable turns primarily on the reasons for which it is performed. By making these very same explanatory reasons the key to justification, one wrongly eliminates the logical gap between justified and creditable action. One makes the earning of credit an automatic corollary of the mere elimination of blame.

The mistake here lies in the failure to bear in mind that reasons for action may vary in quality as well as strength. As I have already explained, other things being equal it is alright to act for any undefeated reason in favour of one's action. But sometimes it is *more* than alright to act for a particular undefeated reason. Sometimes there is also an undefeated second-order reason to act for that particular reason, e.g., a reason to support one's friends out of affection for them, to refuse conscription out of a sense of humanitarian duty, to tell the truth because it is the truth, etc. It does not mean that the other reasons for doing what one does automatically become unacceptable, so that acting on them can provide no justification. It means only that a particular reason is privileged, so that acting for that reason lends special value to one's action, value going beyond what is needed for mere justification. Often, indeed, there are several privileged reasons, and there arises a question which of these one should act for. At this level incomparability of value often precludes a straight answer. By acting in the same way for different privileged reasons people normally exhibit their incomparably different virtues. But whether or not one actually exhibits a virtue in the process, it is creditable to act for such privileged reasons in any case in which both they and the second-order reasons to act for them remain undefeated. This

---

[23] Thus Glanville Williams, *Criminal Law: The General Part* (2nd edn., London, 1961), 26, criticizing the decision in *Dadson*, n. 7 above, complains that 'the law of consummated crimes . . . governs conduct, not purity of intention'.

is not, I hasten to add, the only way in which one may earn credit. One's actions may be creditable because of *how* they are performed rather than why, in which case one should look to the value of skill rather than the value of virtue to supply the explanation. But either way more is required for credit than is required for mere justification. An action may still be justified even though performed without any technical proficiency and for a most banal, trivial, and unimpressive reason. But the key point still stands that, to be justified, it must nevertheless have been performed for an *undefeated* reason.[24]

Does it follow that second-order reasons are irrelevant to justification? If only things were that simple. In many contexts, and notably in the law, the scope of justification is pervasively determined by the operation of second-order reasons. But these are not reasons to act for reasons, of the kind which allow for creditable action. These are reasons *not* to act for reasons. Such negative second-order reasons are in operation whenever an action is required or forbidden. They are therefore the reasons at the heart of *wrong-doing*. This claim should be interpreted with care. We describe actions as 'wrong' in several senses. I already distinguished prima facie wrongness from the all-things-considered wrongness. At the same time one should be aware of a cross-cutting distinction between *advisory* wrongness and *mandatory* wrongness. Actions which are all-things-considered wrong in either the mandatory or the advisory sense can, in appropriate cases, be equally a source of blame. But the distinction between mandatory and advisory wrongness is nevertheless one of great importance. One does the wrong thing in the advisory sense if one does not do what one has reason to do. One does the wrong thing in the mandatory sense—for which we normally reserve more emphatic terms like 'wrongdoing', 'wrongdoer', and 'wrongful'—if one does not do what one has, in Joseph Raz's terms, a *protected* reason to do.[25] A protected reason differs from what I earlier labelled a 'privileged' reason. A privileged reason is a reason which one has reason to act for. A protected reason, on the other hand, is a reason for an action combined with a reason not to act for some or all of the reasons against that action. What happens when a reason is protected is that certain counter-vailing considerations are defeated in advance of any practical conflict. Because these reasons are pre-emptively defeated, action for these reasons does not meet the demands of the basic principle of rationality that one should always act for some undefeated reason. It may be asked how a reason can be defeated in advance of a conflict. Surely whether it is defeated depends on its relative strength when pitted against another reason, and

---

[24] In some extreme cases, if one cannot act for particular reasons, or at a certain level of technical proficiency, then that strips out so much value from one's act that it would be better not to perform it at all. In such cases, the gap narrows between the point at which blame ends and the point at which credit begins.

[25] J. Raz, *The Authority of Law* (Oxford, 1979), 17–19.

therefore must await the conflict? This ignores the role of *rules* in practical reasoning. Rules are devices which improve our prospects of doing what reason demands by settling certain conflicts of reasons before they arise. They obviate the need for reliance on some of the raw pros and cons. It does not mean, as some have thought, that all rules are merely 'rules of thumb', or 'indicator rules', which provide a prima facie reason to believe that the action ought to be performed, without affecting whether the action ought to be performed.[26] On the contrary, real rules are capable of affecting what really ought to be done. In rough outline, they do so because some guiding reasons in favour of certain actions are less likely to be properly followed, or more likely to corrupt the following of other reasons, if one tries to follow them. They are guiding reasons which had better not become explanatory reasons. Since, by the time they are explanatory reasons, it is too late to avoid their distorting effect, they are ruled out of being explanatory in advance by the operation of the rule. Consequently, of course, the price of following the rule is sometimes that one does not act as the underlying reasons apart from the rule would have one act. That in such cases one should nevertheless follow the rule is the small price that rationality pays for avoiding the risk that, by trying to act for some of the raw underlying reasons, one will otherwise very often act against reason. That explains why there are reasons not to act for certain reasons, and why some actions are as a result not merely advisable or inadvisable, but are actually required or prohibited.

In fulfilling its primary functions, the law rarely classifies actions as merely advisable or inadvisable.[27] But it often classifies them as required or prohibited. That is particularly apparent in the criminal law. The very idea of a 'criminal offence' is the idea of an action which is in the eyes of the law not merely wrong but wrongful, i.e., which there is, in the eyes of the law, not merely a reason but a protected reason not to perform. In fact the protected reason which the law creates is, by default, *absolutely* protected. So far as the criminal law is concerned *all* reasons in favour of performing the criminalized action are defeated by virtue of the law's unquestionable and all-embracing authority. It means that one is left with no automatic access to any justificatory considerations, however powerful they might be apart from

---

[26] i.e., that they are prima facie in the lawyer's evidential sense. Some of W. D. Ross's remarks in *The Right and the Good* (Oxford, 1930) may lead one to think that all sound mandatory rules are prima facie in this sense. See also J. J. C. Smart, 'An Outline of a System of Utilitarian Ethics' in J. J. C. Smart and Bernard Williams, *Utilitarianism: For and Against* (Cambridge, 1973), 3 at 42 ff. On rules of thumb and indicator rules see Frederick Schauer, *Playing by the Rules* (Oxford, 1991), 104 ff. (and especially the note at 105).

[27] By 'primary functions' I mean non-self-regulatory functions.. Among the law's functions are the governance of legislation and adjudication. In the fulfilment of these functions the law often avails itself of principles and values which provide merely advisory legal guidance to officials. But of course these functions are parasitic on others. The primary functions of law are its functions in affecting people's actions other than legislative and adjudicatory actions—if you like, outward-looking rather than inward-looking functions. Here the law rarely makes do with mere advice, since it cannot normally count on automatic co-operation. On primary and secondary functions, see Raz, *The Authority of Law*, n. 25 above, at 163 ff.

the law. What the law does, which nevertheless creates a role for some justificatory defences, is to provide us with *cancelling permissions* to perform, under certain specified conditions, the actions which it criminalizes. This may seem like a rather surprising proposition. After all, it was argued above that justificatory reasons do not *cancel* but rather *defeat* the reasons against an action or belief. Now, by contrast, the claim appears to be that justifications arise in the criminal law precisely when reasons are cancelled by permissions. But the air of paradox is dispelled as soon as one realizes that the law's cancelling permissions do not cancel the reasons not to perform the criminalized action, but merely cancel the second-order protective reasons not to act for certain countervailing reasons. Thus justificatory arguments which the law would otherwise disallow are specifically allowed. This means that the law not only regulates the actions which one may perform, but also regulates the reasons for which one may perform those actions. It regulates the actions which one may perform by making some of them into criminal offences, which are prima facie wrongs. It regulates the reasons for which one may perform those actions by picking out certain reasons in favour of their performance as legally acceptable reasons. But, as ever, one benefits from the acceptable reasons in favour of one's action only if one actually acts for these reasons. For even legal rationality, with all of its second-order protection, is governed by the basic principle of practical rationality that one should always act for some undefeated reason. In the case of a criminal act, all reasons are defeated apart from those permitted by law. Thus to claim a justificatory defence, one must not only have, but act for, one of those permitted reasons.

The same is not true in a case to which the definition of the crime does not extend, i.e., in which 'an element of the offence is negated'. In such a case one need rely on no permission to act for specified reasons since the protected reason, which gives rise to the need for such permission, does not apply in the first place. So it does not matter why the defendant acted as he did, so long as that is how he acted. Here we see exactly what the English law student learns by reading *Deller* alongside *Dadson*: in some cases the defendant's motivation is beside the point, whereas in others it is decisive.[28] The real difficulty arises, however, when we try to draw the line in practice between the two types of case, between *Dadson* cases and *Deller* cases. Where we are dealing with raw pros and cons, it is easy to distinguish a justificatory argument from an argument to effect that there is nothing to justify. A justificatory argument is an argument which points to reasons in favour of the action performed rather than to the absence of reasons against it. But when protected reasons enter the equation, this test is no longer adequate to draw the distinction. That is because some of the reasons in favour of an action are already taken into account in the structure of the protected

---

[28] *Deller* (1952) 36 Cr. App. R 184; *Dadson*, n. 7 above. See the excellent discussion in J. C. Smith and Brian Hogan, *Criminal Law* (7th edn., London, 1992), 33–5.

reason. The rule has been shaped with an eye to many of the pros and cons of action in accordance with it. It means that sometimes, when one cites a reason in favour of one's action, one cites a consideration which should bear on the interpretation of the rule one is accused of violating rather than a consideration which bears on whether one is justified in violating it. Accordingly, the mere fact that one points to a reason in favour of one's action does not mean, in this context, that one asserts a justification as opposed to denying the application of the law to the case. Only if one asserts a justification, however, does it matter whether one actually acted for the reason in favour that one cites. It follows that in law one may sometimes benefit from a reason in favour of one's action which was not a reason for which one acted, even though in other cases one must have acted for the reason before one may benefit in law from its application. Unfortunately, there is no general test for telling the two kinds of case apart. It is a question of law, on which different legal systems may of course arrive at different answers, whether a given argument is to be regarded as justificatory rather than as bearing on the scope of the offence. In fact, for all I know, some legal systems may not bother to recognize justifications at all, so confident are they of the moral finesse of their offence definitions. This would tend to lumber them with a regrettable inflexibility, or force them to undesirable vagueness, or both. I will return to these possible moral objections below. But logically it is a perfectly possible solution. It has the pay-off that the legal system in question may take an interest in the reasons in favour of the action which the defendant performed without caring whether the defendant acted for those reasons. All I wish to stress is that this does not turn it into a legal system which endorses an 'objective' rather than a 'subjective' theory of justification, or into a legal system which allows justification to depend upon guiding reasons irrespective of explanatory reasons. It makes it into a legal system which, strictly speaking, does not care about justification at all.

The Priority of Justification Over Excuse

It is widely thought that excuses are more 'subjective' than justifications.[29] In one sense of 'subjective', as we will see, this is perfectly true. But it is not true if we are using the labels 'subjective' and 'objective' to mark the contrast between explanatory and guiding reasons. Over a wide range of cases, excuses, just like justifications, depend on the union of explanatory and guiding reasons. Whenever excuses depend on the union of explanatory and guiding reasons, moreover, they do so precisely because justifications depend on the union of explanatory and guiding reasons. The structure of excuse derives, in other words, from the structure of justification, and thus

[29] Kent Greenawalt, 'The Perplexing Borders of Justification and Excuse' (1984) 84 *Columbia LR* 1897 at 1915–18.

shares in its combination of subjective (explanatory) and objective (guiding) rationality.

Some theorists have associated excuses with character traits.[30] They are mistaken if they think that every excuse is concerned with character. Many excuses are of a technical nature. They relate to levels of skill rather than degrees of virtue. Their gist is that the person claiming them does not possess the skills needed to do better, and should not be expected to possess those skills. Whether one should be expected to possess certain skills, or skills to a certain degree, depends, to some extent, on one's form of life. A doctor who tries to excuse her blundering treatment by claiming lack of diagnostic skill should not get far, whereas an amateur first-aider may be able to extinguish her blame, under similar conditions, by making exactly the same argument. But such excuses, even though they are of great legal importance, will not concern us here. Our concern will be with that major group of excuses which do indeed relate to character evaluation. These include excuses very familiar to criminal lawyers, such as excuses based on provocation and duress. Their gist is similar to that of technical excuses. It is that the person claiming them does not possess the virtues needed to do better, and should not be expected to possess those virtues. Again, which virtues one should be expected to possess, and to what extent, depends largely on one's form of life. A police officer is expected to exhibit more fortitude and courage than an ordinary member of the public, a friend is expected to be more considerate and attentive than a stranger, etc. What exactly does this mean? Essentially, it means that where there is a conflict of reasons, some people are expected to act for some reasons, whereas others are expected to act for other, often incompatible and incomparable, reasons. But obviously the need to claim an excuse from one's action arises only if one fails to establish a full justification. A fully justified action needs no excuse. So the point cannot be that those who act with excuse act for undefeated reasons, i.e., that it is alright for them to act for those reasons. That would yield a full justification for their actions. The point must be that there is something suspect about the reasons for which they act. And indeed there is. They are not valid reasons. They are what the person acting upon them takes to be valid reasons, *and justifiably so*. Thus the structure of excuse derives from the structure of justification. To excuse an action is not, of course, to justify that action. Rather, one justifies one's belief that the action is justified.[31]

This explanation of non-technical excuses has to be modified and extended somewhat to accommodate unjustified actions upon justified

---

[30] See the useful bibliographical note in Michael Moore, 'Choice Character, and Excuse' (1990) 7 *Social Philosophy and Policy* 29 at 40–1. A subtle and sympathetic reconstruction of this approach to excuses is offered by Bob Sullivan in 'Making Excuses', this volume.

[31] Cf. Suzanne Uniake, *Permissible Killing: The Self-Defence Justification of Homicide* (Cambridge, 1994), 15–25.

emotions, attitudes, passions, desires, decisions, etc., as well as unjustified actions upon justified beliefs. Provocation, as Jeremy Horder has explained, involves unjustified action out of justified anger.[32] Duress, or a certain central kind of duress, can be similarly analysed as involving unjustified action out of justified fear. But these are, in a sense, derivative cases. Emotions like anger and fear are mediating forces between beliefs and actions. They enhance or constrain the motivating force of certain motivating beliefs. Their justification therefore turns in part on the justification of the beliefs which partly constitute them. Of course, there is still a justificatory gap: an emotion is not fully justified merely by the justification of its cognitive component. But justified emotion (and in similar vein justified attitude or desire or decision) nevertheless entails justified belief. Thus the most basic or rudimentary case of non-technical excuse remains that of unjustified action upon justified belief. One must therefore consider what is needed to make a belief justified. It is of course one of the great problems of epistemology, and we cannot do justice to it here. Suffice it to say that the general account of justification applicable to action is also broadly applicable to belief. One must have an undefeated reason for one's belief, and that must moreover be the reason why one holds the belief. This explains the nature of epistemic faults, such as prejudice, gullibility, and superstition. One cannot understand these faults unless one appreciates that a belief is justified, not only by the reasons there are for holding it, but also by the process of reasoning by which it came to be held, i.e., not only by guiding reasons but also by explanatory reasons. The same facts also explain why a requirement of *reasonableness* has traditionally been imposed upon excuses in the criminal law. It is not enough that one made a mistake as to justification, if it was not a reasonable mistake, it is not enough that one was angry to the point of losing self-control, if one's anger was not reasonable, etc.[33] By 'reasonable' here is meant, in my view, much the same as 'justified'. There must have been an undefeated reason for one's belief, emotion, etc., which also explains why one held the belief or experienced the emotion, etc. The fact that sometimes this element of reasonableness is dispensed with in the law does not show a drift towards a more purely 'subjective' account of excuses, i.e., one depending on explanatory reasons without regard for guiding reasons. It shows, rather, that some

[32] *Provocation and Responsibility* (Oxford, 1992), 158 ff. This explains why women who have killed after prolonged domestic violence and are denied provocation defences on the ground that their reaction was not immediate do not much like the response that they should instead claim 'diminished responsibility'. They want it to be acknowledged that their anger was (at least partly) justified, and that *this* is why their admittedly unjustified action is (at least partly) excused. 'Diminished responsibility' is a claim which suggests irrationality all the way down (meaning that it is not strictly an excuse: see n. 35 below). It thus reduces the moral status of those who claim it.

[33] See, among many examples, *Albert* v. *Lavin* [1981] 1 All ER 628 (reasonable belief required for mistaken self-defence), *Graham* [1982] 1 All ER 801 ('fear for good cause' required for duress), *Phillips* v. *R.* [1969] 2 AC 130 (loss of self-control must be reasonable for provocation).

excuse-like arguments, in common with some justification-like arguments, may actually serve to negate an element of the offence rather than to excuse or justify its commission. Some mistakes, as the courts put it, may simply serve to negate the mens rea for the particular crime; and if, as may be, the mens rea required is, e.g., knowledge, then of course the reasonableness of one's mistake is neither here nor there.[34] The extent to which legal systems will tolerate such arguments depends on many contingencies about them, including the extent to which and way in which they implement the demand for mens rea. But this has nothing to do with excuses, in which an element of reasonableness, at some level, is conceptually necessitated whether the crime is one of full subjective mens rea or one of no mens rea at all.

Requirements of 'reasonableness' in criminal excuses also sometimes go beyond what the logic of excuses requires, and in that case they normally serve another role. They serve to orientate the law towards general application to people living many different forms of life, rather than tailoring it to suit the expected virtues of a certain kind of person leading a certain kind of life. The debate about the extent to which the reasonable person should be 'individualized' to the characteristics of the defendant in the definition of criminal excuses is partly a debate about the extent to which the criminal law should aspire to this kind of generality. Should the 'reasonable person' in provocation become the 'reasonable police officer' when the defendant is a police officer? Should the 'reasonable person' in cases of drunken mistake become the 'reasonable drunkard'? Once again there is no universal theoretical solution to this problem. Within broad limits, legal systems may quite properly vary in their willingness to individualize excuses and the general principles, if any, upon which they do so. But legal systems cannot, consistent with the logic of (non-technical) excuses, vary in the importance they attach to the combination of guiding and explanatory reasons in the excusatory scheme of things. Thus they cannot altogether eliminate the essential 'objective' dimension of excusatory claims. They cannot ignore the important point that excuses rely on reason, not on the absence of it. That is, they rely on the ability of the person who claims to be excused to believe and feel as reason demands, and because reason demands it. Those people who cannot meet this condition do not need to bother making excuses. Such people are not responsible for their actions, and are free from blame as well as being improper targets for criminal liability, irrespective of

---

[34] That is the logic of the decisions in *Williams* [1987] 3 All ER 411 and *Beckford* v. *R.* [1987] 3 All ER 425, which should therefore not be understood as authorities on the mental element in excuses, let alone as authorities on the mental element in defences in general. At most they show that self-defence is no longer regarded as a genuine defence in English criminal law. Instead, absence of self-defence is regarded as an implied element of every offence, and one to which an implied element of mens rea is automatically attached. It is an absurd rule, and one which should be overturned, but the reliance on *DPP* v. *Morgan* [1975] 2 All ER 347 in both of the cases makes it the only viable interpretation of what they stand for. For excellent discussion, see Andrew Simester, 'Mistakes in Defence', (1992) 12 *Oxford Journal of Legal Studies* 295.

both justification and excuse.[35] Justification and excuse both belong to the
realm of responsible agency, and that is precisely because both depend, to
put it crudely, on the ability to live within reason.

The logical relationship between justification and (non-technical) excuse
helps to explain the so-called 'quasi-justificatory drift' of many familiar
excuses.[36] In English law this is compounded by the law's cautious insistence on having a belt as well as braces: in general no excuse is accepted into
the criminal law which is not also a partial justification, and no justification
is accepted which is not also a partial excuse.[37] The drift of the excuse is not
so much quasi-justificatory as truly justificatory. But neither of these facts
should obscure the crucial conceptual distinction between justification and
excuse. Nor should one be distracted by the paradoxical sound of the claim
that an action which is justifiably believed to be justified is excused rather
than justified. It only goes to show that, as between the concepts of justification and excuse, justification is the more fundamental. The same proposition also brings out the true sense in which excuses may be regarded as more
'subjective' than justifications. For by their nature excuses take the world as
the defendant justifiably sees it rather than as it is. They look to what the
defendant believes to be applicable reasons for action, so long as she does so
on the basis of genuinely applicable reasons for belief. Justifications, meanwhile, look directly to the genuinely applicable reasons for action, without
stopping to look for applicable reasons for belief. But in this whole contrast
the talk of 'reasons' is talk of guiding reasons. It leaves on one side the fact
that, in both justification and excuse, explanatory reasons also play a key
role, and that, in this sense and to this extent, each is just as subjective as the
other.

---

[35] Notice that the effect of this claim is to deny the status of excuses to, e.g., insanity,
infancy, and 'diminished responsibility'. I do not shrink from this pay-off. Excuses have a built-
in precariousness. 'Don't make excuses' is sometimes a legitimate stricture. For many actions
are inexcusable in some situations thanks to the fact that everyone is expected to have the
virtues and skills necessary to perform them in those situations. But even in connection with
these actions in these situations we should not blame the very young or (often enough) those
suffering from serious mental illness. Notice that this does not commit me to the view that very
seriously mentally ill people should get away with everything they do. I share Anthony Kenny's
view that most mental illness is selective in its impairment of rationality, and should only preclude blame by extinguishing responsibility where relevantly operative. See Kenny, *Freewill and
Responsibility* (London, 1978), 80–4. Even so, that is not enough to make an argument based
on mental illness into an excusatory argument, since whether mental illness affects blame
depends not on the nature of the action but on the relevance of the illness to its performance.
Illustrated crudely: even if cannibalism were inexcusable, some mad cannibals would not be to
blame for eating people. The blameless mad cannibals would be those mad cannibals, roughly
speaking, who were cannibals because mad.
[36] I borrow the label from Simon Gardner, 'Instrumentalism and Necessity', (1986) 6
Oxford Journal of Legal Studies 431 at 433.
[37] Hence the Law Commission's difficulties in *Legislating the Criminal Code: Offences
Against the Person and General Principles* (London, 1993), 63–4. The Commission finds
excusatory as well as justificatory strands in the cases on 'necessity' and jumps to the conclusion that there must be two defences rather than one. Not so: one defence, compound rationale.

INSTITUTIONAL OBJECTIONS

Many of the arguments which lawyers give for dividing up justification and excuse along different lines from these are of a broadly institutional character. They are based, not on general considerations of rationality and value, but on views about the limitations which are imposed upon the logic of the criminal law by its legitimate social functions and roles. Such arguments often lead to the conclusion that, while the general spirit of justification and excuse as I have explained them may remain broadly visible and important in the law, the distinction is not one to which the law can or should give exact doctrinal expression. Translation into the legal context means dispensing with some of the finer points. I will briefly mention two arguments which may be thought to point in this direction.

THE RULE OF LAW

One alluring line of argument goes something like this. The question whether an action is justified is, on any view, a question whether it ought, all things considered, to be performed. If they are to have a role in the criminal law, justifications must therefore serve as guidance to potential offenders as to what, in law, they ought to be doing. Justification doctrines must belong to the law's 'conduct rules'.[38] But if it is to be possible to rely upon the law's justificatory doctrines in one's reasoning about what to do, it must be permissible in law to do as the justificatory doctrines require *for the very reason that they are part of the law*. Accordingly, the law cannot consistently demand, in the guidance it gives to potential offenders, that the action be performed instead for some *other* reason. It means that the law must introduce a schism between guiding and explanatory reasons in its institutional adaptation of the justificatory framework. The relevant guiding reasons are, of course, those which the law mentions as justificatory: the fact that one is under attack and self-defence is called for, the fact that crimes are being committed and need to be prevented, and so forth. But the law cannot demand that these also be the explanatory reasons for one's act of self-defence or crime-prevention. The best it can demand by way of explanatory

---

[38] The contrast between 'conduct rules' and 'adjudication rules' which I introduce here is drawn from Paul Robinson, 'Rules of Conduct and Principles of Adjudication' (1990) 57 *University of Chicago LR* 729. Similar contrasts have been drawn by Peter Alldridge in 'Rules for Courts and Rules for Citizens' (1990) 10 *Oxford Journal of Legal Studies* 487 and by Meir Dan-Cohen, 'Decision Rules and Conduct Rules: On Acoustic Separation in Criminal Law' (1984) 97 *Harvard LR* 625. All three authors make interesting remarks on where justificatory defences might fit into such a scheme, and how rule-of-law requirements might apply to them. I should stress that none of the three is seduced by the argument being outlined here, although none of them is entirely immune to its charms either. Dan-Cohen makes the best job of resisting it.

reason is that one acted thus because that is how the law would have one act. Thus even if there is a pros/cons asymmetry which lies at the heart of rationality, it cannot in principle be directly replicated in the institutional context of the criminal law. When justifications are being framed, the law can only state the guiding reasons, and leave the explanatory reasons to look after themselves. Explanatory reasons, however, can readily be counted on the excusatory axis instead. For excuses do not, on any view, bear on what, all things considered, one ought to be doing. Legal excuses therefore do not belong to the law's 'conduct rules' which are there to guide potential offenders, but rather to the 'adjudication rules' which are there to guide judges in dealing with potential offenders. They can thus remain sensitive to considerations which cannot in principle be the subject of guidance directed to potential offenders. It means that, while justifications become more 'objective' in their adaptation to the law's demands, excuses end up taking all the more 'subjective' elements under their wing.

This argument, which I have made as good as I can make it, nevertheless harbours many errors. At its heart lies the idea that justifications, as I analyse them, cannot play a role in the criminal law without violating the rule of law, which requires that the law's conduct rules should be capable of guiding those who are subject to them. But this complaint betrays a false assumption about the sense in which legal justifications are there to provide guidance to potential offenders in the first place. When the law grants a justification, as I explained above, it provides a *cancelling permission* to act for certain reasons which would otherwise be automatically defeated by the prohibition. But a permission to do something is, by itself, no reason to do it. Thus the law does not provide any reasons for one to do what the law holds to be justified. It simply allows that one may have such reasons and act on them. To say that justificatory rules belong to the 'conduct rules' of the law, and must serve to 'guide' potential offenders, is to give the impression that the law gives people positive reasons to do what the justificatory rules allow. But the law does no such thing. Thus the idea of someone who tries to follow a justificatory rule of criminal law, in the sense of acting because of the rule, is the idea of someone who mistakes it for something quite different from what it is. Anyone who sees a justificatory legal rule for what it really is will know that it cannot in itself motivate action in accordance with it since it gives no reasons for action but only cancels the law's otherwise pre-emptive reasons for not acting on certain independent reasons for the justified action, the latter being the reasons which account for its being justified. So there is no point in a law which attempts to turn its justificatory rules into rules which can be followed directly by potential offenders. In the process all that the law does is to defeat its own object, which is that people should act for the reasons which the law permits them to act for, and not for other reasons which the legal prohibition pre-empts. That being so, perhaps justificatory rules of law are not best labelled as 'conduct rules' at all. Of course it is true that sometimes the law *combines* them with what are more perspicuously thought of as 'conduct rules'. Sometimes a police officer may be required by law to arrest using reasonable force, as well as being justified in using such force, which would otherwise be criminal, in effecting a legally required arrest. Such cases may be thought of as self-referential, since they look within the law rather than beyond it for the justifying reasons. But again they create no schism between explanatory and guiding reasons which could conceivably affect the conditions of legal justification. For the legally recognized and protected guiding reason for the arrest must also be, in such cases, among the reasons why the arrest was made if it is to count as fully justified in law. In other words, a police officer who does not act upon the legal rule requiring arrest in such a situation also does not benefit from it.[39]

These remarks show that a stark distinction between 'conduct rules' and 'adjudication rules' is inadequate to capture the complex inner logic of the criminal law. But they also show, for our purposes more importantly, that the rule of law does not militate against a role in the criminal law for justifications as I analyse them. On the contrary, it tends to count in favour of allowing them a significant role. I said earlier that legal systems may differ in the way in which they deal with particular rational conflicts in the structure of criminal liability. Some may incorporate into the very definition of the offence the same considerations which others treat as going purely to justification. But I also added that legal systems which try to follow the former route exclusively are apt to suffer from moral shortcomings, either being excessively rigid or excessively vague. Why do these dangers come of failure to recognize justificatory defences? The answer relates, predictably, to the demands of the rule of law.[40] In a legal system which adheres conscientiously

[39] Opponents will no doubt respond by pointing out that, in English law at least, arrests may be made lawful *either* by the fact that they were made on reasonable suspicion of the commission of an offence *or* by the fact that, although the arrest was not made on reasonable suspicion, it turned out that a real offence was committed: Police and Criminal Evidence Act 1984, s. 24. The second option is a special case of justification, normally known as *vindication*. It is the case in which one is justified in taking a chance that one will turn out to be right. It is not a counterexample to my account of justification nor to my remarks on arrest, since the law still requires, in the vindication cases in s. 24, that the action be an *arrest*, which is *by its nature* an action performed for certain legal reasons. See J. C. Smith, *Justification and Excuse in the Criminal Law* (London, 1989), 33–4. Tony Honoré has suggested to me, however, that there is a more general issue here. Cases of vindication, he believes, point to the need for me to make certain modifications to my analysis of justification. In these cases, one only has a hunch that undefeated guiding reasons exist, and one acts on this hunch. This, in Honoré's words, represents 'a tertium quid between acting for the guiding reason and acting as the guiding reason requires but not for it'. I am not convinced. In vindication cases one does not act because of one's hunch, but because, if I may put it this way, of what it is one hunches. What one hunches is the guiding reason. It is the fact that one acts for this reason, always assuming it is undefeated, that justifies one's taking the chance that one's hunch is right. That one hunches the reason rather than, e.g., knowing of it, does not diminish its explanatory role.

[40] The answer is suggested in George Fletcher, 'The Nature of Justification' in Stephen Shute, John Gardner, and Jeremy Horder (eds.), *Action and Value in Criminal Law*, n. 4 above, at 175.

to the rule of law, offence definitions will be so far as possible clear, accessible, and certain in their application, so that they can be used for guidance by potential offenders as well as by courts and officials.[41] This means that actions which will fall outside the law must be largely decided upon in advance, and closure rules provided for any unexpected cases. But defences in general, and justifications in particular, are largely exempt from these tough demands which the rule of law places upon the definition and drafting of offences. I have just explained why. Legal justifications are not there to be directly followed by potential offenders. They merely permit one to follow reasons which would otherwise have been pre-emptively defeated. So there is no need for them to aspire to standards which apply to legal rules when they *are* there to be directly followed. It means that justifications can introduce an element of flexibility into the law which often cannot be accommodated, compatibly with the exacting demands of the rule of law, in the very definition of the offence. A legal system which tries to do without justifications in its criminal law is thus likely either to violate the rule of law by allowing its offence definitions to remain vague enough to accommodate judicial deliberations in novel and difficult cases, or else it is likely to conform to the rule of law in its offence definitions but at the high price that the novel and difficult cases will be decided without adequate scope for judicial deliberation. Justificatory defences provide a way out of the dilemma. It is not true that the same can be achieved by granting purely excusatory defences. For, as defenders of the 'conduct rules'/'adjudication rules' view of the justification/excuse distinction will be the first to point out, only actions which are all-things-considered wrong need to be excused. What a sophisticated system of criminal law has to have space to do is to grant that some actions covered by a legal prohibition but not properly taken into account or accommodated by the formulators of that prohibition are not all-things-considered wrong in the eyes of the law. By and large that can only be achieved, in conformity with the rule of law, by the continuing judicial development of genuinely justificatory defences.[42]

THE HARM PRINCIPLE

A related but distinct objection to the full legal implementation of the justification/excuse contrast as I have explained it points to the limited moral resources of the criminal law. My analysis depended at more than one point on the invocation of what may be called 'perfectionist' categories, such as those of virtue and skill. I also relied upon the importance of basic principles of rationality. But it may be objected that it is not a proper function of the criminal law in a modern society to reflect judgments of virtue and skill, nor

---

[41] I have explored some aspects of these demands, and in particular the 'so far as possible' proviso, in 'Rationality and the Rule of Law in Offences Against the Person' (1994) 53 *Cambridge LJ* 502.

[42] Contrast Simon Gardner, 'Instrumentalism and Necessity', n. 36 above, at 436–7.

even to enforce norms of rationality. The criminal law in a well-ordered modern society is restricted to the task of harm-prevention. The famous 'harm principle', first defended by J. S. Mill, sets the law's legitimate agenda, and constrains the law's perfectionist ambitions. Some have thought that this prevents legal defences, and in particular legal justifications, from carrying all the baggage of their moral counterparts. Notably, the demand that one acted for the justificatory reason to which the law gave recognition strikes some people as being quite out of place in a legal régime directed exclusively towards harm-prevention. In such a legal régime, acceptable action is action which prevents, or on some versions is expected to prevent, more harm than it brings about. So long as this condition is met there is no further harm-prevention advantage to be gained out of legal inquiry into whether the defendant did or did not have the prevention or avoidance of harm close to her heart at the time when she acted. That did not in any way affect the amount of harm she did or was expected to do. Nor will it affect the amount of harm done by others who, for whatever reason, follow her lead in performing analogous actions in similar situations. Thus her reasons for doing as she does are not the law's proper concern.[43]

Again, errors abound in this argument. The most striking is a far-fetched misinterpretation of the harm principle. The harm principle is a principle which exists to protect people from having to surrender their worthwhile pursuits and ways of life merely because those pursuits and ways of life are morally imperfect. Now, owing to the diversity of ultimate moral values, every valuable pursuit and way of life is morally imperfect. To possess the virtues and skills needed for one way of life one must forego the virtues and skills needed for another. One effect, particularly in a complex and highly mobile modern society in which people are widely exposed to strangers, is that intolerance is widespread. We all find it hard to appreciate and respect fully the different virtues and skills exhibited by those many people that we encounter daily whose ways of life and pursuits are so markedly different from our own. We correspondingly inflate the importance of their limitations, and are continually tempted by the path of suppression. The harm principle, when conscientiously followed, provides some protection against the institutionalization of such temptations in cases in which certain ways of life and pursuits are unpopular with those who hold, whether through democratic or undemocratic channels, the power of suppression. The harm principle, thus defended, is the principle that harmless immoralities should not be officially prohibited or punished, and that harmful immoralities should not be officially prohibited or punished disproportionately to the harm they do.[44] But it is a long way from this to the proposition that

---

[43] This seems to be the key to understanding Robinson's position in 'A Theory of Justification', n. 12 above, at 273 and 292.

[44] I have based my remarks on Joseph Raz, 'Autonomy, Toleration and the Harm Principle' in Ruth Gavison (ed.), *Issues in Contemporary Legal Philosophy* (Oxford, 1987).

official prohibitions and punishments should be tailored solely to the single overarching aim of harm prevention. What is lost in the transition to this proposition is the important point that, within the boundaries set by the harm principle, the law may be tailored to reflect countless considerations which have nothing much to do with harm. Compatibly with the harm principle a legal system may limit its prohibition and punishment of harmful activities to those which are also, e.g., dishonest or malicious or inconsiderate. To put it another way, it does not follow from the premiss that the law should not institutionalize intolerance of any harmless immoralities that the law should not institutionalize the tolerance of some harmful ones. On the contrary, there are many harmful immoralities which should arguably be tolerated by law for the sake of other values, including perfectionist values. This is a matter of particular salience where the scope of criminal law defences is concerned. For, as I explained earlier, when the law grants a defence it tolerates, perhaps regretfully, a prima facie wrong. Assuming that the law is otherwise in conformity with the harm principle, this makes the granting of defences into an act of tolerance rather than an act of intolerance. Thus the harm principle has nothing significant to add beyond what it already contributed to the construction of the offence. Of course that is not to say that the law should ignore considerations of harmfulness in constructing defences. On the contrary, other things being equal, it should always give such considerations whatever rational weight they have, be it great or small. Nor is it to say that there cannot sometimes be positive moral principles requiring that particular harms no longer be officially tolerated. There is certainly no general principle of toleration which would allow the authorities to wash their hands of every problem and dispense with legal regulation altogether. The point is only that intolerance, not tolerance, is the problem which the harm principle, in particular, exists to counter. It is therefore not a general constraint on the legal perfectionism, but a constraint on perfectionist considerations invoked by themselves as if they provided a sufficient ground for official prohibition and punishment.

So, even if it is true that my analysis of justifications and excuses makes them necessarily sensitive to perfectionist considerations, that presents no automatic obstacle to their legal implementation. But, so far as justifications are concerned, I am not even sure that the sensitivity to perfectionist considerations is inevitable. My main argument for the combined subjective/objective (or explanatory/guiding) account of justifications was based on the fundamental principle of rationality that one should always act for some undefeated reason. That principle, I explained, has a broadly instrumental grounding: by acting for an undefeated reason one is more likely to do what one ought, all things considered, to do. That claim, it seems to me, is no less applicable where (let us suppose) what one ought to do, all things considered, is minimize the harm one does. And the claim is therefore no less applicable in some strange legal context to which a reductive harm-prevention objective has (myopically) been applied. Assuming that, e.g., actions in self-defensive situations are generally harm-preventing, one will prevent harm more reliably by acting out of self-defence than by acting in such situations out of, e.g., spite or fear of the legal consequences. One should thus look for and react to the self-defensive aspects of one's situation, not to some other aspects. That is no less true in subsequent cases in which others follow one's example than it is in one's own case. Thus the fictitious, narrow-minded legal system we are considering does well, even by its own excessively parsimonious harm-prevention standards, to reflect the importance of explanatory reasons as well as guiding reasons in the law relating to self-defence. Justificatory defences as I analyse them are accordingly no less at home in a legal system intent on harm prevention and nothing else than they are in a legal system, like our own, with a less monomaniacal outlook.

6

Making Excuses

G. R. Sullivan*

A man has been invited to a flat to discuss some business matters, so he has been led to believe. Once there he is given coffee laced, though he does not know it, with soporific drugs. He is invited to a bedroom where a 15-year-old boy, also drugged, lies unconscious on a bed. The man, a homosexual with pædophiliac predilections, performs non-penetrative sexual acts on the boy. Subsequently, he is charged with indecent assault—*Kingston*.[1]

The drugs at most produced a state of disinhibition.[2] It was not claimed on behalf of the defendant that he was unaware of what he was doing or that he was compelled to do it. The most he could claim by way of excuse was that, had he not been slipped the drugs, he would not have acted as he did.[3] For the trial judge[4] this was not enough—'a drugged intent is still an intent'. The Court of Appeal saw it differently. An intent formed in such circumstances was not to be regarded as a 'criminal' intent and accordingly the conviction was quashed.

The House of Lords regarded this division between the two courts as raising 'a general issue of fundamental importance as well as a more technical question on the law of intoxication'.[5] That issue was whether the absence of blame entailed the absence of *mens rea*. Lord Mustill, giving the judgment of the House, asserted that *mens rea* was a non-evaluative term. If the mental element specified in the definition of the crime was present then *mens rea* was present, the term meaning nothing more than the mental element for the

---

* I am much indebted to Andrew Simester for many valuable suggestions. Thanks are due, too, to Carl Emery, Jeremy Horder, Harvey Teff, Colin Warbrick, and William Wilson. The views expressed are the author's.

[1] [1994] 3 All ER 353 (HL); [1993] 4 All ER 373 (CA).

[2] The actual effects which the drugs produced were not determined at trial. The matter was not pursued consequent upon a ruling by the trial judge that involuntary intoxication did not give rise to a discrete defence.

[3] There was evidence that the defendant had been slipped three kinds of soporific drug with properties which would affect judgment, consciousness, and memory. None of the medical witnesses testified that any of these drugs would give rise to compelled behaviour.

[4] Potts J.

[5] [1994] 3 All ER 353 at 372.

offence. Given that the respondent had *mens rea*, the circumstances of the offence warranted mitigation but did not excuse.[6]

The position to be taken and defended in this paper is that, as far as is practicable, the absence of blame should entail non-conviction for stigmatic offences. It is conceded at the outset that even for stigmatic offences it is not possible to exempt all blameless persons while remaining within the doctrinal parameters of the criminal law. Nonetheless, the impossibility of doing justice to all members of a class is not a reason for failing to do what can be done for some members of it, provided that the grounds of discrimination are not arbitrary or in any other sense unprincipled. Indeed, the House of Lords was not averse to exemptions for the involuntarily intoxicated but took the crafting of any exemption to fall beyond the judicial role. It hoped that the Law Commission might consider whether there was 'a merciful, realistic and intellectually sustainable statutory solution'[7] for such cases. If a solution meeting those criteria can be contrived for cases of involuntary intoxication, why cannot the ideas informing it be more widely deployed?

THE POSSIBILITY OF EXCUSE

How can it be said that a state of involuntary intoxication may give rise to a finding of blamelessness if it does not negate the mental element for the offence nor cause conduct to be compelled? If we take Hart's classic epitome of excusing conditions and ask whether Kingston lacked fair opportunity and capacity to conform his conduct to law,[8] we arguably affirm, not refute, the decision of the House of Lords. The fact that his intoxication was involuntary presumptively engages the issue of fair opportunity. Yet a claim of lack of fair opportunity may be said to founder on the fact that D's conduct was at most merely disinhibited and in no sense compelled. Although self-restraint was made more difficult for D, he seemingly remained in possession of sufficient volitional and cognitive resources with which to conform his conduct to law.

The Court of Appeal's decision to excuse D in such circumstances has been plausibly castigated as unprincipled indulgence.[9] Under that court's

---

[6] A position taken in response to the Court of Appeal's decision by J. C. Smith in [1993] *Criminal LR* 794 and J. R. Spencer in [1994] *Cambridge LJ* 6.

[7] [1994] 3 All ER 353 at 380. The Law Commission declined Lord Mustill's invitation principally because there would have been no time for consultation before including any statutory proposal in its final report: *Legislating the Criminal Code: Intoxication and Criminal Liability*, Law Commission No. 229, paras. 1.5–1.9 (1995).

[8] H. L. A. Hart, *Punishment and Responsibility* (Oxford, 1968), 181–3, 214, 227–30. For an illuminating reworking of Hart's notion of excuse to English case law see K. J. M Smith and W. Wilson, 'Impaired Voluntariness and Criminal Responsibility: Reworking of Hart's Theory of Excuses—the English Judicial Response' (1993) 13 *Oxford Journal of Legal Studies* 69.

[9] See references above at n. 6.

reasoning, D merely has to adduce evidence that his state of intoxication was involuntary. Unless that evidence is refuted, the prosecution is faced with the onerous task of proving the hypothesis that D, had he been sober, would have committed the offence with which he is charged. A claim that one would not have indulged in some reprehensible conduct but for a state of disinhibition induced by drink or drugs is inherently plausible. Moreover, Lord Taylor, in giving judgment for the Court of Appeal, remarked that involuntary intoxication should be a defence for *all* crimes of specific or basic intent.[10] In coming to this conclusion, he invoked an analogy with the defence of duress.[11] There is, however, little point of contact between the respective defences apart from the fact that the involuntary intoxication in *Kingston* arose from the machinations of a third party. Duress, of course, arises only for cases of awful dilemma—offend or be killed or seriously hurt—states of psychic compulsion. By contrast, a condition of intoxication falling short of automatism does not make for involuntary conduct, however loosely the term 'involuntary' is employed. Furthermore, duress is not available if the charge be murder.[12] Although that limitation can be cogently criticized for confusing excuse with justification, granted its existence, to allow non-automatous involuntary intoxication as an excuse for all crimes would further undermine what coherence there is in the current provision of defences.

Lord Mustill was, with respect, correct in ruling that, taken by itself, a state of involuntary intoxication cannot excuse. In *Kingston, mens rea* was present and the conduct uncompelled. There was a powerful case to answer and, *pace* Lord Taylor, it was an insufficient response for D to maintain that he would not have so acted had he not been surreptitiously drugged. Many states of being—anger, apprehension, fatigue, etc.—may arise quite involuntarily and provide a necessary condition for conduct that otherwise would not have occurred. Ordinarily, such destabilization affords no more than mitigation.

Under the Model Penal Code, involuntary intoxication will found a defence to any crime if it deprived the defendant of 'substantial capacity to conform his conduct to law'.[13] Arguably, a significant diminution in the capacity for self-control should excuse completely if the defendant's condition had more affinity with automatism than with a state of mere disinhibition. Absent a clear-cut state of automatism, however, the line is difficult to draw. Many jurisdictions in the United States which formerly used 'substantial capacity to conform conduct to law' as a limb of a Model Penal Code-inspired insanity test have abandoned it because of the impalpable

---

[10] [1993] 4 All ER 353 at 380.   [11] *Ibid.*   [12] *Howe* [1987] AC 417.
[13] Model Penal Code, § 2.08(4). The provision also excuses if his condition precluded him from appreciating the 'criminality [wrongfulness] of his conduct'. This would appear to be confined to situations where the defendant has been rendered insensible or delusional, states more radical than Kingston's.

questions to which it gave rise.[14] The House of Lords was well advised to reject this test as a standard for an involuntary intoxication defence.[15]

Nonetheless, there may have been principled reasons sufficient for the House of Lords to have upheld, rather than reversed, the Court of Appeal. An opportunity may have been missed for creative yet appropriate judicial law-making. Whether a defence should have been provided in *Kingston* depends, it will be argued, on conditions which may, or may not, have been present on the facts of that case. As stated already, disinhibition falling short of automatism cannot *of itself* excuse. But if such a condition arose blamelessly and induced conduct which would not otherwise have occurred, this will attenuate to some extent the culpability of the agent. That culpability would be further attenuated, it will be claimed, if, until the incident in question, the defendant had abstained from practising his pædophilia.

All we know of the defendant in *Kingston* is that he was a homosexual with pædophiliac predilections. The formative influences of sexual preference are obscure. In terms of orientation, our sexuality is something that we have rather than something we have made. If we are dealt a card marked for pædophilia, the most that can be asked of us is that we do not put it into play. The card cannot be surrendered and it would be a barbarity to punish for mere possession. Requiring forbearance in a matter so pervasive and unpredictable as sexual expression is to require a great deal, notwithstanding that the protection of a vulnerable class must always be the overriding concern. If a person of pædophiliac inclinations does not practise his pædophilia, he is entitled to that full dignity and respect which is due to all law-abiding citizens. Indeed, he may claim particular credit for sustaining a non-criminal status. If on a particular occasion he becomes blamelessly disinhibited by drugs and loses self-control when confronted with that temptation he otherwise avoids and resists, it is not obvious that the public interest requires him to suffer the total forfeit of credit which a conviction for a stigmatic offence entails.

The particularity of facts such as those related above renders the consequentialist claims of individual and general deterrence uncompelling. Retributivist claims are less clearly settled. It has already been suggested that his blameless state of disequilibrium must count in his favour, even if only as mitigation. It will be argued more fully below that mitigation may be upgraded to excuse if, until this particular occasion, the defendant had refrained from pædophiliac practices. However, were he a practising pædophile his conduct would not constitute an arguably condonable lapse from a standard he was able otherwise to sustain. Then, at most, he would be a candidate for mitigation. If he is, on the basis outlined above, a candidate for an acquittal, he may yet deservedly be convicted if the conduct for

---

[14] A matter given great impetus by the trial of John Hinckley: see P. W. Low, J. C. Jeffries, and R. J. Bonnie, *Criminal Law: Cases and Materials* (2nd edn., New York, 1986), 663.

[15] [1994] 3 All ER 353 at 369.

which he claims excuse was very grave, for example a killing. We are dealing with uncompelled conduct perpetrated with *mens rea*. In such cases previous good conduct and a blameless state of disequilibrium may be
insufficient to outweigh the culpability evinced by a heinous wrong. We are
not dealing with excusatory claims which, if made out, invariably sustain a
plea for acquittal. It may depend on what it is the defendant has done.

In essence, this paper attempts to found the claim, adumbrated above,
that involuntarily intoxicated persons of previous good character and others in similar case can, if particular conditions be met, be excused for certain
crimes. First, however, we should note the view taken by the House of Lords
in *Kingston* that such cases are adequately treated by way of mitigation. This
standpoint coheres with the unequivocal opinion of Lord Mustill that a conviction for a serious offence need not entail descriptively or prescriptively
that the defendant was in any sense at fault. He endorsed a decision of the
Privy Council[16] to the effect that an undercover policeman acting with the
knowledge and consent of his superiors and without recourse to entrapment
or conduct to the prejudice of third parties would be guilty of trafficking in
drugs notwithstanding that the 'trafficking' (carrying drugs out of the jurisdiction) was done solely in the interests of law enforcement. It follows that
an involuntarily intoxicated person could at most hope for some degree of
mitigation—the policeman's conduct seemed justified whereas the cases we
are concerned with fall, at most, to be excused.

By contrast with the House of Lords, the view taken here is that a conviction for a stigmatic offence is a sanction in its own right and that sanctions should be confined to the blameworthy. The non-conviction of the
blameless should be a pervasive principle of substantive criminal law limited
only by the need to theorize and practise criminal law as a system of rules
and by the exigencies of forensic practicability. Those limitations entail that
many 'normal' life narratives cannot afford grounds of excuse, however
exculpatory the force of the narrative may be. But other accounts, not currently represented in standard defences, can be brought within the framework of substantive criminal law. If it can be done it should be done in order
to diminish the incidence of unnecessary criminal convictions.

DISUNITY OF SELF

Any argument for exculpation in cases such as *Kingston* must demonstrate
that culpability sufficient for a conviction for a stigmatic offence may yet be
lacking notwithstanding the presence of *mens rea* and the absence of any
currently recognized justification or excuse. To clarify the ambit of our discussion, it should be said that we are not concerned with cases where a claim

[16] *Yip Chiu-Cheung* [1994] 2 All ER 924.

of lack of culpability is founded on a judgment of substantive value—for example a claim that to practise euthanasia was right in the particular circumstances. Our concern is with conduct which violates a protected interest, where the grounds of inculpation are met, where no claim of justification legally recognized or otherwise can be maintained and where no standard excuse applies. We have to establish that particular conduct within that class may be excused on grounds that allow, with a sufficient measure of predictability and forensic manageability, similar findings in cognate cases. As alluded to earlier (and to be taken up more fully below) these requirements will exclude many 'normal' life narratives, however compelling the exculpatory story may be. There has to be something exceptional, curtailable about the circumstances that are allowed to excuse.

One exceptional feature in *Kingston* was, in the words of Lord Mustill, 'the temporary change in the mentality or personality of the respondent.'[17] The change in Kingston was at most a change from a state of restraint to a state of disinhibition. More radical are those changes which bring about a completely alien persona. If a case can be made that such profound destabilization should excuse, some purchase will have been gained for an excuse not afforded under current doctrine. It must then be seen whether the grounds of that excuse carry over to less radical destabilizations.

It is sometimes argued that a fundamental change in character brought about by extraneous forces beyond the control of the agent should of itself afford an excuse.[18] The claim must rest on some form of 'character' explanation of criminal liability. Character accounts of criminal liability build on the truism that while liability may be for the deed, it is the perpetrator who is punished. Thus we may only legitimately punish if an inference of bad character may be drawn from the episode of conduct for which the agent is to be sanctioned. Now for certain theorists 'character' is no more than a reference to a notional person of good character. From that perspective, punishment is unwarranted if in the circumstances relating to the offence obedience to law could not fairly have been demanded from any person of good character. This reading of a character conception of liability has no necessary implication for the range and kind of excuses allowed. Typically, it is put forward as the best account of why we provide the excuses that we have.[19]

But there are other versions which focus on the formation and state of the agent's own character.[20] Adherents of these agent-focused versions argue,

---

[17] [1994] 3 All ER 353 at 359.

[18] P. Arenella, 'Character, Choice and Moral Agency' in E. F. Paul, F. A. Miller, and J. Paul (eds.), *Crime, Culpability and Remedy* (Oxford, 1990), 59; P. Alldridge, 'Brainwashing as a Criminal Law Defence' [1984] *Criminal LR* 726.

[19] Accounts of this sort explain defences like self-defence and duress on the basis that otherwise criminal conduct will not manifest bad character when performed in such circumstances: e.g., M. D. Bayles, 'Character, Purpose and Criminal Responsibility' (1982) 1 *Law and Philosophy* 1.

[20] Arenella, n. 18 above.

for instance, with regard to the Patty Hearst saga, that it would have been unjust to punish Ms Hearst for those choices and acts which her alien character inclined her towards. It will be recalled that Ms Hearst was abducted from her wealthy environment and subjected, it was claimed, to effective brainwashing. So it seemed that, through no process of reflection and deliberation of her own, her existing values were erased and a world view imposed on her which conceived of violent bank robberies as legitimate political action against 'capitalist oppression'. It has been argued that if in cases like Ms Hearst's we were to punish on the basis that, notwithstanding her new character, she retained the capacity for practical reasoning and that her conduct was not physically or psychologically compelled, we would, unfairly, be dissociating her punishment from any responsibility she might reasonably be said to have for the state of her character at the time of her offending.[21] A similar but weaker claim has been made that in such cases we should allow the agent a state of temporary immunity in which to adjust to the changed situation and come to terms with the as yet unfamiliar dispositions associated with her 'new' character.[22]

Arguably then, there are occasions when criminal liability should be precluded by invoking some version of 'unity of self' doctrine informed by criteria going beyond mere bodily continuity.[23] Such a doctrine must hold that certain core values subscribed to by a particular agent are constituents of selfhood and that any sudden and fundamental change in those values for which the agent is not responsible make for a discontinuity of the self. A theory of excuse which would exonerate a person such as Ms Hearst while she remains rooted to her alien character (as opposed to the granting of mere temporary immunity) must maintain that she was morally responsible for the state of her earlier (true) character, that her earlier character remains the touchstone of her moral accountability and that she is in a condition of moral irresponsibility in relation to conduct induced by the dispositions emanating from her alien character.

A difficulty in affording an excuse on these grounds lies in demonstrating how any agent, not merely an agent in a predicament such as Ms Hearst's, can be held responsible for the state of her character at any point in her mature life. Ms Hearst's case was, of course, unusual, but unusual in a manner hard to make count within standard criminal law discourse. To be sure, Ms Hearst was not responsible for her alien character in any way which can be linked to a moral theory which explains responsibility for character (as opposed to conduct) in terms of voluntarism. Yet the same holds true for

[21] *Ibid.* The unfairness involved may be underscored by positing, as does Alldridge (n. 18 above), a defendant who had been brainwashed but who was restored to her former character at the time of her trial.

[22] D. Dennett, 'Mechanism and Responsibility' in T. Honderich (ed.), *Essays on Freedom of Action* (London, 1973), 175–80.

[23] For a useful collection of readings on the various versions of 'unity of self' doctrine see S. L. White, *The Unity of Self* (Cambridge, Mass., 1992).

any agent even if living an uneventful, undisturbed life. Genetic and environmental luck are unquestionably major determinants of the modes of self-realization available to an agent. Debate will continue, perhaps indefinitely, concerning the nature and effects of the interaction between endowment and environment. But on our present understanding, many possible modes of identity theoretically available to a new-born agent will be foreclosed before the onset of maturity.

Many will dispute whether it is all a matter of luck. That a mature agent has space for autonomous moral development notwithstanding genetic and environmental constraints is a claim that goes back to Aristotle[24] and which has recently been defended by, among others, Daniel Dennett,[25] Charles Taylor,[26] and Susan Wolf.[27] Persons who have attained sufficient maturity can, it is argued, by introspection and reflection respond to criticism and resolve the tension between first- and second-order desires. Values can be strengthened and secured, thereby developing and enlarging moral selves.

That particular persons are capable of moral and prudential reflection on their conduct and can put into effect those resolutions to which their reflection gives rise is obviously the case. Equally, there are persons who never learn or want to learn. But how, for all that, can we in any way commensurate with voluntarism be blamed for a character which does not include a capacity for effective self-reflection.[28] The presence or absence of such a capacity would seem to be an aspect of character just as are those other traits that make up the character we have. It has yet to be explained how a potential for moral growth (as opposed to the exercise of that potential) is a product of volition in a way that is distinctive from our other dispositions.[29]

The fact of the matter seems to be that, preponderately, the criminal law

---

[24] *Nicomachean Ethics*, Book III, ch. 5.   [25] *Elbow Room* (Oxford, 1984).
[26] 'Responsibility for Self' in A. E. Rorty (ed.), *The Identity of Persons* (Berkeley, Ca., 1976), 281.
[27] *Freedom Within Reason* (New York, 1991).
[28] For claims that just moral censure need not be founded on voluntarism see J. R. Silber, 'Being and Doing: A Study of Status Responsibility and Voluntary Responsibility' (1967) 33 *University of Chicago LR* 47; R. M. Adams, 'Involuntary Sins' (1985) 94 *Philosophical Review* 11; L. Fields, 'Moral Beliefs and Blameworthiness' (1994) 69 *Philosophy* 397. Some sort of non-voluntarist account must underlie the justification for treating psychopaths as fit subjects for the criminal justice system, as we commonly do. The fact that a person is in a condition of moral worthlessness typically affords no ground for not censuring his anti-social conduct. Yet, if his crimogenic character is something that he has been given rather than made, the censure is akin more to an æsthetic than to an ethical judgment. That we should allow excusatory force to psychopathy is well argued by P. Arenella, 'Convicting the Morally Blameless: Reassessing the Relationship between Legal and Moral Accountability' (1992) 39 *University College of Los Angeles LR* 1511. Doubtless prevailing 'reactive attitudes' towards psychopaths may change, should effective treatment for the condition ever become available. As it is, a claim of psychopathy can usually only count if a psychopathic defendant does something strange as well as bad, as in *Byrne* [1960] 2 QB 396.
[29] A point made with particular force and clarity by G. Vuoso, 'Background Responsibility and Excuse' (1987) 96 *Yale LJ* 1661.

is not concerned with how we become what we are. Responsibility indeed does not 'go all the way down': we are subjects of the criminal law provided we are capable of a minimum standard of practical reason.[30] If this threshold is attained, the state of our character is irrelevant to any question of criminal capacity unless our character can in some sense be pathologized in a manner germane to the defences of insanity or diminished responsibility. Arguably, the unusual fate of Ms Hearst could lay claim to an analogous, if problematic, status.[31] Be that as it may, the most salient feature of her story was the unusual nature of the bad luck she ran into. Contrast a good luck story, a case where an affectless psychopath, say, suffers a fall and thereby is changed into a person of compassion and concern. Her compassion is aroused by the practice of hunting and as a hunt saboteur she perpetrates criminal acts. She would not be excused; she would be expected to obey the law like any other good person.

In English law to date, a radical change of character *per se* has not excused. This may be illustrated by the trial case of *R. v. T*[32] which, on first impression, may seem to indicate the contrary. D took an active and violent part in a street robbery. Three days earlier, she had been brutally raped. She contended that at the time of the robbery she was in a state of post-traumatic stress disorder (PTSD) and that, accordingly, she should be allowed the defence of automatism. Thus, in terms of formal doctrine, she claimed that at the time of the robbery her condition was tantamount to a state of unconsciousness or that her consciousness was so vestigial as to render her incapable of agency.[33]

Although D was allowed to raise automatism, her condition, as related in a brief report, seems hard to square with the doctrinal requirements of the defence. Her conduct seemed goal-directed. There were indications of resolve and a capacity to respond to fast moving events.[34] If she had been in a state analogous to sleepwalking, or if it could have been explained that in

---

[30] On the centrality of a capacity for practical reasoning for criminal responsibility see M. S. Moore, 'The Moral and Metaphysical Sources of the Criminal Law' in J. R. Pennock and J. M. Chapman (eds.), *Criminal Justice*, Nomos XXVII (New York, 1985), 11.

[31] It would have to be demonstrated that 'brain-washing' not merely imposed alien values but in some way rendered defective her reasoning and evaluative capacities. Claims by Arenella and Alldridge (n. 18 above) that she should be excused rest on the radical change of character *per se*.

[32] [1990] *Criminal LR* 256. Valuable discussions of this trial decision can be found in Smith and Wilson, n. 8 above, at 83–8 and J. Horder, 'Pleading Involuntary Lack of Capacity' [1993] *Cambridge LJ* 298 at 312–15.

[33] In *Attorney-General's Reference (No. 2 of 1992)* [1993] 4 All ER 683, the Court of Appeal reasserted that a plea of automatism was a claim to be wholly unaware of what one was doing at the material time.

[34] In *T*, it was argued on the defendant's behalf that PTSD had produced a state of dissociation or psychogenic fugue depriving her of a conscious mind or will, a claim not easily squared with the facts as briefly reported, at least in terms of externalities. Dicta of the Court of Appeal in *Toner* (1991) 93 Cr. App. R 382 indicate that a state of dissociation will be accepted as a condition of automatism.

140   *Harm and Culpability*

some way her conduct was psychologically compelled,[35] a sufficient affinity
with standard cases of automatism might have been made out. The nature
and effects of PTSD are controversial. Yet clinical information to date about
the condition does not indicate that subjects are rendered automatons.
Rather, the subject may undergo 'flashbacks', episodes of psychic disturbance whereby she experiences a sense of unreality, becomes disengaged,
and lacks affect.[36] In that condition she may perpetrate violent acts untypical of her mainstream life. Yet during such episodes she remains conscious
of what she is doing and her conduct is seemingly volitional, if unconnected
to her 'deep-self'.[37]

The fact that such a condition requires presentation as a state of automatism in order to give effect to the compassion that these circumstances properly arouse indicates that it is not enough simply to say that until I was raped
I did not rob. But it does not do to excuse on the basis of a fiction, however
well-intended. Moreover there may, in such cases, be factors grounding a
distinct, principled defence. It would be pertinent if she were not, save when
in a condition of disequilibrium brought about by the syndrome, of a violent disposition. So, too, if the condition, though leaving intact sufficient
cognitive and volitional resources to form *mens rea*, produced a state of dis-
engagement or disinhibition similar to more familiar conditions, such as
intoxication.[38] Also relevant would be what was done. Some very bad things
may be inexcusable under the terms of excuse argued for below.

DISEQUILIBRIUM AND LAPSE

The current metaphysics of Anglo–American criminal law debar any ground
of exculpation rooted in the sources of the agent's character unless
those sources can be presented as constitutive of some form of individual
pathology.[39] There is, however, a thin account of character that is widely

---

[35] Scottish courts, while not recognizing a defence of irresistible impulse *per se*, have allowed
a defence of automatism in a case where drugs taken involuntarily (LSD and Temazepam) had
rendered the defendant incapable of self-control: *Ross* v. *HM Advocate* [1991] SLT 564. The
same does not follow if drugs taken involuntarily merely produce disinhibition: *HM Advocate*
v. *Kidd* [1960] SLT 82. The discussion of these cases by Lord Mustill in *Kingston* indicates that
Ross would be followed in England.

[36] E. B. Blanchard *et al.*, 'A Psychophysiological Study of PTSD in Vietnam Veterans' (1982)
52 *Psychiatric Quarterly* 220; R. A. Kulka *et al.*, *Trauma and the Vietnam War Generation:
Findings from the National Vietnam Veterans Readjustment Study* (New York, 1990). PTSD
is recognized medically as a discrete syndrome: American Psychiatric Association, *Diagnostic
and Statistical Manual of Mental Disorders* (3rd edn., Washington, D.C., 1987).

[37] On 'deep-self' see S. Wolf, 'Sanity and the Metaphysics of Responsibility' in F. Schoeman
(ed.), *Responsibility, Character and the Emotions* (Cambridge, 1987), 46.

[38] *A fortiori* if further research into PTSD were to reveal that conduct induced by the condition is, despite its seemingly volitional quality, akin to compelled conduct.

[39] For a trenchantly expressed view that the criminal law cannot accommodate any notion
of social pathology see S. J. Morse, 'The Twilight of Welfare Criminology: A Reply to Judge
Bazelon' (1976) 49 *Southern California LR* 1247.

employed in the criminal law in the spheres of evidence and sentencing practice. This, of course, is the notion of 'good character', indicating merely that a defendant has no previous convictions or has convictions of such staleness or for matters of such veniality as not to count against him.

It is common practice to discount the 'tariff' punishment for a crime on the ground that it is the offender's first or first relevant offence. Why a defendant should be punished less because it is her first transgression rather than, say, her tenth has been much disputed.[40] As Andrew von Hirsch has explained, were we to take a puritan view of human frailty, we would straightforwardly abominate particular kinds of conduct and punish with unvarying rigour.[41] More catholic or secular outlooks can accommodate the notion of *lapse*:

[A] transgression (even a fairly serious one) is judged somewhat less strictly when it occurs against a background of prior compliance. The idea is that even an ordinarily well-behaved person can have his or her moral inhibitions fail in a moment of weakness of wilfulness.[42]

The fact of the matter is, however, that we still punish and not exempt first-time offenders. But where the lapse was a product of exceptional circumstances which had destabilized the agent and for which she was not responsible, we should, in certain instances, extend the condoning principle of lapse to the point of exemption. Within the present framework of the criminal law this can only be allowed where the state of disequilibrium in which the agent found herself was in some sense exceptional and not a vicissitude of normal life (a matter developed below). The destabilization must be sufficiently radical as to give rise to conduct which would not have occurred had the agent not been destabilized. Arguably, a defendant should bear the burden of proof on that question.

If these conditions are satisfied and we are dealing with a first or first relevant episode there is not an obvious case for punishment in retributivist or consequentialist terms. One's status as a non-convicted person is, perhaps, the most important civic asset one can have. To forfeit it in circumstances not of the agent's making and where compliance was rendered very much more difficult is to punish beyond just deserts, notwithstanding the presence of *mens rea* and the absence of compulsion. Any element of defiance of law in her conduct[43] must be set against her previous pattern of conformity in normal circumstances. As the circumstances are exceptional, the claims of

[40] J. D. Stuart, 'Retributive Justice and Prior Offences' (1986) *Philosophical Forum* 40; A. Durham, 'Justice in Sentencing: The Role of Prior Record of Criminal Involvement' (1987) *Journal of Criminal Law and Criminology* 614.

[41] A. von Hirsch, 'Criminal Record Rides Again' [1991] *Criminal Justice Ethics* 2. I am indebted to Andrew von Hirsch for drawing my attention to this point.

[42] *Ibid.*, 55.

[43] For an argument that 'defiance' should be central to criminal liability, see J. Hampton, 'Mens Rea', in E. F. Paul, F. A. Miller, and J. Paul (eds.), n. 18 above, at 1.

individual or general deterrence and of societal protection lack cogency. In normal times an unyielding *in terrorem* criminal law is not required.

There is an important qualification to be made. The agent under discussion retains some capacity for moral agency; notwithstanding her condition she is able to form *mens rea*. Implicit in the notion of lapse is a plea for understanding, for tolerance. We have argued that such appeals can, on occasion, found complete exemption. Yet if some capacity for moral agency is retained, certain exercises of such capacity may result in conduct which is inexcusable, for which offsetting claims based on an exceptional state of disequilibrium and previous compliance with law are simply not enough. Certain awful deeds will constitute not a lapse on the part of a person otherwise of good character but the very destruction of any claim to that status. An act of killing, if deliberate, uncompelled, and unjustified, taints the agent with a negative, indelible, and defining status. Such an act retains its constitutive potency however exemplary the agent's life up to that point in time, notwithstanding that the agent would not have perpetrated such a deed but for very particular circumstances.[44] In respect of exceptionally grave wrongdoing, if sufficient cognitive and volitional resources were possessed by the agent to afford proof of *mens rea*, destabilization should afford mitigation but not excuse.[45] Arguably this reasoning applies to those who seriously injure others and/or perpetrate a non-consensual penetrative sexual act. The factors which favour the defendant must be balanced against the thing the defendant has done. They do not categorically foreclose liability in every case.

The disapplication of a defence in the case of particularly heinous crimes is not a novelty. Duress, in England, is not available on a charge of murder.[46] That limitation can be criticized for confusing excuse with justification: a threat of immediate death or serious bodily harm might be thought to excuse anything. Here, by contrast, we are proposing to excuse certain agents whose conduct met the grounds of inculpation and who were not compelled. In like case are defendants who invoke the American defence of entrapment, a defence unavailable for defendants who have perpetrated violence.[47] A limitation on the ambit of the excuse proposed here is in principle correct, though it is not pretended that the appropriate 'cut-off' point will be a matter of easy agreement.

---

[44] For an account of the constitutive potency of grave wrongs in otherwise exemplary lives see M. S. Moore, 'Choice, Character and Excuse' in Paul, Miller, and Paul (eds.), *ibid.*, 29 at 52–8.

[45] Something, of course, which cannot be done if grave offences, such as murder, carry mandatory penalties.

[46] *Howe* [1987] AC 417.

[47] In the leading case of *Sorrells* v. *United States*, 287 US 435 (1932) it is cautioned that the defence may not be available for 'heinous' or 'revolting' crime, and the Model Penal Code formulation at § 2.13 makes the defence unavailable in respect of causing or threatening to cause bodily injury save against the entrapper himself.

Outside the realm of heinous conduct, however, a combination of previous good character and exceptional circumstances of disequilibrium should ground an excuse. A salient feature of this proposal is the review of the previous convictions of the defendant. If an agent's conduct does not fit the grounds of inculpation or was justified or compelled, any previous criminality has no bearing on her claim to be exempt from criminal sanction. But where a plea for excuse relates to conduct which meets the grounds for inculpation and rests on a claim that she did something untypical of her in circumstances where compliance with law was rendered more difficult, the agent's past criminality[48] is of central relevance. Recalling the facts of *R. v. T*, if the defendant had been previously involved in robberies, then, whatever traumatic impact the rape might have had, it cannot plausibly be said that it generated a propensity to rob. An excuse based in part on previous good character must, definitionally, allow a broader narrative than is required to resolve issues arising under conduct-based conceptions of excuse. Such a defence, which allows in previous relevant convictions, need not require examination of the entirety of a defendant's history. But it must allow in any past convictions which are material[49] to the question whether the particular conduct at issue in the trial was genuinely untypical of the agent. Whether, in the light of her past conduct, a defendant should be allowed to raise this 'character' defence should be a matter to be resolved by the judge in the absence of the jury. Moreover, any acquittal obtained on the basis argued for here should be recorded in an earmarked and retrievable way. It should be available as part of the record in any future case where the defendant raises this 'character' defence. A refusal by a judge to allow the raising of a defence of this kind should be regarded as raising a question of law from which there may be an appeal.

There is an important, subsidiary reason for making previous convictions relevant to a character-based defence. The application of such a defence to conditions like PTSD and pre-menstrual tension will be argued for directly. But defences based on psychological and physiological data encounter considerable judicial scepticism both as to the very existence of particular conditions and as to whether the condition produced the effects claimed by the defence. Nor is that scepticism necessarily misplaced. It cannot be said that attributions of violent conduct to, say, post-traumatic stress, however graphic and convincing when presented in terms of self-report, meet scientific standards of prediction and refutability. Difficulties by way of

---

[48] It is important that the question whether a person is of good character should be confined to the issue of past relevant convictions (and, on occasion, past acquittals; see the text below). Testimony as to general character would involve impalpable matters, be vulnerable to special pleading and be difficult to curtail.

[49] It would be for the trial judge, in the absence of the jury in the procedure outlined in the text above, to determine questions of materiality. One would not anticipate that previous convictions for theft would be material on a charge for violence although a conviction for a violent robbery may well be perceived as material on a charge involving non-acquisitive violence.

providing satisfactory predictive tests, agreed error rates, and adequate control groups entail that such syndromes will, for the foreseeable future, remain in the realm of clinical assumptions rather than causal analysis.[50] If we are to make use of such assumptions in our forensic practice, then the more that is known of the relevant predispositions of the defendant, the better.

Reference at trial to the previous history of the defendant is not unknown in Anglo–American criminal law. A parallel may be found in the predominant version[51] of the American defence of entrapment. Under this variant of the defence, condonation is explained in terms of a combination of attenuated culpability and overreaching police conduct. A defendant must adduce evidence that he was induced to offend by the subterfuge or persuasion of law enforcement officials or their agents and that he did not have a pre-existing disposition to commit a crime of the kind he was inveigled into committing. This version of the defence has been cogently criticized for running together the disparate elements of the personal culpability of the offender and the conduct of the police.[52] Nonetheless, the copious critical literature does not indicate that adducing previous convictions at trial has been forensically unmanageable.

STATES OF DESTABILIZATION

Our proposal will now be concretized by reference to particular states of destabilization. As previously argued, such states must act as a catalyst of conduct which is untypical of the defendant. A review of the circumstances of destabilization, the conduct perpetrated, and the defendant's previous record must indicate that a conviction is unwarranted on retributivist or consequentialist grounds. It must be said immediately that many narratives which satisfy these requirements must, perforce, be excluded from the scope of the proposal.

Attributions of culpability in Anglo–American criminal law rest on certain key assumptions. There is an assumption of free will or a version of compatibilism or at least that certain reactive attitudes[53] to conduct and the punitive responses they engender remain acceptable practices even if 'hard' determinism be true. Genetic or environmental luck is disregarded unless features thereof can be presented as forms of individual pathology. It is assumed that all agents can attain a minimum standard of self-control—

---

[50] For a valuable discussion of the reliability of 'syndrome' evidence, see I. G. Freckelton, 'When Plight Makes Right' (1994) 18 *Criminal LJ* 29.

[51] *Sorrells* v. *United States*, 287 US 435 (1932); *Sherman* v. *United States*, 356 US 359 (1958); *United States* v. *Russell*, 411 US 423 (1973).

[52] B. G. Stiff and G. G. James, 'Entrapment and the Entrapment Defence: Dilemmas for a Democratic Society' (1984) 3 *Law and Philosophy* 111.

[53] On the inevitability of certain 'reactive attitudes' to harmful conduct irrespective of whether we do or do not subscribe to an account of human conduct in terms of free will see P. Strawson, 'Freedom and Resentment' in *Freedom and Resentment* (London, 1974), 1.

unless the circumstances leading to loss of control can be characterized as exceptional[54] or the agent is a member of a legally recognized abnormal class. These assumptions are rooted in a metaphysics that separates moral agency from naturalism. They arc unsettling for those who believe that the world 'is only partly intelligible to human agency and in itself not necessarily well adjusted to ethical aspirations'.[55]

Be that as it may, any proposal which seeks to influence the current practice of criminal law must work with these current assumptions. Accordingly, we must distinguish between different stories which have the same exculpatory potential. A man is devastated by some bad news. He drinks by way of immediate reaction and, being unused to drink, becomes intoxicated. He is taunted by someone about the source of his distress and he reacts violently. Though his life was exemplary to that point, and despite his contrition for what he has done, the circumstances can only mitigate and not excuse. As argued for before, we can excuse if the intoxication was involuntary.[56] The variable is immaterial to culpability. Yet the variable renders the story exceptional, curtailable, and forensically manageable. It can be slotted in. If we were to take in the first account, however, we would be committed to entertaining any story of how 'normal' life had borne down hard. The key assumptions of the criminal law keep such stories out.

Nonetheless, we should take out of the criminal justice system, with all its vagaries, such blameless persons as we can. One set of candidates are the involuntarily intoxicated if the circumstances, including the good character of the defendant, meet the requirements already explained. Clearly intoxication resulting from the surreptitiousness, trickery, or force of others should be regarded as involuntary. A strong case can be made for including persons who become disinhibited from the effects of medication when no warning was given as to the mind-affecting properties of the drug.[57] Of course, such a person is allowed to make a claim of no *mens rea* if such be the fact, the *Majewski*[58] presumptions[59] having no application to such a

---

[54] As is done, unsatisfactorily, within the current parameters of the defence of provocation: see J. Horder, *Provocation and Responsibility* (Oxford, 1992), particularly chs. 8 and 9; G. R. Sullivan, 'Anger and Excuse: Reassessing Provocation' (1993) 13 *Oxford Journal of Legal Studies* 421.

[55] B. Williams, *Shame and Necessity* (Berkeley, Ca., 1993), 164.

[56] A person unused to drink who becomes drunk on resorting to drink as a reaction to some personal trauma is, it is submitted, blamelessly intoxicated (save, of course, unless he was about to drive or whatever) but blameless in a way that cannot be made to count in terms of liability rather than in mitigation.

[57] The effects of medication may be very potent as in *Re H* [1990] 1 FLR 441 where D, a happily married man, killed his wife in a motiveless attack consequent on an aberrant reaction to an anti-depressant drug. In accepting D's plea of diminished responsibility to a charge of murder, the trial judge sentenced him on the basis that, 'there was no responsibility at all' (at 443). Subsequently he was allowed to claim under his wife's will.

[58] [1977] AC 443.

[59] Which, of course, attributes the culpability for 'basic' intent crimes to a state of voluntary intoxication.

case. Additionally, however, the protection of a character-based defence should be extended to persons merely disinhibited by medication.

Less clear-cut is the position of a person of good character who has become destabilized by his medication in circumstances where he is open to criticism for the condition he is in. Such a case was *Hardie*,[60] where D in an agitated condition took double the standard dose of tranquilizers in order to calm his nerves. The case establishes that such a person is not to be inculpated on the basis of *Majewski*. Should such a person be merely disinhibited rather than lack *mens rea*, his exclusion from the proposed character-based defence, given exemplary previous conduct, would be founded on a careless use of medication. It is questionable whether this should prove dispositive. One might contrast the case of *Quick*,[61] where the defendant frequently mismanaged his medication and was prone to violence when disinhibited. Once acquainted with this propensity, subsequent mismanagement is indicative of carelessness as to the interests of others as well as indifference to one's own welfare. Sufficient recognition of the difficulties occasioned by the need to take regular and potentially destabilizing medication is afforded if such persons are removed from the shadow of *Majewski*, but otherwise assessed according to standard doctrine.

Assessment according to standard doctrine should also be the position for alcoholics and those with cognate addictions, even though an argument can be made that addicts should come within a character-based defence. That argument would find a measure of support from recent cases on the diminished responsibility defence for murder, where appellate courts have used the term 'involuntary intoxication' in relation to the drunken condition of an alcoholic.[62] Such a description is only applicable, however, according to these authorities, if the first drink taken was 'compelled' and so, too, each drink taken thereafter.[63] These conditions are so exclusionary that practically all, if not all, alcoholics would fail to meet them. Nonetheless, it would be problematic to describe as 'involuntary'[64] those states of intoxication which are a regular feature of the lives of alcoholics and other addicts. A condition of addiction and the states of disequilibrium arising therefrom should be regarded as emanations of a constitutive trait rather than the product of exceptional circumstances. If we were to allow addiction to destabilizing substances a privileged status it would be impossible to deny

---

[60] [1984] 3 All ER 848.   [61] [1973] QB 610.

[62] *Tandy* [1989] 1 All ER 267; *Inseal* [1992] *Criminal LR* 35. The cases are discussed in G. R. Sullivan, 'Intoxicants and Diminished Responsibility' [1994] *Criminal LR* 156.

[63] Thus in *Tandy*, a chronic alcoholic of some 10 years' standing was disallowed a defence of diminished responsibility on the ground that she had a degree of choice as to when to have the first drink of the day.

[64] The classification of alcoholism as a disease is disputed: H. Fingarette, *Heavy Drinking: The Myth of Alcoholism as a Disease* (Berkeley, Ca., 1988); G. Edwards, 'The Status of Alcoholism as a Disease' in R. V. Phillipson (ed.), *Drug Dependence and Alcoholism* (London, 1970), 140.

similar claims based on other personal characteristics with criminogenic properties. Indeed any proposal to take addicts outwith *Majewski* would be controversial.

By way of contrast with addicts, for whom states of disequilibrium are endemic and integral, there are persons afflicted with such potentially desta-bilizing conditions as diabetes, epilepsy, arteriosclerosis, cerebral tumours, and severe pre-menstrual tension.[65] These conditions can produce states of being which induce outbursts of irrational violence in persons otherwise well disposed. Violent episodes may occur unpredictably however conscien-tious a particular subject may be in the management of her condition.

If legitimate public safety concerns can be met, subjects within these cat-egories should be afforded a defence of the kind argued for here. Whereas the nature and blamelessness of a state of addiction may be disputable, no censure of any kind attaches to the afflictions we are presently discussing. An alternative to current ways of dealing with dangerous conduct induced by these conditions has long been required in English criminal law. Present dispositions may be inappropriate and unjust. If the condition produces a state of mind incompatible with *mens rea*, the disposal of the case may depend on the exact ætiology of the particular condition. For instance, in the case of a diabetic, if an episode of hypoglycæmia is occasioned by adminis-tering insulin, then, because an 'external' factor is at work, a straightfor-ward plea of no *mens rea* is available with the burden of proof on the prosecution and an unqualified acquittal resulting from a successful plea.[66] By contrast, if a state of hyperglycæmia comes about because of excessive blood sugar, the 'internal' nature of the malfunction triggers the bizarre legal category 'disease of the mind' and the appropriate plea is not guilty by rea-son of insanity,[67] with all that that entails. Unsurprisingly, defendants plead guilty rather than suffer the indignity and the risks inherent in a successful plea of insanity.[68] Persons such as epileptics must plead insanity in relation to conduct perpetrated during a seizure and so, too, any other persons who rely on whatever underlying condition they may have rather than the med-ication that they take. The justification for this state of affairs is public safety. Even if that were to be regarded as sufficient reason, in the case of diabetics at least, the differential outcomes in no way track the dangerous-ness of respective defendants.

Were we free to start again, lack of *mens rea* should lead to an unquali-fied acquittal and public danger concerns should be addressed through the

---

[65] Cases involving pre-menstrual tension have yet to be considered at appellate level in England. For a useful discussion of the excusatory claims the condition may warrant see L. Luckhaus, 'A Plea for PMT in the Criminal Law' in S. Edwards, *Gender, Sex and the Law* (London, 1986), 140.

[66] *Quick* [1970] QB 610.   [67] *Hennessy* [1989] 2 All ER 9.

[68] Notwithstanding the more flexible regime for cases other than murder brought in by the Criminal Procedure (Insanity and Unfitness to Plead) Act 1991, a verdict of insanity in such cases remains an unwarranted exercise in public stigma.

process of civil commitment. But the present way of doing things is entrenched[69] and can at best be only outflanked. This could be done, at least in part, were judges prepared to accept a supplementary character-based defence in these cases. This defence would also be in point should the condition in question be not obviously incompatible with proof of *mens rea*. States of hyperglycæmia and hypoglycæmia, for instance, may vary in intensity as between episodes and within a particular episode.[70] The level of consciousness may be commensurate with awareness of one's action.[71] The same applies to *petit mal* seizures and to acts done while in a state of premenstrual tension. What unites all agents subject to these fluctuating unstable conditions is an occasional propensity to impulsive violence.

Persons in these classes should be left free to pursue current grounds of defence, if that is where they consider their interests lie. Alternatively, they should be allowed to plead that even though the grounds of inculpation may be present in their case, the incident was untypical of them and was a product of their condition. In such a case an absence of previous convictions and of relevant acquittals, as explained above, would serve as one of the planks of the defence and also indicate that the public safety concerns which have driven the interpretation of the insanity defence are unlikely to be present. It should be possible to proceed in this way without risk of entanglement in the insanity defence. The defendant is not asserting that he did not know what he was doing (even if the condition produced that effect). He is not claiming that he was, in M'Naghten terms, unaware of the nature and quality of his act. He is, rather, conceding the grounds of inculpation and seeking exculpation on grounds which in no conceivable sense put his sanity in issue.

Clearly, public safety concerns must impose limits. Previous convictions for violence and previous acquittals obtained on the basis argued for here should be available to refute any claim that a defendant's conduct was untypical for him. As already proposed, this defence should not be available whatever the cause for cases of causing death, serious injury, or perpetrating a non-consensual penetrative sex act. Arguably in all cases which are defended on the grounds argued for here, the defendant should have the burden of proving that he would not have offended but for the state of disequilibrium brought on by his affliction. Though limited in this fashion, it would, on a significant number of occasions, offer a better option than pleading guilty or insane.[72]

---

[69] Particularly following the House of Lords decision in *Sullivan* [1984] AC 156, a case where the facts pressed hard for a different approach.

[70] E. L. Diamond *et al.*, 'Symptom Awareness in Diabetic Adults' (1989) 8 *Health Psychology* 15.

[71] S. R. Heller and I. A. McDonald, 'Physiological Disturbances in Hypoglycæmia: Effect on Subjective Awareness' (1991) 8 *Clinical Science* 1.

[72] Such an option would surely attract persons such as the defendant in *Sullivan*, who opted to plead guilty to aggravated assault rather than not guilty by reason of insanity. It will be recalled that Sullivan was a man of good character who, at the material time, was afflicted with a *petit mal* seizure.

Finally, we must consider conditions of psychological destabilization brought about by exceptional and traumatic events. PTSD has been used to support a claim of lack of *mens rea*.[73] If trauma was consequent upon an incident or incidents falling beyond 'normal' life events, insanity will not be an issue.[74] Yet many of the psychological states that such stress may produce are largely compatible with *mens rea*. As alluded to earlier, the nature and effects of the syndrome are not scientifically established, but studies and clinical accounts of the effects of such trauma depict psychic disturbance predominantly compatible with awareness of one's conduct.[75] There is a substantial clinical acceptance, however, that the syndrome may induce behaviour untypical of the agent in the mainstream of her life. Thus such states should be considered eligible for the form of exculpation considered here. The somewhat impalpable nature of the data involved in these cases may be seen to justify placing the burden of proof on the defence.

A proposal that the criminal law should make some provision for persons whose conduct satisfies the grounds of inculpation but who have acted in a state of destabilization is not novel. Jeremy Horder has suggested extending the boundaries of diminished responsibility to offences additional to murder.[76] Under his scheme, a verdict of diminished responsibility would not result in an unqualified acquittal. The defendant would remain within the authority of the court and would be, where appropriate, subject to treatment and/or custodial measures. The defence would be available for persons who have voluntarily caused harm (in the sense that their conduct was the product of their own agency) but who were, because of the condition they were in, 'unable to evaluate their conduct or control it through moral evaluation'.[77]

Horder's criteria provide a more refined ethical foundation for a defence than the disequilibrium/character excuse canvassed in this paper.[78] Indeed, if his conditions are met, there is a powerful case for a complete acquittal with, in an ideal world, public danger concerns addressed through appropriate civil commitment procedures.[79] But, in the light of the fact that we are

[73] As in *R. v. T* [1990] *Criminal LR* 256.

[74] Matters are otherwise if stress is caused by 'normal' if traumatic events as in *Rabey* (1980) 114 DLR (3d) 193 (ending of a relationship), or where no explanation can be given for the psychic disturbance as in *Burgess* [1991] 2 QB 92.

[75] See n. 36 above and associated text.   [76] Horder, n. 32 above, at 316–18.

[77] *Ibid.*, 316.

[78] Under the proposal argued for in this paper, the defendant need only establish that she would not have offended on the occasion in question but for a blameless state of destabilization. That of itself would be enough provided she was of good character.

[79] If and while a person is in a condition where she cannot address the moral quality of her conduct or is compelled to do what she does, then she would seem to be no longer a member of the moral community to whom the precepts of the criminal law are addressed. To hold to this view consistently would leave some very dangerous persons, notably psychopaths, compulsive arsonists, etc., beyond the criminal justice system. As already noted, a verdict of diminished responsibility under Horder's proposal would leave the defendant within the authority of the court.

dealing here with a class of persons who have the volitional and cognitive resources to satisfy the grounds of inculpation, determining whether such agents meet his conditions could give rise to considerable forensic difficulties.[80] By way of illustration let us go back to *R.* v. *T.*[81] All that we know of the defendant is that her conduct was seemingly volitional but that she had been brutally raped three days before she took an active part in the robbery. She asserted a state of PTSD by way of defence; a condition of uncertain nature and effect. On that rather insecure footing, the jury, under Horder's proposal, would review the expert testimony for answers to the alternative questions whether the condition, if established, either precluded the defendant from knowing that her conduct was wrong or prevented her from controlling herself (a matter of irresistible impulse rather than an impulse more difficult to resist because of PTSD). Contrast the issues presented by the form of excuse argued for here. Assuming a burden of proof on the defence, in a case such as *T* they would be:

(1) Was it probable that D was in the condition known as PTSD at the time of her act?
(2) Would D have perpetrated the act had she not been in PTSD at the time?

Recall that this defence would not be allowed to go before the jury had D prior convictions for robbery or sufficiently cognate offences or any previous acquittals for such offences obtained by raising the defence canvassed here. If the defence is successfully invoked, a complete acquittal follows. Given also that certain very serious crimes are excluded from the defence, it is submitted that this proposal is forensically practicable and involves an appropriate trade-off between fairness for defendants and public safety concerns.

HEARING EXCUSES

To return to the decision which prompted this paper, *Kingston*,[82] a pleasing aspect of the Lord Chief Justice's judgment was his sensitivity to the plight of the appellant and his willingness to treat the issue of blamelessness as a matter of substantive defence rather than remainder the question to post-conviction mitigation. For reasons sufficiently rehearsed, an untrammelled defence of involuntary intoxication would be unsustainable. Nonetheless, the openness shown in the matter of defence doctrine is very welcome. Welcome, too, is the firm statement by Lord Mustill in the House of Lords

---

[80] His proposal is a considerable refinement upon the current defence of diminished responsibility, under which the jury has to decide whether an abnormality of mind 'substantially impaired his mental responsibility for his acts': Homicide Act 1957, s. 2.
[81] N. 32 above.   [82] N. 1 above.

that the creation of novel defences is a proper judicial task[83] even though one may regret that he was disinclined to shoulder that task in the instant case.

The judicial role is well suited to the crafting of new defence doctrine.[84] A useful distinction may be drawn between the grounds of inculpation and those factors which argue a case for exculpation on particular facts. In respect of the grounds of inculpation, clarity and generality of application are to be prized, and any significant enlargement in what may not be done should be determined by the legislature. For exculpatory questions, however, there can be creative and principled responses to the quiddity of a particular case without undermining the normative framework of the criminal law.[85] The response argued for here does involve significant innovation in the use of previous convictions and a particular form of acquittal. On the other hand it provides more safeguards than would have been afforded by the Court of Appeal decision in *Kingston*.

Much can be done on the development and individualization of excuses. Such judicial work as is done in this field may employ concepts which are too coarse-grained to capture the particularities that arise for decision. Judges, when considering novel grounds for excusing or when extending the boundaries of existing categories look, understandably, for analogies within existing doctrine. Employing broad and disparate heads of comparison may lead to forced and dysfunctional doctrine. So it has been that, for instance, the nature of the defence of duress has been explicated by reference to aspects of the law of provocation[86] and, similarly, the Court of Appeal in *Kingston* sought purchase for a defence of involuntary intoxication by invoking an analogy with duress.[87] In neither case is the analogy instructive, given the radically different frailties that the respective excuses address.

What has been argued for here is a more fine-grained focus when employing concepts of exculpation. The paper has proposed conjoining the notion of lapse from good character with circumstances of destabilization but for which the agent would not have done what she did. By good character is meant nothing more than the absence of relevant previous convictions or relevant character-based acquittals. The causes of destabilization must in some sense be exceptional. The defence would not be available for certain very serious crimes. Arguably the burden of proof should be on the defence.

It would not be easy or desirable to cast this proposal in statutory form.

---

[83] N. 7 above.

[84] The judicial reluctance to shoulder the burden of creating new defence doctrine continues: *Clegg* [1995] 1 All ER 334 at 346–7 (Lord Lloyd). The Draft Criminal Code expressly preserves a judicial capacity to develop new defences: Draft Criminal Code, cl. 14(4), *Law Commission* No. 177 (1989).

[85] As argued in G. Fletcher, 'The Individualisation of Excusing Conditions' (1974) 47 *Southern California LR* 1269 and M. Dan-Cohen, 'Decision Rules and Conduct Rules: An Acoustic Separation in Criminal Law' (1984) *Harvard LR* 625.

[86] As in *Graham* [1982] 1 All ER 801.   [87] See n. 11 above and associated text.

Certain areas where it might be deployed have been suggested. It may well be that unanticipated difficulties of implementation could arise in respect of different causes of instability—what works for, say, involuntary intoxication may not prove feasible for PTSD. This is best resolved forensically, by way of argued law. It is submitted that implementation of the proposal would filter out of the criminal justice system some persons who lack sufficient culpability for its stigma and coercion. *Pace* Lord Mustill in *Kingston*, non-conviction of the blameless should be an informing principle of the substantive criminal law. A conviction for a stigmatic offence is a sanction in its own right and parsimony in the distribution of sanctions should be fostered.

7

Crimes of Ulterior Intent

Jeremy Horder*

We often blame people simply for having ignoble beliefs or intentions; but, contrary to the impression sometimes given by commentators, it is not only blame that is determined or influenced by mental states or processes. The normative significance of people's conduct may also be profoundly affected by the beliefs or intentions which accompany or motivate that conduct.[1] This general truth is recognized across much of the criminal law. If X picks up a brick, it is the knowledge that X intends to use the brick to kill Y that licenses the use by Y of necessary and proportionate force in self-defence to prevent X so doing. If X demands his property back from Y, intending to use it in the commission of a crime, X's intention (probably) deprives his demand of any legal force it might otherwise have had, and Y is under no obligation to return the property.[2] If X slaps or spanks Y, the question whether this is ordinary social contact or a criminal indecent assault may be resolved in the light of X's purpose in so acting.[3] Most importantly for present purposes, if X engages in conduct that is not *ipso facto* regarded as a crime (or, indeed, as a wrong of any sort), that conduct may none the less become criminal if X engages in it with the intention of committing a crime.[4] Similarly, if X engages in what might otherwise be regarded as relatively minor criminal conduct, but with the intention of committing a greater crime, the self-same act may thereby be transformed from a relatively minor

* I am very grateful to the participants in the criminal law discussion group at Gonville & Caius College, Cambridge, for their penetrating criticisms of a much earlier draft of this paper. Special thanks are also due to Andrew Simester for his detailed and perceptive comments on earlier drafts.

[1] On the neglected or misunderstood significance of the distinction between normative and ascriptive rules in the criminal law, see John Gardner, 'Criminal Law and the Uses of Theory: A Reply to Laing' (1994) 14 *Oxford Journal of Legal Studies* 217 at 220–2.

[2] *Garrett* v. *Arthur Churchill (Glass) Ltd* [1970] 1 QB 92; see the discussion by Glanville Williams, in his 'Obedience to Law as a Crime' (1990) 53 *Modern LR* 445.

[3] *Court* [1988] 2 All ER 221 at 231.

[4] See, e.g., the Criminal Damage Act 1971, s. 3 (having something in one's possession, without lawful excuse, intending to use it to destroy or damage another's property); also the Offences Against the Person Act 1861, s. 64 (hereinafter OAPA 1861).

into a serious criminal offence.[5] In all of these cases the normative significance of X's conduct changes dramatically when viewed in the light of his or her intent; whereupon that conduct becomes eligible for criminalization, and may also change the normative position of those such as Y (in the earlier examples) who are confronted by that conduct.[6]

The last two examples that I gave are both instances of what have been called crimes of 'ulterior intent'.[7] Crimes of ulterior intent seem to have first come into use and become relatively common in statutes of the later eighteenth and early nineteenth centuries.[8] Amongst them are numbered some of the most serious crimes in the criminal calendar,[9] a number of them carrying a maximum sentence of imprisonment for life.[10] I shall try to explain and justify the place of crimes of ulterior intent in the criminal law, a task given fresh impetus by the Law Commission's recent misguided proposal to abolish one of the most important crimes of ulterior intent, wounding with intent to do grievous bodily harm.[11]

RATIONALIZING ULTERIOR INTENT CRIMES

The vast majority of crimes of ulterior intent are crimes where the criminal intent that the prosecution must prove relates to wrongdoing 'beyond' (to use a somewhat misleading but convenient metaphor) the act—whether itself wrong or not—which the accused has in fact done.[12] To take the

---

[5] As in the contrast between unlawful wounding, contrary to the OAPA 1861, s. 20, and wounding with intent to do grievous bodily harm, contrary to the OAPA 1861, s. 18.

[6] In taking this view, I side with Andrew Simester and John Gardner against Paul Robinson in this volume, on the relevance of intention and fault to issues of justification.

[7] *DPP* v. *Majewski* [1977] AC 443 at 478 ff. (*per* Lord Simon); J. C. Smith and Brian Hogan, *Criminal Law* (7th edn., London, 1992), 71.

[8] See, e.g., 26 Geo 2, c. 19 (1753) and the better known 43 Geo 3, c. 58 (1803).

[9] Some very varied examples of ulterior intent crimes include: the OAPA 1861, ss. 18, 21, 22, 24, and 29–33; the Theft Act 1968, s. 9(1); the Protection From Eviction Act 1977, s. 1(3); the Taking of Hostages Act 1982, s. 1(2); the Public Order Act 1986, s. 18. In a sexual context, see the Sexual Offences Act 1956, s. 6. Such crimes are now one of the most common statutorily defined species of non-fatal crime of violence.

[10] See, e.g., the OAPA 1861, ss. 18, 21, and 22; Taking of Hostages Act 1982, s. 1(2). The offence of assault with intent to rob is also punishable by a maximum sentence of life imprisonment: see the Theft Act 1968, s. 8(2).

[11] See n. 5 above. The proposal to abolish this offence is implicit in the shape of the new scheme of non-fatal offences against the person devised by the Law Commission in its Report: *Offences against the Person and General Principles*, Law Commission No. 218 (Cm 2370, 1993). For whilst there are proposed crimes of assault, intentionally or recklessly causing injury, and intentionally or recklessly causing serious injury, there is to be no crime or crimes of assault *with intent to* cause (serious) injury, or of causing injury *with intent to* cause serious injury. For further, more general, consideration of the Law Commission's proposals, see Peter Glazebrook, 'Structuring the Criminal Code: Functional Approaches to Complicity, Incomplete Offences and General Defences', this volume.

[12] One occasionally finds crimes, more broadly, of ulterior *mens rea* rather than of ulterior direct intent. One such is the crime of intentionally *or recklessly* damaging or destroying another's property, intending thereby to endanger life *or being reckless* whether life would be

example mentioned just now, wounding with intent to do grievous bodily harm is an ulterior intent crime because the *mens rea* (the intent to do grievous bodily harm) goes 'beyond' the *actus reus* (the wounding). In spite of the proliferation of crimes of ulterior intent since the beginning of the nineteenth century, there is hardly any coherence in their relationship, even where there are strong family resemblances. There is a crime of assault with intent to rape, or to rob, but no crime of assault with intent to murder or to do grievous bodily harm (despite the fact that it is an offence to wound with intent to do grievous bodily harm).[13] It is a crime to trespass in a building with intent to steal, but no crime to commit such a trespass with intent to obtain by deception. It is a crime to possess a shotgun with intent to endanger life, but no crime to possess poison with such an intent. Doubtless, the apparent mess can all be explained by reference to the haphazard growth of the law, and to the traditionally parochial concerns of criminal statutes,[14] but little attention has been paid to the problem by academics. This is almost certainly because of the entrenched habit of thinking about crimes primarily in terms of the interests they supposedly protect (the person, property, public order, and so forth).[15] Thinking in these terms obscures important subtleties in the quality of the wrongs underlying particular crimes: are they, for example, essentially destructive, acquisitive, or exploitative wrongs?

More importantly for present purposes, thinking of crimes in terms of the interests they protect distracts attention from the way in which criminal wrongs are constituted, whatever the interests they protect. The significance of the difference can be traced into a fundamental question about the limits of the criminal law. Those who conceive of the criminal law in terms of interest-protection will tend to be those who think of the limits of the criminal law as governed by some version of the 'harm principle', according to which a necessary—even if not sufficient—condition of legitimate criminalization is a finding that harm has been caused to another.[16] For this principle naturally generates a set of dependent rules framed in terms of prohibiting the infliction of particular harms, such as harm to the person, to property, or to the State. There has, however, always been an inherent objectivism—or 'outcome bias'—in the way that the harm principle is commonly

endangered thereby, contrary to the Criminal Damage Act 1971, s. 1(2). I will not be dealing here with crimes of ulterior *mens rea*; only with crimes of ulterior *direct* intent.

[13] Contrast the position under the U.S. Model Penal Code, § 5.01, comment 2.

[14] For an excellent historical examination, see P. R. Glazebrook, 'Should We Have a Law of Attempted Crime?' (1969) 85 *Law Quarterly R* 28. In a sense, the present contribution is an attempt to carry a little further forward the debate that Glazebrook sought to initiate in his somewhat neglected article.

[15] See the contents page of any modern textbook on Criminal law.

[16] For more general discussion, see Andrew Von Hirsch, 'Extending The Harm Principle: 'Remote Harms and Fair Imputation', this volume.

stated.[17] This has made the principle difficult to reconcile, not only with the fine discriminations often made in the criminal law between species of *mens rea* in relation to harm done, but also with the proliferation of crimes whose *raison d'être* and seriousness derive from the harm intended, such as those presently under consideration, rather than from the harm done or (objectively) risked. Such difficulties can be overcome if one thinks of the justification for proscribing such crimes as centred on the *wrong* rather than on the harm done.[18] *Mens rea*—sometimes of a very particular kind—can be as essential to the constitution of a wrong as the conduct that embodies that *mens rea*. An example, discussed below, is provided by the case of attempts.[19] It follows that conduct can sometimes be wrong irrespective of whether one can identify a harm done or (objectively) risked, just in virtue of the intention with which one engages in that conduct. Such is the case with many crimes of ulterior intent. 'Wrongdoing' is clearly not *per se* a sufficient condition of criminalization, since there are many non-criminal and non-civil wrongs;[20] but it provides a better starting point in seeking to understand crimes of ulterior intent than does the 'harm principle'.

In this regard, it is possible to make some analytical distinctions between kinds of ulterior intent crime, even if these distinctions are not always hard and fast. Crimes of ulterior intent usually fall into five broad categories (although some crimes cross the boundaries[21]):

1. Committing a lesser crime, intending to commit a greater one.[22]
2. Committing a crime, intending to do some non-criminal wrong.[23]
3. Committing a civil wrong, intending to commit a crime.[24]

---

[17] See, e.g., H. L. A. Hart, *The Morality of the Criminal Law* (Oxford, 1965), 32: 'For the justification of punishment . . . it must be shown that the conduct punished is either directly harmful either to individuals or their liberty or jeopardises the collective interest which members of society have in the maintenance of its organsation and defence.'

[18] See generally Alan Brudner, 'Agency and Welfare in the Penal Law', in Stephen Shute, John Gardner, and Jeremy Horder, *Action and Value in the Criminal Law* (Oxford, 1993), 21–5.

[19] See Gardner, 'Criminal Law', n. 1 above.

[20] Whether, properly understood, wrongdoing is always a necessary condition of criminal, or indeed civil, liability is a question beyond the scope of this essay: see Brudner, 'Agency and Welfare', n. 18 above.

[21] See, in particular, the 'public disorder' crimes under Part 1 and 'racial hatred' crimes under Part 111 of the Public Order Act 1986. Conspiracy is a good example of a crime that neatly traverses the boundary (such as it is) between categories 3, 4, and 5. In one sense, the crime is by its nature ulterior, since one must intend to do something more than simply 'agree': one must agree *intending to play a (future) part* in the plan; yet conspiracy obviously also has close affinities with the preparatory crimes of ulterior intent falling in categories 3 and 4: see text at n. 71 below.

[22] As in the case of wounding with intent to do grievous bodily harm (mentioned earlier), or assault with intent to rape.

[23] As in the case of unlawfully and maliciously administering poison with intent to annoy, contrary to the OAPA 1861, s. 24; see also the Taking of Hostages Act 1982, s. 1(1).

[24] See, e.g., the Computer Misuse Act 1990, s. 1 ('hacking'), and the Theft Act 1968, s. 9(1)(a) (burglary).

4. Doing something overtly innocent intending to commit a crime.[25]
5. Crimes where the intent is by its nature ulterior.[26]

I wish to focus on the ulterior intent crimes (hereinafter: 'UICs', for short) within category 1, although I will say something about those in categories 3, 4, and 5. I will call crimes within category 1 'crime-Crime' UICs, crimes within categories 3 and 4 'preparatory' UICs, and crimes within category 5 'natural' UICs. As we will see, far from seeking to cut back the number and scope of such crimes, Parliament might seek to make more use of them. Our explanation must start with the relationship between UICs and attempts to commit crimes.

REPRESENTATIVE LABELLING, ATTEMPTS, AND 'CRIME-CRIME' UICs

In his ground-breaking work on this area of the law, Peter Glazebrook put forward the startling suggestion that if more use were made of crimes of ulterior intent (although this was not the term he used), we could do without the law of attempts almost entirely.[27] His principal target is the notoriously vague and uncertain 'proximity' requirement, which defines the *actus reus* of an attempt. This is the requirement—in English law—that a defendant's conduct be 'more than merely preparatory' to the commission of the offence, or—under the US Model Penal Code—that the defendant have taken a 'substantial step' towards the commission of the crime.[28] The Legislature should instead seek painstakingly to prohibit all the specific kinds of conduct worthy of condemnation as criminal, when done with the intention to commit the crime. For example, instead of relying on a charge of attempted robbery,[29] one should seek to make separate crimes of the discrete kinds of conduct that one is really seeking to prohibit through the catch-all notion of an 'attempted' robbery, such as (say) being equipped with intent to rob, entering [part of] a building with intent to rob, and assault

---

[25] See n. 4 above for examples, or see the Theft Act 1968, s. 25 (possession of articles for housebreaking etc.). Examples so closely analogous to those within this category that they can be included here are cases where D does something overtly innocent intending to endanger life: see the Firearms Act 1968, s. 16 (possession of a firearm with intent to endanger life).

[26] Examples would be attempt, contrary to the Criminal Attempts Act 1981, s. 1; theft, contrary to the Theft Act 1968, s. 1 (where the intent permanently to deprive goes beyond the appropriation, except in a few contrived examples); blackmail, contrary to the Theft Act 1968, s. 21, and 'having' an obscene article, contrary to the Obscene Publications Act 1959, s. 2(1).

[27] See P. R. Glazebrook, 'Attempted Crime', n. 14 above.

[28] Criminal Attempts Act 1981, s. 1(1); Model Penal Code, § 5.01(1)(c). Glazebrook convincingly dates the 'proximity' requirement to the decision in *Eagleton* (1854–5) Dears 515, and argues that its introduction was a matter more of expediency than principle: see his 'Attempted Crime', n. 14 above, at 32–5.

[29] A charge that has proved seemingly arbitrary in its scope: see especially *Campbell* [1991] *Criminal LR* 268.

with intent to rob (all 'UICs', in modern terminology).[30] Such an approach
seeks to cut neatly through the seemingly intractable debate over how to
understand the proximity requirement, if one is not to deem *any* act to be an
attempt—whether proximate or not—when done with intent to commit a
crime.[31]

More than twenty years on, Glazebrook's suggestions have been given
contemporary significance by the recent decisions of the Court of Appeal
interpreting the version of the proximity requirement embodied in the
Criminal Attempts Act 1981, and by academic criticism of those decisions.[32]
I will not rehearse the detailed arguments Glazebrook put forward to support his own views, but will consider them as I defend my own position. I
will argue that there is an argument focussed on the value of 'representative
labelling'[33] that justifies both a law of criminal attempts *and* the separate
criminalization of certain limited kinds of UICs, namely those where the act
done—with intent to commit the crime—*itself* constitutes a kind of partial
success for the defendant in what she or he set out to do. Other kinds of
UICs require separate justification, as we will see.

Two crime-Crime UICs will serve as a focus for discussion: wounding
with intent to do grievous bodily harm, and assault with intent to rape.[34]
Historically, crimes of this type have given the law relating to non-fatal
offences against the person much richness in moral detail. None the less, in
the Law Commission's latest proposals for reform of this area of the law[35]
wounding with intent to do grievous bodily harm is to be abolished,
although no explanation is given for the abolition. The ground is instead to
be covered by the combined effect of three crimes in the Commission's draft
Criminal Law Bill: intentionally causing serious injury (clause 2), recklessly
causing serious injury (clause 3), and intentionally or recklessly causing
injury (clause 4). The enactment of these crimes will not, of course, make up
for the loss of wounding with intent to do grievous bodily harm; only the
enactment of a further (replacement) crime of committing a clause 4 crime
with intent to commit a clause 2 crime could, in part, do that. So why has
no such crime been proposed? Since there is no direct answer, the answer

[30] See also Glazebrook's discussion of attempted rape in his 'Attempted Crime', n. 14 above,
at 43; on this example, see the text below at n. 57. For further discussion of assault with intent
to rob, see the text below at n. 52.

[31] The latter—the older English—approach is criticized by Glazebrook, 'Attempted Crime',
n. 14 above, at 40. See most recently, Glanville Williams, 'Wrong Turnings on the Law of
Attempt' [1991] *Criminal LR* 416; K. J. M. Smith, 'Proximity in Attempt: Lord Lane's "Mid-
Way Course" ' [1991] *Criminal LR* 576.

[32] See K. J. M. Smith, n. 31 above. The wisdom of Smith's suggestion that guidelines be
drawn up to aid judges and juries, in relation to each offence, in deciding whether the conduct
in question was 'more than merely preparatory' to the commission of the offence itself, is
doubted by Glazebrook, 'Attempted Crime', n. 14 above, at 36.

[33] On this term, see the text at n. 44 below.

[34] On the origins and authority of the latter crime, see Smith and Hogan, n. 7 above, at
459–60.

[35] See n. 11 above.

must be gleaned from what the Commission says elsewhere about crime-Crime UICs based on assault. The Law Commission's Report is silent on the status of assault with intent to rape, which is surprising given the recent controversy surrounding the very existence of the crime.[36] In its earlier Consultation Paper, however, there is some discussion of a crime bearing a strong family resemblance, assault with intent to rob.[37] The Commission's discussion of the crime seeks to justify the making of no proposals at all with regard to it. Assault with intent to rob is said to be 'itself a robbery or an attempted robbery . . . and [hence] it is hard to think that the offence is not in effect redundant.'[38] It is the relationship between the law of attempts and crime-Crime UICs, such as assault with intent to rob, that the Commission here rightly identifies as the key issue in theoretical terms.

The important puzzle that arises in understanding this relationship is as follows. Assaults with intent to rape or rob, or woundings with intent to do grievous bodily harm, could be seen as nothing more than detailed examples of a more general criminal wrong, namely an *attempt* to rob, rape, or do grievous bodily harm. Needless to say, in general, attempts to rob, rape, or do grievous bodily harm would seem to cover a far greater range of courses of conduct than the highly specific crime-Crime UICs which exemplify such attempts. For example, the *actus reus* of an attempt to do grievous bodily harm to someone may be committed when D thrusts a knife at V, whether or not V is wounded by that act, and thus whether or not an offence contrary to section 18 of the 1861 Act is committed. So if one could always charge D with an attempt to commit rape, robbery, or grievous bodily harm when D had committed an assault with intent to rob or rape, or wounded with intent to do grievous bodily harm, these more particular crime-Crime UICs might well seem to be redundant, as the Law Commission claims.[39] In fact, there are important reasons why this claim is mistaken. In order to understand these reasons, it is necessary to consider aspects of the theoretical underpinnings of the law of attempts.

In order to be convicted of an attempt to commit a crime, one must be found to have done an act (with the intention of committing the offence) that was 'more than merely preparatory' to the commission of the crime in

---

[36] See S. Spencer, 'Assault with Intent to Rape—Dead or Alive?' [1986] *Criminal LR* 110.

[37] See Law Commission Consultation Paper No. 122, paras. 9.31–9.33. The existence of the crime of assault with intent to rob is acknowledged by statute in the Theft Act 1968, s. 8(2).

[38] N. 37 above. It is important to note that the Law Commission is unwittingly turning Glazebrook's argument on its head. The Commission argues that it is UICs that are made redundant by the existence of the law of criminal attempts, rather than (as Glazebrook argued) the other way around. Ironic though this is, it does suggest that it is now far too late in the day to be recommending the wholesale abolition of the law of criminal attempts. Criminal attempts have become an entrenched part of the criminal calendar.

[39] With the caveat, absurd as it might seem, that wounding with intent to do grievous bodily harm, contrary to the OAPA 1861, s. 18, carries a maximum sentence of life imprisonment, whereas an attempt to commit grievous bodily harm, contrary to s. 20 of the same Act, carries a maximum of 5 years' imprisonment.

question.[40] This means that an attempt to commit a crime only begins when 'the defendant embarks on the crime proper [or] the actual commission of the offence'.[41] The rationale of the proximity requirement has been said by Smith and Hogan, amongst others, to be the need or desire 'to prevent too great an extension of criminal liability, by excluding mere acts of preparation'.[42] Yet this rationale cannot be the whole story, since there are a large number of precursor offences, such as being in possession of an article for use in connection with a burglary,[43] focussed on merely preparatory conduct. A further, more direct argument for the proximity requirement is informed by the value attributed to 'representative labelling' in the criminal law.[44] The principle of 'representative labelling' requires, *inter alia*, that the crime for which the offender has been convicted properly reflect the nature and gravity of what she or he has actually done. The crime must fit the conduct (and vice versa), because conviction for a particular crime stands as an enduring feature of one's record, a testimony to the precise respect in which one failed in one's basic duties as a citizen.[45] As Antony Duff puts it, elsewhere in this volume: 'blame, at least in its second-person form, should . . . be understood as a participant activity of communication with the wrongdoer: a response to him, which expresses and seeks to communicate a moral understanding of what he has done.'[46] The proximity requirement safeguards this principle within the law of attempts, because it insists on a close connection between the conduct engaged in by the accused, and the (kind of) offence which she or he is alleged to have attempted.

Suppose that the proximity requirement were so wide that it included *any* conduct 'forming part of a series of acts which would constitute . . . actual commission of [a crime]'.[47] On this view, if D takes a hacksaw to a shotgun in order to shorten the barrels to an illegal length,[48] intending to use the gun as modified to kill V, D would at that moment be guilty both of an attempt

---

[40] Criminal Attempts Act 1981, s. 1.

[41] The words of Lord Lane CJ in *Gullefer* [1990] 1 WLR 1063 at 1066. See Glanville Williams' 'Wrong Turnings', and K. J. M. Smith's 'Proximity in Attempt', both n. 31 above.

[42] Smith and Hogan, n. 7 above, at 309.

[43] For a complete description of this crime, see Theft Act 1968, s. 25. Other examples of preparatory offences are found in the OAPA 1861, s. 64; Criminal Damage Act 1971, s. 3; Explosive Substances Act 1883; Firearms Act 1968, s. 16; Criminal Justice Act 1988, s. 139.

[44] On the importance of the representative labelling principle, see Andrew Ashworth, 'The Elasticity of *Mens Rea*', in C. F. H. Tapper (ed.), *Crime, Proof and Punishment* (London, 1981), 45 at 53. I try to explain this principle in more detail in my 'Rethinking non-Fatal Offences Against the Person' [1994] *Oxford Journal of Legal Studies* 335.

[45] See further Horder, 'Rethinking Non-Fatal Offences Against the Person', n. 44 above, at 338–9.

[46] 'Subjectivism, Objectivism and Criminal Attempts', this volume, 38. I would wish to add that, as a 'participant activity of communication', judgments of blameworthiness are communicated to the public as well as to the defendant.

[47] i.e., the 'Stephen test' of proximity: see Stephen's *Digest of the Criminal Law* (5th edn., London, 1894), art. 50, cited by K. J. M. Smith, 'Proximity in Attempt', n. 31 above, at 578. See also *Gullefer* [1990] 1 WLR 1063 at 1066.

[48] Contrary the the Firearms Act 1968, s. 6.

to shorten the barrels and of attempted murder; for picking up the hacksaw was an act forming part of a series of acts which would ultimately involve the commission both of the offence under the Firearms Act and of murder. It follows, on this view, that if someone were found guilty of (say) attempted murder, knowledge of this fact alone would as a matter of principle give one very little idea what that person might have done. He or she might have shot at or stabbed someone, but might instead have done no more than acquire a gun or knife, with intent to kill later. It is the big disparity between these possibilities, all nevertheless falling within the scope of attempted murder, that would compromise the principle of representative labelling. The law, however, excludes merely preparatory conduct from the scope of a criminal attempt. The defendant must have 'embarked on the crime proper [or] the *actual commission* of the offence'.[49] This makes it possible to insist on a much closer association between what defendants have actually done, and the (kind of) crime they are alleged to have attempted. In the example given, we can say that, whilst there is clearly an attempt illegally to shorten the barrels of a shotgun, there has so far been no more than mere preparation for the commission of murder. So saying ensures that the defendant will not be *mis*representatively labelled as someone who has attempted murder. For as Duff has argued, in relation to attempts:

If I try to injure another person, I relate myself as closely as I can to that harm . . . my intention to injure [the victim] and the steps I have actually taken towards that end, define my action as *essentially* injurious . . . [T]o call [an action] an attempt is . . . to emphasise its close relation to, as an incomplete version of . . . the paradigm of responsible [criminal] agency . . . the complete[d] offence.[50]

So far, so good. Now, although the distinction between someone who has 'embarked on the crime proper' and someone who is merely preparing to commit a crime is a qualitative distinction,[51] judgments of degree are in practice inevitably involved in the process of differentiation. If someone (D) stands outside my house, reaches for a knife when I emerge, waits for me to come near enough, raises the knife, and then strikes a blow aimed at killing me, a question of judgment and degree seems inevitably to enter into the process of deciding when D has actually embarked on the crime of attempted murder. In consequence, marking the differences between the point at which D is guilty of no more than a minor precursory offence,[52] the point at which D is guilty of (say) a psychic assault, and the point at which he or she becomes guilty of the very serious crime of attempted murder,

---

[49] My emphasis. See n. 47 above; *Gullefer* [1990] 1 WLR 1063.

[50] Duff's emphasis. The passage cited is from his *Intention, Agency and Criminal Liability* (Oxford, 1990), 202–3. Duff is more concerned with the 'ordinary' meaning of attempts here than with the principle of representative labelling, but what he says is of equal relevance to that principle.

[51] See further Duff, 'Criminal Attempts', n. 46 above, at 23.

[52] Such as the offence, mentioned above (n. 4), under the OAPA 1861, s. 64.

involves a significant element of judgment and degree in the hands of the jury. The inescapability of difficult questions of degree at the heart of the proximity requirement is a key factor in providing one justification for having some crimes of ulterior intent.

I pointed out at the start that whereas there is a crime of assault with intent to rape, and one of possessing a shotgun with intent to endanger life, there is no crime such as assault with intent to murder, or possessing a knife with intent to endanger life.[53] Such gaps in the law may have significant consequences in a case with facts such as those in the example just given. Suppose D is arrested while still waiting for me outside my house, and charged with attempted murder. Knowing of D's intent, jurors may be tempted to stretch the proximity requirement beyond its proper limits, because a conviction for attempted murder is all the law offers them, in the circumstances, to secure the representative labelling of the defendant as a would-be murderer. Yet, on these facts, a conviction for *attempted* murder would clearly conjure up a misleading picture that the defendant came much closer to killing me than he or she in fact did: it would be a case of mislabelling. It is just as true on these facts, though, that a conviction for nothing more than possession of an offensive weapon[54] would also misrepresentatively label the defendant, because it leaves out of account the criminal intention with which D's actions were done. Were there, for example, a crime-Crime UIC of possessing an offensive weapon—or (respecting some of D's later acts) of assault—*with intent to murder*, this would fill what would otherwise be the unacceptably large 'representative labelling' gap between one of the most serious offences against the person (attempted murder) and comparatively minor offences, like possessing offensive weapons or common assault. Conviction for attempted murder rather than for the minor offences may turn on nothing more than the question of degree inherent in the proximity requirement, despite the significant qualitative distinction between them in terms in what they represent as labels. The possibility of conviction for possessing an offensive weapon with intent to murder, or for assault with intent to murder, obviates the need for any such bending of the rules governing the proximity requirement, thus ensuring that the principle of representative labelling is not undermined as it applies to attempts. Moreover, conviction for such crime-Crime UICs of this sort is an exemplification of that principle in its own right, correctly labelling D as an offender bent on serious violence.[55]

The point can be further illustrated by reference to the existing crime-

---

[53] Although see the Prevention of Crime Act 1953, s. 1, dealing with possession of an offensive weapon in a public place.

[54] See n. 53 above.

[55] Cf. the maximum penalty for assault with intent to commit buggery of 10 years' imprisonment. Assault with intent to rob is punishable by up to a maximum of life imprisonment: see Theft Act 1968, s. 8(2).

Crime UIC of assault with intent to rape.[56] Consider the facts of *Kelly*.[57] In this case, the defendant dragged a woman off a road, and pulled her to the ground. He then kissed her, knelt astride her, and having threatened her with a metal bar, put his hand up her skirt. Before his assault could be taken further, however, the defendant was frightened into desisting by the voice of a passer-by calling out. Kelly was convicted of attempted rape. He appealed, *inter alia*, on the ground that the evidence was not sufficient to disclose an act amounting to embarkation on the crime 'proper', as required by *Gullefer*.[58] His claim on this point was robustly dismissed by the Court of Appeal, but a strict interpretation of *Gullefer* would suggest that the case is marginal. Here, of course, the 'crime proper'—the *actus reus* in rape—is vaginal penetration,[59] but at the time he desisted Kelly was still some way from achieving this. No doubt it was right to leave the question of proximity to the jury. Yet this meant that the defendant's conviction for a very serious sexual crime (rather than for mere sexual assault) depended, in the circumstances, on a highly elastic judgment of fact and degree in the jury's hands. What *is* clear, however, is that Kelly was guilty of a crime-Crime UIC at two points in his attack on the victim. When he dragged her from the road, he was almost certainly guilty (perhaps even under the present law) of assault with intent to rape, as he was—*a fortiori*—when he sat astride the victim and put his hand up her skirt. The crime of assault with intent to rape representatively labels the offender as a serious sexual offender, through its focus on the intention with which the defendant acted, without the need to face up to the intractable practical difficulties of the proximity requirement.

The case just made for crime-Crime UICs depends in part on there being some logical space, separate from that occupied by attempts, for such crimes to be committed: in circumstances where substantial doubt may exist over whether an attempt to commit the crime intended has begun. With some crime-Crime UICs, such as wounding with intent to do grievous bodily harm, it is less easy to see how such space might exist. For almost every plausible example of such a wounding must unequivocally be an attempt to do grievous bodily harm. In fact, however, there can be a justification for crime-Crime UICs even where is no doubt at all that the self-same conduct will amount to an attempt to commit the crime specifically intended. In order to understand this justification, more needs to be said about attempts and representative labelling. Other things being equal, if I take aim at and shoot Bill dead (as I intend to do), this is properly described as 'murdering' Bill but *not*

---

[56] What is said here would apply equally to the similar crime of assault with intent to commit buggery (in the Sexual Offences Act 1956, s. 16(1)), or to the crime of assault with intent to rob (Theft Act 1968, s. 8(2)), even if assault with intent to rape is not a crime.

[57] [1992] *Criminal LR* 181. See also Glazebrook's discussion of a similar example, 'Attempted Crimes', n. 14 above, at 43.

[58] [1990] 1 WLR 1063.   [59] Sexual Offences Act 1956, s. 44.

as 'attempting to murder' Bill, even though an attempt is intrinsic to the successful outcome. For the label 'murderer' is reserved for those who are successful in achieving what they set out to do, whereas labelling a crime as an attempt characteristically implies the failure of the endeavour.[60] As Duff explains, the distinction between success and failure is not merely analytical but moral:

> The actual outcomes of actions matter to us, in various ways . . . If the attempt fails . . . there is no (or at least less) room for . . . sorrow or sympathy, and no (or less) harm for which compensation can be required . . . If I have attacked you . . . I owe you an apology, even if you fortuitously suffer no material harm. If my hostile . . . action does cause you some material harm, I have more to apologise for: I have done a greater injury to your well-being.[61]

As it has moral significance, the difference between success and failure has implications for representative labelling. These implications go beyond the simple need to distinguish between labels for successful and labels for unsuccessful criminals. So the distinction must be examined in more detail.

The difference between what counts as a 'success' and what counts as a 'failure' is open to various interpretations.[62] For example, one can think of attempts as failures in both a narrow and a broad sense. In the narrow sense, the sense that is central to the law of criminal attempts set out in the Criminal Attempts Act 1981, an attempt is a failure if there is a mismatch between the actual outcome brought about and D's goal in trying. If I aim to shoot Bill dead, but end up causing him only grievous bodily harm, then my action was a failure, in this narrow sense. In a broader sense, though, my action *may* only have been a partial failure. I may often say of the outcome, 'well at least I managed to do him *some* injury', where doing the injury was no mere matter of moral luck but was done as part and parcel of what I set out to do, namely to kill the victim. In the broader sense, an attempt can be more than just a failure: it may be a partial success, or an almost complete success, even when the outcome the trier had in view does not come about.[63] It may be, thus, that the description of conduct merely as an 'attempt' conceals something of potential importance to representative labelling, namely harm done that constituted partial success in what D set out (ultimately unsuccessfully) to do.

---

[60] Cf. George Fletcher, *Rethinking the Criminal Law* (Boston, Mass., 1978), 131, cited by Smith and Hogan, *supra* n. 7, at 314.

[61] 'Criminal Attempts', n. 46 above, at 36–7.

[62] *Ibid.*, 41–2. Duff does not advert to the interpretation of the distinction discussed here.

[63] In a trivial sense, of course, whenever a defendant takes an unimpeded step towards the commission of the offence, such as buying the gun he intends to shoot at the victim, that step will count as 'partial success' in his enterprise. Whether or not there is a case for making such conduct in itself criminal (on which see the section 'Preparatory UICs', below), since such conduct is (as I have already argued) insufficiently proximate to amount to an attempt, it cannot be an example of an *attempt* that is also a partial success.

It might be said that, whilst the law of 'attempts' as governed by the Criminal Attempts Act 1981 is focally concerned with attempts as failures in the narrow sense, 'attempts' as failures in the broad sense—those which involve partial success—are often more properly the province of crime-Crime UICs such as wounding with intent to do grievous bodily harm. Care must be taken, though, in the drafting of such crimes, as the following example shows. Suppose D wrongfully administers a drug to V, in order swiftly and painlessly to kill V, to avert what is known to be the certain alternative: an agonizing 'natural' death due to an incurable illness. Tragically, and unknown to D, the drug is of the wrong sort for this purpose, and (to D's horror) simply prolongs and intensifies V's agony. Suppose that a prosecutor has a choice between charging D with attempted murder or with a hypothetical crime-Crime UIC of 'inflicting torture with intent to kill'. Which crime provides a more representative label? The answer seems unclear unless and until one has regard to what counts as success for D. Then the answer is clearly attempted murder. What D does, in inflicting torture upon V,[64] is done neither with intent to torture nor (more importantly) with intent to kill V; indeed, V's suffering frustrates D's intent. D intends to kill V, but not through torture. The hypothetical crime-Crime UIC thus risks misrepresenting the torture of V as partial success for D in his enterprise. So it is best to draft such crime-Crime UICs in such a way that it will be clear when the harm done constitutes a partial success. Had the hypothetical crime-Crime UIC consisted of 'inflicting torture with intent to kill *thereby*', then there could have been no doubt about the appropriateness of the attempted murder charge in these circumstances.[65]

This kind of analysis can be followed through when considering existing crime-Crime UICs. Suppose D_1 and D_2 try to to cause grievous bodily harm to V. D_1 thrusts a knife at V, but misses V entirely, whereas D_2 succeeds in wounding V, although neither succeeds in causing V grievous bodily harm. Both defendants are guilty of conduct sufficiently proximate to amount to an attempt to do grievous bodily harm to V. There is an argument for saying, however, that the principle of representative labelling would only be completely respected (putting issues of complicity on one side) by marking the fact that D_2 has been partially successful in his endeavour, given that he

---

[64] Or, perhaps more properly, in causing V to suffer torture.

[65] Another way of expressing the appropriate crime-Crime UIC might be 'intentionally torturing V with intent to kill', but this places insufficient weight upon the causal link between the act done and the intention in acting. Compare the offence under the Criminal Damage Act 1971, s. 1(2) of intentionally or recklessly damaging or destroying property, *thereby* intending life to be endangered, or *thereby* being reckless whether life is endangered. Here, arguably, the insistence on the causal link between the danger and the damage itself is an unnecessary restriction. If I drop a brick from a bridge through the window of a car, what should matter is that through the act which damaged the window I have intentionally or recklessly endangered life, whether or not the damage itself (breaking the glass) was what caused the danger: see further *Steer* [1987] 2 All ER 833, and the highly misleading discussion in Smith and Hogan, n. 7 above, at 706.

has deliberately inflicted a wound in pursuance of it, whereas D_1 has completely failed in that endeavour.[66] 'Wounding with intent to do grievous bodily harm' thus provides the right representative label for D_2's partial success (in the broad sense of attempt), given that D_2 has gone beyond mere preparation, just as 'attempt to do grievous bodily harm' likewise provides the right label for D_2's complete failure (in the narrow sense of attempt). For 'wounding with intent to do grievous bodily harm' marks the important fact that D_2's conduct actually brought about a harm to V of the same kind (broadly construed) as that intended, whereas D_1's did not; although given what was said above, the crime would be better drafted as 'wounding with intent to do grievous bodily harm *thereby*'.[67] So crime-Crime UICs such as wounding with intent to do grievous bodily harm supplement the law of attempts in a different, but no less important, way to crime-Crime UICs such as assault with intent to rape. Given that the proximity requirement is satisfied when D wounds V with intent to do grievous bodily harm, the justification for convicting D of this crime-Crime UIC is that it represents D's partial success in the (broad sense of the) attempt. Charges of 'attempt' under the Criminal Attempts Act 1981 are only absolutely necessary and appropriate, for representative labelling purposes, where D completely 'misses' in the attempt, or in (rare) cases where any harm done other than that intended will actually frustrate D's intent, as in the case above of the would-be mercy killer.

More is the pity, then, that by the enactment of the Criminal Law Act 1967 Parliament saw fit to repeal, rather than to reform and extend, those parts of section 38 of the Offences against the Person Act (OAPA) 1861 that had previously created the general ulterior intent offence of assault with intent to commit a felony. Section 38 could have been reformed and extended to create the following (not necessarily exclusive, and very roughly drafted) list of ulterior intent crimes:

(A) Any person who assaults or injures another with intent thereby to do serious harm or to murder another is guilty of a crime.

(B) Any person who threatens, assaults or injures another with intent to rape is guilty of a crime.

The presence of the qualifying 'thereby' in (A), and its absence in (B), signify the different functions that each proposed section is meant to perform.

---

[66] It is, of course, possible to wound someone with intent to do them grievous bodily harm, without the wounding itself being intended, although the wounding must be subjectively recklessly inflicted (but for a contrary view, see Brian McKenna, 'The Undefined Adverb in Criminal Statutes' [1966] *Criminal LR* 548, at 553–5). An example would be where V puts up his hand in self-defence as D aims a blow at V's body with a knife, with the result that V suffers a foreseen but unintended wound to the hand from D's knife, even though this deflects the blow intended to do grievous bodily harm.

[67] On the drafting of the existing offences under the OAPA 1861, see John Gardner, 'Rationality and the Rule of Law in Offences against the Person' (1994) 53 *Cambridge LJ* 502.

Whereas (A) aims to represent D's partial success in an attempt to inflict serious injury or to murder, (B) aims to fill the representative labelling gap that exists between simple threats, an assault or the causing of injury, and attempted rape.[68] Clearly not every crime by the commission of which someone might seek to kill, rape, or cause serious harm is mentioned in sections (A) and (B). One might, for example, threaten someone with an intent (thereby) to cause serious harm or to kill. For better or worse, though, it is now thought acceptable to include in legislation only those crimes which are (as one might put it) *characteristically* the means—harmful in themselves—by which one seeks to do, or following which one does, the greater wrong.[69] A justification for such restrictiveness may be that legislative attempts to anticipate and proscribe every means through which one might seek to further a criminal purpose run the risk of drawing within the law's 'net' conduct very far from that at the heart of the mischief. One way to respect the 'principle of parsimony' in the drafting of criminal statutes is to cut back on over-inclusiveness;[70] and one kind of over-inclusiveness stems from undue weight being given to hypothetical possibilities for engagement in criminal conduct whose likely manifestation in practice is unknown.

PREPARATORY UICs

English law is home to a number of offences where conduct purely preparatory to an offence, and not in itself criminal, may be turned into criminal wrongdoing when it is aimed at committing a specified crime or crimes. One example would be having anything in one's custody intending, without lawful excuse, to use it to damage or destroy another's property contrary to section 3 of the Criminal Damage Act 1971. 'Overt innocence' UICs cannot be justified in quite the same way as crime-Crime UICs, because whilst the *actus rei* are steps on the way to a recognized crime, they are not part and parcel of what are intended to be (in the broad sense, explained earlier) the

---

[68] Bearing in mind the earlier discussion (text at n. 51 above) one might want to add a further 'section' (C), combining elements of the offence of being in possession of an offensive weapon, contrary to s. 1 of the Prevention of Crime Act 1953, aggravated burglary contrary to the Theft Act 1968, s. 10, and possessing a shotgun with intent to endanger life, contrary to the Firearms Act 1968, s. 16:

> (C) Any person who without lawful authority or reasonable excuse, the proof whereof shall lie on him, has with him in any public place any weapon of offence with intent to kill, to endanger life or to rape is guilty of a crime.

Some aspects of such 'Preparatory UICs' are discussed in the final section.

[69] An analogy will be found in the definition of burglary, contrary to the Theft Act 1968, s. 9(1)(a), where not every conceivable criminal intent with which one might trespass in a building warrants a mention, even if there is a case for minor extensions (as with the intent to obtain by deception).

[70] For an illuminating discussion of various principles of criminal law, including the principle of parsimony and the principle of fair warning (mentioned below), see Andrew Ashworth's *Principles of Criminal Law* (Oxford, 1991), ch. 3.

successful outcomes themselves. For example, the *actus reus* of the offence just mentioned may be a very long way from partial success in, or even embarkation on, an attempt to commit criminal damage, unlike the *actus reus* of a wounding inflicted with intent to cause grievous bodily harm. Taking custody of the 'thing' is nothing more than a preparatory step on the way to committing criminal damage.

The existence of 'preparatory' UICs might be thought to bring most sharply into focus Smith and Hogan's question of how far back into what might be called a 'possible crime history' one can legitimately extend the reach of the criminal law.[71] In two (or more) party situations, the basis on which the parties' conspiracies and incitements to commit crimes are themselves criminalized is controversial, as such conduct is so far back in the possible crime history.[72] So, likewise, it would seem that the criminalization of the one party situation, where D does some purely preparatory act with intent to commit a crime, should also be controversial. For in all of these cases there seems to be a danger that the criminal law is in breach of the principle of parsimony, by enjoining with ruthless instrumentalist zeal any conduct that itself might be thought to increase the risk of criminal activity.[73] The apparent controversy may be much diminished, however, in some cases at least, by bearing in mind the point made right at the start of this essay about the normative implications of intention for conduct.

To engage in conduct with a (particular kind of) wrongful intention may make that conduct *ipso facto* unjustified.[74] What then matters for criminalization is that one has actually changed the normative character of one's conduct, which affects one's normative position, in acting with the relevant intent. For example, a doctor who performs an operation intending that it should kill the patient will be guilty of attempted murder, even if the selfsame operation could legitimately have been performed by a doctor who intended thereby to save the patient; for the normative character of the conduct changes with the agent's intention. Similarly, one's normative position may change *vis-à-vis* others, depending on one's intention: a man intending to endanger life with a shotgun in his possession may legitimately be dispossessed—using reasonable force if necessary—by another who has knowledge of that intent.[75] The criminalization of 'preparatory' UICs is justified in part by this change in the normative character of the relevant conduct when it is viewed in the light of the criminal intent; but there is more to the justification than this.

---

[71] For further reflections on the legitimate limits to the inculpatory power of subjectivism, see A. Duff's 'Criminal Attempts', n. 46 above, at 27–32.

[72] See I. Dennis, 'The Rationale of Criminal Conspiracy' (1977) 93 *Law Quarterly R* 39.

[73] See, generally, the contributions of Andrew Von Hirsch and Peter Alldridge in this volume.

[74] But see Paul Robinson, 'Competing Theories of Justification: Deeds v. Reasons', this volume. Contrast the position where recklessness or negligence is in issue. Here the unjustified character of conduct must be established separately, before any issue of the mental element can come into play.

Plain risky conduct, undertaken with no ulterior intent, may also change its normative character if and when the risk is of such a kind or degree that one is unjustified in posing it, intentionally or unintentionally. None the less, the criminalization of the posing of unjustified but unintended risks *per se*[76] is normally confined—outside the specific regulation of particular industries and the like—to cases where the conduct in question is generally known to involve a vivid danger of tragic consequences.[77] The reason for this is not simply respect for the principle of parsimony in criminalization. It is also because where the unintended posing of risks *per se* is in issue, the principle of fair warning[78] can only have been respected where the defendant can reasonably have anticipated that his conduct might involve criminal liability.[79] Whilst one may very well be posing an unjustified risk of injury or damage simply by running too fast down a street, to regard such conduct—without more—as *criminally* culpable threatens to offend against the fair warning principle.

This extra condition—that the risk be generally known to be palpable— is not necessarily satisfied where 'preparatory' UICs are concerned. Even if the intention to commit the wrongdoing in question is present there is, for example, clearly no palpable risk in simply agreeing on a course of criminal conduct or in being in possession of a 'thing', for the purposes respectively of section 1 of the Criminal Law Act 1977 and of section 3 of the Criminal Damage Act 1971. But the difference between such 'preparatory' UICs and cases of simple risk-posing is that the principle of fair warning is not in issue where the former are concerned, because the former are crimes of ulterior *criminal intent*. After all, if one intends to commit criminal damage with something in one's possession, another's knowing intervention to frustrate one's plans and the ensuing prospect of criminal prosecution can hardly come like a bolt from the blue. One may, drawing on the principle of parsimony, often object to individual 'preparatory' UICs on the grounds that they are futile (and perhaps this is so in the case of section 3 of the Criminal Damage Act 1971, or even in the cases of incitement and conspiracy), or because they put too much power in the hands of arresting and prosecuting

[75] I should not be taken to be implying that defensive force may *only* be used against an aggressor who *intends* wrongdoing. The point is merely that knowledge that an aggressor has such an intention is one—but only one—of the ways in which defensive force may be justified: see now Suzanne Uniacke, *Permissible Killing* (Cambridge, 1994).

[76] i.e. where harm has not ensued.

[77] For a recent example see, e.g., the Road Traffic Act 1988, s. 22A, as amended by the Road Traffic Act 1991, s. 6. For further discussion of the criminalization of endangerment, see my 'Varieties of Intention, Criminal Attempts and Endangerment' (1994) 14 *Legal Studies* 335 at 341–4.

[78] See n. 70 above.

[79] Again, it should be stressed that this very general 'fair warning' condition does not apply where operators in particular industries etc. should be aware of special risks attending their activities. It should be noted that the way in which I have interpreted the 'fair warning' principle is at variance with Ashworth's understanding: n. 70 above, at 64–6. For an analysis similar to mine, see Gardner, 'Offences against the Person', n. 67 above.

officials. But if these specific objections can be overcome,[80] there is not much
of a general case against such crimes based on the principle of fair warning.
If true, this is important, as it weakens one objection to using the creation of
'preparatory' UICs to resolve problems that have arisen in relation to 'natural' UICs.

THEFT, UICS, AND THE INDIVIDUATION OF NORMS

I have already dealt with one kind of 'natural' UIC within category 5, where
the intent is by its nature ulterior; namely, criminal attempt. But there are
other important kinds. Of these theft is the most important and topical
example. In this concluding section I will compare and contrast its definition
with that of burglary, in relation to a little-discussed problem encountered
in defining criminal offences. This problem might be called the problem of
the individuation of norms. Where trespass to property is concerned, it can
sometimes be difficult to identify the norm transgressed by the wrongdoer.
This is because one may commit a trespass for so many different purposes,
each of which changes the normative character of one's conduct in a different way. If one turns to the definition of burglary in sections 9 and 10 of the
Theft Act 1968, one finds the relevant norms individuated in a way that
identifies the relevant normative changes in the character of the trespasser's
conduct. As is well-known, burglary is divided into three species. One
species, set out in section 9(1)(a), creates a series of 'civil wrong' (category
3) UICs focused on entry as a trespasser with intent to commit certain
crimes. The second, in section 9(1)(b), creates a series of instances of 'constructive' burglary, where if whilst a trespasser one commits certain crimes
one becomes automatically guilty of burglary as well. The third species, set
out in section 10, creates the specially heinous crime of 'aggravated' burglary, where one commits a section 9 burglary whilst one has with one any
weapon or explosive. Whatever other problems of interpretation may arise
out of sections 9 and 10, about one thing there can be little complaint. The
wrongdoing involved in burglary is set out with admirable specificity, in that
the different norms transgressed are separately categorized into their three
separate types, with different sentencing maxima.

    As Glazebrook presciently anticipated, many of the problems attending
the definition of theft have stemmed from the fact that in 1968 the legislature tried to avoid having to set out the norms actually transgressed in a
theft, by creating an almost absurdly open-textured *actus reus*.[81] The result

---

[80] As, surely, they are in many cases: see, e.g., the Firearms Act 1968, s. 18 (having with one
a firearm or imitation firearm with intent to commit an indictable offence).

[81] 'Attempted Crime', n. 14 above, at 28 and 43–4. At 28, Glazebrook says, 's. 3(1) [of the
Theft Act 1968] states that "*any* assumption by a person of the rights of another amounts to
an appropriation." Since such assumption need have no legal effect on the rights of the owner,
there seems little, if any, room left for talk of an attempt to assume the rights of an owner.'

has been that judges are left (in effect) to define the scope of theft for themselves, leading inevitably to over-extension.[82] As we now know, one is guilty
of the *actus reus* of theft, not only where one takes possession of another's
property perfectly lawfully,[83] but where one merely touches or purports to
sell that property.[84] One answer to these difficulties may be to model the
definition of theft and related UICs on the definition of burglary, by more
clearly individuating and grading the relevant norms transgressed. Consider
the facts of *Morris*.[85] When D wrongfully switched the labels on the goods
intending to pay the lower price on the substituted label, it is contrary to
common sense to say that he had at that moment stolen the goods, and it is
contrary to principle to say that he had attempted to steal the goods (there
being no more than a merely preparatory act). None the less it is certainly
true that he was guilty of a trespass to goods with intent to steal or obtain
by deception. So here is a category 3—'civil wrong'—UIC which could be
expressly created to supplement (rather than fall under) the definition of
theft.

By creating a series of such UICs, theft itself could be defined to include
only 'central' cases, cases where D takes unauthorized *possession or control*
of another's property with the intention of wrongfully and permanently
depriving that other. The *actus reus* of attempted theft would accordingly be
confined to more than merely preparatory acts aimed at taking unauthorized
possession or control. Having said this, it would be tempting to seek to relo-
cate the problem of generalized definition, by creating an all-inclusive 'overt
innocence' (category 4) UIC based on the wording of section 3(1) of the
Theft Act 1968, namely 'assuming any of an owner's rights to property, with
intent wrongfully and permanently to deprive another of that property'.
Whilst this would not resolve questions such as whether the facts of *Pitham*
and *Hehl*[86] ought to fall within the scope of such a crime, at least the very
separate existence of the crime—and perhaps a lower maximum penalty
applying to it—would indicate that the wrong done is a different and (usually) less serious wrong than central cases of theft. Whatever one makes of
this suggestion, if it has proved possible and desirable to individuate the relevant norms in crimes such as burglary, blackmail, false accounting, computer misuse, and so on, then it ought to be possible to do this—through the
creation of new 'overt innocence' and 'civil wrong' UICs—in relation to the
crime of theft.[87]

[82] As noted by Nicola Lacey, Celia Wells, and Dirk Meure, *Reconstructing Criminal Law*
(London, 1990), 471.
[83] *Gomez* [1993] AC 442.
[84] See generally E. Griew, *The Theft Acts 1968 & 1978* (6th edn., London, 1990), paras.
2–65 to 2–95.
[85] [1984] AC 320.
[86] (1976) 65 Cr. App. R 45. Here D wrongfully offered V's goods for sale to a third party.
The mere offer was held to be itself capable of amounting to an 'appropriation' of V's property.
[87] For the historical basis of such an approach, see Glazebrook, 'Attempted Crime', n. 14
above, at 30–2.

CONCLUSION

It should by now be apparent that crimes of ulterior intent have deserved much more theoretical attention than they have received. For example, in seeking to justify them, but also to limit their scope, I have had to invoke a number of important principles underlying the criminal law, including those of representative labelling, of fair warning, and of parsimony in offence definition. Meanwhile, Parliament continues to rely heavily on such offences in its attempts to secure an ever-widening conception of 'public' order.[88] The need for further theoretical reflection on the nature of these crimes as wrongs, and on the justification for their criminalization, thus seems even more pressing.

---

[88] See, e.g., the Criminal Justice and Public Order Act 1994, s. 68(1), creating the offence of 'aggravated trespass' where a person:

> trespasses on land in the open air and, in relation to any lawful activity which persons are engaging in or are about to engage in on that or adjoining land in the open air, does there anything which is intended by him to have the effect –
> (a) of intimidating those persons or any of them so as to deter them . . .
> (b) of obstructing that activity, or
> (c) of disrupting that activity.

See also, in a very different context, the crime of intimidating witnesses, in s. 51(1).

8

Criminal Liability in a Medical Context: the Treatment of Good Intentions

Andrew Ashworth

When the criminal courts have to decide issues involving the conduct of medical practitioners, the general doctrines of the criminal law are sometimes subjected to considerable strain. The standard formulation of intention in criminal law texts consists of either acting in order to bring about the prohibited result or, if the actor's purpose is otherwise, acting with awareness that the result is virtually certain to follow.[1] Yet in *Gillick* v. *West Norfolk Area Health Authority*,[2] the House of Lords held that a doctor who gives contraceptive advice to a girl under 16 for clinical reasons, whilst realizing that this would facilitate acts of unlawful sexual intercourse, would lack the intention necessary for conviction of aiding and abetting unlawful sexual intercourse. The precise significance of the case is discussed below. But Lord Scarman's explanation, that 'the bona fide exercise by a doctor of his clinical judgment must be a complete negation of the guilty mind' required for criminal liability, seems at odds with the basic proposition that a person acts with intention as to a certain result if he or she knows that the result is virtually certain to follow. This raises the question whether the standard formulation merely describes a general approach, or should be stated subject to exceptions, or is simply wrong.

Another example may be found in the famous case of *Adams*,[3] where a doctor was accused of the murder of an elderly patient. He had administered large doses of heroin and morphia that proved fatal. The prosecution case was that Dr Adams intended to kill the patient in order to hasten his

---

[1] Law Commission No. 177, *A Criminal Code for England and Wales* (1989), vol. 1, cl. 18, as slightly re-drafted by Sir John Smith, 'A Note on Intention', [1990] *Criminal LR* 85.

[2] [1986] 1 AC 112. This was a civil action, in which the question of criminal liability arose incidentally.

[3] Unreported; extracts from the summing-up may be found in H. Palmer, 'Dr. Adams' Trial for Murder', [1957] *Criminal LR* 365, and Lord Devlin, *Easing the Passing* (London, 1985), 171–2.

inheritance, since he was a beneficiary under her will. The defence case was
that the drugs were administered in order to relieve pain. At the trial, Devlin
J directed the jury that it is just as much murder if a life is cut short by weeks
or months as when it is cut short by years. However, where a patient is in
severe pain, a doctor is entitled to do all that is proper and necessary to
relieve pain and suffering even if these measures may incidentally shorten life
by hours or even longer. The jury, having considered these and other points,
acquitted the defendant.

Whether this decision is regarded as turning on causation or on intention,
it appears difficult to reconcile with standard legal doctrine. The direction to
the jury contains a causal proposition that has been widely cited with
approval: causing death means accelerating death, and that can be done by
hours or even minutes. Yet that leads to the conclusion that Dr. Adams did
cause the death, unless a special medical exception to ordinary principles is
being relied upon.[4] An alternative interpretation of the *Adams* direction
might be to suggest a distinction between purposes and 'intended' side-
effects: Devlin J may have meant to suggest, not that the doctor had not
caused the patient's death, but rather that, if the doctor's purpose was to
relieve pain, he should not be held to have intended death even if he knew
for certain that his conduct would accelerate death. This requires considerable reconstruction of the judge's words: the argument would be that, so
long as doctors in these situations have a benevolent purpose, in terms of
acting 'in the patient's best interests', they should not be regarded as intending to accelerate the patient's death.[5] Yet this goes against the standard definition of intention. The decision in *Adams* cannot therefore be supported
on standard approaches to either causation or intention.

These brief descriptions of two examples should suffice at least to raise
doubts about the ability of standard criminal law doctrine to accommodate
medical interventions. But one might ask what this 'standard criminal law
doctrine' is—for, plainly, it is not the doctrine that the courts are invariably
applying. Thus one issue arising from these decisions is whether writers on
criminal law have tended to construct for themselves an artificially rigid
framework of basic concepts, perhaps assuming that conceptual consistency
is an overriding goal and therefore dismissing decisions such as *Gillick* and
Adams as aberrant, perhaps believing that 'rule of law' precepts such as the
principle of maximum certainty should always be accorded priority. John
Gardner and Heike Jung have complained about the 'passion for uniformity'

---

[4] Replying to a criticism from Glanville Williams in *The Sanctity of Life and the Criminal
Law* (London, 1957), 289–90, Lord Devlin went so far as to claim that 'proper medical treatment consequent upon illness or injury plays no part in legal causation; and to relieve the pains
of death is undoubtedly proper medical treatment': *Samples of Lawmaking* (London, 1960),
95. See generally I. M. Kennedy and A. Grubb, *Medical Law: Text and Material* (2nd edn.,
London, 1994), 1206.

[5] See the opinion of Lord Goff in *Airedale NHS Trust* v. *Bland* [1993] 1 All ER 821 at 868.

permeating much writing on criminal law.[6] Nicola Lacey has argued against the over-optimistic assumption 'that subtle distinctions of [moral] culpability can ever be captured in *invariant* conceptual distinctions embedded in concepts which have to be applied across a wide range of substantive offences and concepts.'[7] The courts, evidently, do not make this assumption, and in the decisions described above responded to the moral dilemmas by breaking away from what others assume to be the standard doctrine.

The purpose of this essay is to offer further analysis of two questions. First, how have English courts dealt with claims that certain conduct is justified on medical grounds? Secondly, how should the criminal law deal with such claims?

CONCEPTS OF RECKLESSNESS

When an offence is said to require *mens rea*, this usually indicates that it is committed if the defendant either intended to produce the prohibited consequence or was reckless as to causing that consequence. In practical terms this means that the prosecution need only prove recklessness in order to establish *mens rea*. There is no need here to dwell on the differences between the concepts of recklessness that are to be found in the criminal law—for example, advertent or 'subjective' recklessness as awareness of the risk,[8] inadvertent or 'objective' recklessness which includes unawareness of a risk that would have been obvious to a reasonable person,[9] and 'indifference' recklessness in terms of not caring whether or not the risk is present.[10] It is more relevant that the main formulations of recklessness seem to have one particular objective element in common: the risk should be an unjustified one. Thus the Model Penal Code defines recklessness in terms of 'the conscious taking of an unjustified risk'.[11] The Law Commission's Draft Criminal Code Bill defines a person as acting recklessly in relation to a result 'when he is aware of a risk that it will occur; and it is, in the circumstances known to him, unreasonable to take the risk'.[12] What is the function of the terms 'unjustified' and 'unreasonable'? In one of its early working papers the Law Commission offered this answer:

---

[6] J. Gardner and H. Jung, 'Making Sense of Mens Rea: Antony Duff's Account' (1991) 11 *Oxford Journal of Legal Studies* 559 at 562.

[7] N. Lacey, 'A Clear Concept of Intention—Elusive or Illusory?' (1993) 56 *Modern LR* 621 at 626.

[8] *Cunningham* [1957] 2 QB 396; for general discussion of recklessness, see A. Ashworth, *Principles of Criminal Law* (2nd edn., Oxford, 1995), 175–83.

[9] *Caldwell* [1982] AC 341.

[10] *Sheppard* [1981] AC 394, *Kimber* [1983] 1 WLR 1118, *Breckenridge* (1984) 79 Cr. App. R 244.

[11] § 2.02(2)(c).   [12] N. 1 above, cl. 18(c).

The operation of public transport, for example, is inevitably accompanied by risks of accident beyond the control of the operator, yet it is socially necessary that these risks be taken. Dangerous surgical operations must be carried out in the interests of the life and health of the patient, yet the taking of these risks is socially justifiable.[13]

These are plainly judgments of social value, in which 'the responsibility line is drawn according to an evaluation of the nature of the activity and the degree of the risk'.[14] English courts have rarely needed to make such evaluations because so few prosecutions have been brought in this type of case. For example, of the several disasters in recent years that have resulted in large-scale loss of life, only one has resulted in a prosecution for manslaughter, and that prosecution failed when the judge withdrew the case from the jury.[15] Neither in that case nor in any other have the social justifications for risk-taking by transport operators been judicially considered. But that does not mean that this element in the definition of recklessness has no impact: on the contrary, it might to some extent both reflect and reinforce the views of prosecutors and some others that offences against the person have little place in the response to transport 'accidents', which in turn may explain why so few prosecutions for serious offences are brought in this type of case, and why there is so little open discussion in legal contexts of these critical value judgments.[16]

Does the same apply to the medical cases? The Criminal Law Revision Committee referred to them specifically in its discussion of recklessness: '[e]ven where the person acting knows that there is a high probability that his act will cause death, it is not necessarily an unlawful act. He may be a surgeon acting in circumstances which make it reasonable to take even this grave risk.'[17] Cases of this kind are simply not prosecuted, and this is presumably because there was valid consent by the patient (or consent was unobtainable) and because it is not thought that there was any unreasonableness in the doctor taking even such a grave risk.[18] There are occasional prosecutions of doctors for manslaughter, but these tend to be cases where it is alleged that the wrong treatment was given or that the treatment was administered without proper care.[19] The focus of discussion in those cases is whether the defendant doctor's conduct was so far from accepted practice that it amounted to gross negligence or recklessness in law; the issue of social

[13] Law Commission, *Working Paper on the Mental Element in Crime* (Law Commission No. 31, 1970), 53.
[14] Cf. D. Galligan, 'Responsibility for Recklessness' (1978) 31 *Current Legal Problems* 55 at 70. Glanville Williams has made a similar point by stating that recklessness involves negligence: *Criminal Law: The General Part* (2nd edn., London, 1961), 58.
[15] *DPP* v. *P & O European Ferries Ltd* (1991) 93 Cr. App. R 73, and generally the discussion by Celia Wells, *Corporations and Criminal Responsibility* (Oxford, 1993).
[16] A. Norrie, *Crime, Reason and History* (London, 1993), 81.
[17] Criminal Law Revision Committee, 14th Report, *Offences against the Person* (1980), 8.
[18] Non-prosecution might be justified by reference to the *Code for Crown Prosecutors* (3rd edn., London, 1994), ch. 6.
[19] For a recent example, see *Adomako* [1995] 1 AC 171.

justification for taking risks with patients' lives tends not to arise (presumably because, had the treatment been carried out properly, it would have been legally justifiable). It might arise where, for example, a surgeon performed an operation on a patient who did not need it, in order to further research purposes.[20] If, however, a surgeon were to consult a lawyer before performing an operation on an unconscious patient that carried a distinct risk of the patient dying, whilst being the only or most promising way of saving the patient's life, the lawyer might reasonably advise that it is justifiable and lawful to take the risk.[21]

The result, therefore, is that the standard doctrines of recklessness in criminal law are capable of dealing with medical decisions taken on clinical grounds, without the need for a separate defence of 'medical necessity' or 'clinical justification'. However, only a small proportion of these medical cases would raise questions of recklessness, as distinct from intention. The case must be one in which there is either no valid consent or no intention to cause the relevant injury to the patient: it must be a case in which there is an incidental risk (say) of death, but where such a result is not foreseen as virtually certain to follow.[22] In those circumstances, questions of justification and reasonableness are encompassed within the concepts of recklessness.[23]

THE DEFINITION OF INTENTION

In the opening paragraph it was stated that the standard definition of intention in criminal law includes both purpose and what we might call, for brevity, 'foresight of virtual certainty'.[24] It is therefore no excuse for the defendant charged with causing Y to say that his purpose in behaving thus was only to do X: if he realized that, by doing X, he was also virtually certain to bring about Y, he is deemed to have intended Y. This is the test established by *Nedrick*:[25] thus if a defendant who knowingly caused a certain result seeks exculpation, this may only be found if one of the defences to criminal liability can be invoked. There is no evaluative element in the

---

[20] P. D. G. Skegg, *Law, Ethics and Medicine* (Oxford, 1984), 127.

[21] This would, of course, be in substance a prediction of the view that a court might be expected to take. Since the question of reasonableness or justifiability implies an objective standard, neither the doctor's own view nor an individual lawyer's opinion could be determinative (for discussion of reliance on a lawyer's advice, see Ashworth, n. 8 above, at 233–7). In court, the matter would be one for the jury, provided that the judge thought there was sufficient evidence that the risk might be regarded as unreasonable.

[22] This assumes death followed by a murder charge. If the prosecution is for a non-fatal offence, such as wounding with intent, the argument would have to be adjusted.

[23] The Court of Appeal could have used this mode of analysis in the reckless driving case of *Renouf*, but instead relied on the justification of prevention of crime: see the report and commentary at [1986] *Criminal LR* 408.

[24] *Nedrick* [1986] 1 WLR 1025, and Law Commission, n. 1 above, vol. 2, para. 8.14.

[25] [1986] 1 WLR 1025.

concept of intention. In this respect, it is narrower, functionally speaking, than concepts of recklessness: we have just seen that conduct is not reckless if it is deemed to be socially justified.

In contrast to this stand the various decisions in which judges have propounded much wider or much narrower definitions. The decision of the House of Lords in *Hyam*[26] is well known for its wide definition of intention, which included some cases of foresight of mere probability, and yet in his speech Lord Hailsham stated that a doctor who wounds a patient by 'opening him up' would not be guilty of an offence because he would not have the required intent.[27] At face value this seems extraordinary: was Lord Hailsham claiming that the doctor cut the patient open by accident? A more likely explanation is that Lord Hailsham was equating the legal concept of intention with the vaguer moral term 'guilty mind', and assumed that because the doctor ought to be exculpated the best or only way of ensuring this would be to say that there was no intention.[28] This seems similar to the statement of Lord Scarman in *Gillick*[29] that 'the bona fide exercise by a doctor of his clinical judgement must be a complete negation of the guilty mind which is an essential ingredient' of a criminal offence. Both these judicial statements import into the concept of intention an evaluative element which finds no place at all in the standard doctrine.

Another case which may demonstrate the courts' occasional narrowing of the concept of intention is *Steane*,[30] where the Court of Criminal Appeal quashed the defendant's conviction under wartime regulations for the offence of doing acts likely to assist the enemy with intent to assist the enemy. The Court held that if the act was as consistent with an innocent intent (such as saving his family from a concentration camp) as with a criminal intent, the jury should be left to decide the matter. There are three grounds on which this case may be distinguished from the two just cited: first, the offence here was one of ulterior intent; secondly, it is arguable on the facts that not only did Steane not wish to assist the enemy, but he also may not have thought it virtually certain that his actions would assist the enemy; and thirdly, there was the basis for a defence of duress. However, the terms of the Court's judgment suggest that none of these distinctions was relied upon, and that the Court, in its evident haste to quash the conviction, took the view that Steane's intention to save his family might negative an intention to assist the enemy. This is inconsistent with the standard doctrine, according to which it would be perfectly possible to act with the purpose of saving one's family whilst also realizing that the enemy is virtually certain to be assisted by those acts, or even to act with the purpose of saving one's family by means of assisting the enemy.

---

[26] [1975] AC 55.   [27] *Ibid.*, 77.
[28] A similar approach may be found in the decision of the House of Lords in *Kingston* [1995] 2 AC 355.
[29] N. 2 above, at 190.   [30] [1947] KB 997.

One might argue that these three cases undermine the standard definition. Further examples might also be suggested—for instance, much of the judicial talk in the leading decisions[31] about the 'ordinary meaning' of intention and then about 'inferring' intention from foresight of virtual certainty may be designed to leave juries with the opportunity to infiltrate some social judgments into their determination.[32] The academic criticism of this approach has been strongly worded.[33] Some writers would prefer to classify the three cases as ones of intention, thereby preserving a consistent usage of the concept, and to construct a defence to exculpate the doctor in circumstances such as arose in *Gillick*. Sir John Smith, indeed, commented that the decision of the House of Lords in *Gillick* gave effect to a 'concealed defence of necessity'.[34]

We have already established that the 'standard' definition of intent is not the one adopted invariably by the courts: it may therefore be wrong to describe it as standard. A separate argument is that it is insupportable in principle, being a distortion of the proper meaning of intent. This argument has three steps.[35] First, the true meaning of intention is purpose. One intends to do those things that it is one's purpose to do. But purpose here does not refer to the ultimate objective of the conduct: it refers to whether one has chosen to produce the prohibited consequence. One may choose to produce it either as an end in itself or as a means to an end. Thus the death of another person is intended if it is chosen as an end in itself, or chosen as a means to some different end. In the wounding example given in *Hyam* the surgeon surely chose to cause the consequence as a means to a further end (i.e., restoring the patient's health). It would certainly be fallacious to argue that, because a surgeon's purpose is to restore the patient's health, it is not also her purpose to create wounds by making incisions—that would only be true if it were impossible to act with two purposes in mind, which it is not.[36] The true description is that the surgeon intended to wound the patient in order to restore health: the wound was intended as a means to an end. The situation in *Gillick* is probably closer to *Steane* than to the example from *Hyam*: rather than saying that doctors intend to assist unlawful sexual intercourse in order to preserve the patients' health, it might be more accurate to say that doctors appreciate that in preserving their young patients' health it is

---

[31] *Moloney* [1985] AC 905, *Hancock and Shankland* [1986] AC 455, and *Nedrick* [1986] 1 WLR 1025.

[32] See Lacey, n. 7 above, at 628–36; Norrie, n. 16 above, at 37–47; also nn. 46–8 below and text thereat.

[33] e.g., J. C. Smith and B. Hogan, *Criminal Law* (7th edn., London, 1992) and G. Williams, 'Oblique Intention' [1987] *Cambridge LJ* 417 at 431.

[34] J. C. Smith, *Justification and Excuse in Criminal Law* (London, 1989), 61–70.

[35] Broadly following John Finnis, 'Intention and Side-Effects' in R. G. Frey and C. W. Morris (eds.), *Liability and Responsibility* (St. Paul, Minn., 1991), 32.

[36] A. K. W. Halpin, 'Intended Consequences and Unintended Fallacies' (1987) 7 *Oxford Journal of Legal Studies* 104 at 110.

virtually certain that their acts will have the effect of encouraging the commission of an offence.

This brings us to the second step: it follows from the above that those
cases in which a person acts with another purpose, foreseeing that it is virtually certain that the prohibited consequence will be a side-effect of the
action, fall outside the proper meaning of intent. In these cases the consequence is not chosen either as a means or as an end, and so it is not
intended.[37] If by some remote chance the defendant had achieved the purpose without causing the side-effect of death, he or she would regard this as
a success, not a failure.[38] Thirdly, this does not, however, lead to the conclusion that cases in which death is known to be a virtual certainty should
be excluded from the definition of murder. It merely argues that they should
not be classified as cases where the defendant intended to kill. It might well
be justifiable to classify them as cases of murder rather than manslaughter,
but that should be accomplished by different means than labelling them,
inaccurately, as intended killings.

Now it might be contended that this counter-argument achieves nothing
significant. It avoids the philosophical *faux pas* of maintaining that one
intends every consequence of one's action that one foresees as virtually certain.[39] It also avoids saying that a person who realizes that conduct is virtually certain to cause death has chosen to kill, and that may be important for
those who hold to the view that it is never right to choose to take life.[40] Yet
it does not deny that a person may properly be held responsible for results
that are the side-effects, rather than the purpose, of given conduct. Indeed,
it can be said that the actor brings about those side-effects intentionally—
which is somewhat different from saying that the actor intended to bring
them about. As Anthony Duff argues:

the persisting confusion over whether intention should in law encompass an action's
morally certain side-effects reflects a failure to distinguish these two aspects of intention. . . . The concept of intention both does and does not encompass such side-
effects: it does, in that they are brought about intentionally; it does not, in that the
agent does not act with the intention of bringing them about.[41]

---

[37] For discussion, see A. P. Simester's essay in this volume.
[38] R. A. Duff, *Intention, Agency and Criminal Liability* (Oxford, 1990), ch. 3. It is true to
say that a person who acted with the purpose of achieving X but knowing that Y would be a
necessary means to X would also regard it as a success rather than a failure if by some miracle
X occurred without Y. However, in the first step X and Y are regarded by the actor as insepa-
rable, whereas in this second step Y is merely regarded as virtually certain: Glanville Williams
regards the distinction as too slight to be morally relevant or legally serviceable, but this is
surely debatable.
[39] See, further, Duff, *ibid.*, 74–82, and Finnis, n. 35 above, at 46.
[40] Finnis argues that 'the moral requirement that one never choose—intend—to destroy,
damage or impede any—instantiation of a basic human good' (*ibid.*, 56); cf. Simester's essay in
this volume.
[41] Duff, n. 38 above, at 80.

The target of his criticism is those who claim that 'ordinary language' treats virtually certain consequences as intended. He argues that in ordinary language such consequences are produced intentionally but are not intended. Yet he accepts that, generally speaking, it is right to hold a person responsible for those intentionally produced side-effects.[42] He also seems content with the further step that the degree of that responsibility is better assimilated to intention than to recklessness, in the law's terms.

The standard approach has been defended vigorously by Glanville Williams. He criticizes philosophers such as Duff and Finnis on the ground that:

they mix up the ordinary meaning of the word 'intention' with its desirable legal meaning. To be sure, the meaning of intention as a technical term of the law ought to be close to the literary and popular one, but there are sound reasons for saying that the two should not always be identical.[43]

Whilst the courts veer between 'ordinary language' and other meanings of intention that happen to reflect a moral distinction,[44] encouraged by the seductive similarity between intending to do X and doing X intentionally, Williams and other supporters of the standard view insist that intention in criminal law should encompass both cases of purpose and cases of foresight of virtual certainty. The assumption is that all cases of foresight of virtual certainty are properly placed (for legal purposes) in the same category of culpability as cases of intent.[45] This appears to have been the view of Jeremy Bentham, when he coined the phrase 'oblique intent' to encompass these cases of foresight.[46]

The broader approach to intention endorsed by Williams is challenged by decisions like *Gillick*,[47] which maintain that there are cases in which a person foresees a side-effect as virtually certain and yet should not be held to have intended it. This alternative analysis is intended to exclude from the definition of intention certain 'worthy' cases, but would also have the effect of excluding the person who places a bomb on an aircraft, timed to explode in mid-air, with the purpose of claiming the insurance money on the cargo; and the person who sets fire to another's house, knowing that this is virtually certain to cause death or serious injury to the occupants, but with the purpose of frightening the occupants away from the area. These cases, falling outside a narrow concept of intention, would presumably fall into the category of reckless killings.

---

[42] *Ibid.*, 82–7.   [43] Williams, n. 33 above, at 417.

[44] See Lacey, n. 7 above.

[45] See Williams, n. 33 above, though he does not argue the point out fully. Note the formulation of this proposition in my text: holders of the standard view need not maintain that cases of foresight of virtual certainty are necessarily as culpable as cases of purpose.

[46] J. Bentham, *Introduction to the Principles of Morals and Legislation* (1781; Buffalo, N.Y., 1988) ch. VIII, para. 6; though Bentham included cases where the consequence was known to be 'likely to ensue' rather than virtually certain to ensue.

[47] [1986] 1 AC 112.

Rather than commit themselves to one view or the other, however, the judges seem to have shifted between narrower and broader meanings of intention in order to distinguish between those with 'worthy' and those with 'unworthy' motives. The narrower approach to 'intention' found in cases such as *Gillick, Steane,* and the *Hyam* example was absent in *Smith,*[48] where the defendant's purpose in offering a bribe was to expose the corruptibility of a certain official: he intended to offer the bribe, but only as a means of trapping the recipient. The Court of Criminal Appeal upheld his conviction and held that his motive was legally irrelevant. Similarly in *Chandler,*[49] the defendants' purpose in trying to occupy a nuclear base was to warn of the dangers of nuclear war and not to act 'for a purpose prejudicial to the safety or interests of the State'. However the House of Lords upheld their convictions and regarded their motives as legally irrelevant. These two decisions show the courts adopting a broader definition of intention which excludes consideration of ulterior motives, in contrast to the narrower definition in the medical cases. There are further examples of conflicting approaches. In *Clarke,*[50] a person charged with aiding and abetting burglary argued that he participated in the offence merely in order to frustrate it. The Court of Appeal, whilst incanting the phrase 'motive is indeed irrelevant' to liability, quashed the conviction. It is probable, but not certain, that its decision was based on the recognition of a new defence rather than a narrow definition of intention. The decision was not cited in *Yip Chiu-Cheung,*[51] where the Privy Council held that an undercover agent who entered into an agreement to carry heroin out of Hong Kong, aiming to expose a drug-smuggling ring, should be convicted of conspiracy on the basis that he intended to assist in the commission of the offence:

It was urged upon their Lordships that no moral guilt attached to the undercover agent who was at all times acting courageously and with the best of motives in attempting to infiltrate and to bring to justice a gang of criminal drug dealers. In these circumstances it was argued that it would be wrong to treat the agent as having any criminal intent.[52]

The Privy Council found itself unable to accept this argument, declaring that the defendant 'intended to export the heroin'. Lord Griffiths presented this as if it were merely a finding of fact, ignoring the possibilities of defining intention narrowly or widely or of recognizing a defence.[53] Thus it has been chiefly in the medical cases that the courts have explored these possibilities.

To summarize, in this discussion we have encountered two alternative ways of holding that medical practitioners are not liable for acts done for clinical reasons. (1) The standard approach is to define intention broadly, so as to include both purpose and foresight of virtual certainty. Such a

---

[48] [1960] 2 QB 423.   [49] [1964] AC 763.   [50] (1984) 80 Cr. App. R 344.
[51] (1994) 99 Cr. App. R 406.   [52] *Ibid.,* 409.
[53] See further the discussion of the Law Commission, n. 1 above, vol. 2, paras. 9.33–9.35.

definition leaves little room for any evaluative element, and would (if applied conscientiously by the courts) make it necessary to create a new defence if the medical cases were to result in exculpation. We have noted criticisms of the standard approach, notably that it distorts the proper meaning of intention, but arguments in its favour (including the values of clarity and consistency) have also been canvassed. (2) The courts have adopted a less stringent approach, leading them occasionally to define intention narrowly so as to exclude certain cases from its ambit in an attempt to reflect the moral distinctions relevant to these cases. In effect this provides a concealed defence, but one that can be controlled tightly by the courts, accepting some purposes as legitimate and others as illegitimate. This technique might be claimed to reflect views of moral culpability without creating the danger that false or meritless defences might succeed. Against it are its apparently discretionary nature, in that there is no clear or predictable ground of exculpation upon which individuals can rely in order to guide their conduct, and its failure directly to confront the issue of justification.

The application of these two approaches may be tested against an example put by Sir John Smith:[54]

Take the case of a miner who is trapped by his arm in a roof fall and is unconscious. There being no other way of getting him out before a further roof fall kills him, a doctor amputates his arm. To cut off a perfectly healthy arm looks like grievous bodily harm; and there is absolutely no doubt that it is intentional.[55]

On the first, 'standard' approach this would amount to causing grievous bodily harm with intent, and exculpation could only be achieved by creating a defence based on necessity. The second approach, flexible as ever, could deal with it covertly by holding that the doctor's purpose was to save life rather than to cause grievous bodily harm.[56]

Finally, brief mention may be made of a third approach which the courts appear not to have exploited here, although they might have done. This fastens upon 'unlawfulness' as an element of offences against the person. In a line of cases in which charges have been defended on grounds of a mistaken belief as to the need for self-defence,[57] the courts have held that a requirement of unlawfulness is to be implied into all offences of violence. From this

[54] J. C. Smith, n. 1 above, adapting Law Reform Commission of Canada, Report 31, *Recodifying Criminal Law* (Ottawa, 1987), cl. 2(4).

[55] N. 1 above, at 90. Smith also cites another medical example put by Lord Goff in the course of a House of Lords debate, but that example, as Smith observes, is truly one of recklessness not intention.

[56] Smith, *ibid.* proposes a reformulation which would include as intention not only cases where the person's purpose was to cause the result, but also cases where 'his purpose is to cause some other result and he knows that, if he succeeds, his act will, in the ordinary course of events, cause that result'. It seems that, contrary to Smith's assumption, this would not preclude the conviction of the doctor in his example for causing grievous bodily harm with intent.

[57] e.g., *Gladstone Williams* (1984) 78 Cr. App. R 276, *Beckford v. R.* [1988] AC 130; cf., however, *Albert v. Lavin* (1981) 72 Cr. App. R 178.

they have inferred that a person lacks the intention required for the offence if he or she intends only to use *lawful* violence, believing that there is a justification for using force. This approach is open to objections which cannot be explored here.[58] However, in so far as the courts seem prepared to adopt this approach, they might extend it to medical cases by arguing that a doctor who cuts open a patient for what are believed to be good clinical reasons—as, for example, in Sir John Smith's hypothetical case—does not intend to wound *unlawfully*.

THE CASE FOR A NEW DEFENCE

Much of the argument so far has been concerned to show that there are cases in which exculpation is thought appropriate but in which the courts have adopted doctrinally confusing ways of achieving it. There is no doubt that the issues of medical law and medical ethics raised by these cases are often complex, and that the criminal law is not always the place for legislative guidance on resolving them. However, many cases inevitably raise questions of criminal liability, either directly or incidentally, and an acceptable way of answering them should be found. Would the recognition of a defence to criminal liability be more honest? How might it be formulated? Would it bring more disadvantages than advantages?

Let us begin by rehearsing the reasons in favour of a discrete defence. There are surely circumstances in which a doctor prescribing a course of treatment or performing an operation which is thought necessary on clinical grounds, but which either involves or may cause a wound or the acceleration of death, should have at least the possibility of exculpation from criminal liability. All that English law can now offer is a smattering of dicta to the effect that the surgeon does not have a 'guilty mind', which is loose talk (although it recognizes the problem); some decisions suggesting that the surgeon does not intend to wound the patient with the scalpel because she or he intends to restore the patient to good health, which is a fallacy since the former is intended as a means to the latter; and a body of doctrine and dicta to the effect that a surgeon who knowingly takes a risk of death or injury when carrying out an operation would not be regarded as 'reckless' because and in so far as the risk is a justifiable one to take. This last point forms part of the standard doctrine, but (as we have seen) it does not take us far, since many of the medical cases involve conduct which is intended or known to be virtually certain to cause injury or accelerate death, not merely cases in which this is a risk.

The issue here is one of social justification, not one of *mens rea* narrowly

[58] See A. P. Simester, 'Mistakes in Defence' (1992) 12 *Oxford Journal of Legal Studies* 295; R. H. S. Tur, 'Subjectivism and Objectivism: Towards a Synthesis' in S. Shute, J. Gardner, and J. Horder (eds.), *Action and Value in Criminal Law* (Oxford, 1993), 213.

conceived. The essence of the claim is that the doctor's conduct is justifiable in the circumstances. The courts have striven to reflect the distinction between doctors and other actors by adapting the boundaries of the concept of intention. It can be said that, in doing so, they have placed sensitivity to the moral issues above the goal of consistency in criminal law concepts.[59] However, there is no need to sacrifice conceptual consistency in this way. The courts should abandon the piecemeal and disruptive approach of reinterpreting basic concepts such as intention so as to accommodate these cases: they should instead be brought within a defence. Might one of the existing justificatory defences be appropriate? One of the few decisions that appear to accept this is *Bourne*,[60] where MacNaghten J directed a jury that an obstetrician who performed an abortion on a girl of 14, pregnant as a result of rape, should be acquitted if he acted in good faith and in order to preserve the health and sanity of the mother ('the continuance of the pregnancy [would] make the mother a physical and mental wreck'). The closest kinship of such a defence would seem to be with necessity, in that it embodies the argument that in the situation facing the defendant it was right to act in that way. Of course it is not strictly true to say that action in these circumstances is 'necessary', without more. The implication is that it is necessary in order to preserve some higher value—the defendant's life (inasmuch as cases of self-defence are treated as a species of necessity), or the life of someone threatening suicide (termed 'duress of circumstances' in *Martin*[61]), or the life of someone threatened by an accidental danger he or she has not recognized (the person who sees someone crossing a road and pulls the other out of the path of an oncoming car[62]). In all these cases the necessity is contingent, since the person could simply do nothing and wait for the death to occur. The governing principle is that it is justifiable in such circumstances for a person to use force that would otherwise be a crime, in order to preserve human life. It is a 'balance of evils' test, which can also be applied in cases where the threatened interest is something less serious than human life.

The Model Penal Code contains a general 'balance of evils' defence in section 3.02: the section does little more than announce the defence, and the Commentary accepts that 'deep disagreements are bound to exist over some moral issues, such as the extent to which values are absolute or relative and how far desirable ends may justify otherwise offensive means'.[63] Whilst there may be good reasons for having such a residual provision in the criminal law, there is also a strong case for creating more specific heads of justification to deal with discrete types of case. The law should do its best to give fair warning to doctors, and the presence of a distinct defence, even if it

---

[59] See the quotations from Gardner and Jung and from Lacey, above in text at nn. 6 and 7.
[60] [1939] 1 KB 687.   [61] [1989] 1 All ER 652.
[62] An example given by Lord Goff in *Re F (Mental Patient: Sterilisation)* [1990] 2 AC 1 at 74.
[63] Model Penal Code, § 3.02, commentaries (1981), vol. I, 17.

turns on an open-textured concept such as reasonableness, would give an assurance that the particular problems of medical cases (in which wounds, characteristically, are inflicted deliberately but in order to achieve some greater goal) are recognized authoritatively and not merely dependent on the willingness of the courts to adapt concepts such as intention.

The Structure of a New Defence

How should we approach the creation of a specific defence? A number of models offer themselves,[64] but the discussion here will focus on the main issues that need to be resolved. Six points will be raised for discussion.

SHOULD THE DEFENCE BE RESTRICTED TO DOCTORS?

Criminal codes derived from Sir James Fitzjames Stephen's draft tend to allow the defence to any person. One reason for restricting the defence to doctors, or to 'a doctor or medical professional or a person acting at the direction of such a doctor or professional',[65] might be that this enables the court to insist on higher standards when applying the defence. However, a defence that includes a term such as 'reasonable' will allow courts to apply the standard flexibly according to the qualifications and responsibilities (if any) of the defendant, and also to allow greater latitude in emergency situations. Thus in dealing with a case arising from a situation such as that of the amputation of a trapped miner's arm, in the example given by Sir John Smith,[66] there is no reason why non-medics should be excluded from the defence. The value of a 'reasonableness' standard is further discussed below.

SHOULD THE DEFENCE BE RESTRICTED TO SURGICAL OPERATIONS?

The Stephen-derived codes refer only to 'a surgical operation', whereas the Robinson draft extends to 'administering treatment'. It is surely inappropriate to restrict the defence to surgical operations, since there is now a wide range of medical interventions, including the use of drugs. The facts of the *Gillick* and *Adams* cases, set out in the opening paragraphs of this essay, demonstrate how the issue can arise outside the field of surgery. A more difficult question is whether the defence should extend to non-treatment, such as a doctor's decision not to treat a particular medical condition. The availability of drugs means that a doctor may often be able to postpone death by

---

[64] e.g., s. 45 of the Criminal Code of Canada; ss. 61 and 61A of the Crimes Act 1961 (New Zealand); and, for a model defence proposed as a supplement to the Model Penal Code in the United States, see Paul H. Robinson, *Criminal Law Defenses* (St. Paul, Minn., 1984), vol. 2, 173.

[65] Robinson, *ibid.*, 173.   [66] Above in text at n. 54.

prescribing certain treatment: if it is alleged that the doctor murdered the patient by failing to prescribe a certain drug, should this defence be available? This issue takes us into the realms of euthanasia, and ranges too far beyond the scope of this essay. The question whether the law should provide a defence in such cases should perhaps be kept separate.

WHAT SHOULD BE THE ROLE OF CONSENT?

In principle, any surgical operation or medical treatment should only be permitted if the patient consents. To deal with cases where the patient is unable to consent, for example because of unconsciousness or infancy, the law should incorporate a reference to the consent of a person entitled and able to consent on the patient's behalf, as does section 61A of the Crimes Act 1961 (New Zealand). However, there should also be some provision for cases such as a trapped miner who is unconscious and in respect of whom a decision needs to be made immediately. This might be covered by a general standard of reasonableness, as it is in section 61 of the Crimes Act (New Zealand); but it is essential that the principle of self-determination is preserved by insisting on consent where possible.

SHOULD THE DEFENCE INCORPORATE A REFERENCE TO NECESSITY?

If there is consent, it would seem pointless to insist that the treatment be necessary, but it is right to require that it be for a lawful purpose. Cosmetic surgery, for example, may involve the infliction of a wound but it seems that there can be valid consent to that, in so far as the purpose may be deemed lawful.[67] However, there is a range of cases in which consent is not relevant—not simply the trapped miner who is unconscious, but also a case like *Gillick* where a girl of 15 could not give valid consent to unlawful sexual intercourse. Whether necessity is the most appropriate tool with which to segregate these cases may be debated: the question in *Gillick* was one of clinical judgment in order to prevent an unwanted pregnancy, a judgment that might be encompassed within a broad test of the balance of evils.

'REASONABLENESS': THE PIVOTAL CONCEPT?

It seems hard to avoid incorporating the standard of reasonableness within a defence of this kind, as in defences of justifiable force more generally. In many cases, therefore, the key issue would be whether it was 'reasonable' to administer the treatment. This might well be interpreted consistently with the existing principle that a doctor should act 'in the best interests of the

---

[67] In *Attorney-General's Reference (No. 6 of 1980)* [1981] QB 715 Lord Lane CJ referred to the possibility of valid consent to 'reasonable surgical interference'. Cf. Law Commission Consultation Paper No. 139, *Consent in the Criminal Law* (1995), parts VIII and IX.

patient'.[68] To what extent does compliance with guidance given by one of the professional medical bodies establish that the treatment was reasonable? In the case of *Arthur* Farquharson J directed the jury that professional rules of conduct could not be conclusive as to the proper approach.[69] In *Malcherek and Steel* the Court of Appeal was careful to state that it was not concerned to enquire into the satisfactoriness of guidance from the Royal Medical Colleges or to examine the doctors' reasons for departing slightly from it in that case. Instead, the Court emphasized that 'a medical practitioner adopting methods which are generally accepted [came] bona fide and conscientiously to the conclusion', a test which leaves considerable latitude.[70] In many cases there will be some published guidance, but in others the doctor may be called upon to reach a judgment on the balance of advantages in a given situation. If this approach had been adopted in the *Gillick* case, the question would have been whether the interest of the continuing good health of the patient should outweigh the doing of an act of knowing assistance to the crime of unlawful sexual intercourse with a girl under 16.

Much of the public and legal discussion touching on these issues forms part of the euthanasia debate, with which this essay is not concerned. Judicial statements in the House of Lords in the *Bland* case are relevant here, however. The House held that what is 'in the best interests of the patient' should be determined by reference to whether the doctor's decision is 'in accordance with a practice accepted at the time by a responsible body of medical opinion'.[71] Thus the clinical judgment of the doctor(s) involved (or, in the case of a child, the parents in consultation with the doctor) would be central, although it would be right to make an application to the courts if time allowed. Lord Mustill took a stronger line, arguing that this delegation of authority to the medical profession was inappropriate, in so far as these were often ethical rather than medical decisions and as they raised the question of criminal liability.[72] This is surely right. The propriety of the clinical judgment reached by the doctor ought to be open to review in court. A useful parallel is provided by the proposals of the Law Commission in its Consultation Paper on Involuntary Manslaughter, where it argues that it is for the courts and not for the profession or industry to decide what precautions are reasonable:

---

[68] As Lord Goff put it in *F* v. *West Berkshire Health Authority* [1990] 2 AC 1, 'the action taken must be such as a reasonable person would in all the circumstances take, acting in the best interests of the assisted person'. See also *Re J* [1991] 2 WLR 140, *Re T* (*Adult: Refusal of Treatment*) [1992] 3 WLR 782.

[69] See the discussions by P. D. G. Skegg, n. 20 above, at 128, and by M. J. Gunn and J. C. Smith, 'Arthur's Case and the Right to Life of a Down's Syndrome Child' [1985] *Criminal LR* 705.

[70] (1981) 73 Cr. App. R 173 at 179–81.

[71] In *Airedale NHS Trust* v. *Bland* [1993] 1 All ER 821, *per* Lord Browne-Wilkinson at 882, citing the tort case of *Bolam* v. *Friern Hospital Management Committee* [1957] 1 WLR 582. Cf. now *Frenchay NHS Trust* v. *S* [1994] 2 All ER 403.

[72] *Airedale NHS Trust* v. *Bland* [1993] 1 All ER at 895.

Where the accused acts in a way rejected by his own profession, as in the case of Dr. Adomako, he is likely to be found not to have acted in the way expected of him. In our view, however, the converse should not necessarily be the case. Even if a certain course of conduct is 'industry practice,' or is not regarded as seriously unusual by other operators in that industry, we consider that the jury must retain the right to say that, where a significant risk of death or serious injury exists, the industry's practice is just not good enough.[73]

It is preferable that the courts, rather than any profession or industry, should be the final arbiters of reasonableness in this respect. However, that creates a problem of principle: it detracts from the principle of maximum certainty and fails to give clear warnings to doctors and others about the limits of the criminal law. It is therefore important to ensure that the professional guidance is reasonably full and helpful.

If there is time to apply to a court for guidance, this should be done. In cases where the decisions need to be taken quickly, on the other hand, there are strong arguments for saying that a margin of sympathy (or error) should be extended to doctors caught up in pressing circumstances. No doubt, in these cases, courts would adopt the kind of approach commended by Lord Morris in *Palmer* v. *R.*: '[i]f a jury thought that in a moment of unexpected anguish a person attacked had only done what he honestly and instinctively thought was necessary, that would be most potent evidence that only reasonable defensive action had been taken.'[74] These words, taken from a self-defence case, might have some application in a medical case even though doctors are expected to be able to work under pressure. A defence with this kind of concession would no longer be purely justificatory, and would incorporate an element of excuse.[75] However, it is important to preserve the distinction between cases in which there is the opportunity for reflection, and even for application to a court, and others in which decisions have to be taken rapidly—*a fortiori* if there is little professional guidance relating to the kind of emergency that arises.

SHOULD PROOF OF PURPOSE BE REQUIRED?

The sixth and last question is whether the defence should be defined so that an intention to prevent or to alleviate suffering is required. In most cases this would add little, and it is not proposed to develop the point here since at least three other essays in this volume are devoted to the question of the mental element in justifications.[76]

---

[73] Law Commission Consultation Paper No. 135, *Involuntary Manslaughter* (1994), para. 5.61.

[74] [1971] AC 814. [75] See also *Scarlett* [1993] 4 All ER 629.

[76] See the essays by Robinson, Simester, and Gardner in this volume.

POSITIONING THE DEFENCE

The elements of a defence might therefore be as follows. It should not be limited to medical professionals. It should not be limited to surgical operations, and should extend at least to 'medical treatment'. It should cover decisions and conduct which are either clinically necessary or reasonable in the circumstances, defined in such a way as to make it clear that the courts and not the profession have the last word.

If some such defence is to be recognized, how should this be accomplished in English law? In these days when codification of the criminal law is on the agenda in England and Wales, one might expect the answer to be, 'as part of a criminal code'. If there is to be a code, it would indeed be sensible to include a specific defence. However, in the present codification programme there is no reference to a defence of necessity as such. There are clauses dealing with duress by threats, with the newly-created defence of duress of circumstances, and with the use of force in public or private defence.[77] There is also clause 45(4) of the draft Criminal Code, which provides that a person does not commit an offence by doing an act which is justified or excused by 'any rule of common law continuing to apply by virtue of section 4(4)' (of the draft Code). The intended effect of this is to preserve the power of the courts to develop defences as they have always done, the recent recognition of 'duress of circumstances' being an example.[78] As the Law Commission puts it:

If necessity is properly to be regarded not as a general defence but as the common basis for the recognition of a variety of circumstances of justification or excuse, clause 4(4) will equally enable the courts to declare that the common law accords that recognition to appropriate circumstances coming before them.[79]

The Commission envisages a case-by-case development of the law, and leaves it open to the judiciary to create and shape a defence of medical treatment based on clinical grounds. Such a power appears not to contravene the principle of non-retroactivity, declared in Article 7 of the European Convention on Human Rights, because it involves exculpating people rather than inculpating them for acts done earlier.[80]

There are, however, some different objections to this mode of proceeding. The first is the democratic objection: such decisions of public policy should

[77] Cll. 42, 43, and 44 of the draft Criminal Code of 1989. These clauses have now been superseded by cll. 25–30 of the draft Criminal Law Bill attached to Law Commission No. 218, *Legislating the Criminal Code: Offences against the Person and General Principles* (1993). Cf. also the essay by Glazebrook in this volume.

[78] In *Willer* (1986) 83 Cr. App. R 225, *Conway* [1989] QB 290, and *Martin* [1989] 1 All ER 652.

[79] N. 1 above, vol. 2, para. 12.41.

[80] For further discussion, see Ashworth, n. 8 above, at 67–71.

not be left to the courts and should be taken in principle by the elected leg-islature. Some judges have supported this view, for example in relation to the vexed question of duress and murder,[81] and it is surely right. A second objection is that a defence which turns, in effect, on reasonableness is bound to suffer from uncertainty, leaving considerable leeway to judge and jury. Certainty is an important value in criminal law, but in spheres in which it is not easy to specify situations in advance—and where defences rather than offences are concerned—the flexibility to adapt to differing sets of circum-stances may be considered more important, at least in the short run. However, this leads into the third objection: that the principle of non-retroactivity, and particularly the value of fair warning, cannot be regarded as irrelevant here.[82] It may be true that persons acting under dire threats may not be able or disposed to stop and look up the law, but in the medical field many of the situations will not be of this kind. The law could and should provide some guidance of a general nature, which could then be fil-tered through to the medical profession *via* codes of ethics and other guide-lines.

Following the Law Commission's proposal to abolish the defence of necessity, the arguments which subsequently dissuaded it from this course depended heavily on the impossibility of predicting the circumstances in which people might expect and courts might wish to exculpate an individ-ual.[83] It should be noted that these are not arguments against including var-ious forms of the necessity defence in a code—as indeed has now been done in respect of duress of circumstances. They are arguments against limiting the power of the courts to develop new defences. Some may still contend that defences in this sphere are best left to be developed in response to the experience of individual cases, and that a legislative formulation might cause greater difficulties than it resolves. But that overlooks the importance of a legislative declaration of principle. The existing approach of 'concealed defences', wrapped up in expanding and contracting definitions of intention, recklessness, and legal cause, affords little guidance to courts or to medical practitioners. Of course the criminal law, of itself, could hardly be expected to furnish doctors with detailed guidelines: that is a matter for separate leg-islation, which has not been enacted, and for statements of ethics. It is also likely that the discretion not to prosecute will continue to be used widely in medical cases. But there will be cases appropriate for prosecution, and others in which issues of criminal liability arise incidentally, and at least the criminal law should be clearly consistent with principles of medical law.

---

[81] Lords Hailsham and Bridge in *Howe* [1987] AC 417; see more recently Lord Lloyd in *Clegg* [1995] 2 WLR 80 and Lord Lowry in *C v. DPP* [1995] 2 All ER 43.

[82] See Ashworth, n. 8 above, at 73–6.

[83] See Glanville Williams, 'Necessity' [1978] *Criminal LR* 128, drawing on arguments con-structed by Stephen a century earlier.

Conclusions

The arguments in this essay have dealt with only some aspects of the inter-face between criminal law and medical law. Nothing has been said about the boundaries of consent to treatment, and how they may be manipulated so as to allow paternalism to prevail over self-determination;[84] nor about the many difficult issues surrounding euthanasia.[85] Nothing has been said about the courts' tendency to rely on a distinction between acts and omissions when deciding the criminal liability of doctors, even though such distinc-tions often evaporate when subjected to careful scrutiny.[86] Nothing has been said about the content of a doctor's duty towards a terminally ill patient who has not previously intimated any relevant wishes, although this is clearly important in cases where the doctor's conduct is regarded as an omission.[87] No special attention has been paid to the ambit of the criminal law in relation to cosmetic surgery and to experimentation.

The uncertainties created by the ambivalence and flexibility of the judicial approach to those situations suggest that there are difficulties at various lev-els in the criminal law's response to medical problems—over the principles that should come into play, whether the conflicts between them can be resolved to the extent of stating some general rules, and whether it is desir-able to state rules or preferable to conceal what the courts are doing. All these difficulties are equally apparent in the groups of cases considered in this essay, in which the courts have striven to exculpate doctors for decisions taken in medical contexts which would probably, in almost all other situa-tions, lead to the imposition of criminal liability. The courts have not taken the approach of developing a special defence, but have adapted existing con-cepts in ways that facilitate the exculpation of doctors acting in good faith. We began by suggesting that this amounted to a distortion of the standard approach to criminal liability, but it is now clear that the standard approach is a construct of certain academic lawyers rather than a working model. The courts have not kept to consistent and well-defined concepts of intention, recklessness, or causation, but have striven to adapt them in order to reflect the necessary moral distinctions. Whilst some might argue that consistency is a formalistic and over-ambitious goal, given the variety of situations that call for decisions, the argument here is that consistency and certainty should be promoted so far as possible because they help citizens to know where they

---

[84] I. M. Kennedy, *Treat Me Right* (Oxford, 1988), 331–2.

[85] For discussion and materials, see N. Lacey, C. Wells, and D. Meure, *Reconstructing Criminal Law* (London, 1990), 405–10, and Kennedy and Grubb, n. 4 above, ch. 12.

[86] H. Beynon, 'Doctors as Murderers' [1982] *Criminal LR* 17, and Lacey, Wells, and Meure, *ibid.*, 228–30. Cf. the approach of Glanville Williams, *Textbook of Criminal Law* (2nd edn., London, 1983), 282, followed by Lords Goff and Browne-Wilkinson in *Airedale NHS Trust* v. *Bland* [1993] 1 All ER 821, but doubted by Kennedy and Grubb, *ibid.*, 1208–10.

[87] Kennedy and Grubb, n. 4 above, at 1211 *et seq.*

stand and provide some parameters for judicial discretion. The creation of a new defence is therefore preferable to the continuation of the present *ad hoc* approach.

The dependence of the defence on the term 'reasonable' may be thought to weaken any claims about consistency and certainty. However, an explicit defence might be expected to generate more open argument and discussion in courts, leading to judicial interpretation and development of the defence, which might in turn lead to changes in the professional guidance and perhaps to legislative amendment. Of course, the defence would only be subject to judicial scrutiny when a prosecution was brought and pursued, with the vast majority of cases being neither considered for prosecution nor even reported as possible crimes. But, again, an explicit defence offers a distinct ground for challenge in cases that give rise to concern. Thus it is one thing to recognize that considerable discretionary power will remain in this sphere of criminal law, creating problems for the ideals of certainty and consistency; it is another thing to maintain that there is no point even in statutory recognition of a special defence.

9

Structuring the Criminal Code: Functional Approaches to Complicity, Incomplete Offences, and General Defences

P. R. Glazebrook

The crafting of a satisfactory criminal code—one that is faithful to the underlying principles of the law that is being codified, that strikes a workable balance between (too) general principle and (too) detailed rule, and employs language that is both uniform and as simple as the subject matter permits—is heavily dependent on how the code is structured: on, that is, its basic framework or skeleton.

The more complicated a code is, and the more concepts it employs, the more intricate its drafting becomes, the more likely it is that gaps that are unprovided for will open up between them, and the more opportunity there will be for misunderstanding and confusion among those applying its rules. Each concept employed by a code should, therefore, be shown to be necessary. That it is familiar to those at home with the law which the code is to replace, or that it has played its part in the development of that law, is not a sufficient reason for preserving it in the amber of that code. A good many of the concepts familiar to criminal lawyers completely served their turn long ago.

It is, therefore, unfortunate that the structure adopted by the Law Commission for its 1989 draft *Criminal Code for England and Wales*[1] in several key respects mimics rather too closely for either comfort or simplicity traditional, but no longer very useful, ways of thinking about criminal liability. This is notably so in the way it deals with the law of complicity and incomplete (inchoate) offences. Three lengthy clauses (26–28) elaborately distinguish, among those who commit crimes, 'principals' and 'accessories'. Then, in three equally lengthy clauses (47–49) dealing with those who try,

[1] Law Commission No. 177 (HC 299).

but fail, to do so, it distinguishes between 'incitements', 'conspiracies', and 'attempts'. These unnecessarily complicating distinctions would be deepened and entrenched if the Commission's proposals for replacing the present law of complicity in crime by offences of an inchoate character of 'assisting' and 'encouraging' crimes made in its 1993 Consultation Paper[2] (which acknowledges the critical importance of structuring the law aright) were adopted.

Another instance of the draft code's poor structuring is its provisions for general defences. The currently fashionable, but muddled, concept of 'duress of circumstances' is associated with 'duress of threats' and distinguished from the 'justifiable use of force' (clauses 42–44; 1993 Draft Criminal Law Bill, clauses 25–28), but no provision is made for justifiable contraventions of the criminal law which do not involve the use of force, or for those which are done for purposes as worthy and acceptable (and accepted) as those which are provided for.

There are simpler ways in which the law on these matters might be set out in the Code. This paper, which introduces draft clauses showing how this could be done, may not be wholly out of place in a book devoted to the theory of the criminal law. For the structuring of a code is heavily dependent on both philosophical and historical analyses of the bases of criminal liability. Its general provisions which create this structure (and which are this paper's concern) have, it is perhaps worth stressing, a function different from that of those which define specific offences. The latter will form the basis of directions to juries, and will constantly have to be considered by magistrates. A code's general, structuring provisions, on the other hand, are mainly there for lawyers, one of their principal purposes being to shut off (bad) legal arguments about the application of the code's offence-creating provisions.

I

Sir John Smith having, as it seems to me, demonstrated[3] conclusively that an inchoate structure for the law governing assisting and encouraging others in crime, such as that suggested by the Law Commission in its 1993 Consultation Paper, would not be satisfactory, I would like to direct attention again to the clauses in its 1989 Draft Code. For there is a less complex and, I believe, better way both of codifying the law of complicity and inchoate offences, and of solving the problems identified by the Commission in that Paper: usually, though not always, along the lines which the Commission itself provisionally favours. (The grounds for predicating a principle of joint enterprise liability that is distinct from that applying to

---

[2] No. 131.　　　[3] [1994] *New LJ* 679.

other parties to an offence are, in my view, clearly insufficient, and so I say no more about it.)

Looking, then, to the 1989 Draft Code's clauses relating to complicity in crime, the first thing that may well strike the critical reader as rather odd is the last of them, clause 28. This, in subclause (1), provides:

> A person may be convicted of an offence whether he is charged as a principal or as an accessory if the evidence shows that—
>
> > (a) he was a principal; or
> >
> > (b) he was an accessory; or
> >
> > (c) he was either a principal or an accessory.

For why, she may ask, should one go to the trouble of providing that a person charged with an offence should be *charged* as either a principal or an accessory if one is then going on to say that it does not matter if it should turn out, as the evidence unfolds at the trial, that the prosecution has got it wrong, or that, at the end of the day, it and everyone else (except, perhaps, the defendants) are left completely uncertain on the point?

To this critical, and puzzled, comment the learned criminal lawyer, well-steeped in the cases (and no doubt the Law Commission too) would probably reply that clause 28(1) gives effect to a very well-established principle of the common law of criminal complicity, which is at least a century and a half old. They would point to the well-known, albeit terse, ruling of Pollock CB on the trial of *Swindall and Osborne* in 1846,[4] when the defendants who were charged with manslaughter unsuccessfully claimed that they were entitled to be acquitted because the prosecution had failed to establish whether it was Swindall's or Osborne's cart, or both, that had struck and killed an old man who was attempting to cross the road when they were racing along it.

The critic may, however, respond by asking whether the criminal law has not moved on a bit since 1846? Is it not the case that Parliament has several times stuck its own oar in: notably in the Criminal Procedure Act 1848 (re-enacted in the Accessories and Abettors Act 1861), in the Indictments Act 1915, and in the Criminal Law Act 1967?

Section 1 of the Criminal Procedure Act 1848 sought to assimilate the law relating to parties in felonies to the law governing parties in treasons and misdemeanours. In both treasons and misdemeanours all accessories, and not only those present at the scene of the crime, were principal offenders, so that no distinction needed to be made between accessories and principals in the form of either indictment or conviction. Section 1 accordingly provided (in the language of the same section of the 1861 Act) that:

> Whosoever shall become an accessory before the fact to any felony, whether the same be a felony at common law, or by virtue of any Act passed or to be passed, may

---

[4] (1846) 2 C & K 230.

be indicted, tried, convicted and punished in all respects as if he were a principal felon.

This neatly matched the terms of section 8 of the 1861 Act (deriving from section 26 of the Malicious Injuries to Property Act 1827):

Whosoever shall aid, abet, counsel or procure the commission of any misdemeanour, whether the same be a misdemeanour at common law or by virtue of any Act passed or to be passed, shall be liable to be tried, indicted and punished as a principal offender.

Parliament had thus in 1848 solved, among other things, the difficulty with which Pollock CB had so robustly dealt two years earlier.

These two provisions, in their 1861 embodiment, stood until Parliament eventually got round, in the Criminal Law Act 1967, to abolishing the last few remaining distinctions between felonies and misdemeanours, as Commissions and Committees had for more than a 130 years been urging. Section 1(2) provides that:

Subject to the provisions of this Act, on all matters on which a distinction has previously been made between felony and misdemeanour, including mode of trial, the law and practice in relation to all offences cognisable under the law of England and Wales (including piracy) shall be the law and practice applicable at the commencement of this Act in relation to misdemeanour.

If this means anything it means that Parliament was reaffirming the position reached in 1848 that all parties to all crimes are, as all misdemeanants already were, 'liable to be tried, indicted and punished as principal offenders'. Section 1 of the 1861 Act was accordingly repealed since it was now obsolete and section 8 was amended by substituting references to 'any indictable offence' for the former references to misdemeanours.

If, then, all defendants charged with indictable offences have, ever since 1848, been liable to be indicted (etc.) as principal offenders why on earth, the critic must again ask, did the Law Commission revert, indeed retrogress, in clauses 26 to 28 of its Draft Code, to providing for defendants being 'charged as' either principals or accessories? Does this, perhaps, reflect some provision of the Indictments Act 1915?

The answer is, No. That admirable Act, and the Indictment Rules 1971 made under it, provide that each count of an indictment shall take the simple form with which all lawyers are familiar, distinguishing between the 'Statement of Offence' and the 'Particulars of Offence'. The 'Statement' merely states the name by which an offence is commonly known, saying whether it is an offence at common law or under a specified enactment, while the 'Particulars' will 'disclose the essential elements of an offence: Provided that an essential element need not be disclosed if the accused person is not prejudiced or embarrassed in his defence by the failure to disclose it.'[5] Any disclosure that the charge of the offence specified in the 'Statement'

---

[5] Indictment Rules 1971, r. 6(b).

is based on evidence that the defendant aided, abetted, counselled, or procured another (known or unknown) to do what statute or common law declares to be an offence is accordingly made in the 'Particulars'.

It is, as the House of Lords held in *DPP for Northern Ireland* v. *Maxwell,*[6] only fair, and therefore good practice, that the prosecution should, wherever possible, disclose in the 'Particulars' whether the charge of the offence specified in the 'Statement' is based on evidence that the defendant perpetrated the offence, or aided, abetted, counselled, or procured someone else to do so. But it is not required to do the impossible, and 'disclose' what the evidence in its possession leaves uncertain. So, in a case where the precise nature of the defendant's involvement in the offence he is alleged to have committed is unclear to the prosecution, the defendant cannot object that this is not disclosed in the 'Particulars'. Equally obviously, there can be no question of anyone being prosecuted if the prosecution are not sure what offence to charge him with. It is, therefore, clear beyond argument that no defendant since 1915 has been charged 'as a principal' or charged 'as an accessory'. All defendants have been charged with, and (when convicted) convicted of, offences, whether they were in truth perpetrators, or were in truth accessories. So, as teachers of criminal law point out to their pupils, it is quite possible, and sometimes happens, that a woman is charged with, and convicted of, rape. Indeed, as C. S. Greaves QC, the draftsman of the 1861 Act, tartly observed in commenting on the obscurantist objections of the (original) J. F. Archbold to the (original) 1848 provision:

Now it is obvious that there is no more difficulty in a jury understanding that they may convict A of murder where B is a guilty agent, than where he is an innocent one. In either case all they have to try is whether A caused B to commit the murder. Jurors are perfectly well able to understand that he who causes a thing to be done by another is just as much responsible as if he did that thing himself—*qui facit per alium facit per se*—and there is no more difficulty in satisfying them that a man ought to be convicted of a murder who causes it to be done by another in his absence, than in satisfying them that where one man inflicts a mortal wound in the presence of another, that wound is as much his wound as if he had inflicted it, if they were both concurring in the act that caused it. In both cases a jury must be satisfied that the act of the killer was caused by the other and the advantage of this clause [section 1] is, that it reduces the question for the jury to that single issue, and gets rid of the difficulty, which often formerly arose, whether the evidence proved the prisoner to be a principal or accessory before the fact. In all civil cases, and in the ordinary affairs of life, he who causes an act to be done, though he be absent when it is done, is treated as having done that act, and the same has always been the rule in treason and misdemeanour, and felony was the exception which 11 and 12 Vict. c. 46, s. 1 very properly removed.[7]

---

6 [1978] 1 WLR 1350; [1978] 3 All ER 1140.
7 C. S. Greaves, *The Criminal Law Consolidation and Amendment Acts of the 24 & 25 Vict.* (2nd edn., London 1862), 21–2. Greaves' use of causal terminology is, needless to say, not endorsed.

Greaves' comments, made in 1862, thus underline how badly misconceived is the structure of clauses 26 to 28 of the 1989 Draft Code. For in clause 26(1)(a) and (3) a valiant but unnecessary rear-guard action, worthy of J. F. Archbold, is fought in defence of that venerable doctrine, distilled from the ancient cases, that is familiarly known as the 'doctrine of the innocent agent'. What Greaves perceived, though the Commission does not, was that, with the abolition of the old rule that an accessory to a felony could not be convicted until a principal felon had been (which was another change brought about by section 1 of the 1848 Act), it might be just as difficult for the prosecution to establish that the agent was guilty or innocent as it could be to determine whether a defendant was a principal or an accessory. There are, indeed, some crimes which are almost invariably committed through the agency, unnoticed by most lawyers, of the innocent. Poisonings, fatal and non-fatal, usually occur because the unsuspecting victim consumes the poisoned food or drink. Bank balances are stolen when honest bank staff clear the cheques and debit the victims' accounts. There is, therefore, no need and no point, when restating the post-1848 law, to make provision for this ancient doctrine.

The basic principle underlying the modern law of complicity is, thus, quite simply, that a person may commit an offence in one or other of two ways. He may do so either by doing what has been declared to be an offence or by helping or encouraging someone else to do that. And in either case he may employ an agent (innocent or not so innocent), or have acted jointly with another. For it has long been recognized that a person who aids or abets a criminal act may be just as bad, or even worse, than the person who actually does the dirty work. A modern code should so provide.

Draft clauses 1 and 3, below, which should be read in the light of the General Interpretation Clause (6) of the 1989 Draft Code, and Rule 7 of the Indictment Rules 1971[8] show how I would set about doing so. It will be seen that, with this formulation, the *Bourne*,[9] *Cogan and Leak*,[10] and *Millward*[11] problem, which the Law Commission finds ineradicably troublesome,[12] simply evaporates. What is more, the disappearance of any distinct legal category of accessorial liability means that all the unwanted and unnecessary complications of secondary liability for inchoate offences (of which more presently) do not arise. For with the modern law of complicity thus stated it becomes possible to set out the principles of the law of inchoate offences with comparable simplicity.

---

[8] R. 7: 'Where an offence created by or under an enactment states the offence to be the doing or the omission to do any one of any different acts in the alternative, or the doing or the omission to do any act in any one of different capacities, or with any one of different intentions, or states any part of the offence in the alternative, the acts, omissions, capacities or intentions or other matters stated in the alternative in the enactment or subordinate instrument may be stated in the alternative in an indictment charging the offence.'

[9] (1952) 36 Cr. App. R 125.
[11] [1994] *Criminal LR* 527.
[10] [1975] 2 All ER 1059.
[12] Paras. 2.39–2.46.

II

In Consultation Paper No. 131, the Law Commission, like others before it, makes great play of the fact—if it is a fact—that there is no inchoate offence of offering help towards the commission of an offence by another who does not, however, in the end commit it. If this were true it would, as the Commission rightly says, be a serious gap in the law, which has (because it has been believed to be true) distorted both the law of criminal complicity and the law of conspiracy. The Commission accordingly proposes, as a remedy, the creation of a new inchoate offence of offering such assistance, to parallel the existing inchoate offence of offering encouragement (usually known as incitement) thereby, it is thought, rendering superfluous much, but not all, of the law of complicity. (Not all, because it is thought that 'joint enterprise' liability must be provided for.) But, though the Commission suggests that the Code should contain these two inchoate offences, it does not stop to consider their relationship to the other inchoate offences of attempt and conspiracy, for it long ago fell into the disastrously bad habit of contemplating law reform in penny numbers.[13]

How very seriously astray the Commission is led by this bad habit becomes most apparent when the critical reader of the Consultation Paper asks what the relationship is to be between these two new inchoate offences of assisting and encouraging crime, and that other inchoate offence called conspiracy—a matter barely touched upon, and then only as an afterthought.[14] It is law, both trite and sensible, that if the offence conspired about is committed all the conspirators are guilty of the substantive offence. Is this well-established rule to be retained, or is it to be abolished, along with most of the rest of the law of complicity? Whatever the answer to that question, any satisfactory restatement of the law must take account of those whose participation in a crime consists in agreeing in one way or another with others on its commission.

A little reflection does, indeed, suggest that problems, similar to those which before 1848 bedevilled the law of complicity, may also arise on trials for inchoate offences, for where two or more defendants have embarked on, but not completed, some criminal activity, it may well be quite as unclear who did, or was going to do, what, as when the crime has been completed. It is simply that the problem is largely, though not wholly, veiled from view by the existence of the conspiracy offence which can be invoked in many cases where the prosecution are unsure whether a defendant intended himself to perpetrate an offence, or only to help or encourage someone else to do so.

---

[13] P. R. Glazebrook, 'Criminal Law Reform in Penny Numbers' [1972] *Criminal LR* 622.
[14] Paras. 4.211–4.215.

It may be true that there is no clear and reasoned appellate decision in England that offering help as opposed to encouragement—if the opposition is indeed sustainable—to another to perpetrate an offence which is not in the end committed is itself an offence. Yet the principle on which the decision in *Higgins*[15] in 1801 (the leading authority on the offence of incitement) is based is that the incitor is necessarily *attempting* to commit an offence: as an accessory. He has done all that he has to do, and not merely (in the language of later cases and the Criminal Attempts Act 1981) 'an act more than merely preparatory' to the commission by himself of the contemplated offence. As the Commission frequently reminds readers of its Consultation Paper, he has done 'the last act depending on himself'. For the only reason why he is not guilty of the substantive offence is that the incitee has not responded (or not effectively) to his incitement. There is, moreover, no suggestion in *Higgins* that the principle being applied does not apply equally to the person who is attempting to become an accessory by offering help to a would-be perpetrator. It would be too absurd if there were. For it would mean that the law took more notice of words than of deeds. It is, surely, (almost) inconceivable that a prosecution of *Invicta Plastics*[16] based not on any prior advertisement but solely on evidence that an employee had, in response to a motorist's offer to buy, sold him a Radatec device would have failed.

In earlier generations, when more attention was paid to the principles underlying judicial decisions, and less to the particular words that fall, sometimes rather casually, from judicial lips, the decision in *Higgins* was so understood. So, for instance, the inchoate offence of abetment in section 108 of the Indian Penal Code covers both aid and encouragement. For Macaulay had, in the 1830s, appreciated that it was neither sensible nor practicable to distinguish between them. (There are other Commonwealth code provisions to like effect.[17])

Once, then, the three inchoate offences are seen (as they were by, for example, R. S. Wright[18]) as but three manifestations of a single principle— the attemptor has intended to perpetrate an offence; the incitor has intended to commit an offence by (aiding or) abetting it; while the conspirator will

---

[15] (1801) 2 East 5. Counsel for the Crown had 'contended, that every attempt to commit a crime, whether felony or misdemeanour, is itself a misdemeanour and indictable . . . And if an act be necessary, the incitement or solicitation is an act: it is an attempt to procure the commission of a felony by the agency of another person. By the incitement the party does all that is left for him to do to constitute the misdemeanour; for if the felony be actually committed, he is guilty of felony as accessory before the fact.' Lord Kenyon CJ agreed: 'It is argued [for the defendant], that a mere intent to commit evil is not indictable, without an act done; but is there not an act done, when it is charged that the defendant solicited another to commit a felony? The solicitation is an act; and the answer given at the bar is decisive.'

[16] [1976] RTR 251; cf *Brown* (1899) 63 JP 790.

[17] e.g., Commonwealth Crimes Act (Australia) 1914, s. 7A; Draft Criminal Code for Canada, cl. 4(4); New Zealand Crimes Bill 1990, cl. 67(1).

[18] *Criminal Conspiracies* (London, 1873).

have intended to do either the one or the other, or both—it becomes possible to provide in a code for a single inchoate offence. Draft clause 2 below shows how it may be done. With a single provision for inchoate offences matching the single provision for substantive offences, the sensible answer to many of the questions raised by the Law Commission in the Consultation Paper are readily apparent.

The nightmare of inchoate forms of inchoate offences happily vanishes. The liability of the would-be encourager is not restricted, senselessly, to cases where his encouragement has come to the notice of his would-be perpetrator, for whether or not it has, he has done the last act depending on himself towards committing an offence, and it should be neither here nor there that his letter has been intercepted or lost in the post. Similarly, there is neither need nor sense in letting *Curr*[19] off the hook as, astonishingly, the Commission would continue to do,[20] when it cannot be proved that his stooges were as fraudulent as he was. For if the stooges had collected the Family Allowances (as, of course, they had) he would (had the prosecutor had his wits about him) have been convicted of the completed offence, as either perpetrator or accessory, and in asking them to do so he had done the last act depending on himself towards committing it. He would be caught, and properly so, by my draft clause 2(1) read with clause 3(1)(a). For, if we may descend to mundane considerations of policy, is not the rogue who seeks to employ the imperceptive to do his dirty work for him quite as much a social menace as the rogue who seeks the services of the astute: who may be astute enough to reject his proposal?

On the other hand, an inchoate offence committed by soliciting others to commit crimes should, as an inchoate offence, be limited to the instigation of particular criminal acts, and not extend to incitements to law-breaking in general. This the Commission's provisional proposals do not, but my draft clause does, attempt to do.

III

In the Law Commission's next step towards 'Legislating the Criminal Code', its draft Criminal Law Bill, attached to Report No. 218,[21] the least satisfactory clauses are, perhaps, 25 to 28, dealing respectively with general defences of duress by threats, duress of circumstances, and the use of force in public or private defence. Even the order in which these clauses appear in the Bill suggests that all may not be quite as it should be. For anyone with a nodding acquaintance with the last twenty-five years' writing about the theoretical foundations of criminal liability will think it odd that defences of an excusatory character should be dealt with before any of a justificatory

---

[19] [1968] 2 QB 994.　　[20] Para. 13.7; cl. 47(1)(b).　　[21] (1993) Cm 2370.

nature.[22] It is ominous, too, that the Commission should have hearkened to the siren call of 'duress of circumstances', a recently fashionable, but meretricious and confusing, tune. In the result, clause 26 (duress of circumstances) may well be too widely, as clause 27 (justifiable use of force) is certainly too narrowly, drawn.

This is cause for grave concern. First, because clause 24 indicates that these clauses are designed to provide defences to charges of all crimes, and not just to those of the non-fatal offences against the person which are the subjects of clauses 4 to 19. Secondly, because they fail to cover a number of situations, notably medical situations, where even (and perhaps most typically) defendants charged with non-fatal offences against the person *must* be granted a defence, and where a failure to provide for them in the Criminal Code will mean that resort will still have to be made to 'the common law'.[23] This, being translated, means that instead of being formulated after lengthy, wide-ranging, and well-informed deliberations, for which the Law Commission has both the time and resources, if only it would use them aright, these defences are to be left to be knocked rapidly together amid the hurly-burly, the exigencies, and the emotions of particular criminal trials and appeals. (There are, of course, those who think it better that law should be made in this way—'dog law' as Jeremy Bentham nicknamed it—but they would decline to embark with the Law Commission on its long, and seemingly never-ending, journey down the road to codification.) It may well be wise for a Code to leave to judges a residual power to allow defences in circumstances unforeseen and unforeseeable by the codifiers. But to fail, as the Commission does, to deal with situations which have already arisen, and have been the subject of extensive forensic and juristic debate, is to fall down on the job.

The Commission's odd approach to the codification of general defences, and in particular the prominence and priority it gives to those of an excusatory character, leads, not altogether surprisingly, to some strange conclusions. Even a casual reader of clauses 25 to 27 will, for instance, be struck by the contrast between the opening words of the first two (duress of threats, and duress of circumstances) and the third, dealing with the justificatory defence. Clauses 25 and 26 begin: '[n]o act of a person constitutes an offence if . . .' While clause 27 begins: '[t]he use of force by a person for any

---

[22] The priority of justification over excuse is considered by John Gardner elsewhere in this volume.

[23] It will be apparent that I fully agree with Andrew Ashworth (this volume) in thinking that the explanations usually offered by judges and others for not holding doctors liable for the prima facie harmful and foreseeable consequences of their treatment of their patients are unsatisfactory, and that a justificatory defence must be formulated that will cover these cases. Like him, I consider that this general defence does not need to, and should not, refer specifically to doctors, for it is not only doctors who may, quite properly, provide medical treatment and care. (Special defences will, of course, be needed to cover special procedures, such as abortion and organ transplantation.) My draft cll. 11–13 accordingly represent my own attempt to incorporate a general medical justification within a more comprehensive defence.

of the [specified] purposes . . . does not constitute an offence . . .' (Clause 28 adopts a similar approach.) So the Law Commission is deliberately refraining from laying down any rule about prima facie criminal acts that are justified because done for any of the specified purposes if they do not involve *the use of force*. What can be the reason for this timidity, which then makes it necessary to undertake the otherwise unnecessary task of deciding when non-force is to be deemed to be force (clause 29)? For, surely, if using force for any of the specified purposes may be justified, so also may passivity and acts which are in no way forceful. If I may be justified in, for instance, *assaulting* a police officer in order to prevent him causing serious personal injury to another, I must also be justified in *obstructing* him in order to prevent him causing that injury.

In paragraph 36.2 of its Report the Commission half anticipates the objection, and in paragraphs 40.2 and 40.3 it attempts, but fails, to meet it. In the Consultation Paper[24] that preceded the Report, it had been claimed[25] that 'substantial study and extensive consultation' would be required before the Commission could confidently recommend the enactment of a rule that permitted the doing of any prima facie criminal, but non-forceful, act for any of the purposes for which force may lawfully be used. The short answer to all this is that the question is not one calling for 'substantial study and extensive consultation', but one of principle and, indeed, of common sense. If force is permissible, then so *a fortiori* must all peaceable measures be. If magistrates and juries can be trusted to decide when the use of forcible measures is, and is not, in all the circumstances, reasonable, they can be trusted to decide whether some non-forcible action is, in all the circumstances, reasonable or not. The question for them will not, as the Commission appears to imply, be wholly at large. For the (limited) purposes for which a person may resort to prima facie criminal conduct will have already been specified, and trial judges and the Divisional Court would, in accordance with general principle, retain their power to rule that in the circumstances of the particular case no sane person could suppose that what the defendant did was reasonable. The Commission does not offer a single example to justify its timidity, and it fails to have regard to any of the substantial body of authority that not only confirms the principle that what will justify the use of force will likewise justify non-forceful measures, but also demonstrates that its list of justificatory purposes is woefully incomplete. This is another feature of the clauses which is likely to strike even the casual reader.

Over the years the courts, unlike the Commission, have not hesitated to concede that it may well be proper, and so lawful, to resort to such prima facie unlawful but non-forceful actions as:

> escaping from one's prison in order to avoid being burnt to death in a fire;[26]

---

[24] LCCP 122.   [25] Para. 20.5.   [26] *Reniger* v. *Fogossa* (1551) 1 Plowden 1.

obtaining an abortifacient,[27] or driving whilst disqualified,[28] in order to
avert a threat to commit suicide;

running the risk of spreading an infectious disease,[29] or contravening a
one-way traffic direction,[30] in order to procure medical assistance for
sick or injured persons;

giving drugs which it is known will hasten death in order to keep a terminally ill patient free from pain;[31]

driving while drunk in order to escape assaults likely to occasion bodily harm;[32]

driving in what would otherwise be a reckless or dangerous manner in
order to effect an arrest,[33] or to save someone else from attack;[34]

retaining possession of banknotes known to be forged in order to hand
them in to the police thereby helping the police to trace previous pos-
sessors;[35] and

assisting intending burglars in order to gain knowledge of their bur-
glarious plans for communication to the police.[36]

Is there, one may ask, a single one of these decisions that is not eminently
sensible, and does not represent a clear moral consensus in our society? How
many more decisions concerning how many more varied crimes are required
to persuade the Law Commission that it is safe to codify the common sense
principle that resort to *any* conduct necessary for any of the purposes for
which force may be employed will, if in all the circumstances reasonable, be
lawful and not criminal?

Some of these cases—those where the defendant acts 'because he knows
or believes that it is immediately necessary to avoid death or serious injury
to himself or another'—would, no doubt, fall within the Commission's proposed defence of 'duress of circumstances' (of which more anon), but the
others would not. Yet can it really be doubted that in England and Wales it
is lawful to do *whatever* is known (and not criminal to do *whatever* is
believed) to be necessary and is, in all the circumstances, reasonable, not
only to avoid death or serious injury to oneself or another (the necessary
condition for the application of the 'duress of circumstances' defence), but
also, subject to one important qualification,[37]

to avoid *any* injury (whether unlawful or not), or *any* pain or suffering
(whether caused unlawfully or not); or

to obtain medical assistance to ease or ameliorate injury, pain or suffering (again whether caused unlawfully or not), and not only when suffered by humans, but also when suffered by animals; or

[27] *Fretwell* (1862) L & C 161.					[28] *Martin* [1989] 1 All ER 652.
[29] *Vantandillo* (1815) 4 M & S 73.					[30] *Johnson* v. *Phillips* [1975] 3 All ER 682.
[31] *Bodkin Adams* [1957] *Criminal LR* 365.					[32] *DPP* v. *Jones* [1990] RTR 34.
[33] *Renouf* (1986) 82 Cr. App. R 344.
[34] *Willer* (1986) 83 Cr. App. R 225; *Conway* [1989] QB 290.
[35] *Wuyts* [1969] 2 QB 474.					[36] *Clarke* (1985) 80 Cr. App. R 344.
[37] Discussed below, text at n. 38.

to release any person from unjustified detention (whether unlawfully caused or not); or

to discipline a child who is in one's care; or

to avoid any unjustified loss, damage or destruction of property (again, whether unlawfully caused or not)?

And if it cannot reasonably be doubted, ought not these eminently rational propositions to find a place in *any* codification of general defences, even in one undertaken by so timorous a body as our Law Commission, which has so often put off for another day what should have been done there and then?

This is not, however, the only strange consequence of the Commission's odd and unprincipled approach to the codification of general defences.

The basic principle that acts which are prima facie criminal are, whether or not they involve the use of force, justified (or excused) if done in the knowledge (or belief) that they are necessary for a purpose that the law countenances, and are in all the circumstances reasonable, is, of course, subject to certain qualifications that are almost as equally deeply embedded in the common law. One of the most important of these qualifications is that no one may seek to avert any injury, damage, or harm that is *authorized by law* (and not just not unlawful) even though such action would, in any other circumstances, be considered wholly reasonable. For that—the permitting of resistance to lawful authority—would be the most vicious of all vicious circles. Yet this the Commission's proposed defence of duress of circumstances (at least in the way it is at present drafted) would in certain circumstances allow. A person might well know or believe that he is exposed to risk of death or serious injury from the acts of someone who he realizes is acting with lawful authority, without having knowingly or without reasonable excuse exposed himself to this danger (and thus come within clause 26). An innocent person might well, for instance, be unlucky enough to find himself trapped or caught (as it were) in the cross-fire by the measures being taken, entirely reasonably, to save the lives of third parties, to prevent crime, or to arrest a dangerous offender. The rescuers, or police officers, might not even be aware that they were putting this innocent person at risk. But if he knew or believed that they were doing so, clause 26 would allow him to kill or injure them 'if he could not reasonably be expected to act otherwise', rather than to continue to be exposed to that risk. The innocent hostage is thus to be allowed to join the wanted terrorist in injuring or killing the would-be arresters in order to save himself from serious harm at their hands. This would be to change the present law, and although a fair argument may be mounted for allowing a person in such a dilemma to save himself, it is not self-evidently right to do so. The Commission's readiness to propose a change in a rule that is well-established, not only in England but throughout most of the common law world, is in striking contrast to its reluctance to codify the well-established and uncontroversial principle which the rule qualifies.

There is a second important qualification of the principle, which is equally deeply embedded in the common law, though, perhaps because it is so deeply embedded, there are remarkably few cases in which it has been questioned, and therefore few in which it has been expressly affirmed. This is the qualification that a person may not cause death or personal injury to, or detain, someone whom he does not believe to be threatening or endangering the life or safety or freedom of any other person, or to be committing or about to commit any crime, however necessary a means he may believe it to be to achieve an otherwise laudable, let alone justifiable, end. This stern rule was, of course, affirmed by the Queen's Bench judges in *Dudley and Stephens*,[38] and endorsed by the Privy Council in *Abbott*,[39] and by the House of Lords in *Howe*.[40] A case can, of course, be made for either abolishing or modifying it, and a much stronger one for the exercise of mercy in prosecuting or sentencing. That, however, is not my immediate concern, which is simply that of drawing attention to the justificatory defences being at present subject not only to the overriding qualification that what would otherwise be justifiable (because necessary to serve a laudable end) must, in the view of the tribunal of fact, have been not unreasonable, not disproportionate to that end, but to other and more specific ones as well. The provisions of a draft Code should, I suggest, be structured to reflect this fact.

If this were done, the clauses governing the justificatory defences would begin by specifying the purposes for which actions otherwise criminal may lawfully be performed. They would then qualify that basic principle *first* with any specific restrictions that are to remain on it, and only subsequently by the overriding criterion of proportionality. For there is no point in asking a tribunal of fact whether it considers that what the defendant did was, in all the circumstances that he believed confronted him, reasonable, if there is *any* rule that, whatever it thinks about the reasonableness of his conduct, it is nonetheless not to be countenanced. Draft clauses 11, 12, and 13 that I append incorporate the more logical (and practical) approach.

With the justificatory defences more adequately provided for we may return to those of an excusatory character. The Law Commission's proposal to confer the blessings of codification on a defence of 'duress of circumstances' has, no doubt, a certain superficial attractiveness. If a person is to be excused his commission of a crime because he knew or believed that a thug was threatening to cause death or serious injury to himself or another if it was not committed, and the threat was one which was both believed by him to be immediately implementable and otherwise unavoidable, and was in all the circumstances one which he could not reasonably be expected to withstand, then it seems only fair that he should be excused if a similar threat came not from a thug but from the circumstances in which he

---

[38] (1884) 14 QBD 273.   [39] [1977] AC 755.
[40] [1987] 1 All ER 771. See, too, *A-G* v. *Guardian Newspapers (No. 2)* [1988] 3 All ER 545 at 605h (Donaldson MR).

found himself. For why should the source of the threat be of any legal relevance?

In fact, however, the source of the threat is of very considerable significance, and gives rise to quite different policy issues. The important difference between the duress of threats and the 'duress of circumstances' situation is not that in one case the source of the threat is a human being, and in the other that it is not (indeed, as we have just seen, the Law Commission's 'duress of circumstances' defence would cover cases where the threat arises from human acts), but that in the former case the crime to be committed has been specified by the thug,[41] and in the latter that it has been decided on, albeit reluctantly, by the defendant. In a case of 'duress of threats' there is still, even if the defendant is excused, someone else (the thug) who has indisputably committed the offence and is liable to conviction, and whose resort to the coercion of an unwilling accomplice aggravates his offence. The policy issues that have to be faced are nonetheless highly controversial, time and again dividing the highest tribunals. For they involve not just balancing the interests of the innocent victim of the crime whose commission the thug has demanded against the claims to sympathy and understanding of the equally innocent victim of his threats, but also weighing the undoubted fact that the recognition of the excuse strengthens the arms of thugs and criminal and terrorist organizations, who would never seek to employ coerced accomplices if it did not make the accomplishment of their criminal objectives that much the easier. It enables them to say: 'you have nothing to lose from doing what we want done: for if you do it we won't hurt you, and if you are caught, the law won't hurt you either, since our horrible threats will give you a defence'. A duress of threats defence will, therefore, if allowed at all, have a restricted ambit.

One significant limitation on it will be the rule that threats from another person will not excuse the intentional or reckless causing of personal injury any more than they will excuse an intentional or reckless killing. For if someone acting for a purpose that ordinarily *justifies* otherwise criminal conduct is not permitted to injure, let alone kill, the harmless, a person cannot be *excused* doing so because he believes that his or another's life or safety would otherwise be in danger from a thug. The common law having taken its stand (rightly as many think) on this principle, the draftsman of a duress defence does not have to consider what sort of threats could possibly excuse killing or injuring the harmless. Relieved of this intractable problem he has no good reason for limiting the duress defence to cases where the defendant has been threatened with death or personal injury. For given the great variety of prohibited conduct, not all of it of the same gravity, there are other grave threats which may properly be allowed to excuse other criminalities. Might, for instance, there not be circumstances in which threats to destroy

---

[41] Cole [1994] *Criminal LR* 582.

irreplaceable property, to torture an animal, or to desert a woman and her young children should excuse, say, falsifying documents, possessing a controlled drug, or handling stolen goods? Why, it may be asked, should a person be convicted of crimes which do not involve intentionally or recklessly injuring or killing the harmless when the prosecution is, on the one hand, unable to persuade the jury (or magistrates) that most people in his situation would not have succumbed to the thug's threats and, on the other, able to vindicate the law by prosecuting the thug? The defence of marital coercion is now, no doubt, indefensible but it was not wholly without merit and points to excusatory considerations of a sort which the Law Commission wishes to ignore. The duress of threats defence, therefore, ought to be, and can be, simplified, as my clause 14 shows.

The 'duress of circumstances' situation, on the other hand, gives rise to very different considerations. So different indeed are they that talk of 'duress' serves only to confuse and, by pointing to inapt analogies, results in much muddled thinking. There is no indisputable criminal in the picture: no thug, no criminal or terrorist organization to be considered. The question in such cases is, simply, what should best be done, or what can properly be allowed, in a difficult and unfortunate situation, that has not otherwise been foreseen and provided for by the legislature? The question is, therefore, exactly the same as in any other case of justified conduct: that of balancing (subject to the same qualifications) the harm that would be suffered if recourse were not had to the prima facie criminal conduct, against the harm that will result if it is. What other rule is there that could be devised by the Law Commission after 'extensive study and widespread consultation'?

It is also apparent that a person who, knowing or believing that it is immediately necessary to avoid death or serious injury, acts in the only way that he could reasonably be expected to act (clause 26(1) of the Commission's Bill) will be doing no more than is reasonable in the circumstances as he believes them to be (clause 27(1)). If, then, acting to avoid death or serious injury is one of the approved justificatory purposes specified in clause 27 (as surely it must be), it follows that all cases falling within the Commission's 'duress of circumstances' defence will also fall within any adequately formulated justificatory defence. Such a defence must satisfy two criteria. Its list of justificatory purposes must, while not excluding unforeseen cases, be as complete as possible, and it must effectively break the vicious circle of justified responses to justified measures, while excusing conduct that results from mistakes about the existence of justificatory circumstances. Were clause 27 modified along the lines of the draft that follows, these criteria would be met. There would then be no need for a 'duress of circumstances' defence, no need to take cumulative and potentially troublesome precautions to keep defences of 'duress circumstances' and of acts otherwise justifiable apart (clauses 26(5) and 27(3)), and the occasions on which resort would have to be made to the 'common law', with its attendant risks of decisions inconsistent with the Code's provisions, would be much reduced.

IV

A more simply structured Code thus makes it possible to avoid the complications that arise from having separate provisions for (i) accessories, (ii) those who act through innocent agents, (iii) three inchoate offences rather than one, (iv) a 'duress of circumstances' defence, and (v) justified, but non-forcible, conduct. Ultimately (and this paper *has* reached its end) the question is whether maintaining (or resurrecting) distinctions between principals and accessories, between three different sorts of uncompleted offence, and between those who do what is prima facie criminal because of 'duress of circumstances' and those who do so in order to serve a legally approved objective, serves *any* useful purpose. Or is it just that the Law Commission (like so many other lawyers) is caught in nostalgia's tight grip?

DRAFT CLAUSES[42]

(Words in [square brackets] indicate issues on which the rule to be adopted may be thought to be debatable.)

1. *Committing offences*
    A person commits an offence if he—
    (a) does what this or any other enactment makes an offence; or
    (b) knowingly offers help to another who is doing, or is contemplating doing and then does, what this or any other enactment makes an offence; or
    (c) knowingly offers encouragement to another to do, and that other then does, what this or any other enactment makes an offence.

2. *Attempting to commit offences*
    (1) A person may be convicted of attempting to commit an offence if, intending to, or knowing that he will or may, do what amounts to the commission of an offence, he does an act that is more than merely preparatory thereto.
    (2) A person charged with committing an offence who is proved to have attempted to commit it may be convicted of that.
    (3) A person convicted of attempting to commit an offence is liable (unless otherwise expressly provided) to the same penalties and orders as if he had been convicted of committing it.

---

[42] The corresponding provisions in the Law Commission's draft Criminal Code (1989) are cll. 3, 25–28, 47–51 and in its draft Criminal Law Bill (1993), cll. 25–29.

(4) A reference in this or any other enactment to a person committing an offence is to be regarded as also referring to a person attempting to commit an offence unless (as in this section) a contrary intention clearly appears.

3. *Interpretation of sections 1 and 2*

For the purposes of sections 1 and 2 (and without prejudice to their generality)—

(1) a person is to be regarded as—

    (a) *himself doing*—

        (i) anything which he knowingly induces another to do, and

        (ii) everything which he knowingly joins with another in doing;

    (b) doing *knowingly* what he intends to do [or believes he is/realizes he may be doing];

    (c) *offering help* if, before or during the commission of an offence, he offers advice as to how the other may avoid detection or apprehension (but a mere failure to prevent or impede its commission is not to be so regarded);

    (d) *offering encouragement* when—

        (i) he agrees with another that the other will do what will or would, if what the agreement envisages is done, amount to the commission of an offence; or

        (ii) he seeks to instigate or persuade a person or class of persons to do whatever is an offence (but any such instigation or persuasion addressed to persons generally is not to be so regarded unless the offence is to be committed against a particular person or property, or class of persons or property, or on a particular occasion);

    (e) doing *an act that is more than merely preparatory* to the commission of an offence if he agrees with another that he will do what amounts to the commission of an offence;

(2) a person is *not* to be regarded as—

    (a) having offered *help or encouragement* if—

        (i) what he did could not, in the circumstances, have helped or encouraged the other; or

        (ii) he merely concurs in the statement of another's intention to commit an offence; or

        (iii) [he proves that] after doing so he did everything he reasonably could to prevent the other doing that for which he had offered that help or encouragement; [or

    (b) *doing an act more than merely preparatory* to an offence if paragraph (a) (ii) of this subsection applies to him;]

(3) *another person* is to be regarded as doing what this or any other enactment makes an offence notwithstanding that he belongs to a class of

person whom the enactment (or any other rule of law) expressly or implicitly exempts from liability to conviction.

11. *Justified acts*
Nothing done by a person who believes it to be[43] immediately necessary to achieve any purpose specified in section 12 shall amount to an offence by him unless—
  (a) it falls within section 13, or
  (b) it is, in all the circumstances as he believes them to be, unreasonable for him to do it.

12. *Justifying purposes*
The purposes referred to in section 11 are—
  (a) the prevention of the death of himself or another;
  (b) the prevention or alleviation of injury to, or the suffering of pain or illness by, himself or another;
  (c) the prevention or termination of an assault upon, or the detention of, himself or another;
  (d) the prevention of a crime [or a breach of the peace];
  (e) the prevention of the destruction or damage of, or any trespasses to, any property;
  (f) the prevention of the death of an animal, or the prevention or alleviation of any injury to, or the suffering of pain by, an animal;
  (g) the disciplining of a child who is in his care; and
  (h) the purposes specified in, and in the circumstances authorized by, any other enactment.

13. *Acts not justified under section 11*
Section 11 does not apply to a person who—
  (a) causes the death of, or personal injury to, any person whom he does not believe to be threatening or endangering the life, safety or freedom of himself or any other person, or to be committing or about to commit a crime, unless it is this person's own death, injury, pain or illness he is seeking to avert or ameliorate; or
  (b) causes the death of, or, personal injury to or assaults or detains any person who is, and whom he knows or believes to be, acting for a purpose specified in section 12 in the way specified in section 11, unless he knows or believes this person to be mistaken in thinking that it is immediately necessary so to act; or
  (c) causes the death of, or personal injury to, or assaults or detains, any person who is acting for any purpose specified in section 12 [in the way specified in section 11] whom he knows or believes to be a

---

[43] Professor Robinson (this volume) would, of course, wish to replace the words 'who believes it to be' by 'which is'.

constable, or to be assisting a constable, unless he knows or believes that constable or person to be mistaken in thinking that it is immediately necessary so to act; or

(d) acts only for a purpose specified in paragraphs (b), (c), (e) and (f) of section 12 without the consent of the person who, or whose property or animal, is to be protected unless this person is unable, or too young, to give or withhold that consent; or

(e) knowingly and unreasonably created the danger which he seeks to avert.

14. *Excused acts*

[(1)] A person does not commit an offence by doing anything (except intentionally or recklessly cause death or personal injury to another) if—

(a) he [reasonably] believes that if he did not do it an unlawful act with which another has threatened him would be done; and

(b) this threat was one which a person in his position who shared his physical characteristics and so believed could not reasonably be expected to resist; and

(c) he had not knowingly and unreasonably run the risk of being so threatened.

[(2)] It is for the defendant to prove that he entertained the belief specified in paragraph (a) of subsection (1).]

10

Coercion, Threats, and the Puzzle of Blackmail

Grant Lamond*

A complete theory of the criminal law must be located within wider philosophical perspectives, particularly those provided by moral and practical philosophy. The law has special institutional demands which fashion both its content and process, but underlying these constraints is the role of the law in giving effect to those values which it is obligatory or desirable to uphold. The enterprise of criminal law enforcement presupposes the validity of moral requirements. Hence the concern of criminal law theorists with the normative standards which warrant particular offences.

The aim of this paper is to demonstrate the value of setting problems of criminal law theory within the broader perspective of practical philosophy. Practical philosophy concerns the nature of human action—both individual and collective—and the reasoning which (either explicitly or implicitly) underlies action. A clearer appreciation of the nature of practical reasoning can help to explain some of the specific features of the criminal law. As an illustration of this general thesis I will discuss some of the more important features of coercion, coercive threats, and consent in order to show how a better understanding of these can assist in explicating an intriguing puzzle within the criminal law presented by the offence of blackmail.

The puzzle of blackmail arises in the following way. Statutory definitions of the crime extend its coverage to situations where one person demands money from another in exchange for not revealing some secret. What is puzzling about this is that in many cases of this kind the actual revelation of the secret would be quite legal. Revealing an affair to someone's spouse is legal, but threatening to do so unless paid a sum of money is a standard case of blackmail. If it would be legal to ask another for money, and also legal to

* I would like to thank John Gardner, David Kell, and Andrew Simester for their comments on earlier versions of this paper, and also the participants in seminars held in Cambridge in 1994.

reveal some piece of information, how can it be criminal to request money as the price for non-disclosure?[1]

This puzzle recurs in those definitions of blackmail which broaden it to include threats other than the revelation of information, and to cover demands other than the payment of money. In England, for example, an offence is committed where there is a demand reinforced by threats, made with a view to gain, and where the person making the demand does not believe that the threat is a proper means of reinforcing it.[2] Though there is no authority on the point, it is likely that a credible threat to commit suicide unless another destroyed valuable documents would satisfy this definition. Hunger strikes, for example, are sometimes regarded as constituting a form of blackmail.

Two issues are raised by the puzzle. The first concerns how the addition of a demand can transform a threat to do what would otherwise be permissible into a wrong. To answer this question requires an inquiry into the underlying normative issue of how it can be morally wrong to threaten to perform an action which it would be (morally) permissible to take. A second issue arises for those, such as liberals, who regard wrongful harm as a prerequisite for the criminalization of conduct. If an action does not warrant any legal sanction, whether civil or criminal, how can the *threat* of the same action when combined with a demand constitute a serious criminal offence?

I will argue in the final section of this paper that blackmail is, in essence, a crime which rests upon the moral wrong of depriving another of his property or interfering with his personal autonomy, without his valid consent. It is the use of coercive threats which invalidates the victim's consent to these deprivations and interferences.[3] So understood, it will be suggested that rather than being an embarrassment to the harm principle, the crime of blackmail represents a faithful application of it.

---

[1] This issue is often described as the 'paradox' of blackmail. Whilst the expression is rhetorically harmless, there is nothing strictly paradoxical in treating the combination of two elements differently from the way each element is treated in isolation, nor in treating the *threat* of an action differently from the action itself. See W. J. Gordon, 'Truth and Consequences: The Force of Blackmail's Central Case' (1993) 141 *University of Pennsylvania LR* 1741 at 1742–6 and M. Clark, 'There is No Paradox of Blackmail' (1994) 54 *Analysis* 54.

[2] Theft Act 1968, s. 21(1):

   A person is guilty of blackmail if, with a view to gain for himself or another or with intent to cause loss to another, he makes any unwarranted demand with menaces; and for this purpose a demand with menaces is unwarranted unless the person making it does so in the belief—

      (a) that he has reasonable grounds for making the demand; and

      (b) that the use of the menaces is a proper means of reinforcing the demand.

('Menaces' has been very liberally interpreted to encompass most threats: see, e.g., *Garwood* [1987] 1 All ER 1032.)

[3] Others focussing on the key role of coercion in understanding blackmail include L. Katz, 'Blackmail and Other Forms of Arm-Twisting' (1993) 141 *University of Pennsylvania LR* 1567, S. Altman, 'A Patchwork Theory of Blackmail' (1993) 141 *University of Pennsylvania LR* 1639, and J. Lindgren, 'Blackmail: An Afterword' (1993) 141 *University of Pennsylvania LR* 1975 at 1984–9.

An appreciation of the character of blackmail, however, requires an understanding of the nature of both coercion and threats, neither of which is currently well understood. These raise questions of considerable intrinsic interest which will be explored in the first two sections of this paper before I turn to the question of blackmail itself and (briefly) to the nature of consent. This might seem a very indirect route to the analysis of blackmail, but it is part of the thesis of this paper that problems like that raised by blackmail cannot be properly resolved without being set in the wider context of practical philosophy. Moreover, the issues traversed in the sections on coercion and coercive threats are of more general consequence than the puzzle of blackmail itself.

A number of caveats should be entered concerning the scope of the following analysis. It should be emphasized from the start that the solution to the puzzle of blackmail which will be advanced below is primarily formal rather than substantive in character. It is not concerned to show *which* threats constitute blackmail but why the attempt to secure an advantage through the use of threats requires justification. Its aim, therefore, is not to settle disputes over the boundaries of blackmail, but to identify the nature of the issues which are at stake in such substantive disputes.

Nor is the focus of the following discussion upon what are popularly regarded as the paradigmatic cases of blackmail, namely the threatened revelation of secrets about an individual's personal life.[4] It is situations such as these which ordinarily attract the deepest moral opprobrium and arouse the greatest concern. But the offence of blackmail, as it is defined in England for example, extends beyond such cases to any threat which is not a 'proper' means of reinforcing a demand.[5] My concern is not with one particular class of cases—even one as significant as this—but with understanding the offence as a whole.

One final proviso is that the discussion is almost entirely limited to elucidating the moral wrong which (it is claimed) underlies the legal offence of blackmail. I have little to say about the qualifications and restrictions which must be added to this conception in order to make individual threats proper objects of criminalization. I omit to do this not because I think it is a straightforward task, but rather because it is one which would require considerations well beyond the scope of the present paper. My main aim is to provide an elucidation which will dispel concerns over the coherence and legitimacy of the offence as it is currently defined, rather than to assist those undertaking the difficult task of providing an adequate formulation of the offence.

---

[4] See on this and on the historical development of the offence M. Hepworth, *Blackmail: Publicity and Secrecy in Everyday Life* (London, 1975) and P. Alldridge, ' "Attempted Murder of the Soul": Blackmail, Privacy and Secrets' (1993) 13 *Oxford Journal of Legal Studies* 368.

[5] Or—at least in England—any threat which is not *regarded by the defendant* as a proper means.

Coercion

Blackmail, it will be argued below, is a crime based upon the unjustified use of coercion. But to understand why this is so requires a fuller understanding of coercion—especially the normative aspect of coercion. Part of our conception of coercion is that it is something which stands in need of justification: to attempt to coerce another is to adopt a means which requires good reason to support. Before we can proceed to consider this, however, we need to clarify the nature of coercion by drawing two sets of distinctions which are often neglected in discussions of this topic: (a) between the possible types of coercion and (b) between coercion and duress.

THE VARIETIES OF COERCION

The first set of distinctions relates to the different means by which a person can be coerced. The term 'coercion' is infrequently used outside legal and philosophical discourse.[6] The core idea is of one person *forcing* or *making* another do as the former desires. The person who is coerced acts against his will.[7] This is sometimes expressed in terms of the person who is coerced acting 'involuntarily'. Such usage preserves the ambiguity of the idea of the voluntariness of actions, which ranges from those actions which are merely controlled by the agent to those which are undertaken willingly. There are in fact three types of situation in which we speak of coercion. I will describe them as (i) physical compulsion, (ii) psychological compulsion, and (iii) forced choice. It is coercion by forced choice which is at work in the case of blackmail.

   Physical compulsion involves the use of force against the victim's body to make it move in a particular way. The victim is physically incapable of successfully resisting the pressure brought to bear on him. His body becomes, in effect, an instrument through which the dominant party acts. Psychological compulsion, by contrast, is the rarer condition in which the victim is moved to act by the overwhelming urgency of his own desires. Extreme emotions and sensations, such as terror and excruciating pain, may move an agent to act despite his overall judgment that he should not do so. The torture victim straining to withhold information from his captors, or the petrified soldier trying to steel himself to resist against overwhelming odds, may find themselves incapable of resisting their own desires to speak or flee. They thus succumb not to the application of force but to the reactions instilled by the dominant party. The victim of psychological compulsion

---

   [6] On the language and context-dependence of claims of coercion see A. Wertheimer, *Coercion* (Princeton, N.J., 1987), ch. 10.

   [7] For clarity of exposition I will throughout this paper refer to the party coercing another as 'she' and refer to the party being coerced as 'he'.

acts, unlike the physically compelled, but his action is at variance with his overall judgment.

Coercion by forced choice, on the other hand, acts through the judgment of the victim rather than in the face of it. Here the dominant party is responsible for creating an unwelcome situation in order to engineer the victim's choice of a less unwelcome option. Criminals seeking to make good their get away may wound a bystander in order to hamper a pursuit, knowing that their pursuers will regard the risk of death to an innocent as more unwelcome than allowing the guilty to escape. The choice confronting the victim is 'forced' in two senses: there is no way of avoiding the choice—there is no third option by which both alternatives can be evaded (e.g., there is no-one else to assist the wounded bystander)—and the choice is designed to have the victim act as he would not willingly do. A common way of creating a forced choice is through the use of threats: the dominant party threatens to bring about an unwelcome consequence unless the victim acts as demanded. Forced choices thereby act through the victim's judgment of the unwelcomeness of the alternatives: the victim retains his ability to make a choice between the options and intentionally adopt the less unwelcome one. The victim of a forced choice is not incapable of acting other than as he does; it is simply unacceptable to him to do so.

All three varieties of coercion share the characteristic of subjecting the victim to an external pressure which affects the voluntariness of his actions. But the common terminology can obscure the fact that the effects on the victim in each case are quite different. The common law's traditional attachment to the idea that coercion results in the victim's will being 'overborne' subtly straddles the distinction between psychological compulsion and coercion by forced choice. It relies on an image of the victim's will being moved in a manner analogous to the manner in which the body is moved through physical compulsion. Whatever the usefulness of this image for understanding psychological compulsion, it is inapt as a picture of forced choices. But it is lent a degree of plausibility by the fact that certain threats, such as those of immediate physical violence, are capable of producing overwhelming fear in some cases and a decision to comply in others.[8]

DISTINGUISHING COERCION AND DURESS

The other crucial distinction, which cuts across the first, is between coercion itself and duress. In speaking of 'coercion' as opposed to 'duress' I am not appealing to a distinction consistently represented in our everyday language. Instead I am adopting these terms and seeking to use them to mark an important contrast between two distinct roles which coercion plays.

---

[8] Of course reactions to threats which fall short of psychological compulsion—e.g., fear and panic—can distort the judgment of the victim. I will ignore this complication although it has an important bearing on questions of the victim's culpability for making an unacceptable choice.

'Coercion', as I will use that term, refers to a particular means of affecting human behaviour. 'Duress', by contrast, refers to those situations in which coercion affects the attribution of responsibility to the party who has been coerced. Hence while coercion may lead to duress, and while duress presupposes coercion, coercion does not entail duress. There are cases where a party is coerced but remains fully responsible for his actions.

In the cases of physical and psychological compulsion these two concepts are relatively co-extensive, whereas in the case of coercion by forced choice they separate. In the former cases, the reason for the close link between coercion as a mode of influencing another and as a responsibility-affecting feature is self-evident. Absent considerations of prior fault or constructive liability, physical and psychological compulsion undermine the *preconditions* for the attribution of responsibility. The person subjected to physical compulsion does not 'act' at all: his body is merely an instrument of another's will, and thus he is unable to satisfy any conduct requirement for responsibility. The victim of psychological compulsion, similarly, has his capacity for self-control overwhelmed, like the person subject to an irresistible impulse or provocation. He acts in accordance with one of his desires but against his overall judgment. In a sense, therefore, he acts against his will: his actions do not accord with the usual conception of a fully intentional act. Hence the grounds for a claim to diminished responsibility.[9]

By contrast, a forced choice has no necessary implications for the victim's responsibility. Forced choices operate *through* the victim's judgment: what he chooses depends upon what is an unacceptable alternative *to him*. In order to make the victim choose an option the dominant party must create (or threaten to create) an alternative which the victim finds unacceptable relative to that option. What gives rise to a forced choice is thus dependent on each victim's judgment of what is unacceptable. But the fact that a victim finds an alternative unacceptable does not mean that he is not blameworthy for his particular choice. In order to exonerate himself he must show that he was either justified in taking the option he did or that his choice was at least excusable. If his judgment between the alternatives is morally misguided he may fail to show either of these things.

However, the fact that some forced choices do not exculpate the victim is not, in itself, a reason for regarding them as non-coercive. To do so is to conflate coercion with duress and overlook a series of considerations in favour of keeping them apart. The fact that in the cases of physical and psychological compulsion the two concepts generally track each other is not a reason for restricting coercion by forced choice to situations of duress. Clearly coercion is a necessary component of duress, but it only establishes duress where it justifies or excuses the victim's behaviour.

---

[9] Even if we judge that a person is blameworthy for not possessing greater self-control than he does, the attribution of blame for any action is different from that for a fully intentional action.

Equating coercion with duress turns coercion into a victim-centred concept, since it is only in cases where a victim would be exculpated that it will be possible to say that the dominant party coerced the victim. But there is an important sense in which 'coercion' describes a certain *mode* of influencing human behaviour: a mode which does, in many cases, affect the victim's responsibility but whose conception is independent of this further fact. What is central to this concept of coercion is the perspective of the dominant party. When an agent is contemplating how to affect another's conduct there are a range of options available: requests, persuasion, inducement, manipulation, threats, etc. From the agent's perspective what matters is that the mode adopted *succeed* in altering the other's conduct, whether or not the other is responsible for complying with the agent's initiative.

To identify coercion with duress can also unduly narrow attention to those cases where duress is most pertinent, namely three-party cases in which the dominant agent subjects the victim to a forced choice in order to have him commit some wrong against a third party. It is here that the victim of coercion will seek to exonerate himself by pointing to the choice that he had to make, and arguing that either he made the right choice or that he cannot be blamed for making the choice that he did. It is this issue, of course, which is presented by the criminal law defence of duress. But it is easy to overlook the fact that cases of wrongs to third parties also involve the responsibility of the *dominant* party for the wrong. This is not a matter of apportioning responsibility: the dominant party who uses threats to have a third party wronged is fully responsible for that wrong whether or not she is solely responsible. Even in cases where the victim has no good claim to duress the dominant party will remain responsible for bringing about the harm. What makes the focus of duress on cases of wrongs to third parties misleading is that these are situations where coercion as such is at its least important. After all, the dominant party is the instigator of the wrong, and the particular mode by which she chose to instigate it matters little to her responsibility, i.e., whether she paid someone to wrong the third party, or persuaded him, or misled him into doing so, or threatened him. In this situation, therefore, coercion is almost exclusively of derivative interest because of the victim's claim of duress.

Coercion, however, can be used for many purposes other than wronging a third party. It is more illuminating to consider two-party cases involving only the interests of the dominant party and the victim. A threat can be used to induce the victim to harm his own interests, or even to harm the dominant party, for example to procure active euthanasia from an unwilling doctor. Three-party cases also divert attention from the fact that transactions (such as contracts and conveyances) entered into between the dominant party and victim can be invalid if procured through the use of threats, irrespective of whether those same threats would excuse the harming of another. The victim's responsibility for his actions is sensitive in each of these cases to the details of the circumstances in which the conduct took place.

Most importantly, coercion may be used to promote the good or uphold the right. It can be used paternalistically—to prevent the victim harming himself or even to make him benefit himself. A degree of pressure is often thought to be acceptable to make children attend to their education, for example. Similarly, the law's use of sanctions is presumably directed to having people act as they should.

The case of the law serves as a reminder that our principal normative concern with coercion is not its use to make a victim wrong a third party but its use as a means of making the victim behave in permissible ways. Our concept of coercion includes the idea that its application is, prima facie, wrongful—in the sense that it stands in need of justification.[10] The use of coercion may itself wrong the victim. This explains how it is that transactions procured through the use of threats may be invalid. It also explains part of our concern with the moral limits of the law (whether criminal or civil). The law is partly a coercive system, and its use of sanctions and direct force needs to be justified.[11]

It is important, therefore, that the distinction between coercion and duress is observed. Duress pertains to the potential effects of coercion on the victim's responsibility for his conduct. Coercion denotes a particular means by which an agent can seek to influence the conduct of another. In order to clearly consider the nature of coercion it is necessary to focus upon the permissibility of its use by an agent, rather than upon its relevance to the victim's responsibility.

THE NORMATIVE ASPECT OF COERCION

As noted above, to coerce another is to adopt a means of influencing their conduct which is ordinarily thought to stand in need of justification. This aspect of coercion is easily understood in the cases of coercion by physical or psychological compulsion. The use of force against another and the intentional imposition of fear or pain are all, prima facie, impermissible. But what of forced choices, and in particular those created by threats? The preceding discussion has sought to establish that there is no necessary connection between coercion and exculpation. But this shows only that a forced choice need not excuse in order to coerce. A further question is whether every forced choice is coercive. Let us concentrate on the case of forced choice by

[10] Here, and throughout this paper, 'prima facie' is used to denote a partial judgment which may, all things considered, be defeated, rather than to indicate merely evidentiary support for the truth of some judgment which may later be shown to be false.

[11] The law is, of course, essentially a system of normative directives and requirements, but the pervasive use of sanctions to back up these directives explains the tendency to conflate questions of the limits of the authority of the law with questions of the permissible limits of coercive enforcement of the law.

threats. The question then is whether *every* threat which successfully creates a forced choice is coercive, irrespective of the triviality of what is threatened.

It could be argued that weak threats are simply not part of our concept of coercion.[12] If someone threatens to sulk all night if another does not make her a cup of coffee, the person threatened may feel that complying with the threat is the lesser evil but it is unlikely that we would describe him as having been 'coerced' into doing so. Our ordinary concept of coercion does not extend to such weak choice situations. This may be true, but it should not be regarded as dispositive of the question. It is equally true, for example, that not every hostile touching of another amounts to an 'assault' in everyday usage, but that fact does not settle whether or not there is a significant concept covering all such cases, irrespective of the degree of force involved. It is only if there is a relevant distinction introduced by such gradations that the concept should be so limited in critical discourse.[13]

Other moral terms have a wider scope. We speak of 'lies' to refer to cases which range from minor white lies to the most serious breaches of trust. (The term 'deceit', by contrast, seems to be limited to more serious cases of deception.) But we also regard lies as prima facie wrongful, even if only trifling wrongs. Some lies—for example white lies—may be very easily justified, but they need to be justified nonetheless. Similarly there is a sense in which we refer to the law as 'coercive' in order to indicate its use of sanctions. But some sanctions, such as parking fines, can be quite minor, even though they are intended to deter.

It is in this broad sense that all threats creating forced choices might be regarded as 'coercive'. But this broad sense will be significant only if it can be shown that all threats, like all lies, share some feature which makes it appropriate to regard them as requiring justification. It cannot be the case, for example, that threats are suspect because they intentionally alter another's behaviour: requests, offers, and persuasion all do the same in a morally innocuous way. Offers are wrongful only when they are made to induce the offeree to do something immoral, or if what the offeror proposes to do for the offeree should not be done in exchange for what is requested. Offers, therefore, are not impermissible *per se*, but merely contingently. In the next section I will examine the intrinsic features of threats which make them morally questionable.

COERCIVE THREATS

Threats are a form of social action: the characterization of an individual's action as a threat depends upon the shared understandings of the maker and

---

[12] This seems to be Raz's view: *The Morality of Freedom* (Oxford, 1986), 154.

[13] This is not to reject our common conceptions. There is clearly an advantage in restricting such terms as 'assault' and 'coercion' to serious cases of this type of wrong: to be told that someone has been assaulted is to be informed that a serious violation of their person has occurred.

the recipient concerning the point of certain communications and the intentions with which they are made. An account of threats should be capable of explaining these social functions and meanings. It should also be capable of explaining why certain cases of threats are regarded as parasitic, or secondary—cases such as bluffs, ineffective threats, and futile threats.

By these standards it is generally inadequate to characterize threats through the prevalent approaches to conceptual analysis. Conceptual analyses tend to be concerned with determining the boundaries of what can be appropriately designated as a 'threat' rather than with providing an account of their central or focal cases.[14] That is, they provide an all-inclusive, undifferentiated set of conditions covering every action which can, with linguistic propriety, be referred to as a threat. Marginal and anomalous cases are thereby treated as being of equal status with those cases which are more characteristic of the practice. This approach can result in a set of minimally necessary conditions for the use of the concept which obscure those salient features absent in secondary cases.[15]

An approach which emphasizes the importance of central cases, however, raises the problem of how they should be identified. What makes something a central rather than a peripheral case? Clearly the priority is not meant to be empirical—it is not that focal instances are necessarily the statistical norm. Instead our conception of the central case aims to explain how threats can perform the role they ordinarily discharge in social life and account for how we, as social actors, interpret the actions of others. Our understanding of others' actions is guided in part by our assumptions concerning their intentions and purposes. These assumptions depend heavily on the context in which the actions have taken place. It is the central case which explains why an interpretation of another's conduct is reasonable in the circumstances.

The role of the central case in interpreting others' conduct also explains why secondary cases are brought within the ambit of a social action. One can be held accountable for the reasonably foreseeable consequences of one's actions, and the same point holds for their foreseeable interpretations. One need not actually have performed the action with the appropriate intentions and purposes to be held accountable for it. This means both that (some) actions can be performed negligently, and that they can be manipulated by an agent who has reasons for wanting others to believe that she is acting for the standard purposes. What follows is an account of the central case of coercive threats.

---

[14] 'Central' and 'focal' are the terms employed by J. M. Finnis to describe the form of a social practice which fully characterize it: *Natural Law and Natural Rights* (Oxford, 1980), ch. I. Whilst indebted to this discussion, my account departs from Finnis' in a number of ways.

[15] It is common for this sort of methodology to rely heavily on particular counter-examples, often in highly unusual circumstances. R. Nozick's seminal article 'Coercion' (reprinted in P. Laslett *et al.* (eds.), *Philosophy, Politics and Society, 4th Series* (Oxford, 1972), 101) is an outstanding example.

Threats are either simple or conditional. A simple threat involves communicating the intention to bring about a consequence which is unwelcome to the recipient of the threat. A threat to have someone sacked would fall into this category. A conditional threat makes the carrying out of the consequence dependent upon the occurrence of some contingency: for instance threatening never to speak to someone again if it is shown that he has betrayed one's trust.[16] Coercive threats are a form of conditional threat where the unwelcome consequence is made conditional upon some conduct of the recipient. More precisely, a coercive threat involves the maker of the threat proposing to bring about an unwelcome consequence unless the recipient of the threat does something, in order to make the recipient adopt that course of action. The threat to sack an employee unless he breaks off a personal relationship, for example, is coercive.

There are three features of coercive threats which are crucial to a proper understanding of their nature. The first is that the proposed consequence is *unwelcome* to the recipient. The second is that the maker of the threat proposes to bring about the unwelcome consequence *because* the consequence is unwelcome to the recipient. The third is that the maker *commits* herself to bringing about the consequence if the recipient fails to act as demanded.[17] The key to the normative significance of threats lies in the second feature.

UNWELCOMENESS

The unwelcomeness of the proposed consequence is the most obvious feature which distinguishes threats from offers. Offers involve the proposal to bring about some consequence which the recipient finds welcome. For this reason it is generally desirable to receive offers but undesirable to be threatened. It is the character of the proposed consequence, however, which

---

[16] Some conditional threats are doubly conditional: where P threatens to X unless Q does Y, a common implication is not only that (a) if Q does not do Y then P will X, but also that (b) if Q does Y then P will not X. To avoid certain additional complications I will generally restrict the discussion to single conditional threats.

[17] More technically therefore, the *central* case of a coercive threat can be represented as follows:
P coercively threatens Q when
    (1) P communicates to Q an intention to X unless Q does Y, and
    (2) P intends by (1) to commit herself to X unless Q does Y, and
    (3) P's doing X would be unwelcome to Q, and P knows why this is so, and
    (4) (a) P's reason for (1) is to have Q do Y, and
        (b) P's reason for committing herself to X unless Q does Y is that X is both unwelcome to Q and more unwelcome to Q than having to do Y, and
        (c) Q knows both (4)(a) and (4)(b)
The central case allows secondary cases to be understood: thus bluffs involve P lacking the intent in (2) but seeking to have Q believe that (2) and (4)(b) are true; and threats which P hopes will be defied so that she can rationalize doing X involve (4)(a) and (b) being false but P seeking to have Q believe them. Secondary cases thus turn on Q reasonably believing, in the context in which P communicates that she is going to X, either (i) that P has the listed intentions, reasons, and beliefs, or (ii) that P wants Q to so believe.

determines the nature of the proposal, rather than the recipient's attitude to the proposal as a whole. Some offers we prefer not to receive—such as those we feel obliged to accept out of politeness when we would prefer to decline—whilst some threats may be prearranged by the recipient in order to stiffen his resolve and help him to act as he wishes. What makes a proposal an offer or a threat, therefore, is the recipient's view of what the maker is proposing to do, rather than his view of the proposal itself.

The question of how to determine whether or not a consequence is welcome has received considerable attention.[18] The predominant approach is to say that a consequence is unwelcome when its occurrence would be worse for the recipient than what he would have expected to transpire at the time it is to obtain. So if the proposal to bring about the consequence X is made at time t_1, and X is to obtain at some later time t_2, the nature of X must be determined by considering what the recipient would have expected the situation at t_2 to have been like, absent the proposal. This expected state of affairs at t_2 is generally described as the 'baseline'. X is *welcome* if it makes the recipient *better* off compared to the baseline, and X is *unwelcome* if it leaves the recipient *worse* off. Setting the baseline, however, remains highly controversial. There are at least three possible alternatives, which may be combined in various ways: (a) what *should* occur at t_2 (the 'moral' baseline), (b) what *would* occur at t_2 (the 'statistical' baseline), and (c) what the recipient *expects* would occur at t_2 (the 'phenomenological' baseline).[19]

I will not explore the complications involved in baseline analyses since I think the approach is misguided. A better approach, and one which tracks the phenomenology of threats more accurately, treats unwelcomeness as simply a question of the recipient not wanting X to occur. The gist of the difference between this approach and the baseline analyses is that it dispenses with the idea that the *only* reason we can have for not wanting the consequence to occur is that it leaves us worse off than we would have been (and/or should have been, and/or expected to be) at t_2. Instead we may not want X to occur because it will set back our interests or damage what we value, or because it will block the advancement of our interests or the promotion of what we value. This is so even if we know that the alternative to the dominant party proposing to do X would be her doing something worse than X itself.[20]

What the baseline analyses do address, however, is the fact that what we find unwelcome about a proposed course of action depends in part on what we believe others ought to do and what we expect them to do. (All three 'baselines' can play a role in determining this.) Most noticeably, the threat

---

[18] For an overview of some of the suggestions see J. Feinberg, *Harm to Self* (Oxford, 1986), 219–28.

[19] These alternatives are discussed by Wertheimer, n. 6 above, at 204–11.

[20] A college may, e.g., threaten to set penal exams for a wayward student rather than follow its standard (and legitimate) practice of sending him down.

of an *omission* turns on such responsibilities and expectations. This accounts for how it is that in addition to threatening not to pay a debt we ought to pay, or not to obey a law which ought to be obeyed, we can also threaten not to include someone in a will or not to make a donation to their cause, even though there is no requirement to do either of these things. By contrast, if a stranger accosts us in the street and tells us that she is *not* going to give us £500, this simply seems odd: why *would* she give us £500? Since we neither believe that she ought to do so nor expect her to do so, we have no reason to find the omission unwelcome.[21]

REASONS FOR INTENDING

It is a mistake, however, to suppose that the mere communication of an intention to do something which the recipient finds unwelcome is to threaten him. This is to ignore the distinction between threats and warnings.[22] Warnings do not relate exclusively to unwelcome actions to be taken by others. For example my informing my neighbour that I plan to mow my lawn on Saturday morning may be either a warning or a threat. Which it is depends upon my *reasons* for planning to mow on that day. If my reasons have nothing to do with how much my neighbour dislikes the sound then my communication will be a warning, perhaps motivated by my concern for his comfort. If, on the other hand, I intend to reciprocate for a raucous all-night party by mowing at that time *because* my neighbour dislikes it, then I am making a threat.

This distinction carries over to conditional proposals. I may inform a student that if his work is not submitted by a certain date I will fail him. If I am simply warning him I may emphasize this by saying that I will 'have' to fail him, or I may use the passive voice to say that his work will be failed if it does not meet the deadline. I adopt this phrasing to indicate that the unwelcomeness of being failed forms no part of my reason for intending to fail him. Of course the fact that failing will be unwelcome to the student is one of my reasons for making the communication, i.e., for warning him: indeed it may even be that my reason for giving him the warning is to try to ensure that he does submit his work by the deadline. What are crucial are my reasons for intending to fail the student if the work is late. If one of my reasons is that it will be unwelcome then I am making a threat. I may, for example, have settled upon this response to the student's tardiness because the prospect of being failed seems to be the only thing unwelcome enough to make him more punctual.

---

[21] Expectations play another role in threats (and offers): the force of a threat sometimes turns on expectations. If I regard the chances of my uncle leaving me anything in his will as quite low, the loss of that chance will not be as grave as it would have been if I had fully anticipated a large legacy. And if *P* threatens to bankrupt *Q*, where *Q* knows that another creditor is going to do so in any case, *P*'s threat will carry little weight.

[22] A sensitive treatment of this distinction can be found in Raz, n. 12 above, at 36.

Of course the overall *aim* of a coercive threat is to have the recipient comply with the accompanying demand: the communication is made in order to induce the recipient to act as demanded. The means by which this is sought to be achieved is through the maker of the threat committing herself to bring about an unwelcome consequence in the event of non-compliance. But the reason that the particular consequence is chosen is that it is unwelcome to the recipient (and more unwelcome to the recipient than having to do as demanded). This last element distinguishes coercive threats from conditional warnings.

The fineness of this distinction explains why we are sometimes so cautious in how we frame warnings concerning our own intentions. Hence locutions such as 'having' to fail someone, or 'having no choice' but to do something which will be unwelcome to them. Someone who has doubts about our reasons may well regard a warning as a threat, considering that the proposed action has been chosen (at least in part) because it is unwelcome.

It is the reasons for action of the person making a threat which transform an otherwise permissible course of action into something in need of justification. A coercive threat, therefore, need not involve the threat to bring about something which is impermissible *per se* (i.e., independently of the maker's reasons for bringing it about). Many coercive threats, of course, do involve such wrongs. But what makes a proposal a coercive *threat* is a combination of (i) the unwelcomeness of what is proposed, and (ii) the maker's reasons for proposing to bring it about. The fact that what is proposed is itself wrongful is not what makes it unwelcome, since welcomeness reflects the recipient's beliefs and values. One can just as easily *offer* to perform a wrongful act if the recipient finds it welcome. The recipient may be mistaken over what is morally required, or may not care that what he wants is morally impermissible. It is what someone wants, whether or not because he believes it to be in his interests or believes it to be of value, which makes it welcome to him. The distinctive wrong involved in threats is to propose to take an action *because* it is unwelcome to the recipient, i.e., because he does not want it done.

COMMITMENT

The third significant feature of threats is the role they play in their makers' practical reasoning. A coercive threat does not simply involve the communication of an intention to do something unwelcome. The non-performance of a threatened consequence is made *dependent* upon the recipient doing as demanded. The making of a threat thus creates a *commitment* to the carrying out of the intention. This is reflected in the fact that threats can be made by 'promising' to do something to the recipient. Coercive threats belong to a class of undertakings, including promises and vows, which commit the maker to a certain course of action.

To be 'committed' to a course of action is to have a reason for carrying it out with the same sort of peremptory status as the reasons created by promises and vows. Such a reason pre-empts most ordinary reasons for or against an action. This feature of coercive threats is central to understanding their social function and point. Take the case of bargaining.[23] Where two parties must make choices in succession, the second party can attempt to influence the choice of the first by committing herself to a particular course of action. Consider the following matrix, where two parties, *A* and *B*, must make choices which will result in different distributions of rewards for each, represented by the numbers in brackets (*A,B*):

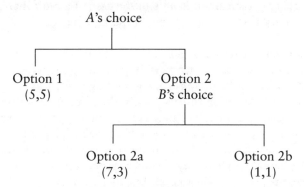

Here it is rational for *A* to take option 2, since it will then be rational for *B* to adopt option 2a rather than 2b. But it would be better still for *B* if *A* were to choose option 1. *B* can seek to influence *A*'s choice by threatening to choose option 2b if *A* does not choose option 1. Were a threat merely the communication of an intention it could not alter the fact that once *A* has chosen option 2 it is rational for *B* to choose option 2a. Threats, however, make it rational to adopt 2b: that is part of what it is to be committed to carrying them out. Threats can only have this effect by creating a reason which pre-empts ordinary considerations and requires action in accordance with the threat. That is, they by-pass action on the basis of the balance of ordinary considerations in favour of carrying out the threat.

There are reasons for people to have the facility to commit themselves to actions: situations like the bargaining example provide one such reason. It is the reasons which support the existence of a facility for creating peremptory reasons which justify the rationality of carrying out a threat even when it is against the balance of ordinary considerations in a particular situation.[24]

---

[23] For a brief account of bargaining, upon which the illustration in the text is based, see J. Elster, *Nuts and Bolts for the Social Sciences* (Cambridge, 1989), ch.14.

[24] That many threats are unjustified does not show that the ability to make such commitments is also unjustified, though it does show that agents are mistaken in thinking that they have a valid peremptory reason in such circumstances. Many promises (e.g., to commit wrongs) are similarly invalid.

Sometimes it is said that the reason for carrying out threats rests in the loss of credibility which would attend the failure to do so. Loss of credibility can, of course, be a reason to act as one has threatened to do. But notice that the fact that failing to carry out a threat entails a loss of credibility only makes sense *because* threats are believed to be peremptory reasons for action. There is, by contrast, no loss of credibility in merely changing one's mind over what one intends to do if it is no longer rational to do it. And significantly, accounts of threats which attempt to reduce them to (ordinary) reasons for maintaining credibility suggest that the reasoning of someone who makes a threat does not differ significantly whether the threat is genuine or a bluff. But characteristically it is only in the case of a bluff that considerations of credibility play a central role in deciding whether to make good on one's proposal.

This section has provided a general account of the nature of coercive threats, identifying their salient features. It has located the prima facie impermissibility of threats in the reasons for committing oneself to bringing about the unwelcome consequence. Threats involve the commitment to bring about unwelcome consequences because they are unwelcome to the recipient; they thus represent an intentional attack upon what the recipient values.[25]

None of this should be taken to deny that many threats are justified. Threats are acceptable when they are an appropriate means of preventing wrongdoing or promoting some good. But there is very little which can be said at an abstract level about *when* this will be the case. Three situations may be mentioned, however. As a general rule, if Q's failure to do Y would be a legitimate reason for P to do X, then P may permissibly threaten to do X in order to have Q do Y. Secondly, it is possible that some threats are justified on the grounds that they are bluffs, i.e., that they will *not* be carried out if they fail. It may be permissible in an emergency to threaten to harm an innocent third party in order to deter an imminent and serious wrong—for example to threaten to kill the child of an assailant in order to deter him from murdering a hostage.[26] More controversial are situations in which it is argued that the making of a (sincere) threat is justified because it will not in fact need to be carried out—as in the case of deterrence.[27]

BLACKMAIL

The puzzle of blackmail, it will be recalled, rests in the impermissibility of demanding something in exchange for abstaining from what would other-

---

[25] That wanting something entails valuing its occurrence follows from the reason-dependence of desires—on which see Raz, n. 12 above, at 140–3.

[26] See, e.g., J. G. Murphy, 'Consent, Coercion, and Hard Choices' (1981) 67 *Virginia LR* 79 at 81.

[27] See G. Kavka, 'Some Paradoxes of Deterrence' and 'A Paradox of Deterrence Revisited' in his *Moral Paradoxes of Nuclear Deterrence* (Cambridge, 1987).

wise be a permissible action.[28] It will be apparent by now that an understanding of blackmail requires an appreciation of the normative role played by reasons for action. I will begin this section by drawing some preliminary distinctions between the kinds of threats amounting to blackmail before going on to consider the nature of the wrong involved in the offence. As I indicated in the introduction, the discussion will range freely over actions which are immoral for the same reason as blackmail threats are criminal. Not all of these cases would, of course, be appropriate for criminalization. I will, in concluding, turn to the question of criminalization, and offer some observations on the compatibility of blackmail with the harm principle.

Blackmail threats can be divided into three categories. The first covers threats of actions which are impermissible *per se* (i.e., irrespective of the agent's reasons), such as physical violence, the destruction of property, and the publication of defamatory information. The second involves threats to perform actions which the maker is already duty-bound (to someone other than the recipient) to perform. A public official may, for example, threaten to revoke a licence where she is aware that conditions requiring revocation have already been fulfilled. Or an opposing party's witness in a civil suit may threaten to give her evidence truthfully unless she is bought off. Or an individual may threaten to report a crime committed against a third party unless her demand is satisfied. Thirdly, there is the category of threats where the action is permissible but not mandatory: the maker of the threat is not bound to take the action but may do so. This would cover cases such as threats to disclose having seen a person in a public place at a certain time, or to foreclose a mortgage which is in default, or to take one's business elsewhere.

The first two categories of blackmail threats are often regarded as unproblematic. The first category certainly is: it is clearly wrong to intend to commit an independent wrong against the recipient unless a demand is met. But the second category is itself puzzling. Why is the recipient of a blackmail demand regarded as the victim when the maker of the demand threatens to fulfil a duty to a third party, thereby proposing *not* to fulfil her duty if the demand is met? In many cases the recipient is better off for not having his licence revoked, or the testimony given, or the crime reported, and would prefer to do as demanded rather than see the duty to the third party discharged. I will return to this issue below. But it is the third category which is generally regarded as the genuinely puzzling one, for how can it be impermissible to threaten what it is permissible to do?

The first step towards elucidating the nature of blackmail is to appreciate that the actions proposed in the third category are not in fact permissible, because the permissibility of actions rests as much on the reasons for taking them as in their consequences. There is, for instance, nothing *per se* wrong

---

[28] A useful collection of articles, with references to the relevant literature, can be found in the Symposium on Blackmail in (1993) 141 *University of Pennsylvania LR* 1565–1989.

in playing music at a reasonable volume or mowing the lawn on a weekend morning, even though a neighbour finds these activities annoying. Nor is there anything wrong in engaging in commercial competition with another, even if one knows that this will drive the competitor out of business. But to do these things *in order* to bring about the unwelcome effects upon another *is* impermissible. To undertake the actions for that reason is to adopt a course of conduct aimed at diminishing another's well-being rather than at pursuing some acceptable goal. The idea that there is a 'puzzle' of blackmail, therefore, rests on too limited a view of which actions are impermissible.[29]

What is involved in blackmail (and in threats generally) is the intrinsic significance of actions—the fact that there are reasons for taking (or refraining from) an action other than the consequences it will bring about.[30] To those with an instrumentalist or consequentialist cast of mind such reasons can seem inexplicable. But they are a pervasive feature of our lives: they account for why it is important not only that my children are cared for, but that they are cared for *by me*. The reasons for which we adopt a course of action are a constitutive part of the action—part of its internal aspect. It is not merely intentions which can contribute to the description under which an action is taken, it is also the reasons for so intending.

Many impermissible actions, of course, lie beyond legal regulation. There are limits to what can be rightly or practically regulated by law. Many immoralities, such as certain types of lies, are not the appropriate concern of the law. In addition, it is generally impractical for the law to adopt regulatory categories other than those based on the consequences of conduct and/or awareness of those consequences, rather than the reasons for bringing them about. Thus if an action is not sufficiently serious in its actual or potential consequences to warrant legal redress, it will be unusual for the actor's reasons to alter this assessment. This explains why many of the threatened actions involved in blackmail are not themselves subject to legal sanction, despite their impermissibility.

The wrong of blackmail, however, does not rest simply in the fact that what is threatened is impermissible. Instead it relates to the way in which the prospect of this action is used by the dominant party against the victim. Blackmail involves the attempt to obtain some advantage from the victim, whether in the form of financial advancement, sexual intimacy, or control over the victim's conduct. The dominant party thus seeks to secure an

---

[29] I ignore a number of complications to this proposition. Most notably, an ill-motivated action may not wrong its victim if it prevents the victim from committing a wrong or if it serves some other value, i.e., if it is better that the action be taken—even for such a reason—than that it not be taken at all. This is well illustrated by freedom of speech considerations which may protect the actual (but not the threatened) publication of some fact whose disclosure is in the public interest, irrespective of the publisher's reasons for doing so. See H. Evans, 'Why Blackmail Should be Banned' (1990) 65 *Philosophy* 89 at 92–4.

[30] On the distinction between action and outcome reasons see Raz, n. 12 above, at 145–6, 279–83, and 305–7. (This is not to be confused with the distinction between agent–relative and agent–neutral reasons.)

advantage which it is permissible to enjoy only with the victim's consent. It is the effect of such threats upon the validity of the consent so induced which is the key to understanding blackmail.[31]

Consenting is a complex normative activity involving the manifestation of an intention to alter (or permit the alteration) of a normative situation. But a consent is effective only where it is the *valid* exercise of a normative power.[32] Broadly speaking, a normative power exists where there are reasons for a person to be able to bring about an alteration in her own (and/or others') normative situation when she intends to do so. A person's normative situation is the set of her rights, duties, privileges, and immunities. Promises, for example, alter the promisor's normative situation by putting her under a duty to the promisee; the same act alters the promisee's normative situation by conferring on him a right to the performance of the promised act. Consent is a common way of granting permissions and transferring rights. There are a variety of reasons which justify normative powers,[33] but a particularly important reason is that it enables individuals to exercise a degree of control over certain states of affairs. In some cases, such as the possession of personal property, the value of enjoying such control is regarded as outweighing the possibility of that control being used unwisely or incorrectly. In other cases the value of an activity is constituted by its being controlled by the participant: sexual intimacy, for example, has value only when participation is both willing and motivated for a particular range of reasons.

Whether a consent is valid depends upon whether the act manifesting the intention to consent is effective in those circumstances to bring about the normative change. One must distinguish, therefore, between the fact that a person intended to consent and the question whether it was valid.[34] Whether a consent induced by a threat is valid is a matter of whether the circumstances are compatible with the purposes for which the power exists, *viz.* enabling the individual to control that state of affairs.

This is sometimes thought to be a matter of whether the consent is 'voluntary' or not, but such an approach does little more than restate the problem. It is of course a useful test where 'involuntariness' refers to physical or psychological compulsion: as consent is an intentional action it cannot be produced by physical compulsion, and it is unlikely that anything other than

---

[31] The importance of consent in blackmail is recognized by J. Feinberg, *Harmless Wrongdoing* (Oxford, 1988), 254–6 and by Katz, *supra*, n. 3, at 1595–8. I attach no particular importance to the fact that blackmail offences are often complete upon the making of the threat rather than upon compliance with the demand: blackmail could just as easily be treated as an attempt.

[32] On normative powers see J. Raz, *Practical Reason and Norms* (2nd edn., Princeton, N.J., 1990), sect. 3.2.

[33] For a discussion see Raz, n. 12 above, at 80–8.

[34] For an interesting consideration of this problem in a legal context see Lord Goff's judgment for the Divisional Court in *Whittaker* v. *Campbell* [1984] QB 318 (discussing the offence of taking a vehicle without the owner's consent—Theft Act 1968, s. 12).

a fully intentional action would suffice, thereby ruling out psychological compulsion. But as most threats do not produce psychological compulsion this is beside the point. On the other hand, it is incorrect to say that consent must be voluntary in order to be valid if it suggests that the validity turns on the *degree* of pressure (either psychological or factual) under which the party acts. A person facing a hard choice, for example on the brink of bankruptcy, may be under immense pressure, but this does not in itself vitiate any transactions entered in those circumstances. Similarly, the fact that a country defeated in a war has no alternative but to surrender does not of itself affect the validity of that surrender. If 'voluntary' is not used to refer to compulsion, nor to the degree of pressure under which a person acts, it seems merely to describe those circumstances in which a consent will be effective in bringing about the purported normative consequences.

Where a party's consent is secured through his being presented with the choice of avoiding an impermissible action, that consent does not serve the purpose of allowing that party to control a state of affairs. Prima facie, therefore, such a consent is defective. There may be countervailing reasons in some cases (or classes of cases) which override this, but otherwise the consent will be invalid. This point is not limited to coercive threats: it also explains the (prima facie) invalidity of consents induced through (i) *offers* not to perform actions which are impermissible *per se* (i.e., irrespective of the offeror's reasons), and (ii) conditional *warnings* that an impermissible action will be taken if the recipient does not consent to something.

A coercive threat, I have argued, involves the maker of the threat committing herself to bringing about an unwelcome consequence because that consequence is unwelcome to the recipient. It follows that unless the threat is justifiable (or unless there are overriding countervailing reasons), any consent it induces is defective. The harm, then, which is involved in the crime of blackmail is the non-consensual obtaining of whatever is demanded from the victim. This explains why blackmail has traditionally been treated as a property crime[35] and its analogues have been located with sexual offences[36] and offences against the person.[37]

FOUR PROBLEMS FOR BLACKMAIL THEORIES

Understanding blackmail as a crime where threats invalidate the victim's consent helps to account for four issues which have been canvassed frequently in the literature on blackmail. The first issue is the underlying unity of the offence, despite the three separate categories of threatened actions mentioned above. The second issue concerns the apparent permissibility of

---

[35] e.g., Theft Act 1968, s. 21 ('Blackmail').
[36] e.g., 'Procurement of woman by threats' (Sexual Offences Act 1956, s. 2).
[37] e.g., 'Criminal Coercion' (Model Penal Code, § 212.5). See also the Oregon offence of 'Coercion' discussed in *State v. Robertson*, 649 P 2d 569 (1982).

'reverse bribery', i.e., cases where the transaction between the parties is instigated by the 'victim'. The third relates to the uncertain status of 'market price' blackmail. And the fourth concerns 'claim of right' defences to blackmail threats. I shall deal briefly with each in turn.

The unity of the offence of blackmail is perplexing not so much because of the 'puzzling' third category of threats (i.e., to take actions which would otherwise be permissible), but because of the second category of threats—those which are regarded as impermissible because they violate the rights of a third party. One influential theory, for instance, argues that all of the puzzling cases of blackmail involve wrongs to third parties, since P uses leverage over Q which rightly only 'belongs' to another person R.[38] A blackmailer of an adulterous spouse, for example, uses the leverage of the ignorant spouse to obtain something for herself. But this analysis is unable to account for cases where no third party is involved, for instance where P proposes to do something to herself (such as commit suicide) or where P threatens to foreclose a mortgage and demands something unrelated to the commercial transaction (e.g., that Q consent to sexual intimacy). In addition, locating the wrong of blackmail in the use of the third party's (R's) leverage over Q leaves unexplained the sense that blackmail wrongs the *victim Q*, even when he acquires some side-benefit from compliance with the demand. The wrongfulness of non-consensual deprivations, on the other hand, explains why the victim of blackmail is wronged whether or not a third party is also wronged. In all three categories of cases the threat has the effect of invalidating the victim's consent to the advantage that the dominant party wishes to acquire. It is this feature which supplies the unity of the offence as a wrong against the victim of the threat.

'Reverse bribery' refers to an asymmetry in the roles of the two parties in the puzzling cases of blackmail.[39] It may be blackmail for P to threaten to do something if Q does not pay her a sum of money, but there is nothing impermissible about Q initiating the same transaction by offering P money not to do that thing. P cannot, for example, threaten to take indiscreet photos of herself and Q to the press unless Q pays her a sum of money, but Q can offer P money to forestall the possibility. The explanation of why it is significant which party initiates the transaction follows from the role of threats in constituting the wrong in blackmail. Where Q initiates the transaction there is no reason to question the validity of her consent to that transaction.[40]

[38] J. Lindgren, 'Unravelling the Paradox of Blackmail' (1984) 84 *Columbia LR* 670.

[39] See S. W. DeLong, 'Blackmailers, Bribe Takers and the Second Paradox' (1993) 141 *University of Pennsylvania LR* 1663 especially at 1664–5, 1677–9, and 1685–8; also G. P. Fletcher, 'Blackmail: The Paradigmatic Crime' (1993) 141 *University of Pennsylvania LR* 1617 at 1620, 1624–5 and 1628, and Altman, n. 3 above, at 1649.

[40] Of course the question is then who really initiated the transaction. If P let it be known that she was going to do something in order to solicit a bribe from Q, she is in much the same position as a direct blackmailer.

It should also be noted that where P possesses information which a third party R is entitled to have but which P will suppress if (and only if) Q complies with her demand, any agreement between P and Q to suppress the information amounts to a conspiracy against R, irrespective of who initiates it. So if P knows that Q has committed a crime, or if P is a key witness in an action by R against Q, or if P is under a duty to inform R of something which Q wishes suppressed, then both P's blackmail of Q and Q's bribery of P will wrong R. But the offence of blackmail is only committed when P threatens Q.

'Market price' blackmail refers to the sort of situation where, for example, a writer (P) discovers information concerning Q in the course of her legitimate research, and the (quite permissible) publication of the information would considerably enhance the value of her work.[41] P informs Q that she is willing not to publish the information if Q will pay a sum equivalent to the amount she will have to forego. Some theorists consider such transactions to be permissible. What accounts for this view, on my analysis, is the perception that such a proposal need not amount to a threat. A coercive threat is a proposal to bring about an unwelcome consequence unless Q complies with a demand. But sometimes P can *offer* to *not* bring about an unwelcome consequence which P already intends to carry out for reasons independent of its unwelcomeness to Q. The market price element plays an evidentiary role in indicating that P is not seeking to threaten Q but to do something welcome for her. P is *warning* Q of her intentions and offering to forego the action.[42] Consequently, if Q accepts P's offer then P is committed to non-disclosure, whilst if Q rejects it P is not committed to publication, as she would be if her proposal were a threat. As this all turns on P's reasons for action, it is clearly a difficult distinction to draw; hence the ambivalence of most criminal law theorists over such cases. Some regard it as impractical to distinguish from blackmail proper,[43] others suggest the possibility of a positive defence.[44]

The appropriateness of 'claim of right' defences to blackmail concerns whether it may be acceptable for P to threaten X in order to have Q do Y in cases where P has a *right* that Q do Y, despite the fact that Q's failure to do Y would not be a legitimate reason for P to do X.[45] P might, for example, threaten to reveal Q's adultery unless Q repays an overdue debt. Whilst it is

[41] See, amongst others, R. Nozick, *Anarchy, State, and Utopia* (Oxford, 1974), 85–6; J. G. Murphy, 'Blackmail: A Preliminary Inquiry' (1980) 63 *The Monist* 156 at 164–5; Feinberg, n. 31 above, at 263–4 and 276; and Altman, n. 3 above, at 1647–9 and 1650.

[42] Note that if the proposed action were a wrong against Q *irrespective* of P's reasons for doing it (e.g., an infringement of privacy), then a consent induced by the intention of P to commit a wrong against Q would also be defective: it would not matter that P's proposal was an offer rather than a threat.

[43] e.g., Altman, n. 3 above, at 1647–9 and 1650.

[44] e.g., Feinberg, n. 31 above, at 276.

[45] Lindgren, n. 38 above, at 677–9; Feinberg, n. 31 above, at 264–6; and Altman, n. 3 above, at 1649.

generally accepted that some threats are always illegitimate (e.g., those to commit criminal offences) there is no consensus on the threat of other actions unrelated to the source of the claim. This reflects the fact that some threats are permissible even though carrying them out would not be.[46] Our uncertainty over allowing this exception reflects the uncertainty over which situations justify bluffs, and an unease over the effects of making such threats. In some cases what began as a bluff may, upon reflection, lead the person making the threat to carry it out.

CONCLUSION: BLACKMAIL AND THE HARM PRINCIPLE

It is sometimes thought that blackmail presents a particular challenge to the harm principle.[47] This is due to the apparent anomaly of permitting an action whilst criminalising demands backed up with the threat of such an action. But as the preceding discussion has sought to demonstrate, there is an important distinction between the two situations. The harm principle provides that wrongful harm is both necessary for criminalization and a reason in favour of it. Where an action is carried out it must be shown that the result of the action is a wrongful harm. In the case of coercively threatening the same action, on the other hand, the harm rests in obtaining whatever is demanded without the victim's valid consent.

The harm principle is primarily concerned with outcomes—causing death, destroying property, violating the person. When these outcomes are brought about wrongfully they satisfy the prerequisites for criminalization. The focus of the criminal law is on outcomes which are (prima facie) impermissible to bring about, or actions taken with such outcomes as further aims. An outcome does not amount to a harm merely because someone does not want it to occur: there must be a setback to some worthwhile interest. If an outcome is not regarded as a harm (or a serious enough harm) warranting criminalization, the reasons of the party bringing it about will rarely alter this. Where, on the other hand, a party secures an advantage from another through the use of threats, the validity of the other's consent is directly put in issue. The harm then resides in the infringement of the control which the victim enjoys over some sphere.

At a deeper level, the crime of blackmail is fully compatible with the rationale for the harm principle. The harm principle is a moral principle guiding the law on the question when it is permissible to punish conduct. It is a limiting principle: it does not require criminalization but merely provides a reason in favour of it. Nor does it necessarily exhaust the principles justifying the coercive use of the law. Civil law, welfare law, and public law may

---

[46] See the text above at n. 26.

[47] Feinberg, n. 31 above, ch. 34, and M. Gorr, 'Liberalism and the Paradox of Blackmail' (1992) 21 *Philosophy and Public Affairs* 43.

all rest on separate justifications.[48] The harm principle sets limits on the scope of the use of sanctions to influence conduct through punishment and deterrence. It represents part of a concern with the limits of justifiable coercion. But coercion is of concern whether it emanates from the state or some other source. Just as it is wrong for the state to overstep these limits, so, too, is it wrong for others to do so. The prevention of wrongful harm not only sets limits to the use of coercion by the state—it licenses its application against the unjustified use of coercion by others.

[48] Regulatory offences, too, may have a separate basis, though by 'regulatory offences' I do not necessarily mean those offences as they are currently conceived. Many serious offences involving health and safety are often treated as 'merely' regulatory.

11

Dealing with Drug Dealing

Peter Alldridge*

Drug dealing is not a matter which has occupied theorists of criminal law very much. Their staple remains issues of responsibility—intention, recklessness, voluntariness, acts, and omissions—centred around the small body of crimes—usually offences against the person—in the context of which 'general principles' are discussed. The refined consideration of questions of responsibility in those areas provides a marked contrast to the treatment of drug offences.

One of the incidents of concentration upon this small group of offences is that the theorist seldom has to consider what exactly is wrong with a given offence. Either that is sufficiently obvious as not to require any explanation (most clearly in the case of all non-consensual offences against the person), or it is regarded as the appropriate study of a different discipline (political philosophy) or there are so many other considerations of a pragmatic nature which militate for or against criminalization that the moral quality of the act becomes a marginal consideration or, perhaps cynically, it is an enquiry best avoided for fear of what might be discovered. Only recently, in consequence, have questions such as 'What exactly is wrong with blackmail or money laundering?'[1] seriously been addressed. So long as the purpose of dividing material is solely to cover ground, its ordering is at best a matter of pedagogical convenience and at worst something purely arbitrary. The analyst can, however, be more ambitious. An answer to the question 'What exactly is wrong with the offence in point?' should produce two things:

> (i) a basis for an analytical critique of non-coherent rules. It will say to legislators (including judges, if they are legislating), 'If *this* is the moral objection to this form of conduct, then *this* is the criminal law norm which follows.' Now of course that will not be determinative of the

* Cardiff Law School. I am grateful, for helpful comments, to participants in a seminar at Gonville and Caius College, Cambridge in Dec. 1994, to Stewart Field and to Andrew Simester.

[1] Regarding blackmail there is now a huge literature, to which (1993) 141(5) *University of Pennsylvania LR* 1565–1975 is central. On money laundering, see B. Fisse and D. Frazer, 'Some Antipodean Skepticism about Forfeiture and Confiscation of Proceeds of Crime and Money Laundering Offences' (1993) 44 *Alabama LR* 737, 740–1.

shape or content of the criminal law,[2] but it will be a point from which to start.

(ii) a basis for the analytical critique of non-coherent sentences, because it will say to sentencers, 'If this is what is thought to be bad about this offence, then this is what makes them worse and that not so bad, and this is how they should be graded relative to other offences.'[3]

WHAT IS WRONG WITH DRUG DEALING?

In this paper I shall examine one offence (or group of offences), drug dealing.[4] There is no offence which is having a greater impact, whether measured in terms of policing, the prison population, or almost any other index, upon the development of contemporary criminal justice systems all over the world. Many of the changes which the British criminal justice system has undergone in the last fifteen years have been driven by drugs. If there is to be a criminal law of the European Union, it, too, will be dominated by drugs. Drug offences give rise to arguments for greater police powers and resources, alteration of police ethics (because of the use of *agents provocateurs* and various surveillance techniques) and greater internationalization of criminal law. Drugs offenders form a very substantial proportion of our prison population. The latest set of criminal statistics[5] shows that there has been a 200 per cent increase in the last ten years in the number of offenders found guilty at all courts of indictable drug offences. On 30 June 1993 27 per cent of all women in prison in England and Wales, and 10 per cent of the prison population as a whole (excluding fine defaulters) were there directly as a result of drug offences[6] and an unquantifiable further proportion to drug-related property offences.[7] Yet drug offences are marginalized from the mainstream study of criminal law and criminal law theory. They do not rate a serious mention in *Smith and Hogan*,[8] and get only two pages

---

[2] This is particularly important in the context of drug dealing: what it means is that *even* if a convincing account is given of what is wrong with drug dealing, nonetheless it may not be a good idea to prohibit it. Considerations of aggregate social value may be thought important here.

[3] This assumes, of course, that the recognition of such factors is and should be part (though not all) of the sentencing function.

[4] That is, offences of manufacture, supply and possession with intent to supply controlled drugs contrary to Misuse of Drugs Act 1971, ss. 3, 4, and 5(3) and Customs and Excise Management Act 1979, ss. 50(2), 50(3), 68(2), and 170.

[5] *Criminal Statistics 1992* Cm 2401 (London, 1993), table 5.19.

[6] *NACRO Briefing paper No. 24* (Aug. 1994): 310 of 1,130 women and 2,880 of 31,380 men.

[7] Even within the areas traditionally encompassed by the 'general part' drugs offences have their effect. (My speculation is that) the burden of proof in duress would not be a serious issue (Law Commission No. 218, *Legislating the Criminal Code: Offences Against the Person and General Principles* (1993), paras. 31.1–31.16) were it not for the claims made by persons smuggling drugs into the jurisdiction to have done so under duress in their country of provenance.

[8] This is not because of the relative newness of the offences: offences under the Computer Misuse Act 1991 are included. J. C. Smith and B. Hogan, *Criminal Law* (7th edn., London, 1992), contents.

in Ashworth's *Principles of Criminal Law*[9] (which lumps together possession and dealing). Perhaps most surprising of all, drug dealing gets no consideration independent of drug use in Feinberg's *magnum opus*.[10] For those
interested in having an ethically defensible criminal law, it provides a most
pressing set of issues. Put briefly, the problem is that on the one hand, very
extensive resources are being devoted to the issue of drug dealing and, on the
other, it is not clear exactly what is wrong with it, and it may well be that
arguments for controls upon (at least) some drugs cannot rationally be distinguished from arguments for controls upon alcohol. If it is the case that
drug dealers are just people trying to make a decent living by buying and
selling a commodity which other people want to consume for recreational
purposes, then there can be no moral justification for the prohibition or the
consequent expenditure. My question here is not whether there are sound
practical reasons for prohibiting the practice, or whether it is practically
possible to prohibit it, or as to the rights of persons who wish to take drugs,
but whether there are grounds for disapproval of drug dealers, and how, if
there are, drug dealing can defensibly be graded as against other offences.

Extrapolating from the current rates of escalation in drug-related crime,
the next ten years will either see measures of decriminalization enacted, or
the preponderance of the resources of the criminal justice system devoted to
drug offenders. No doubt this gives rise to enormous practical problems for
legislators and criminal justice officials. But it also challenges theorists who
want to find a moral basis for the discriminations between forms of behaviour made in the system of condemnation and sentence. A morally defensible criminal law must have a satisfactory account both of what is wrong
with drug dealing, and of the sentencing differentials made in drugs offences.
If the treatment of drugs offenders cannot be justified on a moral basis,
either for reasons of internal inconsistency or in comparison with other
offences, then any attempt to give the entire system moral legitimacy by
making sophisticated and apparently plausible differentiations elsewhere is
at best something of a diversion.

Within a framework which assumes that moral disapproval is a prerequisite for serious criminal offences, I want to consider the consequences for the
treatment of drug dealing of various accounts of what actually is objectionable about it. It may very well be that the principal justification for prohibiting simple possession of drugs[11] is a paternalistic one. But it does not
follow that offences of manufacturing, importing, supplying, or possessing
with intent to supply drugs are simply varieties of complicity in, or procur-
ing of, simple possession. The debates surrounding drugs give the impression that any participant other than the eventual user (who is often
stereotyped as somewhat pathetic) is *caput lupinum*, and that the kinds of

---

[9] A. Ashworth, *Principles of Criminal Law* (2nd edn., Oxford, 1995), 53–5.
[10] Joel Feinberg, *The Moral Limits of the Criminal Law* (New York, 1984–8).
[11] I shall consider this question only in so far as it bears upon the liability of the dealer.

gradations in seriousness which inform different classifications and sentencing practices elsewhere[12] are not necessary. All persons involved are tarred
with the same brush. There is a trend current in drugs legislation towards
the return of legal mechanisms equivalent to forfeiture for felony.[13] It is regularly claimed that drugs offences are particularly bad, and therefore that
especially strong police powers are needed to combat them.[14] In addition to
giving rise to intrusive rules of procedure and harsh standards for punishment, this anathematization of drug dealing has also meant that the normal
kinds of constraints in the definition of the offence have been side-stepped.
By 'constraints' I mean, for example, that if harm to users is the focus of the
legislation, then foresight of the harm might be expected to be expressed as
a *mens rea* requirement, that the remoteness of the harm might be regarded
as a limitation upon criminal liability,[15] and that (at least in the case of
offences commanding a prison sentence) the imposition of strict liability
might be viewed with considerable suspicion.

In seeking descriptions of what actually is wrong with any particular
offence, and how to make differentiations in gravity between differing ways of
committing it, one place to start is with the cases on sentencing. The
leading 'guideline' case on sentencing for drugs offences is *Aramah*.[16] The
judgment[17] discloses three major reasons for criminalization: profits, consequential crime (both by users and distributors), and harm to the user. The
guidelines for sentencers which Lord Lane CJ laid down differentiated sentences for drugs offences according to the class of the drug (class A more serious than class B, class B more serious than class C), 'street value' (higher 'street
values' more serious than lower) and category of involvement (importation
more serious than dealing, dealing more serious than possession *simpliciter*). It
is these guidelines, with some subsequent modifications, which govern sentencing in drug cases today, and which deserve to be considered closely as indi-
cators of what is taken by the courts to be wrong with drug dealing.

PROFITS

Are the profits what is really objectionable in drug marketing?[18] The guidelines in *Aramah* specifically linked the penalties to the 'street value' of the

---

[12] Cf Horder, this volume, regarding offences against the person.

[13] Drug Trafficking Act 1984.

[14] They are also the driving forces behind such extensions in the scope of the domestic criminal law as s. 20 of the Misuse of Drugs Act 1971 (assisting in or inducing commission outside
the United Kingdom of an offence punishable under a corresponding law) and the amendments
to s. 1 of the Criminal Law Act 1977 contained in the Criminal Justice Act 1993, s. 5.

[15] See Andrew von Hirsch, 'Extending the Harm Principle: "Remote" Harms and Fair
Imputation', this volume.

[16] (1982) 4 Cr. App. R (S) 407.   [17] See especially the passage at 408–9.

[18] And see *Couzens and Frankel* (1993) 14 Cr. App. R (S) 33—conspiring to produce
NMDA (a class A drug) on a small (experimental) scale in U.K. with a view to larger scale pro-

drugs which were in point:[19] the greater the 'street value', the greater the penalty.[20] The principal justification for this factor is that it was the profit which the courts found to be significant, irrespective of any danger which the drugs represented. Motive has never been thought irrelevant to sentence, and in spite of the often-repeated statement that motive is irrelevant to criminal liability,[21] there are a number of mechanisms for making it the determinant. One mechanism for making motive relevant to liability is to make transactions lawful unless commercial. There are, in the United Kingdom, some transactions which are illegal only when commercial.[22] There are others some preparations for which are illegal only when the final arrangement is commercial.[23] Rules relating to bribery and corruption generally provide that it is entirely lawful for an official to be helpful to a member of the public, but that if she receives remuneration otherwise than from her employer, however, it becomes illegal.[24] It is lawful (without more) to keep information about another person secret: it becomes blackmail when done for money. It is a good thing that Parliamentary questions are asked: it is not a good thing that they are asked for money. In the present case, however, it is not clear whether and to what extent drug dealing is to be condemned because of the profit motive. Actual or potential profits are irrelevant to *liability*: thus profits might be an aggravating feature, but cannot of themselves be a reason for criminalization. Nonetheless the fact that the dealer acts for a profit is not irrelevant to the account which will be developed later.

CONSEQUENTIAL CRIME

One of the matters mentioned by Lord Lane CJ as being of increasing concern is that of consequential criminality—the argument that drug takers will steal, deal in drugs, enter into prostitution or commit other crimes in order to finance their habit, or that those engaged in the supply of drugs will engage in 'gang wars' with their competitors. A rational legislator might well take the view that each of these considerations argues for decriminalization. So far as concerns the first (addicts will commit crimes to finance the

duction elsewhere generated a sentence of 9 years owing to the prospect that they were trying to make 'a considerable profit' (at 34).

[19] See Les Kay, '*Aramah* and the Street Value of Drugs' [1987] *Criminal LR* 814. *Aranguren et al.* (1994) 99 Cr. App. R 347, 16 Cr. App. R (S) 211, [1994] *Criminal LR* 695 represents a move away from the use of 'street value', but the reasons—that street values had been going down—are extraordinary.

[20] And see P. Green, C. Mills, and T. Read, 'The Characteristics and Sentencing of Illegal Drug Importers' (1994) 34 *British Journal of Criminology* 479 at 482.

[21] J. C. Smith and B. Hogan, n. 8 above, at 79: cf Robinson, this volume.

[22] Human organ transplants (Human Organ Transplants Act 1989, s. 1) and surrogacy arrangements (Surrogacy Arrangements Act 1985, s. 2).

[23] Commercial sex work. Street Offences Act 1959, s. 1.

[24] Public Bodies Corrupt Practices Act 1889; Prevention of Corruption Act 1906.

addiction), the argument is well known—decriminalize, cut out the 'crime tariff', cut out (or cut down) consequential crime. As for the second it is clear that the sort of internecine strife to which Lord Lane referred is an effect of, rather than a reason for prohibition. There has not been violent competition between alcohol suppliers in the United States since the repeal of prohibition. This is not to say that competition between alcohol suppliers is crime-free.[25] But it is no longer attended by serious violence. Neither the first (profits) nor the second (consequential crime) argument advanced by Lord Lane give independent reasons for criminalization, and they can only explain the crime being accorded greater gravity than would otherwise have accrued.

HARM TO USERS

In denouncing drug dealers Lord Lane CJ placed most emphasis on the fact that addicts may lead unpleasant lives or die. This argument can be presented in two ways. Drug dealing can be expressed either to be a form of inchoate offence against the person, or as a form of complicity in the self-harm of the user, that self-harm being prohibited either on paternalist or on moral grounds. The distinction, between treating drug dealing as an act of complicity in self-harm and as an offence against the person in itself, reflects the complaint von Hirsch[26] makes against the 'standard analysis' for imposition of criminal liability when harm is caused—that it fails to recognize the significance of intervening choices. An analysis which regards drug dealing as a harm against the addict and characterizes the dealer as committing an offence against the person disregards the choice made by the user to take the drug. One which regards the dealer as complicit in wrong by the drug taker does not. I consider these in turn.

Drug Dealers Commit Inchoate Offences Against the Person

There are many sentencing remarks, other than those in *Aramah*, to the effect that what is wrong with drug dealing is that any involvement in a chain of supply constitutes a step towards harming the eventual user.[27] If this is indeed the major vice of trafficking then further questions arise. First, why it is that the consent of the user is not regarded as a relevant consideration?[28] Where the drug is actually administered by another person it

---

[25] Witness the Guinness/Distillers saga. Peter Pugh, *Is Guinness Good for You? The Bid for Distillers* (London, 1987).

[26] See von Hirsch, 'Extending the Harm Principle: "Remote" Harms and Fair Imputation', this volume.

[27] There is, e.g., a reference to 8 deaths from ecstasy (MDA) by Beldam LJ in *Allery* (1993) 14 Cr. App. R (S) 699 as being an account of a harm which flows from the drugs and which should inform sentence, and, of course, many trial judges passing sentence make the same sort of statement.

[28] I except, for the purposes of this discussion, questions of youth, which give rise to some theoretical and many practical problems.

appears that consent is no defence,[29] but how far that rule extends is unclear. In its recent consideration of consent the Law Commission[30] confined its attention to offences against the person, and drug offences were not regarded as falling within the ambit of the review. Secondly, even if consent does not affect liability, it might be thought to mitigate. If supplying drugs is an inchoate offence against the person, we need an account of why it is that no mitigation can come from the fact that the actual consumption of the drug generally takes place in private and is, if not for pleasure, then for relief. These are precisely the grounds upon which sentences were reduced by the Court of Appeal in *Brown*.[31] Is drug dealing, expressed as an offence against the person, really different? This question at least needs to be considered. Thirdly, and even more fundamental than the first two objections, it is not even clear that harm is done to a voluntary user of drugs by supplying her.

Drug Dealers are Complicit in Self-harm by the User

So far as users are concerned, the courts have been somewhat diffident about explicitly adopting the paternalistic position, even when simple possession is charged. Rather than say to a user, 'I am sending you to prison for your own benefit and for the benefit of those like you', judges have tended to say, 'Like it or not, this is the law here. If you don't like it, go somewhere else.'[32] Nonetheless, assuming that it is paternalism which supports the prohibition on possession, where does that leave the supplier? Even if (and I do not propose to rehearse those arguments[33]) it were legitimate to deploy the criminal law paternalistically, or in order to enforce some particular moral position, there would remain the question of sanctions. If what is going on really is an exercise in paternalism then one might expect the sentences on the user to be of the same order as those for seat belt and crash-helmet offences.[34]

---

[29] *Cato* [1976] 1 WLR 110; [1976] 1 All ER 260.

[30] Law Commission Consultation Paper No. 134, *Consent and Offences Against the Person* (1994).

[31] Lord Lane CJ differed from the trial judge in accepting consent to be one of the mitigating factors, 'chief among which is the fact that the victim of the assault was not only a consenting party but seemingly derived pleasure from the infliction upon him of pain by the other. That, coupled with the fact that the acts were carried out in private and in the belief that they were not criminal [operates as mitigation].'*Brown* [1992] QB 491 at 500H–501G.

[32] See, e.g., Griffiths LJ in *Robertson-Coupar and Baxendale* (1982) 4 Cr. App. R (S) 150 at 151.

[33] Joel Feinberg, *Harm to Self* (New York, 1986), 3–26; Douglas Husak, 'Recreational Drugs and Paternalism' (1989) 8 *Law and Philosophy* 353.

[34] Road Traffic Act 1988, s. 14 and s. 17 respectively: maximum penalty, fines at levels 2 and 3 on the standard scale, respectively. Road Traffic Offenders Act 1988, sched. 2. This kind of argument (that some types of offence are sufficiently unimportant that very heavy sentences are not appropriate) is not really known at a constitutional level in the U.K., but might become so known under the jurisprudence of art. 3 of the European Convention on Human Rights. In *Bowers* v. *Hardwick*, 478 US 186 (1986), (*per* Powell J at 197–8) a less liberal U.S. Supreme Court than is currently constituted was apparently prepared to support the view that where the

ALCOHOL AND TOBACCO

But there is a much more fundamental objection, which applies to all three of Lord Lane CJ's rationales. Any satisfactory explanation of what is wrong with drug dealing must account for legal regulation of tobacco and alcohol. It is of course possible to provide histories of how things have turned out as they have,[35] but that does not amount to a moral justification. A justificatory analysis must either explain in what respects tobacco and alcohol are different, or must advocate similar treatment for tobacco, alcohol, and other drugs. If profits are the matter in issue, then supplying alcohol or tobacco has the same acquisitive objective. If consequential crime is the matter, then alcohol-related crime is, in the United Kingdom, far more of a problem than other drug-related crime, and it is reasonable to conjecture that the disparity would only be amplified were alcohol to be prohibited or other (currently illegal) drugs permitted, or both.[36] Thirdly, regarding the 'harm to users' rationale, there is again no defensible distinction to be made between tobacco, alcohol, and other drugs. There are indeed drug-induced deaths in the United Kingdom, but the numbers are about 300 a year, which compares very favourably to deaths from alcohol or tobacco.[37] It might be said that the numbers of deaths are low because drugs are illegal, but given their relatively wide availability this seems implausible. Indeed, the mortality rate may well be able to be reduced by ensuring that users have better information as to the strength and purity of the product they use, in the way that such information is available for alcohol and tobacco. That can better be achieved by regulation of than by outlawing the trade in drugs. Whether the wrong which drug dealers do is described as profiteering, as generating consequential crime, or as an act of complicity in self-harm or some kind of inchoate offence against the person, then either it is impossible to justify the current levels of sentences and legal and political *brouhaha* regarding drugs, or those same levels should apply to alcohol and tobacco.

Instead of working within these possible justifications, what I hope to show is that, once a decision is taken to criminalize the supply of addictive drugs, the basic relationship which is created is one in which the supplier exploits the addict. What this implies is that dealing in addictive drugs cannot be a trivial offence. Either it must be decriminalized, or it will be sufficiently (morally) serious and sufficiently widespread to drive the entire

crime was one whose foundation was a particular set of moral views and there was no 'victim' then to imprison at all could amount to cruel and unusual punishment (which is unconstitutional under the 8th amendment). If that is the case for the perpetrator, so too, so long as accessorial liability is derivative, for the accomplice.

[35] Nigel South, 'Drugs: Control, Crime and Criminological Studies' in Maguire *et al.* (eds.), *The Oxford Criminology Handbook* (Oxford, 1993), 393 at 394–8 and sources there cited.

[36] Ibid., 419–22.

[37] Ibid., 394. This argument applies equally to the case where the supplier is taken to be complicit in self-harm, and it is no less powerful through being obvious and disquieting.

criminal justice system. The idea that criminalization of drugs is criminogenic is not, of course, a new one. The way in which it is most often stated is that criminalization of drugs gives rise to other criminal behaviour (violence, theft, and so on) amongst both buyers and sellers.[38] But that argument is usually made while treating criminalization itself as effecting little or no alteration to the moral position. The argument of this essay is that the interaction of market forces and criminalization actually alters the moral quality of the act of supplying drugs, by increasing significantly its wrongfulness (if it was wrongful) or making it wrongful (if it was not). It follows that whilst criminal law is a means of applying moral standards by classifying and grading conduct,[39] it can also affect the wrongfulness of behaviour even for those who do not believe that the a criminal injunction necessarily carries moral force.

Unlawful Dealing in Drugs As A Form of Exploitation

I do not propose to consider the competing explanations of the existence or the comparative gravity of the crime of blackmail,[40] and in this essay will assume that it is and should be a serious crime. Rather, my purpose is to identify the wrong in drug dealing by drawing attention to certain analytical similarities with blackmail. Even those who assert the rights of autonomous individuals to take drugs[41] tend not to defend the activities of dealers, and the low esteem in which drug dealers are generally held might be the pointer to a better account of the wrong in drug dealing, one which concentrates upon the way in which a dealer takes advantage of the market. It is a market which has crucially been altered by being made unlawful. In an unlawful market the 'crime tariff' will apply, and there is no legal means of preventing the tendency of such markets to local monopoly. These matters give rise to the risk of exploitation of addicts.

Once a person is addicted to a particular drug, whenever she is denied it she confronts its withdrawal symptoms, which can be very unpleasant (for otherwise addiction would not be such a problem). The 'exploitation thesis' is that a dealer threatens an addict with whatever the withdrawal symptoms are for the drug in question. That is a serious physical or psychological threat. If the addict does not buy, she suffers the harm. The immediate drug dealer, the one who deals with the user, deploys that menace to assist him in

---

[38] Sandford Kadish,'The Crisis of Overcriminalization' (1967) 374 *Annals of the American Academy of Political and Social Science* 157.

[39] Paul Robinson, 'A Functional Analysis of Criminal Law' (1994) 88 *Northwestern University LR* 857.

[40] (1993) 141(5) *University of Pennsylvania LR* 1565–1975 contains an important symposium dealing with blackmail. See also Lamond, 'Coercion, Threats and the Puzzle of Blackmail', this volume, and Leo Katz, *Ill–Gotten Gains* (University of Chicago Press, 1996).

[41] Douglas Husak, *Drugs and Crime* (Cambridge, 1992).

selling the drug to generate profits. Of course, the usual act/omission distinction in blackmail is reversed, because in the normal case of blackmail the perpetrator is threatening to do something which causes harm to the victim. Inactivity (silence) is what is for sale. In the drugs case, by contrast, the dealer threatens (implicitly or explicitly) by inactivity to harm the victim. Drugs are for sale.[42] But morally that distinction is neither here nor there. Dealers in addictive drugs obtain money by very unpleasant menaces. They sell protection from withdrawal symptoms. This is blackmail or its moral equivalent.

Whether sale of addictive drugs to an addict constitutes blackmail in English law[43] as it stands will turn largely upon two things. The first is whether victim-initiated transactions can be thought of as giving rise to 'demands' upon the victim.[44] The second is whether 'menaces' can include a threat to do nothing. In English law the 'demand' question probably turns upon whether the ordinary literate person would understand the drug dealer to be making a demand when she purports to be making an offer so as to exploit the addict's fear.[45] The courts have been prepared to give a very wide reading to the term 'menace' within the Theft Act 1968 and the legislation which preceded it. It is clear that 'menace' is wider than 'threat'.[46] A conditional promise to cause harm by doing nothing can amount to a menace.[47] Leo Katz[48] gives the example, 'Pay me $10,000 or I won't throw you that life jacket', and draws attention to the German Criminal Code's provision which covers 'defendants who exploit the distress, inexperience . . . or the pronounced weakness of will of another' for material advantage (and would clearly cover the case of a drug dealer selling to an addict). If 'Pay me $10,000 or I won't throw you that life jacket' is extortion, so too is 'Pay me $10,000 or I won't give you drugs'. But for the purposes of this argument it does not matter whether the formal definition of blackmail is satisfied so long as the moral wrong is equivalent. That moral wrong has recently been characterized by Fletcher:

> The proper test . . . is whether the transaction with the suspected blackmailer generates a relationship of dominance and subordination. If V's paying money or rendering a service to D creates a situation in which D can or does dominate V, then the action crosses the line from permissible commerce to criminal wrongdoing. The essence of D's dominance over V is the prospect of repeated demands.[49]

---

[42] On this account, supplying a non-addict in an attempt to generate addiction, or in the knowledge that of a number of non-addicts supplied some will become addicted, can be treated as an inchoate form of this kind of wrongdoing.

[43] Theft Act 1968, s. 21.

[44] This is the problem to which Grant Lamond refers as the 'reverse bribery' case: 'Coercion, Threats and the Puzzle of Blackmail', this volume, 235.

[45] *Treacy* v. *DPP* [1971] AC 537 at 565 *per* Lord Diplock.

[46] *Thorne* v. *Motor Trade Association* [1937] AC 797.

[47] W. H. D. Winder, 'The Development of Blackmail' (1941) 5 *Modern LR* 21.

[48] Leo Katz, 'Blackmail and Other Forms of Arm-Twisting' (1993) 141 *University of Pennsylvania LR* 1567 at 1570, and 1599.

[49] George P. Fletcher, 'Blackmail: the Paradigmatic Crime' (1993) 141 *University of Pennsylvania LR* 1617 at 1626.

This, too, is the essence of drug dealing. The relationship between simple possession and dealing can now be restated. The addict is the victim of exploitation, not a participant in it. On this account of drug dealing, the focus moves from the actual injecting, smoking, or otherwise ingesting of the drug to the transaction by which the drugs are acquired. The vice is no longer to be found in the relationship between the user and the drug, but is in the relationship between the user and the supplier (or between users in general and suppliers in general).

Even if selling drugs to addicts does not fall within the definition of blackmail in English law, it is sufficiently near to show what is wrong with drug dealing. The real *gravamen* of the offence is such that it should be grouped with other offences of exploitation, and differences in the gravity of particular cases should be assessed by reference to the criteria which identify and differentiate exploitation offences. The offences with which drug dealing can be grouped, on this account, include, in addition to blackmail, living off immoral earnings, and harassment of tenants and debtors.[50]

The blackmail analogy also generates an account of the difference between supplying alcohol and tobacco (on the one hand) and controlled drugs (on the other). Recall that if the rationale for the prohibition upon dealing in drugs is the supposed need is to prevent harm to the user, then there is no categorical distinction between the sale of drugs, alcohol, and tobacco. At the very most, distinctions of degree are appropriate. A corner shop selling cheap drink to alcoholics does just as much damage to individuals' lives, in very much the same way, as does a drug dealer. But they *sell* differently. The relationship in the corner shop case is not an illegally exploitative one. The account advanced here of the wrong in selling addictive drugs states that people should be prevented from demanding money by the threat (implicit or explicit) of withdrawing supplies from the addict. The factors which differentiate the alcohol case are that the withdrawal symptoms for alcohol are significantly less serious than they are at least for some drugs and that the corner shop does not have the local monopoly which, in effect, a drug dealer is likely to hold over an addict's supply, and which is a necessary part of the economics of blackmail.

NON-BLACKMAIL RETAILS

The extortion account I have outlined applies most clearly to the retail sale of addictive[51] drugs to addicts who are on the point of suffering withdrawal

---

[50] Harassment of tenants (Protection from Eviction Act 1977, s. 1(3)), harassment of debtors (Administration of Justice Act 1970, s. 40), living off immoral earnings (Sexual Offences Act 1956, s. 30).

[51] Questions like, 'How addictive?', 'What proportion of prospective users addicted ?', 'How quickly?', and so on are ones upon which expert evidence would be required. See Ronald Akers, 'Addiction: The Troublesome Concept' (1991) 21 *Journal of Drug Issues* 777.

symptoms. This is the central case of the exploitative sale. It is probably not
the most common, but other types of involvement in the production and sale
of drugs should be assessed by reference to it. The central case needs to be
differentiated in particular from two other types of dealing—consumer sales
other than those which fall within the blackmail argument, and sales other
than to the final consumer. I shall deal first with non-blackmail retails.
Assuming all other things (in particular, the effects of the drugs) to be equal,
the blackmail argument establishes that it is significantly worse to sell addictive drugs to addicts than to engage in one of three lesser practices. The first
is sale of non-addictive drugs. If particular drugs are not addictive, then,
even though the consequences of one bad session might be unpleasant, since
their sale does not involve exploitation of the buyer, dealing in them should
be regarded, at most, as less serious.[52] If the type of threat is something to
be considered in sentencing for blackmail,[53] then the type of withdrawal
symptoms (rather than the actual effects of the drug) should be taken into
account when sentencing dealers. Secondly, *gifts* of addictive drugs to
addicts may be discouraged, but should not attract the same sort of blame
which operates in respect of sale to addicts, again because coercive exploitation of the buyer is not involved. It may be that the gift is made with the
intention of creating addiction as a basis for subsequent exploitation, but in
that case the gift should be punished (if it is not too remote) as an inchoate
form of the sale offence. Thirdly, the sale of addictive drugs to *non-addicts*
also does not involve such an exploitation (though it may be thought of as
a 'pump-priming' exercise done in the hope of securing addiction, and it may
be that liability should be determined by an 'ulterior intent' to secure later
addiction). What of the scrupulous dealer who understands how wrong it is
to sell to addicts, and decides only to sell to non-addicts, so as not to exploit
her clients? Whatever we say is wrong with her behaviour, one thing we cannot say is that it is the moral equivalent of blackmail, or that it forms part
of the large-scale protection racket which trade in unlawful addictive drugs
involves. Likewise, the prudent addict who always keeps a reserve supply
will never be the victim of this kind of wrong.

The anathematization of drug dealing has meant that gradations have not
been sought or made as to what might be appropriate definitional elements
for dealing. I suggest that as long as drug dealing is to be an offence it
should, on a charge of supplying, be a complete defence, a significant mitigation, or a less serious offence that: (i) that no charge was made for the
drugs; or (ii) that the drug was not, or was believed not to be, addictive; or
(iii) that the purchaser was not, or was believed not to be, an addict. The

---

[52] Douglas Husak, n. 41 above, at 100 ff. considers the argument against treating addicted
users as autonomous individuals respect for whom implies allowing them access to the drugs
(and concludes that they have such a right). He does not consider the moral position of the supplier.
[53] D. A. Thomas, *Current Sentencing Practice* (London, 1982), B6–6.

alternative is to resile from the kind of *mens rea* requirement proposed in (ii) and (iii) and to say that knowledge or recklessness whether the purchaser is an addict or that the drug is addictive is irrelevant both to liability and sentence. This could not be reconciled with the general precepts as to *mens rea* in serious offences. The kind of differentiation suggested here is by no means abnormal in other areas of the law.[54] It has hitherto been regarded as unnecessary in the field of drugs only because enquiry into the wrongfulness of drug dealing has been neglected.

My analysis also offers something of an answer to a difficult 'conflict of duties' case. An addict is on the point of suffering serious withdrawal symptoms. Should the person who supplies drugs to her have any defence on the ground that the supplying prevented a worse harm occurring? If the supplier was (causally) responsible for the addiction, then under *Miller*[55] there is (at least arguably) a duty to continue supplying, whereas under the Misuse of Drugs Act 1971 there is a clear duty not to supply. This raises the issue of whether prior fault can negative an excusing condition.[56] The supplier wishes to resist a conviction upon the grounds of choice of evils—that by supplying drugs she was relieving the distress of the addict. Assume for the sake of argument that there is no other way by which the addict might obtain the drug in question. We may want to grant a defence to the supplier who performs a reasonable act of supplying in order to relieve the distress: this without charging, or at the very most, charging cost price. But the dealer could not be heard to say that she had acted reasonably on the basis of choice of evils if she was acting for a profit.

RESPONSIBILITY OF THE VARIOUS PARTICIPANTS

Thus far I have dealt only with retail sales to the user, and I have been employing some moral distinctions which are immediately relevant to the sale transaction in order to suggest a better grading of drug dealing offences, and to suggest provisions which should form part of the legislation. It is the retail transaction, within the context of prohibitions upon drug use, which provides the central vice in drug dealing. The next consideration is how that analysis affects the evaluation made by the law of other participants in the

[54] It is, e.g., the kind for which Horder argues in this volume, in respect of offences against the person.

[55] [1983] 2 AC 161. In this case D lit a cigarette, and went to sleep. He woke to find that that cigarette had started a fire in property of P, but did nothing to prevent the spread of fire. He was convicted of reckless damage to property on the ground that the fact of his having started the fire, albeit inadvertently and—as the case was argued—without negligence, in the property of another created a duty to take reasonable steps to prevent or reduce damage, and that recklessly failing to take such steps, although insufficient for liability where D had not in fact started the fire, here sufficed.

[56] Paul Robinson, 'Causing the Conditions of Ones Own Defence' (1985) 71 *University of Virginia LR* 1.

chain of supply and sale of drugs, and how does it affect the particular questions raised by importation? Generally justifications are not required for higher sentences for manufacturers and wholesalers than retailers because (in so far as they get caught) they can be held to account for a great deal more drugs than the retailer, so any 'moral distance' or 'intervening agency' mitigation is more than outweighed by the quantum of drugs. But assuming equal quantity, what kind of account should be taken of the fact that the manufacturer and wholesale suppliers do not know and need not care about the eventual consumer, whilst the retail supplier does?

As to supplying, it has been argued here that the wrong in illegal drug dealing is to be found in the exploitative relationship with the addict. All other participants in the chain of manufacture and supply are complicit in that wrong. The question is how to allocate liability between them.[57] The current treatment of offenders in English law is that for the purposes of naming the conduct no distinction is to be made between retailers and wholesalers. They are all suppliers. How might it that view be altered to reflect the changed nature of the wrong which this paper identifies?

Assuming equal quantities of drugs are involved, the fact that a person who is a link in the chain of supply of drugs is not the one who finally delivers the drug may be thought to mitigate, for two reasons. The first is the moral distance involved between production and consumption and the intervening agency of the final vendor. We know from evidence of social psychologists that perceptions of guilt and responsibility can be diluted by 'moral distance'.[58] The idea that it is less reprehensible, especially when done passively or by the willing agency of another, to harm a victim who is neither seen nor heard, nor perhaps identified, and who may be several thousand miles distant, has been mooted in moral philosophy but seems very difficult to justify.[59] It does, however, underlie much of our behaviour (it is much easier to eat more than is necessary to survive when there is not someone starving in the corner of the room: the knowledge that people are starving elsewhere is able to be suppressed) and Milgram[60] provided compelling evidence of its currency. A law which had regard to this difference would regard the guilt of the retail supplier as greater than that of the producer.

As for moral distance, so, too, for agency. It is the general (highly individualistic) assumption of much of English criminal law that the perpetrator, the performer of the prohibited act, is the most significant participant. This is not, of course, a distinction to be found mirrored in the legal designation of their crimes. The kinds of distinctions which are recognized in

---

[57] Andrew Ashworth, 'Sentencing Reform Structures' in M. Tonry (ed.), *Crime and Justice* (Chicago, 1992), xvi, 181.

[58] Jonathan Glover, *Causing Death and Saving Lives* (London, 1977), ch. 20.

[59] Ted Honderich, 'Our Omissions and their Violence' in *Violence for Equality* (London, 1980), 58. The principal area for discussion of these issues in criminal law is the case of corporate liability.

[60] Stanley Milgram, *Obedience to Authority* (London, 1974), 122.

other jurisdictions[61] between instigators and other participants are not known to the criminal law of the United Kingdom, at least so far as concerns liability (though they inform sentence). If it is the nature of the consumer sales transaction which is objectionable, rather than the final effect of the drug upon the taker, then rules for ascribing responsibility should differentiate between that transaction and others in the chain of supply. There are two major ways in which to do this—either by means of general rules of complicity or by developing specific rules to deal with drugs suppliers.

The retail supplier is the perpetrator of an exploitative and criminal wrong, and her supplier is an accessory. The 'general principles', which do not (yet[62]) distinguish instigation from other forms of complicity, suggest, if anything, that the former should attract more serious punishment. An alternative would be to reject the possibility of treating the varying degrees of complicity of participants in a chain, supplying drugs, under the 'general principles'[63] and instead to regard the differences in their respective responsibility as something to be dealt with as *res integra*. This is what is done in the law of theft, in which the handler, who might be a remote participant,[64] can incur greater liability than the actual thief. Since the days of Jonathan Wild[65] it has been recognized that the receiver of stolen goods has a degree of responsibility going beyond that which would be assigned by application of the normal rules of complicity in theft. Today's archetypal master criminal does not deal in stolen goods but in drugs.

These reflections upon the division of responsibility between participants might also inform redefinition of the supplying offences, so as to include ulterior *mens rea* provisions relating to dealing. If dealing offences were brought into the mainstream of criminal law and looked at alongside the Law Commission's review of assisting and encouraging crime,[66] then it would be seen that whether we apply the usual English rules of complicity, or borrow from some area where, for particular reasons, those rules have been departed from, some kind of *mens rea* provision will have to be made. Since there will be so many different cases and since there will always be a wide sentencing discretion, it may not be too significant whether the rules for drug dealing are borrowed from the law of theft or are simply applications of the more general law of complicity. What does matter is that the

[61] George Fletcher, *Rethinking Criminal Law* (Boston, Mass., 1978), 671. See Law Commission Consultation Paper No. 131, *Assisting and Encouraging Crime* (1994), para. 4.10 ff.

[62] See Law Commission Consultation Paper No. 131, *Assisting and Encouraging Crime* (1994).

[63] Which are here as elsewhere little more than a default setting—laying down what is the case absent specific provision to the contrary.

[64] A handler of stolen goods, who is liable under s. 22 of the Theft Act 1968 to a sentence of up to 14 years.

[65] See Jerome Hall, *Theft, Law and Society* (2nd edn., Indianapolis, Indiana, 1952), 71–4.

[66] Law Commission Consultation Paper No. 131, *Assisting and Encouraging Crime* (1994).

present position, which imposes strict liability upon the supplier, should be changed. If we insist that the dealer, to be guilty of the most serious case of dealing, should know that the drug is addictive and that the purchaser is addicted (or buying for an addict) then, before the serious punishments which are current are imposed, we should also insist that the wholesaler/ courier be shown to have had have some culpable mental state—probably contemplation[67] of the possibility that the drug is addictive and will be sold to addicts.

IMPORTATION

A related puzzle about the law relating to drug dealing is that it seems to go without argument in sentencing cases that it is more serious to attempt or conspire[68] to import drugs than simply to deal or to possess them with intent to supply. Can any morally satisfactory explanation be developed for this disparity? Or is it that possession of drugs in a customs hall with intent to supply is just another version of possession with intent to supply, and that possession in a customs hall for personal use is just another variety of possession, the only significant difference in each case being that the chances of detection are greater in a customs hall? In English law the convictions will be under a different statute,[69] but that is not in itself enough to account for what is a most significant sentencing disparity. Nor is the differential treatment explicable in terms of the kinds of criteria normally said to distinguish offence seriousness for the purposes of sentence.[70]

The most significant difference occurs in the case of a person who imports drugs purely for personal use. Should her sentence be on the basis that she has possessed drugs for personal use (which is the least serious form of involvement in drugs) or that she is an international drug trafficker (which is the most serious)? The authorities are inconclusive.[71] In one case in which the higher sentence was imposed, Simon Brown J (as he then was) said:

[67] *DPP* v. *Maxwell* [1978] 1 WLR 1350.

[68] The offences under the Customs and Excise Management Act provide clear examples of legislation which are generally prosecuted in the inchoate rather than the complete mode, but where the usual discount for attempts does not seem to obtain. Recent sentences include: 9 years for *attempting* to import cannabis—*Sturt* (1993) 14 Cr. App. R 440; 9 years for *conspiring* to import and *conspiring* to supply cannabis—*Rescorl et al.* (1993) 14 Cr. App. R 522; 5½ years for conspiring to import LSD (class A) which was treated as an importation—*A-G's References (Nos. 3, 4, & 5 of 1992)* (1993) 14 Cr. App. R (S) 191.

[69] Customs and Excise Management Act 1979, ss. 50(2), 50(3), 68(2), and 170. Sentences are set by sched. 1. Sentences under the Misuse of Drugs Act 1971 are set by sched. 4.

[70] Andrew von Hirsch and Nils Jareborg, 'Gauging Criminal Harm: A Living Standard Analysis' (1991) 11 *Oxford Journal of Legal Studies* 1—who are concerned with the effect of crime upon the 'living standards' of victims.

[71] *Dolgin* (1988) 10 Cr. App. R (S) 447; *Meah and Marlow* (1990) 12 Cr. App. R (S) 461. *McLean* (1994) 15 Cr. App. R (S) 706 suggests that the fact that importation is for personal use is slight mitigation only (6 years reduced to 5).

The vice in the offence consists in the very fact of importation, of increasing the stock of the prohibited drugs within our shores. There is always the risk that the drug once here may be stolen, and there is the possibility, particularly if it is a large quantity that even if the importer had not initially been intent on supply, as time passes he may become tempted for whatever reason to make supplies of it.[72]

That is to say, 'By importing the defendant makes the drugs our problem rather than somebody else's, whereas in the case of the retail dealer the drugs are already our problem.' This does not seem to be a very sound foundation upon which to build such substantial differentials.[73]

The difference between sentences for drug dealing and for drug importation is also a large one. The preponderance of sentences for importation are now in the range four to seven years,[74] which places it on a par, for example, with robbery. If the moral wrong they each commit is to serve as members of a chain of supply and if the only difference between the importer and the dealer is the place at which they are apprehended, then it is difficult to provide a moral distinction to support the differences in penalty. I suggest, so long as dealing in drugs is unlawful, that wholesale suppliers' guilt should be taken to be diminished for moral distance and (generally) raised for quantity as against retail suppliers. Couriers should be regarded as complicit with dealers, and their offence should not be taken to have been aggravated simply on account of the border crossing.

DECRIMINALIZATION

Thus far I have made the case that if drug dealing is to remain criminal, each individual extortionate sale to an addict is the moral equivalent of a blackmail or a robbery. Non-extortionate sales are less grave but may well be regarded as so closely bound up in the whole enterprise of extortion as to attract significant censure. There will be thousands of such sales every day, and many people who can reasonably be regarded as complicit in each sale. If the criminal justice system is to deal with these people within a framework which emphasizes moral differentiations in offence gradation and in sentence, then drug dealing will remain the motor of the criminal justice system. *Agents provocateurs*, stings, state access to bank accounts, reversed burdens of proof, intimate searches, abduction, telephone taps, seizure of assets, and very long prison sentences, with all the concomitant expense, follow naturally. The alternative is decriminalization. There is no *via media*. It is impossible for drug dealing to be a relatively unimportant offence.

Thus the question arises, 'How are we to determine whether or not drug dealing should remain a criminal offence?' The pragmatic reasons for

---

[72] *Dolgin* (1988) 10 Cr. App. R (S) 447, 449.

[73] If that is the rationale the test case is one where the drugs are only passing through this jurisdiction *en route* to another. It is unlikely that this will provide a mitigation.

[74] See Green, Mills, and Read, n. 20 above.

decriminalization are well known and will not be discussed here. Drawing upon the account which von Hirsch[75] presents of the 'harm principle', there is a strong case for decriminalizing. According to the standard version of the harm principle which he describes, in considering whether to criminalize the following considerations are appropriate:

(i) The gravity of the eventual harm and the likelihood of its occurrence. In the case of a serious addictive drug (say heroin), abuse gives rise to lowered economic productivity and various social problems. People addicted to drugs tend to lie, cheat and steal.

(ii) Counterpoise the degree of intrusion upon the actor's choices that criminalization would involve, and the social value of the conduct involved. Whether or not there is any social utility in taking (say) heroin there is a clear infraction upon the actor's liberty to make that choice.

(iii) Side constraints (in particular, privacy) that would preclude criminalization.

The standard harm analysis contemplates a process of aggregating the social value of criminalizing or decriminalizing an action. It may very well be that even on those (admittedly vague) criteria the case for decriminalization is a good one. But there are two considerations which make it more powerful. The first matter which might be included (or which might be subsumed under the second head) is whether or not there is any prospect of success in using the criminal law, or whether the legislation is essentially futile—that is, what kinds of rates of compliance are in prospect and what sorts of effects upon behaviour is the prohibition likely to have? Obviously the greater the security measures which are taken to enforce the prohibition on drugs, the more chance there is of diminishing the incidence of unlawful possession. But it is clear that even in a strictly controlled environment (typically, in prisons) heroin is fairly readily available. A jurisdiction which made every effort to stamp out heroin would impose security measures on its populace at least as strict as those governing prisons. To do so would, of course, be simply unacceptable. But anything less would concede that the overwhelming preponderance of (say) heroin usage would go unapprehended. Thus society suffers the deleterious effects (expense, expanded police powers, and so forth) of criminalization without much by way of the benefit, and with general loss of respect for law.

The additional factor which is introduced by von Hirsch—that wrongful action needs to be imputed to the initiator of remote harms—militates against the imposition of liability, not merely in the case he posits (the soft target of marijuana), but also in the case of addictive drugs with much more powerful effects. If one excludes from the harms for which the drug dealer is to account, first, those consequences which are not a function of drug

---

[75] See von Hirsch, 'Extending the Harm Principle: "Remote" Harms and Fair Imputation', this volume.

dealing but of the fact that drug dealing is unlawful, and secondly, those consequences in respect of which there is some intervening choice, it is not evident what, if anything, is wrong with it.

CONCLUSIONS

The debate on drugs can take place at many levels—embracing libertarian arguments as to the rights of the taker, practical arguments about what is to be done, and also historical and sociological discourse about how we got where we are. What I hope this paper has added is to explain in terms of blackmail the nature of the wrong done in the typical case by a dealer in unlawful addictive drugs, and to suggest that if proscription is to continue some of the distinctions which are drawn in English law as to liability and sentence could with profit be revised. The account shows that dealing in illegal drugs is sufficiently serious that if the prohibition upon drugs remains (together with commitment to a criminal law which encapsulates defensible moral judgments) then drugs will continue to be a driving force propelling the criminal justice system along lines which may be far from welcome. The recognition that drug dealing cannot be a relatively trivial offence, and the consequences of maintaining criminalization[76] may well be thought a reason for legalizing such transactions altogether.

---

[76] Randy E. Barnett, 'Bad Trip: Drug Prohibition and the Weakness of Public Policy' (1994) 103 *Yale LJ* 2593, reviewing Steven Duke and Albert Gross, *America's Longest War* (New York, 1993).

12

Extending the Harm Principle: 'Remote' Harms and Fair Imputation

Andrew von Hirsch*

Formerly, proposals to extend the reach of the criminal law often were rationalized on paternalistic grounds, or on grounds of the conduct's supposed 'sinfulness'. Such efforts could be challenged by appealing to the harm principle—that is, the requirement that the conduct involved be harmful to others. The harm principle thus served as a valuable antidote, a way of keeping the scope of the criminal law modest.

At present, however, efforts to widen the law's scope are often rationalized in a different manner, that is designed to co-opt the harm principle: appeal is made to the conduct's supposed *long term* risk of harm to others. A variety of prohibitions (for example, those relating to drug use[1]) have been defended by reference to the eventual deleterious social consequences to which the conduct leads. Extending 'harm' in this fashion, thus may erode the usefulness of the harm principle as a constraint on the state's punitive power. This raises the present question: what limitations of principle should there be upon the invocation of more 'remote' forms of risk, as grounds for criminalization?

My thinking on this question has not reached the point where I can offer a full, positive account. I shall, however, suggest how and why a conven-

* I am grateful to the participants of two exploratory meetings on the subject of remote harms which were held at Brasenose College, Oxford (13 Feb. 1993) and Stirling University (27 Nov. 1993). Funding for those meetings was generously supplied by the Fulbright Commission, London, and by the Fund for the Study of Criminal Jurisprudence, School of Criminal Justice, Rutgers University. I benefited also from discussion with the other authors of this volume, in meetings at Gonville and Caius College, Cambridge, at various times during 1994.

I am particularly indebted to Andrew Ashworth, who helped me conceptualize the whole approach, and to Andrew Simester and Antony Duff who supplied me with extensive written comments. I am grateful also to Stanley Cohen, Hyman Gross, Douglas Husak, and Nils Jareborg for their suggestions on earlier drafts.

[1] See John Kaplan, *The Hardest Drug: Heroin and Public Policy* (Chicago, Ill., 1983).

tional harms analysis does not suffice; and point to certain other issues that need consideration—particularly, those relating to what I shall call 'fair imputation'.

The reader should bear in mind that the present topic concerns *criminalization*: whether the legislature should proscribe certain types of conduct on grounds of its remote risks of harm to others. A legislature has the power to proscribe conduct for any reason (subject to whatever constitutional constraints the particular legal system affords). A conscientious legislator, however, should support proscription only when good reasons exist for so doing. The conduct's potential harmfulness to others has long been considered a good prima facie reason.[2] My question is whether and to what degree this holds for remote risks of harm.

THE PROBLEM OF 'REMOTE' HARMS

Much of the attractiveness of the harm principle derives from its having been applied to fairly immediate harms, where certain other vital normative concerns (namely, those concerning liberty and the imputation of fault) are readily satisfied. When applied to ordinary victimizing conduct, the harm principle serves well as a limitation of state punitive power: ordinary citizens' freedom of action is not greatly restricted by prohibiting, say, violence or thievery. This holds also for prohibitions that concern the more immediate risks of harm: barring people from driving while intoxicated still leaves them with a wide variety of other permitted choices, not least getting drunk at home or at the corner pub. Indeed, one of the principal justifications that has been offered for the harm principle is that—unlike paternalistic rationales, for example—it helps to preserve personal freedom.[3]

Once a straightforward harms analysis is extended to include more remote harms, however, matters change—because all sorts of seemingly innocent things I (or we) do may ultimately have deleterious consequences. It will not be easy to identify conduct which confidently can be said to be without substantial risk of injury in the long run. As a result, the harm principle—unless suitably modified or supplemented—can lose much of its liberty-safeguarding role.

When the harm principle is applied to individual, victimizing harms, the attribution of fault is also relatively straightforward, because of the close links between the actor's culpable choice and the resulting harm. If I intentionally assault you, and you are injured as a result, I am to blame for (at least, the forseeable) injury that results. This holds not only for actual

---

[2] See J. S. Mill, *On Liberty* (London, 1859), ch. 4; Joel Feinberg, *Harm to Others* (New York, 1984) (hereafter '*Harm to Others*').

[3] See, e.g., Joseph Raz, *The Morality of Freedom* (Oxford, 1986), ch. 15.

injuries but for the more immediate forms of risk: when I drive recklessly, I should be accountable for the hazard my driving foreseeably creates.

When more remote risks are involved, however, holding the actor to blame for the possible injurious results becomes more problematic. Typically, what is prohibited is a present act, A, which (in the legislature's judgment) creates or helps create an unacceptable risk of some eventual harm, X, and the *mens rea* required is merely an intent to perform the present act A. In such circumstances, it is not always obvious how or why the actor should be held sufficiently accountable for the eventual harm that his current conduct can legitimately be deemed blameworthy. And if it is not blameworthy, how can the censure of a criminal penalty be warranted?

THE STANDARD HARMS ANALYSIS

How, then, has the issue of 'remote' harm been addressed? While the subject has not received a great deal of attention, a mode of analysis has developed which focuses on the likelihood and magnitude of the risk, and on certain countervailing concerns and constraints. This approach has by now become sufficiently established to merit being termed the 'Standard' Harms Analysis.[4]

Stated schematically, the Standard Harms Analysis involves the following steps for deciding whether a given type of risk satisfies the requirements of the harm principle:

Step 1: Consider the gravity of the eventual harm, and its likelihood. The greater the gravity and likelihood, the stronger the case for criminalization.

Step 2: Weigh against the foregoing, the social value of the conduct, and the degree of intrusion upon actors' choices that criminalization would involve. The more valuable the conduct is, or the more the prohibition would limit liberty, the stronger the countervailing case would be.[5]

Step 3: Observe certain side-constraints that would preclude criminalization. The prohibition should not, for example, infringe rights of privacy or free expression.

(The Standard Harms Analysis does not, of course, require that conduct automatically be criminalized whenever its criteria are met. Existing

---

[4] For an exposition, see *Harm to Others*, n. 2 above, at 190–3, 216.

[5] While this 'balancing' approach seems utilitarian in its focus on the extent of injuriousness of the conduct and on the countervailing benefits, it does not presuppose a general utilitarian outlook. Harm concerns the deleterious consequences of conduct. Why not, then, assess those consequences in terms of their likelihood, gravity, and countervailing benefits? This mode of analysis concerns only the issue of criminalization, and would not necessarily be applicable to other issues of criminal justice, such as that of sentencing—where non-consequentialist concerns (particularly, those about desert) seem to matter more. See Andrew von Hirsch, *Censure and Sanctions* (Oxford, 1993), ch. 2.

prohibitions may suffice to deal with the problem. The potential difficulties and costs of enforcement need also to be considered.)

The eventual harm, under the Standard Harms Analysis, should be of a kind which could be criminalized itself, were it to occur immediately. Claims about supposed eventual risks sometimes address bad societal consequences of a non-criminal nature: John Kaplan, for example, contends that widespread drug use undermines the work ethic, leading to lowered social productivity.[6] Laziness, however, is not in itself criminal. That drug use might lead to declining work habits thus is not a valid ground for criminalization— unless those altered work habits lead, in turn, to something else that qualifies as a harm.[7] Kaplan's argument thus would need to be revised so as to assert that drug abuse leads to laziness and lowered economic productivity; and the consequent increase in poverty is likely to lead, in turn, to (say) more theft and violence.

When applied to the more immediate sorts of risks, the Standard Harms Analysis works nicely. Why, for example, might a legislature wisely prohibit driving while intoxicated, while not proscribing walking in a similar state? The reason has something to do with the likelihood and magnitude of the risks involved. Why should the legislature abstain from proscribing the more strenuous forms of political advocacy, even if those involve some enhanced risk of public disorder? The reason concerns the side constraint of free expression. And so forth.

Does the Analysis perform so well, however, when extended to remote risks? It has been thought so: Feinberg, for example, recommends its use, and suggests no fundamental distinction between the more immediate and remoter forms of danger.[8] Yet there are reasons for doubt.

The Standard Harm Analysis does at least recognize the issue of liberty, by making the degree of restriction of choice a counter-consideration to be weighed against the magnitude and likelihood of the harm. But liberty is treated merely as a weighing factor, which means that the greater the predicted harm, the more extensive loss of liberty would be permitted.[9]

With imputation of fault, matters are worse: the Standard Harms Analysis provides no framework for dealing with this issue. In its concerns about the

---

    [6] N. 1 above, at 131–4.
    [7] See Douglas Husak, 'The Nature and Justifiability of Nonconsummate Offenses', (1995) 37 *Arizona Law Review* 151. Feinberg makes essentially the same point, asserting that those purportedly harmed (in this case, those eventually harmed) by the conduct must have interests the protection of which is supported by a valid claim; see *Harm to Others*, n. 2 above, at 109–14.
    [8] *Harm to Others*, n. 2 above, chs. 5 and 6.
    [9] It might be responded that the Analysis's counter-consideration concerning 'intrusion on actors' choices' could make a difference, if it is given sufficient weight. If little restriction of choice were tolerated, only a narrow ambit of criminalization would be permitted. This, however, only shows how sensitive the analysis is to the weight which such counter-considerations are given. Were these given reduced weight, much restriction of liberty would become permissible. Unhappily, the Standard Harms Analysis does not suggest how this critical weighting issue should be resolved: it merely says that the counter-considerations should somehow be 'balanced' against the degree and likelihood of the harm.

likelihood of the harm, it addresses the empirical link between the prohibited conduct and the undesired harmful result. But the normative link—why and to what extent the defendant committing a given act should justly be held accountable for its remote consequences or risks—is not systematically addressed at all.

I do not wish to suggest that the Standard Harms Analysis should be jettisoned, for it has an important role to play in assessing the usefulness of prohibitions, as we shall see. What I wish to contend, however, is that the Analysis cannot stand alone: there need to be further principles, designed to deal with the special problems raised by remote harms.

WHAT ARE 'REMOTE' HARMS?

Before proceeding with our analysis, we need to define what is meant by 'remote' risks. It is not literal spatio-temporal remoteness that should matter: I would see no problem, for example, in punishing the act of secreting explosives in a populous area, timed to explode months hence. I am speaking, instead, of risks that are remote in the sense that they involve certain kinds of contingencies. Let me enumerate a few kinds:

ABSTRACT ENDANGERMENT

Traditional criminal legislation, where concerned with risk, addresses actual danger: the prohibition is couched in terms of creating an unreasonable probability of hurting someone. (Reckless driving is the stock example.) Included may be conduct the riskiness of which depends on the existence of a contingency, but where it is not known or knowable to the actor *ex ante* whether that contingency will materialize in the particular situation. Overtaking on a blind corner endangers another only if there actually is a car behind the curve, coming in the opposite direction. But as the driver cannot know whether there is a car coming when he overtakes, this is an unreasonable risk to take.

Modern criminal statutes dealing with remoter forms of risk, however, often couch their prohibitions *abstractly*, in terms that cover instances of the conduct known to be harmless. Sometimes this is done because the behaviour ordinarily is dangerous. Consider a prohibition against driving with a high (e.g., over 0.8 pro mil) blood-alcohol level. Since most streets are frequented, and most persons drive badly with so much alcohol, this usually constitutes dangerous conduct. But a defendant is liable even if he knows full well that the street is empty, or that his tolerance for alcohol is especially high.[10]

---

[10] We are speaking here of the conduct's potential to harm other persons. The driver on the empty street may endanger himself, but to criminalize that endangerment would be a paternalistic measure, outside the scope of the harm principle.

Typically in such legislation, the feared risk is not even included in the legal definition of the crime: the statute proscribes (say) driving with over a given blood-alcohol level. The conduct's tendency to produce accidents comes into the picture merely as the legislature's reason for the proscription.

Abstract-endangerment liability may also include, more problematically, prohibitions of conduct which ordinarily is not risky, but which is proscribed because *some* actors may endanger others. An example is Sweden's recent prohibition of driving with quite low (0.2 pro mil or more) blood alcohol levels.[11] Most people at that point can still drive reasonably safely, but a minority who hold their liquor badly cannot. Many thus are barred from choosing conduct that involves tolerably low risks, in order that the less competent few are prevented from endangering others.

INTERVENING CHOICES

Legislation concerned with remote risks may also proscribe conduct which has no ill consequences in itself, but which is thought to induce or lead to further acts (by the defendant or a third person) that create or risk harm. Gun-possession is an instance: ordinarily, the danger materializes only when the gun-possessor (or another) handles or uses the weapon in certain ways.[12] The harm thus is 'remote' in the sense that it arises upon the making of an intervening choice; but the conduct is punishable whether that choice occurs or not. Indeed, the feared subsequent choice may occur only in a minority of cases: most people who possess guns, for example, do not misuse them.

While gun control is widely considered a sensible step, other intervening-choice claims seem more dubious. An example is provided by the House of Lords' decision in *Brown*,[13] where it was argued that consensual sadistic/masochistic sex among adult males should continue to be proscribed—in part, because permitting such conduct might encourage the seduction of young boys unable to give proper consent.

The Standard Harm Analysis assigns no special status to the fact of an intervening choice. The Analysis simply addresses the magnitude and likelihood of the harm, and the applicability of the counter-considerations and side constraints. If gun-control is thought acceptable and the bad-example

---

[11] This reduction in the permitted blood-alcohol level for drivers was approved in 1990 (see Swedish Session Laws 1990: 149).

[12] But see the further discussion of gun control, in the text accompanying n. 29 below.

[13] [1993] 2 WLR 556. What was directly at issue in this case was immediate harm—namely, the defendants inflicting minor wounds on one another in the course of their sexual activities. The defendants contended, however, that since the participants were all adults and expressly had consented, the state's intrusion was an inappropriate exercise of paternalism. In arguing that the public interest called for continued proscription notwithstanding the participants' consent, one of the concurring majority opinions in the House of Lords—that of Lord Jauncey—adverted to the risk of eventual harm not involving valid consent: *viz.*, 'the possiblity of proselytization and corruption of young men'.

theory in *Brown*[14] rejected, it would be on account of the respective degrees of likelihood of harm involved, or the applicability of (say) the side-constraint of privacy.

ACCUMULATIVE HARMS

In yet other situations—those involving accumulative harms—the conduct does the feared injury only when combined with similar acts of others. Dumping household garbage in the river is treated as a health hazard, but the conduct actually endangers health only when numerous other persons do likewise. In such situations, however, the proscribed act is a token of the type of conduct that cumulatively does the harm: the actor cannot draw a moral distinction between his behaviour and that of the others who contribute to the injury. This is to be contrasted with intervening-choice situations, in which the conduct is harmless in itself even when cumulated and leads to possible injury only because it supposedly induces or permits harmful choices of another kind.

REMOTE HARM AND FAIR IMPUTATION

WHY IS IMPUTATION IMPORTANT?

An essential characteristic of the criminal sanction is that it conveys censure.[15] The sanction is thus visited appropriately only on conduct which is in some sense reprehensible. Criminalizing conduct should thus call for an explanation of why the behaviour merits the condemnation of the criminal law.

One important aspect of blameworthiness concerns whether fault can be *imputed* to the actor. Not only should the conduct have injurious consequences, but it needs to be explained why the actor can be held accountable for those consequences. The harm principle traditionally focused chiefly on individual, victimizing harms, where (as mentioned earlier) attribution of fault is relatively straightforward: so long as the act is committed with the requisite *mens rea* and acceptable excuses are not present, wrongdoing can usually be inferred directly from harming.

When the law is extended to include more remote harms, however, the inference from causing harm to doing wrong becomes more tenuous. Suppose the conduct to be proscribed is not immediately injurious to anyone; but it triggers a series of events (possibly initiated by independent agents) that eventually risk harmful consequences. It then becomes

---

[14] See the text accompanying n. 13 above.
[15] For a fuller account of the connection between punishment and censure, see von Hirsch, n. 5 above, ch. 2; also Joel Feinberg, *Doing and Deserving* (Princeton, N.J., 1970), ch. 5.

necessary to ask whether, and for what reason, those consequences are ones for which the defendant should properly be held accountable.

The clearest examples of this problem of fair imputation concern intervening-choice risks. Suppose, for example, that there actually were evidence that unregulated premarital sex, by yielding higher rates of illegitimate births, leads to more children growing up in impoverished households with weakened parental control, which in its turn generates higher crime rates by offspring.[16] If the Standard Harm Analysis were applied without more, there might (depending on the likelihood and extent of the eventual harmful consequences) be a prima facie case for the intervention of the criminal law, subject only to the applicable counter-considerations and side constraints. Whether or not the latter (that is, the side constraints) apply depends on how the prohibition is couched. Direct proscription of fornication seems objectionable as a violation of privacy, but indirect restrictions— say, a curfew on teenagers attending discotheques and other places deemed to encourage premarital sex—might arguably be less so.

A second case is the familiar one of drug prohibitions. Suppose evidence were indeed available that widespread use of a given drug leads to lowered social productivity which, in turn, creates a criminogenic social environment.[17] The Standard Harm Analysis would then make prohibition depend in large part on estimates of the likelihood and magnitude of such effects.[18]

In both of these cases, however, simple reliance on the Standard Harm Analysis would overlook something fundamental: the question of fair imputation. The harm is produced not by the actor's own behaviour, but by the subsequent choices of third parties whom he does not control (the offspring of fornicators, or the persons influenced by the changed social atmosphere generated by drug use). Criminalizing the conduct thus raises the question: why should I be punished for conduct of a kind that does no harm in itself, merely because it might influence other persons to decide to engage in acts that are potentially injurious? The problem is not the factual link: my behaviour may well influence others' choices, in a variety of ways.[19] Nor is the

[16] Charles Murray has been vocal in asserting the existence of such links. See his *The Emerging British Underclass* (London, 1990); and also his *Underclass: The Crisis Deepens* (London, 1994). I am sceptical of his claims, but they serve as a useful hypothetical for present purposes.

[17] See Kaplan, n. 1 above, and the text accompanying nn. 6 and 7 above. It is sometimes claimed that drug use leads more immediately to harm, in that users must steal in order to pay for drugs. That need to steal, however, appears to derive largely from the inflated price of drugs that prohibition itself generates.

[18] Feinberg deals with intervening-choice situations in such terms. For example, with so-called 'imitative harms' (say, the showing of a violent film which evokes actual violence on the part of some viewers), he argues that the conduct would be covered *pro tanto* by the harm principle (provided that the actor knew or should have known of the possibility of imitations), but that countervailing concerns—particularly, interests in free expression—militate against criminalization. See *Harm to Others*, n. 2 above, at 232–45.

[19] I thus agree with Feinberg that a person's voluntary act can be influenced by another's behaviour; see *Harm to Others*, n. 2 above, at 235–7, and Feinberg, n. 15 above, ch. 7. My point, however, is that X's having influenced Y's action does not necessarily render X morally accountable for Y's behaviour.

problem one of conventional *mens rea*: let us assume that the prohibited act (say, drug possession) is intentionally committed. The problem is, rather, the imputational link: should I be held responsible for the potential ill consequences that flow from the choices of other agents?

Under certain circumstances, an actor may properly be held accountable. The most obvious case is that of solicitation: X solicits Y to commit a crime. Another well-known case is the sale of hazardous products: the manufacturer knowingly sells a product the standard use of which creates (say) dangers to health. In these situations, however, it is not merely the actor's having influenced the subsequent choice that matters; rather, it is his having, in some manner, underwritten that subsequent choice.

Where there has been no such involvement on the part of the defendant, he should not be held accountable. The reason why not concerns the idea of personal agency in the criminal law.[20] An actor may properly be held responsible if he brings about a harmful result himself, or if he brings it about through another person, say, by inducement or persuasion. But to hold him liable merely because another person chooses to follow his example, or otherwise permits herself to be influenced, infringes basic notions of the separateness of persons as choosing agents. It is that other person who has made the culpable choice of doing harm, not the original actor.

The traditional causation doctrines of the criminal law also contain a principle that the intervening act of a third party ordinarily relieves the original actor of causal responsibility.[21] That principle likewise appears to be based, at least in part, on notions of culpability: that in such situations, the original actor is not the person who should be deemed at fault.[22] Does that mean that we can resolve imputation questions concerning intervening-choice liability simply by invoking traditional causation doctrines? I think not, for the context is different. The original actor, in the intervening-choice situations of which I am speaking, is not being charged with direct responsibility for the injury; instead, his conduct is proscribed on probabilistic grounds, because it is thought to contribute to the harm's eventual likelihood. Rather than trying to import traditional causation doctrines wholesale, it would be preferable to examine these doctrines to see how they might be suggestive for developing imputation principles suited to this new context. One aspect of those traditional doctrines does thus seem suggestive: namely, the strictures concerning intervening actors.

[20] See Andrew Ashworth, *Principles of Criminal Law* (Oxford, 1991), 100; also Glanville Williams, *Textbook of Criminal Law* (2nd edn., London, 1983), 390–3.

[21] Ashworth, n. 20 above, at 100.

[22] Glanville Williams thus notes: 'When one has settled the question of but-for causation, the further test to be applied to the but-for cause in order to qualify it for legal recognition is not a test of causation but a moral reaction. The question is whether the result can fairly be said to be imputable to the defendant . . . If the term "cause" must be used, it can best be distinguished in this meaning as the "imputable" or "responsible" or "blameable" cause, to indicate the value judgment involved. The term "imputable" is chosen as best representing the idea.' N. 20 above, at 381–2.

It is not only intervening-choice cases that raise questions of fair imputation, but abstract-endangerment liability as well. Consider the 55 mph limit
on many American superhighways. The limit (let us assume) is well below the
speeds that would be safe for the ordinary driver of a properly inspected car.
Why, then, have the limit? It appears to be based (at least in part) on the statistical expectation that lower driving speeds would help reduce the number
of accidents: the driver is being called upon to refrain from doing something
he himself could do without undue risk, in the common interest of greater
overall public safety. If driving over that limit is worthy of the criminal law's
censure, that cannot rest merely upon the empirical (in this case, statistical)
connection between the conduct and accidental injury. There must be a normative basis as well: that drivers have an obligation to co-operate in a safety-
promoting scheme by observing certain speed limits, and that an offending
driver may properly be held to blame for his or her refusal to co-operate in
that scheme. Seeing the crime in this light, however, squarely raises the question of what limits there should be on such obligations of co-operation.[23]

The point holds also for accumulative harms. There, the proscribed act is
a token of the type that does the feared injury when accumulated. Why,
however, should I refrain from conduct that in itself does no harm, merely
because it becomes injurious when combined with the behaviour of others?
The answer must lie, again, in an obligation of co-operation: we ought to
work together—by each of us foregoing some choices—for the sake of our
joint interest in preventing certain harmful consequences. Such co-operative
obligations, however, cannot be unlimited: I surely should not be held
accountable for *everything* which might lead to harm when combined with
the actions of others. At some point, the actor—when confronted with the
question 'What if everyone did what you are doing?'—should be entitled to
say that that is not and should not be made her business.

When speaking of such co-operative obligations, it is important to consider not only whether such obligations exist, but to whom they should
extend. It is one thing to assert that manufacturers, specializing in the making of a product, should have an obligation to co-operate in a scheme of
legal regulation (backed by criminal sanctions) that is designed to minimize
the product's harmful environmental effects. It is quite another to say those
obligations should be extended to casual users. Co-operative obligations are
related to roles, as we shall see below.

THE CHARACTER OF IMPUTATION PRINCIPLES

Imputability should thus be an important element in a theory of criminalization. With respect to any proposed criminal prohibition aimed at pre-

---

[23] For more on these limits, see the discussion below. Feinberg seems to imply that there
should be some such limits, in his discussion of purely statistical risk-assessments as grounds
for criminalization; see *Harm to Others*, n. 2 above, at 199–202.

venting the remoter sorts of risks, the question should be asked: *how, and why, can the supposed eventual harm fairly be imputed to the actor*? The reasons will be complex—and will vary with the specific context. But it will not do simply to disregard the question, or to assume that a purely empirical account of causality suffices.

Dealing with this question calls for a different vocabulary. It would seem natural to speak of whether the actor is 'responsible' for the eventual outcome, but responsibility in the criminal law has mainly been concerned with the character of the offender's present choice: with whether that choice is made voluntarily, with intent or foresight of consequences, without undue constraint, and so forth. The question of which I am speaking is different. Even if the prohibited conduct is done intentionally, and even if the conduct does empirically increase the risk of eventual bad consequences, it needs to be determined whether, and why, those consequences should be treated as the actor's responsibility in the imputational sense—the sense of being his 'business' or 'proper lookout'.[24] I am using the term 'fair imputation' to convey this idea.[25]

The issue is not necessarily one of the actor's intentions or foresight of the consequences. Where sound reasons for imputation exist, prohibition may be appropriate, whether or not actors ordinarily can foresee the eventual harmful consequences that provide its basis (as may be true, for example, of various environmental offences[26]). Conversely, knowledge or foresight does not necessarily suffice as grounds for imputation. In the Charles Murray hypothetical mentioned above,[27] for example, it should not matter whether fornicators consider the possible long-term societal effects of their consequences: as far as the criminal sanction is concerned, those effects should not be their lookout.

Imputation also is conceptually distinct from the fair-warning principle. As criminal legislation ordinarily is not well publicized, it largely relies on citizens' everyday moral sense for securing compliance: not so much the legal prohibition as the ordinary person's sense of right and wrong counsels her not to assault, steal, or riot, and to pay her taxes. The more attenuated the link to the ultimate harm is, the less the law is apt to provide such 'fair

---

[24] For different possible meanings of 'responsibility', see also H. L. A. Hart, *Punishment and Responsibility* (Oxford, 1968), 210–30. One of Hart's categories is 'liability-responsibility', in which he lists several subcategories. One of these subcategories concerns 'whether some form of connexion between a person's act and some harmful outcome is sufficient according to law to make him liable'. Included in this subcategory are the criminal law's traditional causation doctrines. However, Hart does not specifically discuss imputation issues of the kind which I am addressing here.

[25] I have taken the term 'imputation' from Glanville Williams (see n. 22 above), but extend its use beyond traditional legal causation contexts to what is being discussed here: the normative link, warranting attribution of fault, between the proscribed behaviour and the eventual resulting harm or risk.

[26] See also the text accompanying n. 33 below.

[27] See the text accompanying n. 16 above.

warning' to ordinary citizens. Fair warning, however, might be provided by publicizing the prohibition adequately. Imputation, by contrast, is not a matter of actors' awareness of the prohibition. Even if a prohibition has been widely publicized, it still raises imputation problems if—for the variety of reasons mentioned above—the feared harmful consequences are none of the business of the persons to whom the prohibition is addressed.

Imputation cannot be a matter of satisfying any simple general test. What is involved, rather, is constructing reasons why the ultimate harm is appropriately deemed the proper concern of the actor or actors.[28] Those reasons will, in significant part, be role-dependent. The extent of responsibility of a vendor, for example, depends on his social role—which provides clues about what he is implicitly representing to customers concerning his product. The responsibilities of manufacturers or civil servants likewise will depend on their respective roles. Beyond these particular roles, every person has certain responsibilities as a citizen—for example, the obligation to contribute his or her share of taxes. Such grounds for imputation cannot be drawn straightforwardly from everyday morality, because the roles involved often presuppose certain social or institutional frameworks. This makes issues of criminalization more difficult to deal with: they are not resolved by simple general criteria of the sort provided by the Standard Harms Analysis. Yet such complexity is unavoidable if we wish to deal adequately with remote harms.

An imputation doctrine can perform an important liberty-safeguarding role. Consider again intervening-choice liability. I have suggested that if a person engages in conduct that is innocuous in itself, it should not be proscribed *merely* because the conduct induces others to take further injurious steps. The fault-oriented reason, just discussed, is that the actor has done nothing that makes him responsible (in the imputational sense) for those other persons' harmful choices. However, restricting intervening-choice liability is also important as a means of protecting personal liberty—for otherwise virtually anything a person might do could be criminalized on grounds of its potential for harmful imitations.

Introduction of imputation doctrines will require more attention to be paid to precisely how the conduct is linked to the eventual risks. Take the example of gun control. When one inquires how gun-possession might lead to harm, various answers might be given, each carrying different fault-imputation implications. Is the risk mainly that of weapons going off spontaneously?[29] This account (if factually plausible) involves no intervening choice at all: the basis for prohibition would be akin to that concerning the

---

[28] Citizens' prima facie obligation to obey the law cannot, obviously, supply the imputation grounds. The legislature needs good reasons (including those relating to fair imputation) for prohibiting conduct. It cannot provide those reasons, bootstrap-style, merely by prohibiting the conduct—and then pointing to citizens' duty of obedience as the justification.

[29] See *Harm to Others*, n. 2 above, at 195.

keeping of easily-combustible substances such as nitroglycerine. Is it that guns kept in the household may become accessible to children? This still would not involve true intervening-choice liability, as the child is not a fully responsible agent. (There may also be a special basis for holding the actor answerable: namely, his or her duty of care toward minor offspring.) Is it the risk of guns being used in domestic or personal altercations? This does involve intervening choice, as the risk materializes only when a participant in the altercation resorts to the weapon. However, one is speaking here of the gun-possessor's own subsequent conduct, and of conduct occurring under considerable emotional pressure—namely, in the stress of a domestic fight. Would this suffice as grounds for imputation, and if so why? Is it, finally, the risk of guns being acquired by criminals? This rationale does seem troublesome from an imputational standpoint: the ordinary person is being barred from possession because (with no encouragement on his part) that could permit other persons to acquire the weapons and use them for further nefarious ends.

Important as imputation principles are, they can serve only as prima facie constraints that might sometimes have to be superceded. Suppose, for example, we were to conclude that none of the just-cited reasons justifies a broadly-drafted prohibition of possession or ownership of weapons. Such a measure might still be defended, however, on grounds that the potential injuriousness is so grave and widespread as to trump ordinary concerns about imputability. The argument would be a Dworkinian-style one: that the constraints of justice (in this situation, the fair-imputation constraints) may be overridden in exceptional situations where the countervailing concerns about preventing harm are of extraordinary urgency.[30] This argument depends, however, on demonstrating a high likelihood of extraordinarily grave and pervasive harm—sufficient to overcome the normally-applicable fairness constraints. Possibly, gun control legislation could meet this special burden, given the widespread carnage that appears to result from the easy availability of guns. But few other measures could do so; drug prohibitions, for example, are unlikely to be defensible on this basis.

GENERAL VERSUS SPECIAL PROHIBITIONS

A familiar distinction exists between criminal prohibitions applicable to the general public and those which deal with more specialized activities. It may be worth trying to reinforce this distinction, as far as it concerns prohibitions which aim at preventing remote harms. Restricting the number and scope of proscriptions of general applicability would help provide 'fair

[30] See Ronald Dworkin, *Taking Rights Seriously* (Cambridge, Mass., 1977), ch. 7. For application of such an 'override' argument in sentencing contexts, see von Hirsch, n. 5 above, ch. 6.

warning': it would safeguard the citizen against liability which she cannot readily anticipate. Even if, in aggregate, the use of aerosol sprays damages the ozone layer and creates long-term health hazards, criminalization of the purchase of such sprays would remain problematic: for it is asking much of the ordinary citizen to understand the environmental effects sufficiently to develop a sense that she should refrain from using such products.[31] A company that specializes in manufacturing the product, by contrast, is in a better position to familiarize itself with the applicable rules. Restrictions on manufacture will, of course, affect the options of citizens indirectly, for they can no longer readily purchase aerosol sprays. But the means of prevention are considerably less coercive of ordinary people than is threatening them directly with punishment.

Distinguishing between general and special penal measures also alleviates the problem of cumulative prohibitions. Generally-applicable prohibitions, when accumulated, impinge together to restrict the life and freedom of the ordinary citizen. If, for example, the use of each hazardous product is generally proscribed, an ordinary person would have to inform himself of and observe a broad band of constraints. Special prohibitions are different, in that persons are not likely to engage in more than one or a few specialties. The aerosol manufacturer would have to concern itself with the restriction on sprays, and the lobsterman about the restrictions on undersize catches, but few are likely to have both specialties and thus need worry about both kinds of prohibition.

Can notions of fair imputability give support to this distinction between general and specialist liability? While a confident answer would require fuller development of imputation theory, especially as it relates to accumulative harms, the answer would seem to be affirmative. There are, I have suggested earlier, certain basic duties of co-operation which each person owes in his capacity as citizen. These would concern such matters as the payment of taxes, the protection of the administration of justice, and so forth. It is such basic duties of citizenship that would support generally-applicable prohibitions.

Beyond these basic duties, responsibility for co-operating to prevent remote harms should be role-related. On a role-based conception of imputation, the duty of co-operating to forestall a given eventual risk would seem to fall, most logically, on those most closely associated with the activity involved: i.e., on the specialists in that activity. A firm which manufactures aerosol sprays *makes* the consequences of that activity its business, in a way that a mere occasional user does not.

---

[31] This concern about fair warning could be met (as noted above) by giving adequate publicity to the prohibition. However, that remedy could only be achieved selectively: a few measures aimed at remote harms might be publicized, but the more numerous the proscriptions are the less feasible it would be to provide the public with any real notice. Imputation concerns are different, in that they are not a matter of notice at all.

The general–special distinction exists in the law already, in the sense that there are a great many more specialized regulations and prohibitions than there are prohibitions of general applicability. What I am suggesting, however, is that the distinction be reinforced in the following respects.

(i) The scope of general prohibitions should be kept narrow. Not only should the harm be imputable to the actor, as discussed above, but the conduct should be sufficiently obviously reprehensible for its wrongness to be apparent to ordinary persons. Included would be *mala in se* crimes of ordinary victimization,[32] plus infringement of certain basic and well-understood public duties.

(ii) The scope of prohibitions affecting specialized activities would not be so greatly restricted. No requirement of *obvious* reprehensibleness need be imposed. Accumulative harms (for example, those affecting the environment) could be addressed, and abstract endangerments could be proscribed.[33] However, basic imputation constraints should continue to apply: if good reasons (including reasons relating to public obligation or duties of co-operation) cannot be supplied for holding the actor accountable for the eventual injury, then the prohibition should fall. Intervening-choice risks, for example, should ordinarily be considered suspect as grounds for criminalization.[34]

The difficulty with maintaining any such distinction between general and specialist liability will be in the details. It may not be easy, for example, to specify which kinds of public goods are fundamental enough to support general criminal prohibitions, and which are not. But the distinction strikes me as being of sufficient interest to warrant further exploration.

WHAT PRACTICAL DIFFERENCE?

Even if remote-risk prohibitions raise the theoretical problems this essay has addressed, are they problems in practice? Some of the examples I have cited are imaginary. Much as conservatives like to thunder about family values, it has not (to my knowledge) been seriously proposed that fornication be outlawed in order to prevent its supposed long-term criminogenic consequences.[35] The aerosol spray ban is also hypothetical. Other cases I have cited, however, are true to life. Drug prohibitions exist in most jurisdictions, and have been defended in part on grounds of the long-run social harms that

---

[32] Most of these, in any event, would involve actual harm or concrete endangerment.

[33] My view thus differs from that of Winfried Hassemer, who holds that abstract-endangerment crimes should be largely be eliminated—even for specialized activities. See Winfried Hassemer, 'Kennzeichen des Modernen Strafrechts' in Raimo Lahti and Kimmo Nuotio (eds.), *Criminal Law Theory in Transition* (Helsinki, 1992), 113.

[34] See the discussion of intervening-choice risks in the text accompanying nn. 16–22 above.

[35] See n. 16 above; Charles Murray advocates sharp reductions in welfare benefits for single mothers, but does not propose new criminal legislation.

use of the drugs would create. The House of Lords has upheld a ban on consensual sado-masochistic activity among adults, with reference made to the
possibility of imitation by pædophiles. Outlawing child pornography on the
ground of its tendency to promote violence against children has become a
hotly-debated issue in a number of jurisdictions, including (most recently)
Sweden. A fuller survey of criminalization efforts in the past few years
would doubtless uncover many further instances.

Could not such measures, however, be disposed of straightforwardly by
the Standard Harms Analysis, without need to address the admittedly more
complex questions of imputation? The Standard Harms Analysis does, after
all, supply a basis for challenging dubious harm claims, in its requirements
concerning the extent and magnitude of the eventual harm. Has the potential harm in the instances just cited—drug use, child pornography, and so
forth—really been properly documented?

Insisting on adequate evidence, however, may not be a sufficient safeguard. That is because estimates of the gravity and likelihood of harm tend
to become progressively more indeterminate, when the envisioned harm
becomes more remote. When speaking of not-very-remote risks such as
those involved in driving while intoxicated, one can speak fairly definitively
about the likelihood of driving impairment, the potential extensiveness of
the anticipated injury, and the like.[36] But what about applying the Standard
Harm Analysis to claims that drug possession should be proscribed because
widespread drug use will tend to accelerate social decay, with its attendant
poverty, social disorganization, and crime? Here, estimates of the magnitude
and likelihood of the risk necessarily become quite speculative.

We could bar such speculative risks in applying the Standard Harm
Analysis, but such a strategy would encounter the following dilemma. It is
not only the more debatable prohibitions which involve difficult-to-estimate
risks; so do seemingly more attractive areas of possible intervention such as
those regarding the environment. It is very hard, for example, to gauge the
effects of global warming. A stringent standard—one barring all but reasonably clear risks—might not only call into question the marijuana prohibition, but much environmental legislation as well. Loosening the standard
of evidence could have the reverse disadvantage of being too permissive.

The ultimate drawback of relying solely on the Standard Analysis, in the
area of remote risks, is that it yields insufficient arguments of principle.
Those who desire parsimony in extension of the criminal laws will be rele-
gated to making arguments about the benefits and costs of criminalization.
That criminalization is just plain wrong—because the feared outcome
should not be the actor's business—is something that cannot be contended.

Supplementing the Standard Harms Analysis with further restraining
principles, particularly those concerning fair imputation, could change the

---

[36] See James B. Jacobs, *Drunk Driving: An American Dilemma* (Chicago, Ill., 1989), ch. 3.

character of the debate. An opponent of (say) the marijuana prohibition would no longer need to argue merely that the evidence of ultimate social harm is insufficient, that the countervailing costs (and difficulties of enforcement) are too great, or that (say) privacy concerns protect the user. He could raise the more fundamental objection, about whether the feared eventual result is the actor's proper lookout.

Suppose that A, B, and C, typical users, enjoy smoking cannabis but continue to work (as so many do). Why is it their business that their example might induce D and E to become users, like the drug too much, and stop working—causing productivity to fall, so that F and G might lose their jobs, and decide to turn to crime?[37] The objection is not just to the factual plausibility of these links, for (who knows?) supporting evidence might be discoverable, at least in certain social settings. The real objection is to the fault-imputation link: A, B, and C have gone about their business, and have not abetted larceny or violence by any other person. Why, then, should F's and G's subsequent decision to offend be their proper lookout? And if not, why the imposition of the blame-ascribing criminal sanction?

Raising these issues of imputation will not, of course, settle debates over criminalization. Proponents of a broad ambit of criminal prohibitions may not even acknowledge the idea of fair imputability. Questions of imputability are also highly context-dependent, so that the grounds for denying imputation must be constructed in the particular situation. That means it will be necessary to *argue* why, in the marijuana case, F's and G's misconduct is not A's, B's, or C's business.[38] But it is nevertheless important to be able to make such arguments, and sometimes they may prove persuasive.

None of what I have just said should be read as suggesting that the Standard Harms Analysis should be abandoned altogether, as far as remote harms are concerned. The Analysis is helpful in addressing the *usefulness* of a given prohibition—where it does matter how likely and how grave the expected harm is, how socially valuable the conduct is, and so forth. Consider the drinking-and-driving prohibition: why should persons who drive when having over a stated blood-alcohol level be punished but not, say, those found with only trace amounts of alchohol? Here, the likelihood and magnitude of the prospective harm matter. The counter-considerations of the Standard Harms Analysis are also illuminating: it constricts citizens' options less to bar substantial alchohol consumption by drivers than to prohibit even a casual sip of wine.

What the Standard Analysis does not resolve, however, are certain questions of principle. The drinking-and-driving prohibition (unlike a prohibition on driving when actually intoxicated) is a species of abstract-

---

[37] For the 'contagion' argument, see William Bennett, *National Drug Control Strategy* (Washington, D.C., 1989), 11; for the loss-of-productivity argument, see Kaplan, n. 1 above, and the text accompanying nn. 6 and 7 above.

[38] For such arguments, see the text above at nn. 16–20.

endangerment legislation: it covers even those who are capable of driving carefully after having ingested the proscribed level of spirits. We need to ask why and to what extent those 'safe' drinkers should have an obligation to co-operate in such a scheme of driving safety, sufficient to render them at fault if they violate the rule—and thus become fit subjects of the criminal sanction. This latter question, of imputation, is not answered just by assessing costs and benefits.

Fair imputation can concern matters of political obligation: for example, about the extent of duties of citizenship.[39] Is this 'political' character a serious drawback? Would the Standard Harms Analysis be preferable, because of its apparent 'neutrality'? I do not think so. When we debate the permissible scope of the criminal law, the relevant doctrines must rest ultimately, at least in part, on notions about citizens' freedoms and obligations. It is best, I think, to try to make those doctrines and their underlying assumptions explicit. The Standard Harms Analysis merely *seems* apolitical: its politics actually are buried, only slightly below the surface, in its formula that the risk of ultimate harm should be 'weighed' against the need to preserve the liberty of the subject.

One final caveat: the issue of imputation relates to only one possible ground for criminalization: the conduct's supposed tendency to generate remote risks. Even where this argument fails, there may be other bases for sustaining a prohibition. Consider the drug laws once more. I have raised doubts about the Kaplan-style argument for criminalization, that drug use affects productivity, which in turn affects crime rates. But supposing that argument were rejected, there may yet be other grounds for criminalization—for example, paternalistic grounds. Some drugs, at least, do appear to damage the health and the lives of those who take them (glue-sniffing being an example). These effects are less remote—although they raise squarely the issue of the state's entitlement to use its laws to protect persons from themselves.[40] However, a restricted paternalism may be less threatening to citizens' liberty than reliance instead on a broad harm principle not adequately hedged by imputation constraints.

This essay has been of an exploratory nature. I have argued why it is important to develop fair-imputation principles when dealing with remote risks, but have not sketched how those principles should be formulated in any detail. I think, however, that the idea of imputation is important enough to make further efforts to elucidate it worth undertaking.

[39] See the discussion accompanying n. 28 above.
[40] See Joel Feinberg, *Harm to Self* (Oxford, 1986); Douglas Husak, *Drugs and Rights* (Cambridge, 1992).

Index